SOCIAL POLITICS AND MODERN DEMOCRACIES

THE MACMILLAN COMPANY
NEW YORK · BOSTON · CHICAGO · DALLAS
ATLANTA · SAN FRANCISCO

MACMILLAN & CO., LIMITED
LONDON · BOMBAY · CALCUTTA
MELBOURNE

THE MACMILLAN COMPANY
OF CANADA, LIMITED
TORONTO

SOCIAL POLITICS
AND
MODERN DEMOCRACIES

BY

CHARLES W. PIPKIN, D.Phil. (Oxon.)

Professor of Comparative Government at
The Louisiana State University
Author of "The Idea of Social Justice" and
"World Peace Is Not a Luxury"

VOLUME I

NEW YORK
THE MACMILLAN COMPANY
1931

· PRINTED IN THE UNITED STATES OF AMERICA ·

To

My Father and my Mother

EDGAR MALONE PIPKIN

and

ELLA CATHERINE JEWELL PIPKIN

who have lived in
Courage and in Beauty
the Good Life

PREFACE

A LARGE body of political experience for the whole world has been provided by England and France. The contributions these great peoples have made to the story of human progress are written large in the thought and in the institutions of all nations. I am glad that this study of social politics which deals with two great states attempting to meet the problems of a changing world industrial system can appear at this time. It is perhaps true that men are today more willing to consider the foundations of national security in terms of human welfare and happiness than at any time since 1914. This means, of course, that the English and the French national character and the record of modern democratic conflict in these two countries have significance for all students of popular government. We can hope that the dull and sordid days which came after the War and which denied the nobler aspects of its sacrifice have about passed. The prophets of prosperity have said all they have to say. They have departed. Again men and nations turn to the study of government, and the object of their study is both practical and speculative. At no time in democratic experiment have so many minds put their best thought upon the conditions of its success, and what this reveals of England and France today is of consummate importance.

It is important because we can better understand the enduring greatness of England and France when we see plainer the clash of ideals which is revealed in their industry and politics and national life. This understanding was never so needed before, simply because now the first steps are being taken to direct the civilization of the world by co-operation rather than by war. If reason and justice fail within the national community they are certain to be defeated in the international community. This fact is significant for all men of good will. It is suggested in the the remarkable book of Herr Wilhelm Dibelius, Professor of English in the University of Berlin, *England, Its Character and Genius* (1930) when he discusses the embodiment

vii

of modern ideals in national life. "The English State," he says, "rests on two specifically English assumptions, common sense and the transformation of the antagonist into a privileged colleague. It is characterized by freedom. . . . It is good for the world, and good for nations with other ideals, that the world contains a state such as has made the State well-nigh superfluous, where most of the functions of the State are administered by society. England's contribution to civilization is this free state. It is a structure in which free play is given to the natural forces that go to the building of society. It rests on the *instinctive* forces of humanity; on naïve egotism, naïve imitativeness, and on the instinctive need of men to lead and be led. The Englishman has shown that great things can be achieved along these lines. His achievement is, in the last analysis, not the individual achievement of single statesmen, single legislators, single generals or single thinkers, but the collective achievement of the Anglo-Saxon race. It is, in truth, not the ideal state; its faults are plain to see, nor could it work at all with other than Anglo-Saxons; but it is an advantage for humanity that the English model is there, to enable the one-sidedness of other systems to be improved and offset by comparison with it."

It is very interesting to put along with this comment the words of M. André Siegfried, Professor of Economic Geography at the School of Political Science, Paris, in his *France, A Study in Nationality* (1930). "Our democracy," he writes, "is Latin in origin, and therefore unlike the Anglo-Saxon democracies where practical social accomplishments are the first consideration. Their programme is to increase the comfort and material welfare of mankind, but they do not worry very much about its intellectual freedom. They have a practical aim which they expect to achieve through moral co-operation. 'We give people leisure so that they can read books', writes M. Étienne Flournol, 'but they (the Anglo-Saxons) give them leisure so that they can have an automobile.' This democratic formula which arose from Puritanism is an Anglo-Saxon invention and has no connection with our rational conception. Politically the Anglo-Saxon state is moral rather than intellectual; and although it fully recognizes the rights of man, it drags in social duties which from our point of view seriously hamper his liberty. . . . Yet, if mankind is ever again preoccupied with the question of the individual, his thoughts, and his right to think for himself, it is not talk about

vacuum cleaners, refrigerators, and adding machines that will move
the world. French idealism, with its motive power still intact, will
regain its old interest. Our old mystical way of viewing politics,
although insufficient in its social efficiency, explains itself and to a
certain extent justifies itself by an instinctive and a persistent determination to safeguard the individual : and there lies the vital interest whose promptings France will likely never deny." The evidence
of this book on the social politics of England and France will often
confirm the wise reflections of Herr Dibelius and Monsieur Siegfried.

This present study incorporates what has been found useful in a
former study of mine, *The Idea of Social Justice,* but in these chapters the reader will find fresh material. My obligation and my
appreciation to Professor W. G. S. Adams, Gladstone Professor of
Political Theory and Institutions at Oxford University, have deepened with the years I have been privileged to know this distinguished
Oxford scholar. This study could not have been carried on without
his wise and sympathetic friendship. Professor Adams as the teacher
and the friend of American students at Oxford has become one of
the powerful personal influences for understanding between his
country and the United States, and in his life he nobly interprets
the high traditions of honour and of public service of Oxford. I am
happy that this study is published while yet my friends Sir Francis
and Lady Wylie are at Rhodes House, for I share with all Rhodes
Scholars a debt to them and glad memory of their delightful
hospitality. They have helped mightily to build a way of understanding around the whole world. To the Rector and Fellows of
Exeter College, of which I have the honour to be a member, I wish
to offer appreciation and respectful homage. I am grateful to the
Master of Balliol, Dr. A. D. Lindsay, for his interest in this study,
and for the keen and penetrating criticism with which he and Mr.
G. D. H. Cole honoured this book. I am indebted to the Rt. Hon.
Margaret Grace Bondfield, Minister of Labour, for valuable services
from her Department and for the outline of the Ministry of Labour
which she kindly had prepared for this volume. It will be found in
the Appendix. I am under obligation to the distinguished Director
of the International Labour Office, M. Albert Thomas, for the use
of the letters which interpret his spirit and leadership, and they are
also a part of the Appendix. My friends at the Louisiana State

University library and the League of Nations library at Geneva
have been unfailing in their library services.

It is a happy privilege to express here my abiding obligation to
my friend Mr. Ralph W. Baucum of the Louisiana Bar for his help
in making this study possible and for unfailing interest in it. The
former administrator of my university, President Thomas W. At-
kinson, generously allowed a year's leave in Europe for special
work, and I express appreciation, and it is a pleasure to record the
interest of President James Munroe Smith of Louisiana State University in this study. I want to express appreciation to my friend and
colleague, Colonel A. T. Prescott, Dean of the College of Arts and
Science, and Professor of Government; and my friends and colleagues, Professor Harriett Spiller Daggett, of the Louisiana State
University Law School, and Professor Taylor Cole, of the Department of Government, know how grateful I am for their generous
and sympathetic help. This comparative study would not in any way
commit my friends to its views and to its limitations, but I am glad
that it has been honoured by the personal interest of my friend, Professor Robert Kent Gooch of the University of Virginia, a foremost
authority on the government of France. And I am unwilling not to
call to mind in a study which has for its field two countries I love, the
friends of Oxford with whom the Oxford years were spent, and they
will know much of the Talk at Oxford and Paris and Günterstal is
here quick again! The Turl, the High, Boulevard Saint Germain des
Pres, Kybfelsenstrasse, and Third Street hold ten years against the
world. My dedication to them cannot reveal the pride and love I bear
my parents who have made their lives a way of honour and of courage and of noble living.

Now this is ended. At All Souls one day my friend wrote: "We
cannot yet discern with certainty the character of our own times.
We can see them more or less darkly against the ages which have
gone before, but we can only dimly speculate how they will compare
with those which are to come. Yet it may well be that our generation
is one in which the struggle of forces is alike more complex and more
uncontrolled than will be that of the future, that gradually the experience of years will guide Society to a clearer, calmer, steadier
way of life, that there will be seen more plainly the true nature,
structure and method of Society, and that this period in which we live

and move will be looked back on as great in its dark struggle and
giving birth to a new order of justice which will gain more and more
complete acceptance throughout the world." This is my hope.

C. W. P.

At Baton Rouge,
    January the twenty-seventh,
        Ninteen hundred and thirty-one.

CONTENTS

CONTENTS

CONTENTS

THE DEVELOPMENT OF SOCIAL LEGIS-LATION AND ADMINISTRATION IN ENGLAND AND FRANCE SINCE 1900

INTRODUCTION

I

THE LESSONS OF POLITICAL DEMOCRACY

The development of social legislation and administration in England and France since 1900 is the story of two great states attempting to meet the problems created by a changing industrial system. England and France throughout a century before the present one had seen the old order giving place to a new; they had by 1900 proved to the world political democracy in action, through an extended franchise and through political institutions directing in significant ways the democratic life of both countries. These two modern democracies offer an opportunity for contrast and comparison in their meeting of the common task of applying the lessons of political democracy. France and England have been selected as the countries of study, because the survey of their social legislation will be a means of discovering how these two modern industrial nations have tried to work out in their national communities the ideas of equality and well-being which the growth of political democracy has made a common possession for both peoples.

A large body of political experience for the whole world has been provided by England and France. They have not only had a continuous influence upon the national life of each other both in political thought and in a standard of social culture, but wherever men have reflected upon the questions of representative government these two experiments have been of predominant interest. The position of France on the continent has never failed to signalize her place among the world powers, while the island democracy of England has through her political leadership directed the expansion of an empire. At the same time domestic problems within the country, arising from the control of industry and the increase of power of the workers demanded more and more attention of Governments. It is also of importance that the forces of nationalism and internationalism have required England and France to take a large part in the decisions of peace in the world.

Within each nation there has been a growing democratic consciousness demanding a liberty for the citizen not before provided for in the old forms and by the old institutions. France since 1789 has attempted to establish the ideals of the Revolution, never failing to give fresh validity to them in her own national life and by her leadership suggesting their application to a constantly enlarging international order. The Napoleonic wars and the war of 1914–1918 ploughed deep the life of both nations; and from the resulting changes made by military force a new order of things in the two countries developed. Each nation under the reaction of wars had to create great public services and adapt the governmental agencies to new duties. In both centuries an old individualism, rooted in conditions which were swept away, had to be undermined and in its place there came larger influences which were to control the lives of men.

The tremendous impact of modern industrialism was first experienced by England, and she has always had to bear the initial costs and the heaviest burdens. The first prosperity—and the later penalties—came to England. The magnitude of her problems has tended at times to minimize the difficulties of France, but each has had the same duty of a modern state organizing its economic life on a new basis. England has through her maturity given the example of a strenuous political discipline, and within her Parliamentary struggles there has been seen with increasing effectiveness the determination to reach higher levels of public service, however much there was reflected the clash of opposing national forces. There has also been a larger communal understanding of the nation's problems and the claims the nation has upon co-operative citizenship. England was first to teach the nineteenth century voter and taxpayer that his century was ended, and that his relations as a citizen of the twentieth century were vastly wider.

This study surveys primarily the social legislation of the twentieth century, but it is obvious that social progress cannot be divided nicely into arbitrary historical periods. This is especially a sound view to take when the legislation on industrial questions in the democratic countries of England and France is to be studied. The genius of the democratic method seems to lie in the gradual evolution of institutions, each generation making plainer through them its will for the well-being of the people. The industrial codes of the present century, in their detail and complexity, had their beginning in the factory legislation of England and France in the nineteenth century. Administration with its high standards today, a virtual government itself in action, is largely the record of the creation of public opinion on social questions and the necessary building up through the central government of a stable supervisory machinery of control. The aim behind legislation and administration, whether it was safety, security, or well-being generally, had to be realized slowly within an industrial system which could be changed only as men were convinced that it should be changed. Then there had to follow the slower persuasion of changing the ideas of men about their government; but the process went steadily on in the nineteenth century in England and France. It is hard to say when the twentieth century really did begin. Therefore, this study, though it deals primarily with a definite number of years, provides a survey at first of the Labour movement down to 1900 in England and France; and the growth of industrial legislation in each nation is outlined. The important developments of democratic progress in this century are based upon the preparation of England and France to use the machinery of their government to change social and economic conditions, and, the effort is made to indicate briefly the preparation of each country for meeting its complex industrial organization.

The historical survey is followed by a review of the legislation of the twentieth century in England and France, dealing with social and industrial questions. This will indicate the conditions the state attempted to improve and the means taken to carry out its purpose. Where it has been possible, the reasons that Governments gave for their social policy, through the responsible Minister, have been set forth at length; for this helps to make plain the intent of the lawmakers and the aims of the legislature. It is true that often an Act of Parliament is the work of long years of intelligent planning by voluntary associations and by disinterested individuals who provide

Governments with this cumulative experience; but nevertheless the final determination of principle is a duty of the Government, and, because this study is concerned with governmental action, primary attention is given to what was done by different Governments when in power. After a law has been passed, the means of administration, or the lack, have been given in each case; for often new principles of administration mark as important an advance in social legislation as the statute itself. The details of the many Acts passed, which are referred to, are not given in full, but each new principle of state intervention is pointed out and the enlarging scope of the enactments is carefully noted. This is especially done for administrative provisions and with regard to the increasing use of the power of delegation to the responsible Ministers of State. It is hoped this method will not confuse the reader with a vast miscellany of laws, but will make it possible to judge the progress of social legislation in each country and to note the means of administration. But two old civilizations with institutions of traditional significance like England and France present for the student of social legislation no clear cut picture of either legislation or administration.

The final passing of an Act is more fully noted than the later amendments and extension of the principle which the original legislation introduced. The debates at this earlier time are often more indicative of divisions of opinion than subsequent discussion, when Parliamentary Acts have been accepted on all sides as part of the established administrative system for which any Government must be responsible. This is especially true of much of the Liberal legislation of 1908–1914. The post-war debates have not been centred upon the principles of social legislation, so much as they have been taken up with matters of public finance and the question of extension to one class of persons or another. It may be noted that no hard and fast definition of social legislation has been followed, for public social services today have a wide scope which it is almost impossible to delimit. Health and education and public recreation services involve vast sums of money, and affect every citizen; but primary attention has been given to those laws which affect directly the wage-earner in the conditions of his employment and in his standard of living. This last condition has included in this study the recognition by the state of the rights of Trade Unions, especially as representative associations for the protection of the interests of the workers.

When the development of legislation and administration has been given, the Labour movement in England and France in its political and industrial organization is reviewed, with special attention given to the programmes of these bodies on social legislation. Social legislation is today increasingly in its economic aspect a non-partisan matter; but it is necessary in this study to direct attention to the political Labour movement which has derived its chief strength in England from its alliance with the industrial Labour movement. The fact that this is less true of the political Labour movement in France, is one of the instructive facts of a survey of the Labour movement in these two countries.

This present study is necessarily limited to social legislation and administration, with the attention to workers' organizations which is required to round out the survey of France and England of the present century. It is by no means suggested that this treatment exhausts the field or covers the wide range of social politics; for there is a wealth of material in voluntary social, religious and humanitarian movements awaiting the student of this period which will yield a rich return for a long time. Likewise it is regretted that significant developments in the national life of England and France must be omitted entirely or only mentioned briefly. The France and England of today have been made strong by many loyalties and by forces which get their strength from many institutions. It would be unwise to under-estimate the practical importance in raising the standard of living among the people of the revolution in the national public health and educational services. Generous humanitarian enterprises have enriched the whole life of the state; there has been a broader social sympathy among many leaders within the Church, and in both countries the Church has accepted a teaching duty to inspire the sense of social obligation; the consumer's co-operative movement has been a training school for many in citizenship; and, finally, the temperance cause, international welfare work, and the crusading zeal which many people feel for the aims of a world at peace internationally—all have strengthened the cause of goodwill by cutting across every class line and by making it possible for the common life to be improved. There are no set boundaries for progress. This fact has made the selection of material for this survey difficult. But it is hoped that what has been done may form a part of the whole story of two great peoples' determined effort to direct their national life along the way which leads to the acceptance of reason and justice as the guide to domestic policies and international relations.

A good deal of attention has been given to the growth of the political Labour and Socialist movements in England and France. The writer has definitely tried to point out that the recognized leaders, supported by an increasing number of the electorate, depended on political tactics as an important factor for bringing about changes in the life of the people. It is true that this is a more significant fact in the beginning of Labour's influence, and it is so considered throughout this study; but the background needs always to be kept in mind, even if the emphasis is tedious for the informed reader. This political or it may be called constitutional allegiance of the Labour movement in both countries has been a means of direct preparation for the power which has come to the Parliamentary Labour and Socialist parties in England and France. This is a necessary emphasis in the development of the English and French Labour movements, the implications of which are of increasing significance as political methods become less useful and as industry becomes better organized.

The give-and-take, which work in Parliament has demanded, can be useful when industry and labour attempt to work out together a policy which both can accept and which at the same time conserves the general interests of the community as a whole. The present day participation of the workers in the life of the state, their co-operation in the organization of trade, and their direction of national influence through their power in Parliament, are best seen when the long story of the political organization is recorded. Between 1870 and 1900 the mind of the workers had been turned by Marx to the capture of the industrial system. His authority was plain in the French programmes, though their sectarian divisions were obstacles to permanent political influence; and in England while Marxianism was weak, Liberalism and Fabian doctrine taught the advantages of political action. Marxian socialism in France had conquered Proudhomian mutualism and the anarchism of Bakunine, both of which were revived in the revolutionary Syndicalist movement and have always had to be reckoned with in the French Labour movement. This same period is marked by a strong struggle between nationalism and internationalism in the French Labour movement, while the solid advance of Trade Union aims in England was hardly disturbed by this consideration of internationalism. But soon in England the ideals of guild socialism were freshening the industrial outlook of labour, and there was the attempt to harmonize syndicalism and state socialism. Reaction followed so closely after the war that men wondered if anything could be salvaged from the hopes of war-time England and France. And recuperation has come so slowly in England (while in both France and England the problem of rationalization in production and organization has unsettled industry), it is as yet only possible to record the programmes of national industrial organizations. Today there are experiments being made by workers and employers and the Government which could not have been possible at any other time in the field of industrial relations.

II

THE UNDEFINED FUTURE OF SOCIAL POLICY

The future of social policy is undefined. Hard lessons have been learned, and all parties in the community have set themselves again to build a sane order for industry wherein there is for the individual and for the whole nation security. This security is, moreover, today seen more closely to be joining the interests of all the community together and calling for a new kind of collaboration among all the producing factors of the nation. This gives weight to a new emphasis upon the principle of constitutional assent on which the French and English Labour movements have been based. Their progress has been within the forms of the existing government. Even the general strike of 1926, which has been interpreted by some as a challenge to the constitutional principle of assent, was interpreted by the leader of the Labour party to mean that never again would the Labour movement allow itself to be side-tracked from the important aim of winning by the only way victory could be achieved finally, a victory given by the majority opinion of the nation. M. Jouhaux, Secretary-General of the French General Confederation of Labour, in discussing the question of industrial peace at the 1929 Congress, declared that the strike today appears no longer in the eyes of the worker as the heroic gesture of other days. If the Labour movements of England and France have now reached the bargaining position where their aims can be discussed as a national problem of the economic organization of industry and the nation, it is because there were long years in which political lessons of compromise were forced home to all leaders in Parliament. It was not Labour alone which needed to be taught this lesson.

It is then, with this point of view to the fore, that in England the political crisis of the famous Budget of 1909 has been discussed, so far as it helps to illustrate the importance of the national programme of social legislation; and, with the same purpose in mind, the debates on industrial unrest in England, and the record of revolutionary French Syndicalism, have been given special attention. The economic organization of labour and the nation have not been under-estimated; but for this study the events have been reviewed from the point of view of political action. Thus the sources most relied upon have been debates in Parliament and official Command Papers and the Reports of Commissions and Special Committees set up by Parliament, together with debates and proceedings of the Trade Union Congress and Labour and Socialist conferences and congresses. The fact that today the economic validity of factory legislation is universally recognized and the Trade Union organization is accepted by Governments to carry out responsible national aims, is proof of how well the organized labour movement has directed the interests of the workers. The organized Trade Union movement of England and France has made it possible for Labour to co-operate upon a basis of equality in the councils of the nation. The standard of living, the conditions of work, and the status of the worker, rest today upon the results of the long years of Trade Union organization. This is perhaps of more importance in the highly industrialized England where there are several million more factory workers than in France, but the demand in both countries for the national organization of the agricultural workers and the inclusion of home-workers in all schemes of welfare, has shown the common bond which unites all the claims to protection on the part of the wage-earner. In both England and France, Governments have been able to utilize Trade Union organization and to carry forward from their first beginnings the aims of a larger security for all the workers, as well as to aid in creating the conditions in industry which will ensure peace for the whole community. It is possible to say that the constitutional growth of the Labour movement in England and France has strengthened the whole foundation of the claim for democratic control.

The outlook of the leaders of Labour has been broadened by their participation in national affairs, and this has had a direct effect upon the proposed programmes for industrial action. The rank and file of the working class at the beginning of the fourth decade of this century have a sounder understanding of what can be done through the action of Parliament and what can be achieved through trade or professional action. This is as applicable to the conduct of foreign policy as in the organization of national effort to combat unemployment. Political training separated the world of Labour of 1900 from 1930. Other groups in the state had for a long time leadership in political activity, which led to power, and this gave a prestige to the old parties in the country which Labour had slowly to gain for itself. But conditions have changed in both England and France. It will be a chief point of this study to make clear how the alliance of the industrial and political labour movements, much more effective in England than in France, has made it possible to call into active collaboration organized labour agencies in the public social services set up by governmental action. By 1930, in fact, most of the new agencies of social legislation in England and France, whether in the conciliation and arbitration of disputes, or the administration of a national system of social insurance, depend upon the active co-operation of organized labour for their successful administration. This is literally a revolutionary change in the place of Labour in the national community. The state has in addition utilized the services of voluntary and statutory consultative bodies. This important advance in co-operation was accelerated by the war, but the beginnings can be seen in the social legislation before 1914 and in the growing power of Trade Unions in both countries. The comparative progress is more remarkable in France, where organized trade unionism has had neither the power in industry as a negotiator nor the prestige of the community's goodwill as in England.

In this study of England and France one other fact has been kept in mind, namely, that the democratic movement has developed slowly in both countries. Reform in laws and in institutions has been a gradual evolution. This is not less true of France where the words of the Revolution have often been heard. Social legislation has had to be created upon a broad basis of assent, until today in both England and France this subject rivals discussion upon the Budget and foreign affairs in the amount of talk that must be heard upon its proposals. And outside of Parliament every newspaper is a forum for conflicting arguments upon the national policy of social insurance. The slow processes of reform have demanded the formation of a public opinion, which breaking down obstructive barriers, has finally been defined in an Act of Parliament accepted by the people and by each succeeding Government. Social legislation has thus been piecemeal legislation which has had to wait until necessity for its provisions has been well-nigh universally recognized. This accounts for the fact that there has been little reaction to social legislation in England and France, once Acts have been put into force. Social legislation in the two countries has not left behind any determined minority bent upon nullifying as soon as possible the intent of the law. This is an indication of healthy progress, and means legislation on social questions has been usually nothing more than the registration of decisions which have already been made by the opinion of the nation. There has been a generative power in the laws which have been passed. Amendments and changes have followed original Acts of Parliament, of course, and the war strained administrative agencies on account of a fluctuating and depreciating currency and a dislocated industrial system; but for the most part existing legislation has been from year to year supported by succeeding Governments through more effective administration. Subsequent legislation has confirmed earlier principles. Dissatisfaction with the Unemployment Insurance Acts in England might be said to be an exception to this, but this national problem goes deeper than reaction to a state system of unemployment insurance and challenges study because unemployment endangers a whole people's security. The economic validity of political action has been accepted. If it is to be of lessor necessity, it is because its successes have created a better understanding of the place of industry in the modern commonwealth. If it is to be no longer so useful, the way has been prepared for the agencies which industry and government are better able to use today to fulfil their aims.

It is of course too early for the permanent results of the war upon democratic governments to be fully known. But even in the midst of the conflict there were those who could see that one of the chief services of the war should be to teach that democracy cannot be brought about by a drift or tendency of unconscious purpose; it needs conscious organization and direction by the co-operative will of individuals and nations.[1] It is exactly this co-operative will which has an increasing part to take in the post-war industrial relations. The effect of the war on the organization of modern democracies was considered by Lord Bryce, who may have had England especially in mind. He believed there was a continuity in the processes of trial and error by which modern states sought to attain economic and political ends. The war might divert but it could not materially change the course marked out by the industrial organization of the century. The tendency toward reform and control would continue working itself out anew in the changed world after the war. He saw that the absorption of men's minds with ideas and schemes of social reconstruction had directed attention from the problems of free government which occupied men's minds when the flood-tide of democracy set in seventy or eighty years ago. That generation, he thought, was busied with institutions, this generation was bent rather upon the purposes which institutions may be made to serve. The conclusion Bryce reached, was that if any of the bold plans of social reconstruction after the war were put into practice they would apply new tests to democratic principles and inevitably modify their working. His belief was plainly put: "The old question,—what is the best form of government? is almost obsolete because the centre of interest has been shifting. It is not the nature of democracy, nor even the variety of shapes it wears, that are today in debate, but rather the purposes to which it may be turned, the social and economic changes it may be used to effect." [2]

England and France have certainly attempted to apply new tests to democratic principles; there is not only difficulty in estimating the forces which were at work in the pre-war social movement but to gauge the strength of the social and economic changes which have come since the war. It may be taken for granted that in England and France the war did not alter materially the conditions which social legislation had sought to change nor did it achieve the ends it seeks to promote. The structure and processes of French government show

---

[1] Cf. J. A. Hobson, *Democracy after the War* (4th ed. 1919), p. 157. Post-war changes would see the extension of the functions of the state for the enlargement and improvement of existing public services, and the extension of state ownership and administration to various economic fields, would necessarily be accomplished by a large increase of taxing power (p. 162).

[2] *Modern Democracies*, vol. I, *Preface*, pp. xi–xii.

no permanent effects of the war; they remain today substantially what they were in 1914. The changes will come and have come not so much as the result of the war, as of tendencies already set in motion before the war, held in suspension during its course, and now given a new impetus, an accelerated pace.[3] Progress quickly came back to its old course, one believed, in Germany toward state paternalism, in England toward autonomous organization, and in France toward political intervention.[4] President Lowell in 1918 in the preface to the first edition of *Greater European Governments* wrote that the general traits of the political systems portrayed ten and twenty years before in his *Government of England* and in his *Governments and Parties in Continental Europe* had altered little. The preface to the edition in 1925 gave Mr. Lowell the opportunity to say that in England and France the general nature and the working of the governments are much the same as they were before the war.

The significance of these observations is increased when the progress which has been made in social legislation and administration is considered since 1920. Even in so short a time a new approach to industrial relations has developed and a new spirit can be seen. This is more important than political change. There have been no great changes in the political systems of England and France, but there has been continuous development of the public policy initiated before 1914 and carried forward by statutory and voluntary effort since the war. It is in the field of social politics that changes can be seen which give most encouragement. The tendency since 1920 has been marked in the reports and researches which have come from the Liberal and Labour parties, from the French General Confederation of Labour and the British Trade Union Congress, and from independent surveys. Research and study have been necessary for informed action, and this has been especially true in connection with post-war social legislation; for even when it has been confessedly temporary, public policy has had to be considered in the light of the changing economic and financial problems of England and France. The wasting and fluctuating currency of France made difficult

[3] Cf. E. M. Sait, *Government and Politics of France* (1921), *Introduction*, p. xi.
[4] Cf. Georges Scelle, *Le droit ouvrier* (1922), pp. 205–206.

measures of reconstruction, and in England the recovery of the pound, the change to a gold standard, and the changing bank rate have had significance for the schemes of social legislation. The changing conditions have made it necessary for every Government to keep constantly advised on the whole problem of national welfare and prosperity, and this has brought into the counsels of the nation many neglected sources of information.

It may be said finally that England and France are modern governments whose future concerns the whole world, and the success of their institutions of industrial control will necessarily affect the authority which democratic government everywhere may command. They have for the most part the same problems as all modern governments. England and France have had to depend for effective administration increasingly upon the efficiency of their civil service; the machinery of local government has had a growing importance as the national government developed its public services, reaching to the remotest *commune* and village, affecting an over-widening sphere of individual and community interest; and the Parliaments of each country have been overwhelmed with the work which they have had to do, initiating legislative programmes and then maintaining the semblance of Parliament's control.

This study of the national life of the two peoples, recording in part what has been done by social legislation to direct the growth of a modern industrial nation, concerns the work and the conditions of living for the workers of England and France, and gives an account of how these problems became a foremost interest of the national community. The story has been told as much as possible in the language of workers' congresses and debates in Parliament and official reports, and, while this has increased its length, this method provides the reader with material from which judgments can be made. Upon such a subject as that of this study, the accumulating evidence of national purpose is of importance. It is difficult to make this story direct and simple; for it tells of two old civilizations working out a new destiny in a century of complex industrialism; then adjusting after a world war the national life to changed economic and social conditions, and through it all attempting to establish the standards of living which the power of the whole community would maintain in the interests of national security.

III

THE EVIDENCE OF SOCIAL CHANGES

The bibliographical sources of this study of the first importance are: the debates in the Parliaments of England and France, the official government documents dealing with social policy and the administration of social legislation, and the reports of the workers' industrial congresses and political conferences. The volumes of Parliamentary Debates (Hansard) and the *Journal officiel de la République française* report the proceedings of the House of Lords and the House of Commons in England, the Senate and the Chamber of Deputies in France. The volumes are now published separately for each House, and this is the case in Reports of Committees and in Reports submitted to Parliament. In connection with the legislative record of social legislation the important Parliamentary Command Papers between 1900 and 1930 have been used, in so far as they concern directly this study and the central government. Many of these official documents both in England and France are of comparative value, because the history of legislation in other countries is recorded for the law-maker to study. The House of Commons and the Chamber of Deputies have received in the years since 1900 many Command Papers and *Rapports,* and, while the ones used are not again listed in the bibliography of this study, they may be quickly referred to in the chapters dealing with legislation. The hearings, the preliminary reports, and the recommendations of Select Committees and Royal Commissions are published, and the more useful of these have been noted in the text. A complete record of the work of the French Superior Labour Council has been given, for this advisory body has had an increasing influence in the development of French social legislation, both in the formulation of new and in the administration of old legislation. There are indications that now a more vigorous support from organized Labour will be given, and with the consistent loyalty of the Government to the *Conseil Supérieur du Travail,* which has been always true, this institution will have an even larger influence in the determination of social policy. There is no reason to assume that the effective organization of the National Economic Council will diminish the Superior Labour Council's special work, for the National Economic Council has been

given the definite task of seeing the whole of French national life
from the point of view of production and the re-organization of
industry and commerce. Its terms of reference, so far as labour
questions are concerned, are only a part of the general problem of
French industrial progress. The service that these two national
advisory bodies are called upon to do corresponds to that put upon
Royal Commissions by Governments in England, for often the work
of Royal Commissions extends over a number of years.

The annual reports of the Departments of State dealing with
labour, health, commerce, trade, finance and local government provide a vast amount of source material for study. Of special significance in England are the reports of the old Local Government Board
—now the Ministry of Health—the Home Office, the Board of
Trade, and the Ministry of Labour. The duties of the Local Government Board were taken over in 1919 by the Ministry of Health, and
the eleven reports down to June, 1930 provide the history of the important post-war years. The annual reports of the Ministry of
Health and the Ministry of Labour, together with the annual report
of the Chief Inspector of Factories and Workshops (which is under
the Home Office) provide the best review of the results of administration of social legislation in England. The current account of
labour and industrial policy, changes in legislation, departmental
orders and the movement of labour, are found in the monthly
Ministry of Labour Gazette. The sources of statistics given in this
study are these annual reports of responsible State Departments for
England; and for France they are taken from the reports of the
*Ministère du Travail, de l'Hygiène, de l'Assistance et de la Prévoy-
ance Sociales*. The *Bulletin* (*37° année, 1930*) of the Ministry of
Labour is published four times a year, and serves both as a means
of official publication of documents and as a useful survey of the
progress of French and international social legislation. The *Bulletin
du Marché du Travail* is published weekly and is the information
publication of the Ministry, dealing with unemployment, employment exchanges, and labour problems in general. The *Bulletin de la
Statistique générale de la France* is a quarterly publication (volume
XIX, 1930), while the *Annuaire Statistique* (XLIV° volume 1928
[1929]) includes the whole of the annual statistical history of
France. This last volume is the one cited in this study; where it is
possible, later statistics have been used from official sources, which

are indicated. It has not been possible to bring the French official figures as nearly down to date as the English in some instances, because of the slow publication of official French documents. It is not even possible to know when the quarterly or other publications of stated intervals will appear, so irregular is the practice in France. The Departments concerned simply say they do not know.

Throughout this study the official debates of the English and French Parliaments have provided the material for the legislative history of an Act of Parliament, and the *Memorandum* of the Bill by the Government Department sponsoring it, and the *exposé* attached to the French Bills, have been used as official information. The index of debates in the volumes of proceedings of the House of Lords and the House of Commons, makes it possible to follow the history from year to year of a problem of social legislation; and in France this service is met by the *Tables Alphabétiques et Analytiques des Chambres des Députés et le Sénat*. There have been changes in the numbering of the volumes of debates and in the use of separate volumes of the two Houses in England, and this accounts for the changes in the form of citation of sources; but references otherwise in English and French debates are uniform. It should also be said that each *Bulletin du Ministère du Travail* gives a legislative time-chart of Bills affecting labour law, and the first issue of each year provides a complete record, up to that time, of the session of Parliament. This is of help in finding out where a particular Bill may be, or where it has been conveniently lodged before a Committee of Parliament by the Government. It has been the long established custom to delay legislation. It has been possible in this study to consolidate into a chronological table the English Acts of Parliament referred to, and this may be easily used as a method of finding an Act and its place in the statutes, a yearly volume of which is published. While the French Labour Code has not progressed far enough as yet in the quarter of a century of codification to include all the labour law, it is possible in this survey to refer to the *Code du Travail* for the law on most of the subjects discussed. All laws are published in the *Journal officiel,* and so are the Decrees and Orders and Circulars of the Ministers. The Ministry of Labour, however, from time to time unites in a single volume the Labour Code of France, and the uncodified Acts affecting the working class, the Decrees, Orders and Circulars embodying the administrative rules in force. The last volume published in 1928 (the next is anticipated in 1932), is the volume cited in this survey, as *Lois, décrets, arrêtés concernant la réglementation du travail*. It has been possible, however, to use the 1930 edition of Dalloz' *Code du Travail* as a basis of reference both in the history of Acts and for Acts, and Decrees of the Ministry of Labour through September, 1929. The earlier citations of editions before 1930 are sometimes given for the purpose of providing a means of contrast, but the 1930 edition is the volume used throughout the study. The *Annuaire de Législation Française,* containing the Acts of the French Parliament, is issued yearly by the *Société de Législation Comparée;* but the easier method of finding legislative and administrative documents is in the current issues of the twice monthly *Bulletin Législatif Dalloz: Lois, Décrets, Arrêtés, Circulaires,* etc. *Trauvaux Législatifs.*

The official reports of the Trade Union Congress and the British Labour party have been used for England, because they represent the industrial and political organization of the labour movement in Great Britain. In France the reports of the French General Confederation of Labour (*Confederation Générale du Travail*) and the Unified Socialist Party Congress (*Congrès Générale des Organizations Socialistes Françaises* [*S.F.I.O.*] (have been used, because they are the central organizations of the French Labour movement. The bibliographical notes at the end of this study treat more fully the source materials which have been used, and a selected list of books consulted is given. But reference should here be made to the help derived from the publications of the International Labour Office (League of Nations) ; in the *Studies and Reports Series,* in the weekly *Industrial and Labour Information,* and in the monthly *International Labour Review,* not only all students everywhere but Governments have for their information and guidance an account of social legislation and its administration in all countries.

The informed reader will note reference to sources which suggest immediately controversial issues and party programmes, and in a study which is of a period yet unfolding its variety and complexity this is inevitable. Because of the subject matter, which has been yearly debated in party conferences in France and England, the student of social policy will find books mentioned which are now of interest simply because they were contemporary testimony to the issues of the day. Likewise a question is sometimes allowed to stand defined in the resolution of a Trade Union Congress or a Socialist party appeal, or in a statement by the responsible Minister— Campbell-Bannerman, Waldeck-Rousseau, Millerand, Churchill, Clemenceau, Asquith, Briand, Lloyd George, Baldwin and Mac-Donald, Herriot and Poincaré. The issue itself may have a better statement in the books written by men removed from the actual Parliamentary fray, and, in years after, even appear a different thing; but this study has tried to keep in mind the value which there is in just such testimony by men who at their worst and at their best were politicians. They had to act, they were responsible. Whatever the forces were that shaped their final policy, at the moment of decision they took the directing step which meant action. This study is then political in this meaning.

It is difficult to judge in a period so near to the changing events and to the chief protagonists, some even yet in places of influence and office, what is the abiding, and what forces a hundred years from now will prove to have been the determining influences of these times. But it is certain that Parliamentary debates and the records of workers' and political organizations hold much of the meaning of modern democratic conflict. If already some of these recorded events seem to belong to a remote era, it is none the less worth while to try to find out what they meant to men organizing their new interests and bringing their power directly to bear upon the policy of Governments.

It has been possible in this study, for the most part, first to give the history of an Act of Parliament and the conditions which made it a matter of legislative record. And then in both England and France the three periods included in this survey naturally fall into the record before 1914, the war years, and the post-war years. One is thus able to see what progress was made to 1914, the temporary and permanent influence of the war measures, and to judge something of the remarkable advances made since 1920. At no time in democratic experiment have so many minds put their best thought upon the conditions of its success, and what this reveals of England and France today is of consummate importance. The chapters of this study deal with material which may help in reaching some conclusions.

ENGLAND

CHAPTER I

THE BACKGROUND OF THE ENGLISH SOCIAL MOVEMENT

I

The Slow and Sure Reform of British Institutions

British institutions are difficult to interpret. The permanent gains in political experience which they represent have their strength in centuries of law and custom. Political liberty was won because men determined to make government responsible and themselves to take part in the decisions which affected their lives and their property. The basis of participation in affairs of local and national government has been so extended that today all citizens have in theory the power to influence the aims of their government. The economic history of modern Britain is no less significant because it tells the story of the industrial revolution and the way in which a great industrial state functioning as a political democracy has tried to organize the industrial system. The meaning of freedom for the average man and woman is closely connected with the political and economic history of England.

This chapter is intended to sketch briefly the English social movement and takes into account labour legislation, the development of the political labour movement, and the growth of opinion which made law an instrument of social peace in the modern democratic community.

The nineteenth century saw the slow and sure reform of British institutions. It was a century in which men were attempting to live together in a new kind of civilization; they were working out an order of security and happiness in an industrial society which was changing the purpose and character of all institutions. The common life of the people was revolutionized, and there was upheaval at the top and at the bottom of English society. The way men and women and children made a living was forced upon the attention

3

of governments by workers. Security in the daily work of making a living became the increasing concern of more and more people; their happiness and welfare finally had to be one of the major concerns of the state. At first elementary decency compelled cautious action through parliament, but this compulsion broadened generously until legislation aimed at the whole of community interest became the basis of governmental intervention.

The growth of social conscience which is reflected in the legislation of one hundred and thirty years, dealing with conditions of work, is important as a principle upon which government policy has depended, and it has not ceased to contribute to the development of social legislation. One writer has observed that, "A population which we have seen a hundred years ago hardened by suffering has become distinguished for compassion to misery and aversion to pain, as a new consciousness arose of the commonwealth as a whole, which must suffer from the weakness of any part." [1] The growth of humanitarian sentiment, by which civilization may be measured, has certainly to be reckoned with, says President Lowell, in the history of the Factory Acts, which made a breach in the tenets of *laissez-faire*. But it is not an adequate interpretation of the substance of later enactments, the history of which parallels the history of the modern Labour movement, which established new duties for the central authority and gave to state departments by statutory rules and orders a power to exercise authority over rights and property till then almost exclusively reserved for parliament.

It is true that this new consciousness demanded from the state a more intelligent protection—even promotion—of the conditions of the workers' lives. The earlier legislation, referred to below, represented a reaction to the blind faith in an all-wise economic law; but the continuance of legislative intervention made more definite the aims behind parliamentary action. Arnold Toynbee anticipated Professor Dicey by twenty-five years in the interpretation of Socialistic Acts "passed by Tory country gentlemen"; adding, in 1892, "I tremble to think what this country would have been without the Factory Acts." Toynbee at the time pointed out that the material

---

[1] Cf. *A Short History of the English People,* by John Richard Green, revised and enlarged with an Epilogue by Alice Stopford Green (1916), *Epilogue,* p. 895; G. M. Trevelyan, *British History in the Nineteenth Century, 1782–1901* (1922), p. 182; A. L. Lowell, *The Government of England* (2 vols., 1st ed. 1908, new ed. 1917), vol. II, pp. 522–523.

inequality of men under existing social conditions was a fact; that the poor law, factory legislation and trade unions might lessen the pressure of the strong upon the weak, modifying and mitigating the inequality of wealth, but notwithstanding all, the fact of inequality remained, and on this fact the maxims of the Radical Socialists were founded. This protest based on equality belongs to a long tradition in the social thought of England. It implied for Toynbee two things; first, that where individual rights conflict with the interests of the community, there the state ought to interfere; and, second, where the people are unable to provide a thing for themselves, and that thing is of primary social importance, then again the state should interfere and provide it for them.[2]

There was yet another, at Cambridge, who saw that a policy of intervention was entered upon by the state. Professor Maitland illustrated this, pointing out that an Englishman has a child born to him; within 42 days, by an Act of 1874 (37 and 38 Vict. c.88) he must register its birth at the proper office, if he does not he can be fined. Within three months an Act of 1867 (30 and 31 Vict. c.84) required he must have that child vaccinated, otherwise he would be fined. By an Act of 1876 (39 and 40 Vict. c.79), it was the duty of the parent of every child to cause such child to receive elementary instruction in reading, writing and arithmetic, and if such parent failed to perform such duty he was liable to such orders and penalties as were provided by the Act.[3] Opposition from the beginning of restrictive legislation by men who have considered intervention as administrative despotism has not diminished the ever-increasing burdens of state control. A policy of regulation has inevitably implied administrative power.

It is thus plain that there was from the beginning of legislative intervention more than the mere humanitarian motive. What is im-

[2] See *The Industrial Revolution of the Eighteenth Century in England* (1st ed. 1884), by Arnold Toynbee, memorial edition, pp. 232–233, the address, "Are Radicals Socialists." Lord Milner's *Reminiscence* of Toynbee, written in 1894, spoke of the striking difference in the social and political philosophy of Oxford during these years. "When I went up (1873) the *laissez-faire* theory still held the field. All the recognized authorities were 'orthodox' economists of the old school. But within ten years the few men who still held the old doctrines in their rigidity had come to be regarded as curiosities" (p. xxv); and compare his post-war commentary, *Questions of the Hour* (1923).

[3] Cf. F. W. Maitland, *The Constitutional History of England*, edited by H. A. L. Fisher (Cambridge, 1908), p. 504.

portant to note is the change which legislation brought in the status of the worker and his family. At the beginning of the nineteenth century the worker was alien from participation in the life of the community as a whole; his progress to responsible citizenship with obligations which demand leadership in the nation is what popular government means today.

The slow and sure reform of British institutions created the conditions which have made constitutional government a reality. There has come from this fact a constitutional morality which has deepened the spirit of unity in the democratic government of the English people, and this spirit has enforced all the efforts of reform, giving them the validity they possess today. The ideal of human good has become constantly more effective as more citizens have joined in common duties, and this has broadened the basis of community action. This is a civic revolution which has silently changed the structure of old institutions when it has not found expression in new ones. It is then important to point out some of the changes in law and opinion which separate the nineteenth and twentieth centuries.

The England of 1900 had recognized the problems before the modern industrial state and had set about to meet them. The factory laws, the oldest and best developed of any nation, were an indication that legislation had been a means to protect labour and to minimize the costs of industrial progress. The strength of the trade unions, the power of the co-operative movement, the extension of municipal trading and the capital it represented, the recognition of the needs of a large group of the employed by the fixing of a standard of life in the wage clauses in public contracts, and the effort of labour and capital to settle disputes by conciliation and arbitration, all indicated there was a growing understanding of the nature of the problems of the twentieth century.

The political schemes by which England has sought to adjust her social ills have been affected very little by the remedies used on the Continent. Social purpose has taken form from the needs of the British people, directed by men often close to the soil. Social progress has depended much upon legislation, and, though its limits are obvious, so long as political jurisdictions remain there is no indication that legislation will not be needed. The claim of the whole community of interest has always been the force behind social legislation, and the growth of the consciousness of this claim throughout the nineteenth century is a proof of its power to compel the allegiance of men. England gave the solid background to its expanding influence, and this is a natural thing, for England's life is the parliamentary system, which depends upon the will of the people being found out, and then executed. "The reformed legislature, and the reformed organs of administration which it created," Trevelyan says, "were helping on the general social improvement and the movements by which the new Britain was striving to remedy the evils attendant on the Industrial Revolution—Co-operation, Factory Laws, Trade Unionism, Free Trade—were all like the Industrial Revolution itself, British in conception and origin." [4]

The originality in conception and origin of the attitude of England toward social reform has often made the British Labour movement a seemingly contradictory thing on the Continent. The history of parliamentary interference is certainly a confused story of compromise. President Lowell has pleasantly expressed an American view of this temperament. He describes the Englishman of today as sanguine, impatient, eager to attack the evils he perceives, and very willing to try experiments in the process. If there is overcrowding in the cities, he at once builds a few dwelling-houses. If the agricultural labourers are not well off, he passes a law whereby some of them may be furnished with plots of land. If neither of these things proves to be a serious remedy, he builds a few more houses, and makes ineffective amendment to the Allotment Act. If the mortality among babies is large there is a supply of municipal milk. President Lowell, early in the century, reflecting upon the ideas dominant three score years before, declared he found political interest in England greater today in the distribution of wealth, and this in spite of the many business men in the House of Commons. [5]

This interest in the distribution of wealth is a direct result of the growth of democracy, and it has meant that when representatives of the people have gone to Parliament they have made an effort to grapple with the problems of modern industrial organization. Business men in the House of Commons, with perhaps no special competence, were as impotent before the march of industrialism as University representatives were of the increase of popular educa-

[4] G. M. Trevelyan, *British History in the Nineteenth Century*, p. 268.
[5] *Op. cit.* vol. II, p. 526.

tion; and President Lowell's earlier strictures on the Labour party as a perverted instrument of popular government which could increase the dangers of paternalistic legislation has to be shared by all the parties of the state. For the purpose of this study it is worth while to ask if the Labour movement has increased this danger or not? Whether it is an inevitable tendency of democracy to imperil parliamentary government by the support it gives to class conscious minorities or majorities? The concentration of power in the hands of the Ministry has often been given as an example of this danger, which is especially true of England.

II

INDUSTRIAL LEGISLATION AND THE CHANGE OF OPINION BETWEEN 1801 AND 1901

It was ninety-nine years from the beginning of factory legislation in England, with the passing of the Health and Morals of Apprentices Act, 1802, to the Factory and Workshop Act of 1901. This was a century in which there was a continuous development of the principle of security within the industrial order for the individual worker. Institutional change was defined in the growth of labour legislation and in the application of the doctrine of collectivism. This period represents a long evolutionary movement and it is difficult to find satisfying interpretations of the dominant influences which were changing the whole life of England. The way men lived and what they thought about their work proved there was a difference in law and a change of opinion between 1802 and 1901. The difference in both law and opinion made it possible for the institutions which had been developed to be used differently by men with a changed social outlook, and this helps in an understanding of the power which great trade and political organizations have had in the lives of men. The nineteenth century slowly gave form and expression to a power which has not yet spent itself. That power was in the development of the industrial system but it left no part of the whole life of the nation untouched by its influence.

It has often been pointed out that the Act of 1802 was not based on any general principle, but "sprung from the needs of the moment and owed nothing either to the advance of democracy or socialism." [6] Professor Clapham says, "It was the rank and file of average sensual parish-apprentice-employing factory owners, including, oddly enough, himself, whom Sir Robert Peel the elder intended to control by his Health and Morals of Apprentices Act." [7] Parliament readily gave what Peel asked, and the rapid passage of the 1802 Act contrasts strangely to the long and exacting Committee work on the Act of 1901. Again this Factory and Workshop Act of 1802 when compared with the Children's Act of 1908 sharply gives the contrast in both law and opinion. The law of the twentieth century, however, had its beginning in the 1802 Act which was a response to the humanitarian impulse of that earlier time, in this instance connected especially with the epidemic in Manchester among the apprentices in the cotton mills. The Act of 1802 provided for the cleansing and ventilation of the cotton mills and factories, hours of labour, and the religious education of apprentices employed therein; and to compare its scant provisions with the hundreds of clauses in the Children's Act of 1908 and the Education Act of 1918, is to gain a fairly accurate impression of the contrast in the two centuries and in parliament's attitude towards the welfare of children.

The enforcement of the Act of 1802 was through inspectors or visitors who were appointed by the justices of the peace, and, even if they had done their full duty under the law, the problems of supervision would have soon changed. The Factory Acts which followed the passing of the Health and Morals of Apprentices Act indicate the changing conditions of work. The inadequacy of enforcement provisions was also true of the Factory Acts of 1819, 1820, 1825, 1830, 1831 and 1833. The Act of 1831 was a consolidating Act, which was repealed by the 1833 Act, the first general factory Act. These Acts were determining the way along which future legislation would go when legislation would have behind it a force of popular opinion which would demand effective administration. The early Acts are also important because they reveal a changing law and opinion in those times. One long familiar with the Home Office, which is in charge of the administration of the Factory Acts, has suggested this by saying that the meaning of existing laws and regula-

[6] Cf. A. V. Dicey, *Law and Opinion in England* (1st ed. 1905, 2nd ed. with Introduction, 1914), p. 110.

[7] J. H. Clapham, *An Economic History of Modern Britain* (1926), p. 372.

tions cannot be understood if the conditions which gave rise to them are forgotten.[8] The Factory Acts of the nineteenth century are to be read as commentaries on the quickly changing industrial life of England. The Act of 1833, "An Act to regulate the labour of children and young persons in the mills and factories of the United Kingdom," known as Lord Shaftesbury's Act, was the first important factory act imposing effective restriction on the employment of children. This Act protected children (9 years to 13 years) and young persons (13 years to 18 years) employed in cotton, woollen, worsted, hemp, flax, tow, linen and silk mills driven by steam or mechanical power. This Act was an advance beyond the Factory Act of 1819 which forbade children being employed in cotton mills before they were nine years of age. The Act of 1833 is also important in the history of factory inspection, because for the first time the Home Secretary was empowered to employ inspectors, limited to four persons, and provision was made for certificates from physicians. The administrative basis of factory legislation was laid, depending upon a central inspectorate. This beginning was the next year paralleled in another field by the Poor Law Amendment Act of 1834, which established for the first time the principle of centralized executive control in the poor law policy of the nation.

The protection of women and children was further extended by Lord Ashley's Mines Act of 1842, which prohibited underground work in mines for all females and for boys under ten years of age. The Factory Act of 1844 consisted of 74 sections, and a central office as set up in London called "The Office of the Factory Inspectors." This Act provided that certifying surgeons were to be appointed by the inspectors, women were brought under the provisions applicable to young persons, children were brought under a half-time system, and there were definite provisions in regard to health. The main lines of factory legislation were being developed.

The first decided triumph of the movement which began in 1802 was in the Ten Hours Act of 1847, which reduced the working hours of women and young persons to a maximum of ten hours per day or 58 hours per week. This Act meant that the regulation of public labour was a concern of the state and laid the basis for a whole system of government inspection and control. The 1833 Act provided for the appointment of inspectors of factories, and the

[8] Cf. *The Home Office* (1925), Sir Edward Troup, note Preface.

Mines Act of 1842—the beginning of the mining code—had put enforcement in the keeping of inspectors who were required to report to the Secretary of State.

Factory legislation was first extended to works by an Act of 1845 which regulated the labour of children, young persons and women in print works, and between 1860 and 1864 Acts were passed which included other works and processes. The Factory (Dangerous Trades) Act, 1864, marked the extension of regulation beyond the textile trades, and began the system of special regulations now applicable to dangerous and unhealthy trades by a clause empowering special rules as to cleanliness and ventilation, but subject to the approval of the Secretary of State. The Factory Extension Act of 1867 extended the earlier Factory Acts to all places where 50 or more persons were employed in any manufacturing process and to certain other enumerated places. This Act also gave the Secretary of State power to make Orders. The Workshops Regulation Act, 1867, brought in all establishments where less than 50 persons were employed. The Factory Act of 1874, directly influenced by the Education Act of 1870, which brought all children alike into public elementary education, provided that after 1875 no child under ten years of age should be employed, childhood should last till 14 years, unless after the age of 13, an educational certificate was gained, and that factory schools should be substituted for schools recognized by the educational authorities.

This brief survey is enough to show that the Royal Commission appointed in 1876 had work to do in studying the whole subject of the law on factories and workshops, which at that time consisted of a great number of regulations contained in nineteen Acts, from 1833 to 1874. The Act of 1878 was the result of the Royal Commission's Report, and this Factory and Workshops (Consolidation) Act, 1878, with amendments was in force until the Factory and Workshops Act, 1901, was passed. Amending Acts of 1883, 1891 and 1895 made it necessary to consolidate the Factory Acts, and this the 1901 Act did, and, while it has been added to by subsequent Acts, is the existing labour code on this subject. The Parliamentary Committee of the Trade Union Congress in 1901, considered it a most important landmark in labour legislation, and advocated consolidation along the same lines of such Acts as the Mines Regulation Acts and the Education Acts.

The comparison of the 1901 Act with the 1802 Act indicates the changes which had taken place in the thought of England, and the giving up of theories which dominated the earlier times. From the Act of 1802 which owed nothing either to the advance of democracy or socialism, to the 1901 Act, which Professor Dicey considered "the most notable achievement of English Socialism," [9] is a period which enlarged the conception of freedom for the worker. The list of Factory Acts extending from 1802 to 1901 proves that men saw what was to be done if there was to be security in industry, and the legislation was a partial attempt to adjust changing ideals to conditions of work. "After 1815," says Dicey, "thoughtful men must have perceived the existence of a want of harmony between changing social conditions and unchanging laws"; and yet the political and economic theory of the years of expanding industrial revolution in England seemed closely joined with a doctrine of social and economic fatalism. Throughout this period there were contrary winds of doctrine. The pioneer legislation was slow but it was necessary that ground work be done, and it has served as the solid foundation for the most comprehensive factory and workshop regulation in the world.

Factory legislation was only one aspect of the England which was changing from the old order into a new. The Combination Act of 1825 repealed the earlier laws of 1799, 1800 and 1824; the Reform Act of 1832 had been passed; the New Poor Law Amendment Act in 1834, though arousing great population opposition, had sought to cure obvious evils; and in 1846 the Corn Laws were repealed.[10] The "State of England question" was before Parliament, and, what is important, the people knew it was there. Public opinion was at work. Legislation was looked to for correction of evils as the reports of the factory inspectors and the working of the Poor Law

---

[9] *Op. cit.*, pp. 328 and 115. The Schedule of the Factory Acts from year to year provide an index of the progress of legislation. A most satisfactory study is Frank Tillyard, *Industrial Law* (2nd ed. 1928) ; and see, B. L. Hutchins and A. Harrison, *A History of Factory Legislation* (1903) ; *Redgrave's Factory Acts* (12th ed. 1916), C. F. Lloyd, revised by W. Peacock; Karl Marx's interesting survey in *Capital* (17th ed. 1920), pp. 214–288; S. and B. Webb, *History of Trade Unionism* (ed. 1920), pp. 310–313; J. L. and Barbara Hammond, *The Town Labourer (1760–1832)* (1917), pp. 194–220, *Lord Shaftesbury* (1923), and *The Rise of Modern Industry* (1925), Part III.

[10] Cf. S. and B. Webb, *English Poor Law History* (Part II.) *The Last Hundred Years* (2 vols. 1929), vol. I, pp. 90–103, and pp. 26–31 (Benthamism).

became known to the public and to Parliament. The Elementary
Education Act of 1870 was followed in 1871 by the Trade Union
Act, and the Combination Act of 1875 (Conspiracy and Protection
of Property Act) was taken by Dicey to represent in the main
the combined influence of democracy and collectivism; an influence,
however, which was still balanced or counteracted by ideas belonging
to individualistic liberalism. It was an individualism based largely on
the social philosophy of Bentham, and with roots deep in the soil of
England itself—an England which had changed before men could
see the terrible results of dearly held beliefs about individualism.
Needs became too acute and the ideas behind the agitation for legislation were too powerful for the *laissez-faire* creed to hold unchallenged authority, and both economic development and political
controversy helped to mark the decline of its great power over men's
minds from 1880.[11] By 1884 the progress of collectivism or socialism
had begun to be felt and to influence legislative opinion. Mr. Chamberlain in 1885, putting before the nation the Radical Programme,
could say the stage of agitation had passed, and the time for action
had come. At last the majority of the nation would be represented
by a majority of the House of Commons, "and ideas and wants and
claims which have been hitherto ignored in legislation will find a
voice in Parliament, and will compel the attention of statesmen."
He saw that new conceptions of public duty, new developments of
social enterprise, new estimates of the natural obligations of the
members of the community to one another, had come into view, and
demanded consideration.[12] A new spirit in legislation became evident
as the democratic revolution of 1866–1884 made plain that the doctrine of *laissez-faire* or individualistic liberalism was at an end.
The Earl of Wemyss on July 31, 1885, in the House of Lords made
a speech deploring the advancement of state interference in business,
and gave a *résumé* of the Acts of Parliament between 1870 and 1885

[11] Cf. Ernest Barker, *Political Thought in England from Spencer to Today*
(1915), pp. 203–204.

[12] See *The Radical Programme,* with a Preface by the Rt. Hon. J. Cham-
berlain, M. P. (1885), Reprinted, with additions, from the *Fortnightly Review.*
The quotations are from the Preface by Mr. Chamberlain. Cf. W. H. Mallock,
Social Equality (1884), and, *Property and Progress or a Brief Inquiry into
Contemporary Social Agitation in England* (1884), especially pp. 167–248; and
of interest, H. M. Hyndman's *England For All* (1881), and the Social Demo-
cratic Federation's *Socialism Made Plain* (1883), together with the first
Fabian *Tracts.*

which showed the progress of socialism. Again on May 19, 1890, he warned that body of approaching danger. There have not been lacking since then speakers who give to both Houses the same instruction. In this connection it is well to remark that M. Hauriou considers that the period of the individualistic philosophy of the French Revolution did not come to an end until the passing of the Act of July 1, 1901, on Liberty of Association and Associations.[13]

There were principles of social legislation and administration, particularly industrial law, embodied in the statutes of Parliament by 1901 which had logically developed from the extension of the reform movements since 1800, but which would not have been accepted by the most radical of the advocates of change at that earlier time. The progress of industrial legislation—the interference of Parliament in the industrial system—was a test of how far the state conceived its functions of control to go; and it also measured the effort to change the organization of modern government to meet the vastly more complicated structure of industrial society. At the end of the century it seemed to one critic that the lines along which state protection of labour advanced in the nineteenth century were illustrated by these four laws of development:[14] (1) A movement along the lines of strongest human feeling; (2) Protective legislation moving from the highly organized to the less highly organized structures of industry; (3) A growing complexity of aims and of legislative machinery; and, (4) An increased effectiveness of legislation with growth of centralized control. These developmental characteristics were well defined at the end of the century, but to complete the survey it is necessary to take into account the better internal organization of trade unions and industry and also the growth of extra-legislative agencies which influenced opinion. When all of these factors are considered it will be seen that the industrial legislation of this century has not departed from the ways which in the earlier time were in part made plain.

The developments which have just been outlined suggest the question which Professor Dicey asked in discussing the relation of democracy and legislation, "Does not the advance of democracy afford the clue to the development of English law since 1800?" It is only necessary to note the fact that between 1804 and 1900 there was

[13] Cf. *Principes de droit public* (2nd ed. 1916), p. 550n.
[14] Cf. J. A. Hobson, *The Evolution of Modern Capitalism* (1902), p. 321.

small part of the English Statute book that had not been changed in form or in substance. This certainly shows a close and immediate connection which exists in England between public opinion and legislation, and helps to explain that throughout the nineteenth century every permanent change of a constitutional character had been in a democratic direction. The advance of society in the democratic direction had by 1900 transformed the English Constitution into something like democracy; it had extended the electorate to a point where parliamentary and other institutions had come to have a direct relation to the democratic sentiment. Yet it is well to keep in mind that the growth of England's democracy and the spirit of her government today has been greatly influenced by the traditions of the aristocratic government out of which it has developed, and this has had its share of influence in the social theory of the Labour leaders.[15] Professor Trevelyan writing in an age in which he believed the law of perpetual and rapid change was accepted as inevitable, and the difficulty was to obtain progress without violence, thought there was profit in the story of a statesman, who after a period of long stagnation, initiated in "our country a yet longer period of orderly democratic progress, and at the critical moment of the transition averted civil war and saved the state from entering on the vicious circle of revolution and reaction." [16] He believes that to understand Lord Grey of the Reform Bill and his paramount influence in the Britain of 1830–1832 is to understand the world of that transition period. It is to understand also the position and outlook of the liberal-minded autocrats peculiar to the history of England, whose existence has been one of the reasons why the political traditions and instincts of the English have differed so profoundly from those of Germany, of France, or even the United States of America.

The beginnings of the advance towards democracy in the nineteenth century were largely political, and it is remarkable that at the beginning of the twentieth century the Labour party of England were at work upon the problems which political democracy had forced upon them, with perhaps more emphasis on the means

[15] Cf. J. Ramsay MacDonald, *The Socialist Movement* (1911), p. 235, and *Socialism: Critical and Constructive* (1st ed. 1921, new ed. 1929), Preface to 1924 edition, and pp. 287–293; also Dicey, *op. cit.*, pp. 48, 58.
[16] G. M. Trevelyan, *Lord Grey of the Reform Bill* (1919), Preface, p. viii and p. 368. Cf. H. W. C. Davis, *The Age of Grey and Peel* (1929), Chapter XI, pp. 267–286, "Whiggism 1830–1850."

that such power gave them than on the development of economic organization. The reactions of opinion throughout the nineteenth century, and even so far in the years of the twentieth century, have indicated that there is a continuing ebb and flow in the modern social movement, between the political and economic method. Mr. Mac-Donald has characterized this for the British Labour party by saying that it, like all movements, is a thing that ebbs and flows. "It flows from emphasis on political action and *vice versa*. The defeat of the miners in the coal lockout turned the tide toward political action. The reason for their final defeat lies in the fact that the starvation point comes before economic victory can come when capital and the Government combine as they did in this case. The effect has been to emphasize the political aspect, the importance of public opinion and parliamentary control. *The British Labour Movement is at heart more political than industrial in its emphasis and it is conscious of this.*" [17]

This post-war interpretation of the British Labour Movement by its responsible leader in Parliament is important to note. The Reform Act of 1832 meant that the parliamentary system of government, which since 1689 has been essentially the English system, would become more democratic and more representative of the cross-currents of politics and social thought in England. It was soon manifest that Parliament as a legislative machine would bring more fully into effective expression the will of the people. This was confirmed in the Reform Acts of 1867, 1872, 1885, the Parliament Act of 1911, the Representation of the People Act, 1918, and the amending Acts of 1926 and 1928. These Acts completed the work of political democracy so far as extension of the franchise is concerned.

Modern democratic government can be taken as starting in England with the passing of the Reform Act of 1867, which gave predominant power to the middle classes and the manufacturers. The Reform Act of 1867, which gave the parliamentary franchise to workers in the towns, was followed by the Reform Acts of 1885, which set, said Mr. Chamberlain, the seal on the great change which the Reform Act of 1832 inaugurated. Parliamentary democracy has tended since 1832 to place the emphasis on the great common

[17] See *British Labour Speaks* (1924, p. 17, "Some Aspects of Labour Ideals," by J. Ramsay MacDonald, (my italics), and the address of Philip Snowden, stressing the political-mindedness of Labour.

interests of the nation, disciplining each political party, and this most characteristic contribution has been the work of the two great political parties of the nineteenth century. The rise of the Labour party under a discipline administered by the two-party system has had a great deal of influence on the leaders of that party and upon the corrective internal discipline of the party itself. There has been in England the hope, if the three-party system is to continue over a long period of time, that it would not lessen but tend by its demand upon co-operation, to raise the level of parliamentary responsibility. The minority Prime Minister of the Labour party made this appeal in 1924 and in 1929 on taking office, and in 1929 gave his pledge to Parliament to keep in mind his leadership of a "Council of the Nation."

The influence of the parliamentary experience of the British Labour party has been so significant in its development as a national party that it is difficult to over-estimate its importance. There is in this experience something profoundly different from what has taken place in France. The implications of this history are seen in the apt statement below by a Labour leader who has given in the past to British Labour perhaps as large a theoretical formulation as any thinker. Lord Passfield (Mr. Sidney Webb) writes:[18] "The working of political democracy, if it is to be a genuine machine for 'government of the people' necessarily involves the existence, in the Parliament of the nation, of an Opposition as well as a Government. Otherwise the electors are given no real choice of Cabinets, and cannot effectually control either their representatives or the Ministers. And the very existence of differences of opinion among the people—which will always prevail—and the continuance of rival political parties—which are indispensable to a genuine Democracy—indicates that no party, not even the one calling itself Labour or Socialist (as it is necessarily only a part of the whole community), can ever expect to be continuously in power. At best, it can only alternate in power with the Opposition party, whatever this may be called, according as the majority of voters—made up of the 'average sensual man' who belongs to no party—periodically expresses its approval of what the Government of the day has done, or is doing, or is proposing to do." This is the Labour statement of

---

[18] *Encyclopaedia of the Labour Movement* (1927), p. 269, in his article on *Fabianism*.

what is referred to below in President Lowell's estimate of British political history.

The British Labour party has thus inherited a parliamentary sense. It has shared in the traditional spirit of controversy in English public life, and this has kept the party from becoming doctrinaire. The party has been opportunist and practical. The parliamentary lesson of compromise has been its very life. It has thus gained a power which makes leadership possible; and on all these points the French Labour movement has failed in the past and is failing today. It is true that the Parliamentary Labour group in France has suffered from internal disputes, but it would have had a more responsible share in the government of France if the French Parliament had the permanence of legislative discipline in party divisions that has obtained in England. The effect of this tradition on the public mind in England has been considerable, and over a long time it has worked for the diminuation of the class struggle in the politics of democracy. Parliamentary democracy has slowly educated the electorate and parliamentary responsibility has made for party discipline. The English Labour Prime Minister can say that the "Socialist transforms by the well-defined processes which a living social organization allows. He is an evolutionist *par excellence*." [19] A foreign observer, seeing the growth of the English parliamentary system to meet the problems of industrial expansion and the extension of empire and governmental powers by legislation and administration, believed the British had made "the greatest contribution of the nineteenth century to the art of government—that of a party out of power which is recognized as perfectly loyal to the institutions of the state and ready at any moment to come into office without a shock to the political traditions of the nation." [20] This was written in the first decade of the twentieth century and its force has not been less in the exigencies of British politics in the third decade. The power of constitutional self-control behind this fact has sustained hope in parliamentary government, and has figured largely in the history of the democratic struggles of Labour in England, where "a degraded House of Commons really means a degraded democratic authority," and where Labour has learned that "parliamentary government without the constitutional instinct or habit is an impos-

[19] J. Ramsay MacDonald, *Socialism: Critical and Constructive*, p. xii.
[20] Lowell, *op. cit.*, vol. I, p. 451.

sibility." [21] It is not yet known what equal contribution may be made to English parliamentary democracy by a minority determined to be a part of the constitutional give and take in the work of Parliament.

The faith in parliamentary government which has steadily increased in the modern British Labour movement has had a constant influence on the movements of agitation, from the earliest agitation in the nineteenth century, the period of old Toryism, 1800–1830, to the Clydeside group within the Labour party today. In the earlier period sensible men perceived that the state of England would soon necessitate a choice between revolution and reform, and the major problem then was the adoption and changing of the political system to meet the new conditions in the social and industrial life of England.

The British Labour movement naturally taking its development from the democratic nature of the state has sought broadly to interpret the social ideal of Labour in the community and to establish it under the sanction of parliamentary democracy. Trade Union history has not been different from the history of the political Labour movement. The New Unionism of 1833–1834 rejected, under the influence of Owenism, political action, but the leaders of the New Unionism of 1889–1890 aimed at using existing social structures in the interests of wage-earners. "Above all," say their historians, "they sought to teach the great masses of undisciplined workers how to apply their newly acquired political power so as to obtain, in a perfectly constitutional manner, whatever changes in legislation and administration they desired." [22] The New Unionism found ready for their use an extensive and all-embracing democratic structure, which it was impossible to destroy and would have been foolish to ignore, and by their use of it they made a vital contribution to its strength.

The trade union leaders from the time of the passing of the Trade Union Acts of 1871 and 1875, legalizing private collective bargaining, underwent a process of political instruction in dealing with the two established parties which stood them in good stead when the time came in the twentieth century for straight effective political action, hastened on by the Taff Vale decision and the Osborne judgment. The development of collective bargaining has progressed with

[21] J. Ramsay MacDonald, *Socialism and Government* (3rd ed. 1910), pp. 116–118.
[22] Cf. S. and B. Webb, *History of Trade Unionism,* p. 474, pp. 557–575.

the increase in political power of the Labour movement, and this has reached national proportions in the post-war industrial agreements. Today industrial disputes are considered less as landmarks in Trade Union history. In their place there are other useful methods, often statutory and political in character, by which the organized labour movement advances in public influence and in a recognized participation in the government of the nation and in the control of industry. A well defined influence mutually operates between the action of trade unionism on legislation, and of legislation on trade unionism. The action is incessant and reciprocal, and the significance of it has not diminished under a Labour Government.

Chief among restrictive laws at the beginning of the nineteenth century were the Combination Act, 1800, and the Act of 1817, for the prevention of seditious meetings. But from the Reform Act of 1832 there was a deliberate attempt to bring the political system into accord with the life of the nation. It was by this continuous effort of reform and re-making of the law of the land that the democratic tradition was strengthened, providing an opportunity for a Labour movement to develop free from the orthodoxy of Marxism, nor bound hopelessly by a futile philosophy of social determinism. The importance of this tradition is written plain in the social programme of the political parties in the England of the last century; the practical social politics of the Conservative and Liberal parties attest the influence of the idea of democratic progress. It was for some time the function of the party, which took soon after the Reform the name Liberal, to extend the franchise, especially in the industrial centres; to reform the Poor Law, the criminal law, municipal government and the civil service; pass laws for the improvement of public health; establish general elementary education; give greater freedom to trade unions; remove grievances of Dissenters; disestablish the Church in Ireland; enlarge the local government and create a system of central control. When the Conservatives won their victory at the election of 1874, the period of Liberal domination had for a time come to an end, because they had worked out their chief problems, "they had brought the state in its most important aspects into accord with modern conditions." [23] It is a mark of British social politics that no party has dominated the progress of social policy, but each has contributed to its development by fresh legislation and by the fact that they have been responsible for administration.

[23] Lowell, op. cit., vol. II, p. 103, pp. 116–117.

The extension of the franchise and the growth of popular education and the wider diffusion of well-being have inspired each generation in England to consider anew the tasks of democratic government; and there has been created a strong body of opinion which no party in England is able to disregard in formulating a Government policy. The Conservative party under Disraeli advocated progressive measures and the Reform Act of 1867 was brought in by a Conservative Ministry. His effort to bring about an alliance of his party with the newly enfranchised working class electors was a venture; but till 1868 only a small number of working men were voters, and a majority were unenfranchised in 1884. Political apathy followed the collapse of the Chartist movement, and this fact combined with the well established tendency of a large number of voters toward non-participation in politics, made any progress in political education difficult. When the struggle for legalizing the trade unions went on, 1859–1875, the Labour movement was weak numerically and financially. The first Gladstone Ministry of 1868–1874 did not affect to any appreciable extent the problems which faced the mass of the workers. It was not until Mr. Gladstone returned to power in 1880, after the fall of the Disraelian Government, that the full force of the Irish question brought out a definite, settled policy of social reform and remedial legislation. In the first year of the triumphant Gladstone Government, Mr. Gladstone wrote to Lord Rosebery that, "What is outside Parliament seems to me to be fast mounting—nay to have mounted to an importance much exceeding what is inside." The agitation for land legislation and the policy which Gladstone pursued, gave an opportunity for the development of the tendencies which grew into the British Labour movement of the modern period.

III

THE BEGINNINGS OF THE MODERN LABOUR MOVEMENT

British Socialism from 1880 was freer from dogma than French Socialism. At the same time that the doctrine of *laissez-faire* was being undermined in England, there was a vigorous growth of freedom in the English Labour movement. When the programme of Marseilles, directly inspired by orthodox Marxism,[24] was being written in 1879, English Socialism was enthusiastic for the optimism

---

[24] Cf. Paul Louis, *Histoire du socialisme Français* (1901), pp. 306–307.

of Henry George. This period began a definite break from the Marxian influence, and from this freedom there has resulted a positive suspicion of theory among the English working class and in the Labour party, which has not always been to its advantage, but it has been possible for the leaders to say that "a reply to Marxian dogma is not a reply to Socialism." [25] There has been a great deal more talk about Marx in the literature of the Socialist and anti-Socialist controversy since the war than can be found in the history of British Socialism before 1914. This is no doubt due to the large place Russia has occupied in the thought of the world. Marx's influence on the economic and political theory of the English Labour leaders has been scant; Mr. Sidney Webb (as he then was) saying that Marx added nothing "whether sound or unsound, which makes for the construction of a Socialist State, as distinguished from Socialistic rebellion against any other form of State." [26] British Socialism learned its lessons at home and the application has been upon native soil from the start.

A compulsion of community interest has helped to discipline the political Labour movement and has also kept its leaders from straying far into mere questions of theory. England has had enough practical problems to keep their attention in Parliament, and there their criticism of the industrial system has been heard. But it has not only been in the ranks of organized Labour and in the propaganda of electoral groups that the social aspects of the economic system have been stressed. The doctrine of Welfare in economic theory has been given a first place, and emphasis has been put upon the social cost to the community as a whole of an unjust economic order. The demand of Labour has fortunately coincided with the conviction of many citizens who have been concerned about a fairer distribu-

---

[25] J. Ramsay MacDonald, *The Socialist Movement*, p. 93; and this fact is elaborated in his *Socialism and Society* (1905).

[26] See *The Encyclopaedia of the Labour Movement*, vol. I, p. 26, article on *Fabianism* by Sidney Webb (Lord Passfield). Cf. A. D. Lindsay, *Karl Marx's 'Capital'* (1926); H. W. B. Joseph, *The Labour Theory of Value in Karl Marx* (1923), pp. 1–28, 148–174. Mr. Beer in his significant *History of British Socialism* (vol. II, 1920), says (p. 202) that "The rise of modern socialism in Great Britain, as well as the whole Labour unrest since 1907, so far as their leaders have been attempting to give them a theoretical foundation, are inseparably linked with Marxism." Compare this with his statement on p. 345, and Egon Wertheimer, *Portrait of the Labour Party* (1929), pp. 192 ff. Also E. R. Pease, *History of the Fabian Society* (1st ed. 1916, new ed. 1925), Appendix I by G. B. Shaw, and pp. 23–24, 236. Pease declared that none of the earlier Fabians had read Marx.

tion of the wealth of the nation. Professor Edwin Cannan was speaking for many of his fellow-countrymen when he said that social reform in England derived no strength from Marxian doctrines, but is "now chiefly dependent upon the popular belief that greater equality in the distribution of wealth is desirable." [27]

It is thus easy to understand why the progress of the Labour movement from the democratic ideas of Chartism, 1838–1848, is reflected in achievements of social and legislative reform. The older democratic revolt sought political change only; the spirit of the times was in the revolutionary propaganda of the struggle. It is a commentary on the growth of democracy that the advocates of change in the 'eighties who sought more adequately to interpret democracy in social institutions and to gain a larger freedom in industry, were moderate in temper and method. They seemed convinced and were persuasive. There was no definite plan of legislation like the Chartists' points, but the working class, so far as there was any theoretical formulation, were inspired by a vague and general programme for the reconstruction of society under collectivist or socialist ideals. The Trade Union Congress aims, however, were set forth as concrete objectives that could be easily understood. The propagandist enthusiasm is seen in the second Fabian Tract in 1884, when George Bernard Shaw, in the concluding affirmation, said "we had rather face a civil war than such another century of suffering as the present one has been." Yet twenty-four years later the retrospective view perhaps more accurately saw the meaning of past events, and Shaw wrote that in 1885 "we set ourselves two definite tasks: first to provide a parliamentary programme for a Prime Minister converted to Socialism as Peel was converted to free trade; and secondly, to make it as easy and matter-of-course for the ordinary respectable Englishman to be a Socialist as to be a Liberal or a Conservative." [28]

[27] *Theories of Production and Distribution* (3rd ed. 1920), pp. 404–405.
[28] See Shaw's *Introduction* to the 1908 edition of *Fabian Essays in Socialism* (American ed. Boston), p. xv. The "political inadequacy of the human animal" has been a doubt which Shaw says has grown on him "during my forty years' public work as a Socialist" (Preface of *Back to Methuselah*, p. 9). This Preface of 72 pages is illuminating in parts for Socialist history, suggesting a contrast with the great literary figure of French Socialism, Anatole France. See also his *An Intelligent Woman's Guide to Socialism and Capitalism* (1928); Archibald Henderson, George Bernard Shaw (1911), chap. IV; Mrs. Sidney Webb, *My Apprenticeship* is a lively survey of the period.

From the beginning of the English Labour movement two influences of distinctly British genius have been at work, modifying and complementing each other. The one is common sense acceptance of compromise by leaders in Parliament—and in industrial agreements—and the other is an unfailing belief of the mass of the workers in gaining reforms by political ways. Parliament has been looked to from the beginning as a means of change. Also in the background of the social movement is the part the intellectuals have taken in providing criticism of the Labour movement and in giving the movement from time to time the fresh energy which comes from taking a new direction. All of these influences have not diminished since 1874, when for the first time two Labour-Liberal members were returned to Parliament, Alexander MacDonald and Thomas Burt. Seventeen years before, in 1857, George Jacob Holyoake was parliamentary candidate for the constituency of Tower Hamlets. It was, he said, the first claim ever made to represent Labour in Parliament. His conclusion in the campaign address to the voters, dated March 23, 1857, is interesting: "All progress is a growth, not an invasion. Legislation can do little more than enable the poor people to help themselves. But this help, given with personal knowledge of their wants, and in a spirit free from the temerity which would precipitate society on an unknown future, and free from the cowardice which is afraid to advance at all, may do much." This is a characteristic statement of the democratic movement in England.

Labour representation in the House of Commons meant at this time the sending of working men to Parliament, a movement which was really given a basis of support by the formation of the Trade Union Congress in 1868. There was no regular body to promote or initiate legislation before the assembly of the Trade Union Congresses.[29] The Congress in 1869 first declared itself in favour of the direct representation of Labour in Parliament, and in that year the Labour Representation League was formed. The prospectus of the League interpreted the point of view of the leaders, and in 1871 the Trade Union Congress affirmed that the direct representation of Labour is a necessity, not only in the interests of the working men

[29] Cf. George Howell, *Trade Unionism, New and Old* (3rd ed. 1900), p. 468; George Jacob Holyoake, *Sixty Years of an Agitator's Life* (1893); A. W. Humphrey, *A History of Labour Representation* (1912), pp. 187–190.

as a class, but also in the interests of the nation at large. Mr. Gladstone that year, in speaking on the Elections Bill, declared the great
blot on their representation system was that they had not been
able to bring working men within the walls of Parliament. He further stated that when the Reform Act of 1867 was passed, so largely
increasing the constituents, there were few honourable members who
did not hope that one result of that change would be that they
would have the pleasure of welcoming, in the House of Commons,
some of their fellow citizens of the working class. Nearly forty
years later Mr. Keir Hardie, in a memoir of the great leader, while
appreciating the love of freedom which was a positive quality in
Gladstone, held that "the modern Labour movement and the conditions which have called it forth, he never understood, and there
was no Labour party to evidence the fact that there was a Labour
movement in existence. Surely, however, this cannot be imputed as
blame to him. The fault lies elsewhere." [30] Another generous critic
has written that "constructive legislation coping with pauperism,
sweating, unemployment, old-age destitution, or engaging the State
in constructive work for the development of the productive resources
of our land and labour lay outside his (Gladstone's) conception of
practical or even legitimate politics." [31] In October, 1897, Mr. John
Morley (as he then was) wrote in his diary: "When will some man
arise to lead and command Labour? I doubt if he will come from
their class. Some men with Mr. Gladstone's genius, devoted to social ends." [32] Of the pioneer leader Keir Hardie, he wrote in a letter
in 1907: "He is an observant, hard-headed, honest fellow, but rather
vain and crammed full of vehement preconceptions, especially on
all the most delicate and dubious parts of politics. Perhaps it is only
the men with these unscrupulous preconceptions—knocking their
heads against stone walls—who force the world along."

[30] *The Labour Leader,* May 28, 1908. Two interesting books on this period
are F. W. Soutter, *Recollections of a Labour Pioneer* (1923), and A. Watson,
A Great Labour Leader, Being the Life of the Rt. Hon. Thomas Burt, M.P.
(1908).
[31] J. A. Hobson, *The Crisis of Liberalism* (1909), p. 3. "The whole conception of the State disclosed by the new issues, as an instrument for the
active adaptation of the economic and moral environment to the new needs
of individual and social life, by securing full opportunities of self-development
and social service for all citizens, was foreign to the Liberalism of the last
generation" (p. 3).
[32] Viscount Morley, *Recollections* (Two vols. 1917), vol. II, p. 76, and p. 235.

A political revolution—a changed House of Commons—was a necessary condition for the realization of a new economic policy, and this revolution waited upon many things. But three Labour members were elected to the House of Commons in 1880, ten in 1886, fifteen in 1892, twelve in 1895, and in 1900 ten. In 1886, eighteen years after the first Trade Union Congress, the Labour Electoral Association was organized with the aim of returning Liberal-Labour men to Parliament. Mr. Henry Broadhurst, for fifteen years the secretary of the Trade Union Parliamentary Committee, says in his *Autobiography,* that the Parliamentary Committee fulfilled the function of the Radical wing of the Liberal Party, exerting itself not merely for the working classes, but on behalf of the community at large. The main work of the Committee up to 1875 was to further legislation for the complete legalization of the trade unions and the protection of their funds. In the 'seventies and early 'eighties the work of the Committee was largely spent on the Trade Union Bill of 1871, the Mines Regulation Act, 1872, and the Nine Hours Bill, 1871. It was also interested in the reform of jury laws, the amendment of the Summary Jurisdiction Act, and the Shipping and Patent Laws. The Committee fought for the codification of the criminal laws; drafted a Bill dealing with boiler explosions; and Broadhurst drew up a Bill for the abolition of property qualifications for membership in local governing bodies, which was introduced by A. J. Mundella in 1876, becoming a law two years later. The Committee drew up a Workmen's Compensation law, which was subsequently read a second time and referred to a Select Committee, and also used its influence to secure the Act consolidating the Factory and Workshop code, and the protective clauses for Labour in the Shipping Act of 1883.[33] However much the opposition of the old-line trade union officials kept the Labour movement from developing into a distinct political party, and whatever the drawbacks of this policy were, there was all the time going on in the ranks of

[33] See Humphrey, *op. cit.,* pp. 72–73 for a summary of the activities of the Parliamentary Committee of the Trade Union Congress. Cf. Sidney and Beatrice Webb, *History of Trade Unionism,* pp. 680–682, and *Industrial Democracy* (1897 ed.), p. 351. From 1873 an official Report of the Trade Union Congress has been issued. W. J. Davis has done for the Congress what Léon Blum did for the Workers' and Socialist Congresses of France, written its chronological record in *A History of the British Trade Union Congress* (vol. I, 1910; vol. II, 1916).

the movement agitation for concrete reforms which was excellent training for future political activity. The leaders too were becoming much stronger in the demands they made upon those responsible for carrying through legislation in Parliament. In the thirty-three years from 1868 to 1901, over sixty Acts of Parliament directly affecting Labour were passed.[34] Political change through this period was indicated in an increasing demand for legislation favourable to Labour, and there was a public opinion which supported legislative action and made it possible. As early as April, 1873, the Federation of Employers was organized to combat the growing parliamentary influence of Labour. In a Manifesto, dated December 11, 1873, the Federation outlined its purpose, pointing out that the growing strength of the trade unions made it possible for them to bring unusual pressure to bear on Parliament.[35]

The increasing demand for factory legislation before 1900 indicates the political power of the growing Labour movement, and this power was also directly affecting the organization of the trade unions. Since 1868 there had been organized such exclusively political trade union organizations as the United Textile Factory Workers' Association, a predominantly political association as the Miners' Federation of Great Britain, together with the formation of a general political machinery throughout the trade union world, in the form of Trade Councils, the Trade Union Congress, and the Parliamentary Committee of the Trade Union Congress. These agencies were directly responsible for an active political consciousness being created in the British Labour movement. They provided a splendid training school for the future Labour party. But in spite of the increasing recognition of how useful in the House of Commons was direct representation of Labour, it was not until 1899 that the Trade Union Congress decided for *independent* Labour representation. A resolution was passed in that year instructing the Parliamentary Committee "to invite the co-operation of all co-operative, socialistic, trade unions, and other working class organizations as may be willing to take part to devise ways and means for the securing of an increased number of Labour members in the next Parliament."

[34] Cf. George Howell, *op cit.*, pp. 469–472, for list of these Acts.
[35] See Frank H. Rose, *The Coming Force: The Labour Movement* (Manchester, 1909), *Appendix,* for extracts from this Manifesto.

A special committee was appointed, composed of delegates from the Congress, the Independent Labour party, the Social Democratic Federation and the Fabian Society, to prepare the agenda for the Conference. The task of drafting the constitution for the proposed Labour party was given to Mr. J. Ramsay MacDonald, by the delegates. Of this committee of ten members, four were from the Parliamentary Committee of the Trade Union Congress, and two from each of the Socialist organizations. The Special Conference on Labour Representation was held at the Memorial Hall, London, February 27–28, 1900. One qualified to judge this Memorial Hall meeting has written that there had come "some to bury the attempt in good-humoured tolerance, a few to make sure that burial would be its fate, but the majority determined to give it a chance." [36] The close connection between the industrial and political Labour movement, which has continued, is seen by the fact that the chairman of the Trade Union Congress, Mr. J. T. Chandler, opened the proceedings. But not being a member of the Conference, he was succeeded by Mr. W. C. Steadman, who in his opening remarks said that although he had only been a member of Parliament for a short time, he had been there long enough to see that "every interest was represented and protected except the interests of Labour." The former chairman had set forth the objects of the Conference, and the Resolution of the 1899 Congress had defined the purpose of Labour representation in Parliament.

The task of the Labour leaders was to direct their increasing influence in Parliament, and to secure the continuance of this strength they had to build up a sure and safe electorate throughout Great Britain. This spirit was made plain by the proceedings of the Memorial Hall Conference of 1900, in the first resolution which was offered and in the opposition which it provoked. The resolution declared, "That this Conference is in favour of the working class being represented in the House of Commons by members of the working class as being most likely to be sympathetic with the aims and demands of the Labour movement." This resolution was described by Mr. John Burns as a "narrow and exclusive proposal," and to proclaim in favour of working class candidates only would be bad enough, but to give a definition to the candidates would be infinitely worse. He said he was "getting tired of working class

[36] J. Ramsay MacDonald, *The Socialist Movement*, p. 235.

boots, working class trains, working class houses, and working class margarine." He voiced the idea of the democratic advance of the Labour movement in politics when he urged that they should not be "prisoners of class prejudice, but should consider parties and policies apart from class organization." The amendment to the resolution moved and seconded by Mr. G. N. Barnes and Mr. Burns, was passed by a vote of 102 to 3, and was also amended to include the co-operators. The resolution was, "That this Conference is in favour of working class opinion being represented in the House of Commons by men sympathetic with the aims and demands of the Labour Movement, and whose candidatures are promoted by one or other of the organized movements represented by the constitution which this Conference is about to frame."

The dissensions between the Social Democratic Federation [37] and the majority of the delegates, who had a definite idea of what could be accomplished by the tactics of "progressive politics," were seen in the resolution of the Social Democratic Federation, when they proposed, through Mr. James MacDonald, that the representation of the working class movement in the House of Commons form there a "distinct party, separate from the capitalist parties, based upon the recognition of the class war, and having for its ultimate object the socialization of the means of production, distribution and exchange." It was said in the discussion on this resolution that nothing would be more unfortunate for the Conference than for it to "label across its front 'Class War'." An amendment to this resolution was offered by the veteran leader Hardie, president of the Independent Labour party, which was unanimously decided upon and which outlined the independent policy of the Labour party which was to be formed, and which really came into being with the Labour Representation Committee, which carried on the first fights of the Labour party during the general election of 1900. The Hardie Resolution is important as the then basis of Labour party electoral policy [38] It is: "This Conference is in favour of establishing a

---

[37] Cf. H. M. Hyndman, *Le Mouvement Socialiste,* "La Crise Socialiste en Europe," October 15, 1901, pp. 449–455, pleading for no compromise in the class struggle. The statement with reference to industrial organization is given in a more picturesque way in *Tom Mann's Memoirs* (1923), a readable account of this period.

[38] *The Report of Memorial Hall Conference* was published in 1900 by the Labour Representation Committee.

distinct Labour Group in Parliament who shall have their own Whips and agree upon their policy, which must embrace a readiness to co-operate with any party which, for the time being, may be engaged in the promoting legislation in the direct interest of Labour, and be equally ready to associate themselves with any party in opposing measures having an opposite tendency; and, further, members of the Labour Group shall not oppose any candidate whose candidature is being promoted in terms of Resolution I (the Barnes Resolution). The Social Democratic Federation in 1901 brought forward the resolution pledging the candidates to recognize the class war, but it was lost, and in August of that year the Social Democratic Federation withdrew from the Labour Representation Committee.

In the Executive Committee of the Labour Representation Committee numbered twelve, composed of seven members from the Trade Union Congress, two each from the Independent Labour party, and the Social Democratic Federation, and one from the Fabian Society. The Labour Representation Committee had only been formed eight months when Parliament was dissolved in September, 1900, and it was not prepared to face the election; but fifteen candidates were run under the auspices of the Committee, of whom two were returned, Keir Hardie and Richard Bell. The formation of the Labour Representation Committee was the determined effort to initiate an independent political movement; and the third annual Conference held at Newcastle-on-Tyne in 1903, definitely set forth the independent political principle: "In view of the fact that the Labour Representation Committee is recruiting adherents from all outside political forces, and also, taking into consideration the basis upon which the Committee was inaugurated, this Conference regards it as being absolutely necessary that the members of the Executive Committee should strictly abstain from identifying themselves with or promoting the interests of any section of the Liberal or Conservative parties, inasmuch as if we are to secure the social and economic requirements of the industrial classes, Labour representatives in and out of Parliament will have to shape their own policy and act upon it regardless of sections in the political world; and that the Executive Committee report to the affiliated associations or bodies any such official acting contrary to the spirit of the constitution as hereby amended." [39] This 1903

[39] *The Labour Year Book 1916*, pp. 306–307.

Conference also established a Parliamentary Fund for the payment of Labour members and for election charges.[40] The years 1903–1905 witnessed the most carefully planned and enthusiastic period of political organization in the history of the British Labour movement; it is no wonder that when the general election took place in 1906, of the fifty candidatures of the Labour Representation Committee, twenty-nine were returned. A compact and coherent Labour group was formed, which had its own officers and Whip, and acted independently of the other parties in Parliament. The appointment of a Select Committee on Housing in 1906 was the first occasion of Labour claiming a distinct right for representatives on such committees in Parliament. The Government announced that "the Labour Party were entitled to have one twenty-third of the representatives on these Committees, and yet, out of seventeen Committees which had been appointed, they were represented on no fewer than thirteen." [41] By a vote of 320 to 43 the Labour claim for a member on the specific Committee was rejected, but their claim was an indication of strength in Parliament.

The name of the Labour Representation Committee was changed in 1906 to that of the Labour party, and the definite establishment of a Parliamentary Labour party in the House of Commons meant that a new element had entered British politics. The entrance of the Parliamentary Labour party just at the time the Government was pledged to a radical social programme affecting "the condition of the people," makes pertinent a consideration of the legislation affecting the aims of Labour. A survey of this social legislation and its administration is the basis of this study.

This chapter has provided an introduction for the long years of agitation for social legislation. In the parliamentary struggles and in the debates there may at times be obscured the background of political liberty in England which made a Labour movement possible; and for this reason this chapter has recorded the preparation

---

[40] In 1904 the Labour party submitted a motion for debate on payment of members of Parliament, by Mr. Arthur Henderson. The vote against was 221—151; for debate, see *Parl. Deb.,* H.C., 4 S., 1904, vol. 134, pp. 1105–1129. The Resolution adopted August 10, 1911, provided for the payment of members, which the Committee on Supply allowed in the appropriations for the year.

[41] *Parl. Deb.,* H.C., 4 S., 1906, vol. 156, p. 1282 (Whitley) ; and pp. 1383–1384, Labour statement, by Mr. Crooks.

of an important part of the community for the responsibilities of citizenship. This citizenship has become increasingly significant in the twentieth century, not only in its influence in the Parliament of the nation but in the community interests of the whole people. Legislation is only one aspect of this growth in democratic government, but it is the part with which this study is concerned. When the twentieth century offered a Parliament where the nation's problems could be heard, at the same time it was made sure that there would be the continuity of progress which only faith in the integrity of popular institutions can make possible.

CHAPTER II

SOCIAL POLITICS AT THE BEGINNING OF THE CENTURY IN ENGLAND

The year 1900 was not the year 1930, and the survey of the social legislation of England in the intervening years will often appear to offer a dull repetition of Acts and amendments, of Bills and Motions. And, in the debates in Parliament which are referred to, one looking back may question the significance now of what seemed at the time of first rate importance. A Government announcement in 1904 on unemployment may seem a quarter of a century later more remote in history than it is, and a Labour motion then by Mr. Keir Hardie may seem unrelated now to the life of Great Britain at the beginning of the fourth decade of the century. The post-war years have changed so much that was familiar, the difficulty is now that the full significance of pre-war years is neglected.

The official statement of the Conservative Government of Mr. Balfour on the internal affairs of the country in 1900 was given in the address at the opening of Parliament as follows: "The time is not propitious for any domestic reforms which involve a large expenditure. Amendments are required in the laws which govern limited liability companies and those which relate to agricultural tenancies. Measures for amending the law of ecclesiastical assessments, and in regard to education in Scotland, and for the relief of tithe-rent payers in Ireland, will also be laid before you. Your attention will also be invited to proposals for better enabling local authorities to aid secondary and technical education in England and Wales; for controlling the contracts of money lenders; for the amendments of the Factory law, of the Law of Lunacy, and of the Housing of the Working Classes Act." [1]

The 1900 election had been fought mainly over the issue of the

[1] *Parl. Deb.,* 4 S.H.C., vol. LXXVIII, 1900, p. 4.

South African War. The embittered feelings of the time were expressed in the extended debate on the Address, finding an outlet in personal bitterness and recrimination. The ugliness of War rumours were in Parliament, and members of the Cabinet had especially to be above suspicion in their financial connections, and at the same time they heard from Mr. John Burns, quoting Burke, that it was "no excuse for presumptuous ignorance that it is directed by insolent passion."[2] The leader of the Opposition, Sir Henry Campbell-Bannerman, centred the attack against the Government on their war policies and their failure adequately to meet the internal problems of the country. He claimed the full right of criticism; it was "the very time for effective criticism," if the nation was to understand the issues of the day. The Address, he said, had omitted any reference to measures dealing effectively with overcrowded and insanitary dwellings and old-age pensions, the two great social questions that the people were concerned with most intimately.[3] The Government, so it seemed, had taken advantage of what appeared a tempting situation. Parliament had been dissolved, and the "Khaki" election, while leaving the relative numbers of the two great parties practically unchanged, seemed to assure the Government an extended lease of power for five or six years. "And this, " reflected Lord Oxford and Asquith in later years, "turned out to be their undoing. For it lead them to introduce reactionary domestic legislation, particularly in regard to education, which was profoundly unpalatable to the Liberal-Unionist side of the partnership. And it gave to Mr. Chamberlain, as the now recognized Empire-builder-in-Chief to the Coalition, the opportunity of raising the flag of Imperial Preference, which had an equally disintegrating effect upon his Tory associates. This was bad enough, but worse was to follow. Almost in the twinkling of an eye it became apparent that the Liberal party had been gratuitously presented with the one specific which was most certain to salve its wounds and to re-establish its unity. The lately warring factions fraternized, without difficulty or delay, in a cause which both by their tradition and their convictions commanded their united allegiance."[4] Thus, a

[2] *Ibid.*, p. 787.

[3] The two chief speeches of Sir Henry Campbell-Bannerman, leader of the Opposition, on the Address were on January 30, *Parl. Deb., op. cit.*, pp. 79–111; and February 6, *ibid.*, pp. 803–814.

[4] Lord Oxford and Asquith (Mr. H. H. Asquith), *Memories and Reflections* (2 vols. 1927), vol. I, pp. 178–179.

united Liberal attack was in the process of formation just at the time that Labour opposition was able to add its protest to the policy of the Government. The strength of this combined attack increased from 1902 to 1905, and prepared the way for the new Liberal victory.

Criticism levelled against the Government because of its failure to consider the insistent claims of social reform was particularly a feature of the 1900 debates on the Mines (Eight Hours) Bill, the Housing of the Working Classes (1890) Amendment Bill and the Old Age Pensions Bill. The Government were reminded time and time again that the pledges of 1895 were to be honoured; that they were responsible for the great majority which the Government received in that election. In the debate on the Sale of Intoxicating Liquors to Children, it was declared that their great majority was given to the Government in 1895 for a specific purpose, and that was to devote their attention to matters of social legislation for the country.[5] The Government accepted this point of view. In the debate on the Old Age Pensions Bill, a Government supporter stated that "in the general election of 1895 prominence was given to subjects of social character," and that "the promise of social amelioration in their programme had very much to do with the return of the Unionist party at the general election of 1895."[6] It was added that the great majority of the promises had been fulfilled.

It was to be expected, when such an issue as that upon which the Khaki Election centred was predominantly to the front, that "democratic control over legislation" would be slight.[7] Nevertheless it was impossible for the Government to be unmindful of the imperative problems of keeping the machinery set up by past legislation functioning and the necessity of bringing the administration of the laws constantly into touch with actual needs. There were Parliamentary achievements in the years 1900–1901 which meant progress in industrial legislation by extension and application of principles of state interference which had before been accepted. Within this period were passed the Mines (Prohibition of Child Labour Underground) Act, an enlarged Workmen's Compensation Act, the Railway Employment (Prevention of Accidents Act, the Merchant Shipping (Liability of Shipowners and others) Act, and the epochal

[5] *Parl. Deb.*, H.C., vol. LXXX, p. 521 (Mr. John Wilson).
[6] *Ibid.*, pp. 312–313 (Sir J. Fortescue Flannery).
[7] Cf. J. Ramsay MacDonald, *Socialism and Government,* vol. II, pp. 7–8; and James F. Hope, *History of the 1900 Parliament* (1908), pp. 1–7.

Factory and Workshop Act, 1901. From 1901 to 1905 the Government had much more definitely before it a complex problem of social politics in dealing with the rights of the Trade Unions and with the whole Government policy toward social reform.

With regard to social reform there was a spirit of compromise and agreement upon many principles. But in 1900 in debate, Mr. Bryce (as he then was), stated that, "We are in a perpetual dilemma between government interference on the one hand and the danger of removing individual responsibility on the other. I don't believe it will ever be possible to find a general principle to guide us satisfactorily between the two extremes of this dilemma. All we can do is, in each case, to try and reconcile individual responsibility with so much government interference as is necessary to deal with the evil. If we look back fifty or sixty years it will be found that we have always had to accept the doctrines of both sides and endeavour to steer between them." [8]

Yet the country became restive under such counsel, for it wanted bolder, larger schemes of action. The South African War brought bitter weariness to many, while it encouraged cautious plans on the part of leaders. Sir Leslie Stephen, who had studied his century honestly and had thought much upon his changing time, wrote to an American friend, "The prospect of coming to an end is sometimes cheered for me by the thought that at any rate, I shall hear no more of preferential tariffs and protection." [9]

On the other hand the veteran Labour leader, Mr. J. Keir Hardie, could appeal to Mr. John Morley to cut himself adrift from the "Rosebery-Asquith" section of Liberalism, and give a lead of democracy. An open letter to Mr. Morley declared that "a section of very earnest Liberals are thoroughly ashamed of modern Liberalism and are anxious to put themselves right with their own consciences. Working-class movements are coming together in a manner, for a parallel to which we require to go back to the early days of the Radical movement. Already, 212,000 have paid affiliation fees to the Labour Representation Committee. What is wanted to fuse these elements is a man with the brain to dare, the hand to do, and the

---

[8] *Parl. Deb.,* 4 S. H.C., 1900, Vol. LXXX, pp. 306–308.
[9] A letter to Charles Eliot Norton, October 12, 1903, in F. W. Maitland's *The Life and Letters of Leslie Stephen* (1906), p. 485.

heart to inspire. Will you be that man?"[10] Of the Trade Union Congress at Leicester in 1903 one wrote that, "The enthusiasm and earnestness for Labour Representation are most marked. One feels as if at last one could almost see the masses becoming articulate and determined to look after themselves and improve themselves by united action instead of grumbling about what the people they elect, who have other points of view from themselves, do or don't do." [11] It could be said that even in 1903 some thought that it was possible for Parliament to help individuals in building the City of God in this world, dwelling upon dwelling, street upon street.[12]

The beginning of the century, April 23, 1901, saw the first complete Socialist declaration made in the House of Commons by J. Keir Hardie, who unluckily was last on the private members' ballot. One wrote that the Prime Minister (Balfour) was drawn there by the metaphysical curiosity of the Scot to amuse himself by hearing what a brother Scot had to say on Socialism.[13] Twenty minutes before midnight Hardie offered his resolution: "That considering the increasing burden which the ownership of land and capital is imposing upon the industrious and useful classes of the community, the poverty and destitution and general moral and physical deterioration resulting from a competitive system of wealth production which aims primarily at profit-making, the alarming growth of trusts and syndicates, able by reason of their great wealth to influence governments and plunge peaceful nations into war to serve their own interests, this House is of opinion that such a state of matters is a menace to the well-being of the Realm and calls for legislation designed to remedy the same by inaugurating a Socialist Commonwealth founded upon the common ownership of land and capital, production for use and not for profit, and equality of opportunity for every citizen." "Socialism," Hardie concluded, "by placing the land and the instruments of production in the hands of the community, will eliminate only the idle and useless classes at both ends of the scale. The

---

[10] *J. Keir Hardie: A Biography*, by William Stewart, with an Introduction by J. Ramsay MacDonald (1921), quoted p. 161. Hardie later made the same appeal to Mr. Lloyd George.

[11] Margaret Ethel MacDonald, in a letter, quoted by J. Ramsay MacDonald in his book of this title (1st ed. 1912, 5th ed. 1920), pp. 182–183.

[12] *Ibid.*

[13] Stewart, *op. cit.*, p. 181.

millions of toilers and of business men do not benefit from the present system. We are called upon to decide the question propounded in the Sermon on the Mount, as to whether we will worship God or Mammon. The last has not been heard of this movement, either in the House or in the country, for as surely as Radicalism democratised the system of government politically in the last century, so will Socialism democratise industrialism of the country in the coming century."

Whether or not this period will be regarded as marking the end, and, therefore, also the beginning, of a new era in political thought,[14] when there was an appeal to economic facts and needs and to new social ethics, it is important as marking the sure and steady turn toward the great upheaval of 1906 in British politics when Liberalism came sweeping into power. The year 1904 has been taken as an especially good example of the trend of sentiment in England.[15] Surveying the year 1904, one writer said it would be memorable in history as the year in which the vested interests first began openly to flaunt their power over the Legislature. The struggle was one between the people and the Interests. What was doubtful was the duration and character of the conflict and the final form of victory. If the enthusiasm of the people was slow to be aroused, if the leaders quarrelled amongst themselves, if the great majority of the well-educated, well-meaning, moderate men and women were content to allow themselves to drift into the camp of the Interests the struggle would be long and bitter, the final result bear the spirit of revenge. But if the people responded quickly to the call, if the leaders were strong and unselfish, if moderate men and women frankly took sides with the people, the struggle would come almost without conflict, and the inevitable result be achieved in merciful justice. But clear insight

[14] Cf. L. T. Hobhouse, *Democracy and Reaction* (1904, 2nd ed. 1909), p. 3; also *Social Evolution and Political Theory* (1913), esp. chap. IX, pp. 185–206; and Beer, *op. cit.,* vol. II, p. 345.

[15] Dicey, *op. cit.,* pp. 295 ff. The temper of the 1904 Parliament can be seen in the prolonged debate on the Address; the lengthy debates on the fiscal question, the Education and Licensing Bills did not stop the flood of new Bills which are noted later. For Address see *Parl. Deb.,* 4 S. H.C., 1904, vol. 129, pp. 1–5; pp. 106–118 for the Government; pp. 118–138, Campbell-Bannerman; pp. 138–147, Chamberlain; and pp. 199–237, Redmond. Cf. J. A. Spender, *The Life of the Rt. Hon. Sir Henry Campbell-Bannerman* (1923), chaps. XXV–XXVI. Vol. I, pp. 136–187, for years 1904–1905, and view of changing political forces. And, John Morley, *Recollections,* vol. II, pp. 140–145.

would be necessary to choose correctly and high moral courage to abandon cherished prejudices.[16]

The Government programme of 1905, as outlined in the Address at the opening of Parliament, stated that legislation would be submitted for the establishment of authorities to deal with the question of unemployment, a Bill for the amendment and extension of the Workmen's Compensation Act, and a proposal for establishing a Ministry of Commerce and Industry.[17] At the end of the session the London *Times,* August 11, 1905, stated that "the session of Parliament which comes to an end today, leaves behind it a record of futile debate and disappointing achievement." The chairman of the Labour Party said at the London Conference in 1906 that, "from the legislative aspect of our work the last session of Parliament was undoubtedly the most barren in modern history."[18] Another critic described the session as "a burning national scandal and dire disaster."[19] But no more sweeping condemnation was given than by the leader of the Opposition, Sir Henry Campbell-Bannerman, in the 1905 debate on the Address. He declared that, "a situation so unthinkable as that of the Government at the present time is unknown in our Parliamentary history. The feeling of the country has been demonstrated beyond all doubt or dispute. The political situation today is of such ingrained falsity, it is so fraught with danger to the public interest, that to prolong it is a betrayal and usurpation of power. A Parliamentary majority is, no doubt, a great instrument and a necessary instrument for the Executive Government, but it is not everything. There is something behind any Parliament or any majority in any Parliament from which both Parliament and the majority derive their power. That is the public conscience. The public

[16] F. W. Pethick Lawrence, in "Preface" to *The Reformers' Year Book, 1905.* The party literature of the period is interesting. See especially *Nine Years' Work,* issued by the Central Conservative Office, a review of the legislation and administration of the Government from 1895–1904; *Ninth Year of Tory Government,* being speeches and party leaflets by the leading Liberal members of Parliament; *The Liberal View,* with Preface by Earl Spencer, being articles on current politics by the '80 Club. Also J. A. Spender, *A Modern Journal: A Diary for the Year of Agitation (1903–1904)* (1904); B. Villiers, *The Opportunity of Liberalism* (1904).

[17] *Parl. Deb.,* 4 S. H.C., 1905, vol. 141, pp. 1–5. The Ministry of Commerce and Industry Bill, introduced by Mr. Sinclair, was House Bill No. 151, 1905.

[18] Arthur Henderson, Chairman's Address in the *Report of the 6th Annual Conference of the Labour party,* London, 1906, p. 42; pp. 39–42 entire.

[19] *The Reformers' Year Book,* 1906, p. 62.

conscience is greater than any constitutional machinery, and no man can say in this case that the public conscience is vague."[20]

A new Government soon came into power,[21] after the Conservative and Unionist party had been in office for over twenty years, with a brief exception—the Rosebery and Fourth Gladstone Ministeries. The Prime Minister, Sir Henry Campbell-Bannerman declared that underlying every proposal of his Government would be a policy of social reconstruction looking toward a greater equalization of wealth, and the destruction of the oppressive monopolies of land and liquor. Mr. Asquith, after Campbell-Bannerman's retirement, succeeding to the leadership of the Commons, declared that the injustice of the existing social system rendered a popular attack upon it inevitable. He said, "Property must be associated in the minds of the masses of the people, with the ideas of reason and justice." England had faced the severest struggles of a democracy attempting to administer an Empire, and, at the same time, making an effort to direct the democratic movement at home.[22] In the years which the Conservative party governed the principles upon which the state interfered in the organization of industry were definitely expressed and greatly enlarged. The years from 1890 to 1905 were a background for that wider and more expansive movement which in this century has sought to bring in the democratic state.[23] From 1905 to 1914 the Liberal party was to have the opportunity to govern, aided and urged to action by a Labour party, with as much freedom and as complete a Parliamentary majority as their opponents had possessed from 1885. The

[20] *Parl. Deb., op. cit.,* pp. 120–141, speech entire.

[21] Social legislation promised in the Address of 1906 *(Parl. Deb.,* 4 S.H.C., 1906, vol. 152, pp. 21–24) were Bills dealing with the law of Trade Disputes, Workmen's Compensation and for amending the Unemployed Workmen Act; note speeches of the Prime Minister, pp. 164–179; Mr. Joseph Chamberlain, pp. 149–164; for Labour: Mr. Hardie, pp. 193–201, and Mr. Barnes, pp. 259–265.

[22] The first public and private speeches of Mr. Balfour, retiring Prime Minister, provide a review of his long period of service and his interpretation of them; on Dec. 9, 1905, at Manchester, the *Times,* Dec. 11, p. 6; on Dec. 18, at Leeds, the *Times,* Dec. 19, p. 7. See also the long editorial survey "1905," the *Times,* Dec. 30, 1905, pp. 9–11. The Albert Hall speech of Campbell-Bannerman, December 21, the *Times,* Dec. 22, p. 7, also at Perthshire, Nov. 30, the *Times,* Dec. 1, may be compared with Mr. Balfour's speeches. These are interesting because the changing tendencies of the time are well expressed by the official leaders. They provided the cues for parties.

[23] Cf. John Morley, *Life of Gladstone* (1903), vol. III, chaps. VII–X, pp. 490–552; also J. A. Spender, *op. cit.,* vol. II, chap. XXVIII, on formation of First Liberal Ministry.

country was ready for a change, and to the new work which had to be done the Liberal and the Labour parties were dedicated. The temper of the Parliament of 1906 was reflected by the Liberal leader, Sir Henry Campbell-Bannerman, when he said in his opening speech of that year that "England must be less of a pleasure ground for the rich and more of a treasure house for the nation." [24] It is well to directly consider now the social and industrial legislation of the century, and in its later developments some attention will again be given to the relationship of politics, so far as there is anything to be gained from party controversies with regard to social politics.

[24] *Parl. Deb.*, 4 S.H.C., 1906, vol. 152, pp. 164–179.

CHAPTER III

SOCIAL LEGISLATION IN ENGLAND AFFECTING THE CONDITIONS OF WORK

I

THE STATE AND THE FACTORY ACTS

This chapter surveys social legislation in England dealing with the conditions of work for the wage-earner. State action is considered with regard to factory legislation, the Shop Acts, the Coal Mines Regulations Acts, the Workmen's Compensation Acts, and legislation dealing with young persons and children as workers.

The historical significance of the Factory and Workshop Act, 1901, has been pointed out in this study. It is well known that this Act constitutes the basis of existing factory law. A permanent administrative official in the Home Office has described this factory code in a very comprehensive way.[1] The Act applies to all factories and workshops, and, some of its provisions, including the inspection clauses, extend also to home work, and to laundries, docks, buildings in course of erection and the railway sidings of factories. The Act provides for sanitation and ventilation, for safety, for reporting and investigation of accidents and industrial diseases, for the regulation of hours, holidays, overtime and night work, and for the fitness of young persons for employment. The Act contains special provisions for tenement factories, for humid textile factories, for bakehouses, and for certain dangerous or unhealthy processes. Other dangerous and unhealthy processes it left to be dealt with after inquiry by the Home Office, conferring on the Home Secretary power to certify "any manufacture, machinery, plant, process or description of manual labour" to be dangerous or injurious, and thereupon to make "such regulations as appear to him to be reasonably practicable and to meet the necessities of the case." It is thus seen that the Act of 1901 is not only a general code for all factories and workshops,

---

[1] See Sir Edward Troup, *The Home Office* (1925), pp. 162–163, the author was Permanent Under-Secretary of State in the Home Office, 1908–1922.

but the source of many special codes, settled carefully and usually by agreement, to meet the conditions of dangerous or unhealthy employments.[2]

The Act of 1901 consolidated with Amendments all previously existing Factory Acts, especially the Factory and Workshop Act, 1878, and the Amending Acts of 1883, 1889, 1891, 1895, and 1897. The Standing Committee on Trade fused two Bills introduced in the House of Commons, the one an Amending Bill, the other a Consolidating Bill. The Act contained 10 parts and 163 sections. The headings of the 10 parts indicate the wide scope of the Act: Part I, Health and Safety; II, Employment; III, Education of Children; IV, Dangerous and Unhealthy Industries; V, Special Modifications and Extensions; VI, Home Work; VII, Particulars of Work and Wages; VIII, Administration; IX, Legal Proceedings; and the last part deals with the application and definitions of the Act. This Act with its modifications and the subsequent legislation which has carried its principles to every phase of the industrial life of England, is often referred to in this survey of legislation. For this reason the protective and humanitarian features of the Act can be passed over without definite enumeration. Part VIII of the Act, dealing with Administration, can now be outlined.

The appointment, powers and duties of factory inspectors and certifying surgeons are given first,[3] then the powers of the local authorities are defined,[4] together with the procedure of Special Orders by which the Home Secretary can extend or curtail the application of the Act to particular industries.[5] Remaining sections definitely set forth the duties of occupiers of factories and workshops with regard to the Act, and the duties which are required of district councils and their medical officers.[6] Where the general provisions of the Act are not sufficient to meet the needs, the Home Secretary is given power to make regulations. Section 79 is so important both in the Act and as an illustration of administrative power, that it is given here: "Where the Secretary of State is satisfied that any manufacture,

---

[2] See *Annual Report of the Chief Inspector of Factories and Workshops for the Year 1927* (Cmd. 3144, 1928), pp. 14–68, and for 1928 (Cmd. 3360, 1929), pp. 34–47, for illustration of this.

[3] Sects. 118–124.

[4] Sect. 125.

[5] Sect. 126.

[6] Sects. 127–134.

machinery, plant, process, or description of manual labour, used in factories or workshops, is dangerous or injurious to health or dangerous to life or limb, either generally or in the case of women, children or any other class of persons, he may certify that manufacture, machinery, plant, process or description of manual labour, to be dangerous; and thereupon the Secretary of State may, subject to the provisions of this Act, make such regulations as appear to him to be reasonably practicable and to meet the necessity of the case." [7]

The great majority of Special Regulations under the power given to the Home Secretary have been made with reference to the health and safety of the worker. It is well to note that there is a difference in the Special Rules under the Act of 1891, which had to be made for each separate factory or workshop, whereas under the 1901 Act Special Regulations apply to every factory and workshop of the class specified. [8] This was a change in administrative enforcement, which has been carried into other Acts. Special Regulations are made by the Home Secretary, largely dealing with means for the prevention of accidents. There were in 1913 under Regulations or Special Rules, 68,432 works or departments. This number increased by 1927 to 194,650 works or departments, and in 1928 to 215,652, as shown by the annual report of the chief inspector of factories and workshops. [9]

Parliament further made it possible for the Home Secretary to extend the workings of this Act by giving power of legislating by Special Order. This was in keeping with the spirit of Parliament of late years to settle principles and to leave detailed decisions and the working out of extensions to "other bodies," creating inferior bodies to whom law-making powers have been delegated. [10] This power was

---

[7] See Act of 1901, Part IV, Sect. 79. Recent examples under this section are the Horizontal Milling Machines Regulations, (S.R. and O, 1928, No. 548) and the Manufacture of Cinematograph Film Regulations, (S.R. and O. 1928, No. 82).

[8] Cf. 1901 Act, ss. 80–85 (Regulations for Dangerous Trades); the earlier procedure is found in ss. 8–10 of the 1891 Act, amended by ss. 12, 24 (3) and 28, of the Act of 1895. Different texts are usually compared.

[9] *Annual Report 1928*, p. 140, Table 8, and *Annual Report 1929*, Table I, p. 129.

[10] Cf. Tillyard, *Industrial Law*, pp. 19–28; "Non-Parliamentary Industrial Legislation," Lord Hewart, *The New Despotism* (1929), chaps. VI and X, "Departmental Legislation" and "Examples from Statutes," pp. 79–101, 239–305. Cf. *Public Administration*, vol. 5, pp. 382–413, vol. 6, pp. 32–40, for general review of recent tendencies towards the devolution of legislative functions to administrative agencies.

given in the Particulars section of the 1901 Act, which is as follows:
"The Secretary of State, on being satisfied by the report of an inspector that the provisions, of this section are applicable to any class
of non-textile factories or to any class of workshops, may if he
thinks fit, by Special Order, apply the provisions of this section to
any such class, subject to such modifications as may in his opinion be
necessary for adapting those provisions to the circumstances of the
case. He may also by any such order apply those provisions, subject
to such modifications as may, in his opinion, be necessary for adapting
them to the circumstances of the case to any class of persons of whom
lists may be required to be kept under the provisions of this Act
relating to out-workers, and to the employers of those persons." [11]

Under the power to extend the provisions of the Particulars section, which originally included only textile factories and workshops,
to non-textile works, the Home Secretary by 1903 had brought under
this section more than 3000 factories and workshops, and by 1913
this number was increased to 27,000. The industries to which Special
Orders have been made applicable have constantly increased, now
being about 40 trades; and 19 Special Orders have been issued to
suit the special circumstances of the industries under the control of
this section.[12] The principle Parliament recognized by passing an Act
has been extended by experiment, and effective inspection has shown
its usefulness. It is convincing proof that administration is legislation
in action, and emphasizes the value of delegating the working out of
labour regulations to responsible departmental heads after Parliament has laid down the general principle of action. The necessity for
this is made plain when one sees the complex and technical matters
covered by Statutory Rules and Orders. When the Factory Extension
Act, 1867, and the Workshop Regulation Act, 1867, were passed,
Statutory Orders were first introduced. At that time a division of
work between Parliament and the Departments of State was set up,
and has constantly increased. The Factory and Workshop Act, 1901,
expressly defined it with regard to factory legislation, and the provisions as to Special Orders by the Secretary of State for the Home
Department is of such importance as to be especially noted.

The Order shall be under the hand of the Secretary of State—in

---

[11] 1901 Act, Sect. 116, subsect. 5.
[12] See Table 8, p. 138 of *Report of Chief Inspector of Factories and Workshops for 1928* for list.

this instance the Home Secretary—and shall be published in such manner as the Secretary of State thinks best adapted for the information of the persons concerned. The Order may be temporary or permanent, conditional or unconditional, and whether granting or extending an exception or prohibition, or directing the adoption of any special means of provision, or rescinding a previous Order or affecting any other thing, may do so either wholly or partly. The Order shall be laid as soon as may be before both Houses of Parliament, and if either House of Parliament, within the next forty days after the Order has been so laid before that House, resolves that the Order ought to be annulled, it shall after the date of that Resolution be of no effect, without prejudice to validity of anything done in the meantime under the Order or to the making of a new Order. The Order while it is in force, shall, so far as is consistent with the tenor thereof, apply as if it formed part of the enactment which provides for the making of the Order.[13] The Power to make Orders is relevant to 45 sections of the Factory Act, and has been exercised in regard to 33 of these sections. Parliament has never disallowed these Regulations or Special Orders. A development in this administrative procedure occurred during the war when the Home Secretary was empowered under the Police, Factories, etc., Act of 1916, to issue Welfare Orders, which do not come before Parliament. Some fifteen of these have been made, requiring such things as drinking water, mess-rooms, washing accommodations, protective clothing, first aid appliances and ambulances. The Act gives power to the Secretary of State to issue Orders "where it appears that conditions . . . in any factory . . . require provision for securing the *welfare* of workers." [14]

The powers of local authorities and their officers for the purpose of their duties with respect to workshops and workplaces under this Act of 1901, and under the law relating to public health were, that they should have, without prejudice to their other powers, all such powers of entry, inspection, taking legal proceedings or otherwise, as an inspector under this Act. The term local authority for the purpose

[13] Act of 1901, sect. 126, subsect. 1-4.
[14] Section 7 of the Act of 1916. For an example see one of the latest Orders, the Bakehouses Welfare Order, 1927, securing the welfare of workers employed in bakehouses (Statutory Rules and Orders, 1927, No. 191). See *Annual Report of the Chief Inspector of Factories and Workshops for the year 1928*, pp. 53–61, for account of administration.

of this Act includes city and town councils, urban and rural district councils acting as the local authority for public health purposes.[15]

The labour code known as the Factory and Workshop Act, 1901, has been added to by nine statutes besides the Employment of Children Act, 1903, and the Notice of Accidents Act, 1906. The Census of Production Act, 1906, authorizing a small alternation in the time for sending in return of persons employed, is the least important, but the remaining six indicate the steady progress of state control in administering the provisions of the Act and in extending it to include more workers.[16] The Factory and Workshop Act, 1907, brought "commercial laundries" under the general law, and applied the Act, subject to modifications, to work such as needlework, embroidery and laundry work carried on in charitable and reformatory institutions, unless the institution was already under government protection. The work of women was further protected by the Employment of Women Act, 1907, repealing section 57 of the Act of 1901 which allowed unrestricted labour by women in flax mills, in order to bring the law of the United Kingdom into conformity with the rules of the 1906 Berne Convention. A further international agreement found expression in the White Phosphorus Matches Prohibition Act, 1908, prohibiting the use of yellow phosphorus in the manufacture of matches or in the sale or importation of matches so made. Parliament again gave authority to the Secretary of State to legislate in the Factory and Workshop (Cotton Cloth Factories) Act, 1911, which superseded sections 90–94 and Schedule IV of the Act of 1901, for the Secretary of State could make regulations as regards cotton cloth factories, which he did in the Regulations of 1912. The systematic growth of industrial regulation is noted in these Acts, and their development seemed only a natural outcome of the state's duty of protection. There was no particular comment when it was decided by Parliament how a laundry should be ventilated, nor

---

[15] Act of 1901, sects. 125 and 154. The Public Health Act, 1875, sect. 91, is the basis for provisions with regard to sanitary conditions of workshops and domestic factories, but the Factory and Workshops Act, 1901, extended that section so as to make provisions for sanitation in factories and workshops, with two minor differences, practically identical—see ss. 1–2, Part I, 1901 Act. Compare relevant provisions in Local Government Act, 1929.

[16] As early as 1904, Bills were presented for substantial changes in the Factory Acts: see the Factory and Workshops Act (1901) Amendment Bill No. 61 (1904), by Mr. Tennant, and the Accidents (Mines and Factories) Bill, by Mr. Cochrane (House Bill, No. 73, 1905).

did it appear an unwarranted interference when certain industries were forced by law to change their method of manufacture or go out of business.

The Employment of Women, Young Persons and Children Act, 1920, carried out four conventions agreed to at the Washington Conference in 1919. They were conventions (1) fixing a minimum age for admission of children to industrial employment; (2) concerning night work of young persons employed in industry; (3) concerning night work of women employed in industry; and (4) the fixing of minimum age for admission of children to employment at sea. A child is one under 14 years of age, a young person is one under 18, and at 18 a woman reaches her industrial age. The administration of the Act is under the Factory and Workshop Act, 1901–1920, to which it is the most recent addition, together with the Women and Young Persons (Employment in Lead Processes) Act, 1920,—an International Labour Convention—and the Lead Paint (Protection Against Poisoning) Act, 1926. This last Act gave the Secretary of State power to make Regulations for preventing danger from lead paint.[17]

Administration of the Factory Act

It is nearly one hundred years from the passing of Lord Ashley's Act in 1833, which began the appointment of factory inspectors, with extensive powers. Today the staff of inspectors and assistants numbers 207, of whom over thirty are women. The Home Secretary in 1929 (Mr. Clynes) announced to the deputation organized by the Standing Joint Committee of Industrial Women's Organizations, that he was in communication with the Treasury and hoped to obtain Treasury approval for a very substantial increase in the number of factory inspectors. The Act now applies to more than 260,000 factories and workshops which are under the inspectorate.[18] At the head there is the Chief Inspector with three deputies. The country is divided into ten divisions each under a Superintending Inspector and

[17] The Secretary of State on December 24, 1926, under section 1 of the Act made an Order and rule for enforcement of this Act (Statutory Rules and Orders, 1926, Nos. 1620 and 1621) and further regulations in 1927 under section 1 of the Act, being Statutory Rules and Orders, 1927, No. 847.
[18] See Table 14 of the *Annual Report of the Chief Inspector of Factories and Workshops for the Year 1928*, p. 149, which is a summary of the administration of the Act from 1914–1928.

his deputy, and into eighty-three districts each with a district inspector. There are technical inspectors—five electrical, five engineering and four medical, and, in the textile centres, five inspectors of
textile particulars. There are also some 1800 "certifying surgeons,"
part-time officers who make reports on the more serious accidents and
cases of industrial disease, certify young persons as fit for factory
work, and examine periodically the persons employed in certain
dangerous trades. They examined in 1928, 334,059 young persons for
employment. The general responsibility for the factory inspectorate
and the Factory Act is upon the Home Secretary. There has been
some effort to combine under the Ministry of Labour this duty, as
well as the Mines Department, now under the Board of Trade; this
consolidation under a Minister of Labour and Industry being advocated by the Report of the Liberal Industrial Inquiry in 1928.[19]

Constant changes and continued agitation have made for a new
Factory Act, the bringing in of which the Government of Mr. Baldwin pledged itself. The Labour Home Secretary introduced in 1924
a Factories Bill which was termed "a new charter for factory
workers." The Conservative Government later rejected this Bill,
which was again introduced in 1926 by a Labour member, undertook
to make such a measure a principal Government pledge. It has been
declared that "probably no departmental bill has ever had more labour
or a greater variety of technical knowledge devoted to it than the
Factory Bill now waiting final approval before introduction in the
House of Commons."[20] The Labour Government is pledged to a new
Factories Bill. It is certain to be an extended work for the House of
Commons. From the Act of 1901 to 1930 is the most important
period of England's industrial history with regard to factory legislation; the Act passed will demand a tremendous amount of legislative
effort and departmental research. It can in no sense be mere party
legislation.

It is significant that since the end of the War the Home Office
has taken a share in the scientific research into the causes and conditions of industrial fatigue. There has been an effort to better understand the relation between the worker and his industry. The whole
tendency of rationalisation has increased the necessity of intelligent
labour supervisors. The practical value of this study can be suggested

[19] *Britain's Industrial Future,* pp. 220–222.
[20] Troup, *op. cit.,* p. 168.

by the figures given by the Ministry of Health dealing with industrial incapacity in 1926. In England and Wales there was lost to the nation in the year, among the insured population only, a total of 28¼ million weeks' work, or 543,270 years. The Ministry's report suggested it was not only the year's working equivalent of some 540,000 persons that was involved, but also the labour and expense entailed in their care during their incapacity. In his address as president of the Industrial Hygiene Section of the Royal Sanitary Institute, July 1928, Mr. Ramsey MacDonald urged that a new Factory Act was long overdue. Legislation, he said, had not kept pace with scientific research, and his illustrations were those above, taken from the Ministry of Health's Report. Such comments as these with regard to a new Factory Act indicate the progress of England's factory legislation and the science of industrial hygiene. This was also confirmed in the Trade Union Congress resolutions of 1928 and 1929 dealing with the proposed new Factories Bill.

The first session of the Labour Government came to an end on August 1, 1930, and the new Factories Bill had not been introduced.

II

The Shop Acts

The tendency at the beginning of this century toward unifying labour laws, of which the Factory Act is the pre-eminent example, was also indicated in the Shop Hours Act, 1904. An Act passed in 1886, and made permanent in 1892, had restricted the employment of young persons under eighteen to 74 hours a week including meal times: another Act in 1899 required that women shop assistants should have seats, one seat for every three assistants; and the Act of 1904 consolidated the law on the subject.[21] The movement for the voluntary closing of shops had failed. In the year 1904 three Bills on the question of shops and early closing were introduced, which brought a warning from Sir Francis Powell and Sir Frederick Banbury that it was "very hazardous to pass legislation having for its object the limitation of adult labour." However, this argument

[21] *Parl. Deb.*, 4 S. H.C., 1904, vol. 132, p. 802; pp. 794–802 for second reading debate on the Dilke Shops Bill. The Bills were House Bills 1904, Numbers 24, 31 and 165; the last (Cochrane's) becoming by adoption of Government the Act of 1904.

seemed to have little effect on the majority of the members of Parliament, especially those who looked back to 1847 to the beginning of legislation dealing with adults. There was hardly an important debate between 1900 and 1914 on labour legislation when from one side or the other a member did not confess that an opponent's speech could just as well have been made three quarters of a century before. So it was in the debate of 1904 on the Shop Hours Act. Professor Dicey in commenting on this Act was moved to say that "the time is rapidly approaching when the state will, as regards the regulation of labour, aim at as much omnipotence and omniscience as is obtainable by any institution created by human hands." [22]

Yet there has been no tendency to be less interested in the detail of regulations, and the Home Department in asking for a Select Committee in 1911 indicated the progress that had been made since the first Committee on the subject was appointed in 1886.[23] The Report of the Select Committee in 1928 brought the history of the Acts down to date. This Committee made the following recommendations: (1) The discontinuance of the Shops Acts 1920 and 1921, and the Orders enacted therein; (2) The principle of compulsory closing of shops be embodied in permanent legislation; (3) The closing hour to be fixed at 8 p.m. on days other than the late day and the day of the weekly half-holiday; (4) Local authorities to be given power to fix by order the day of the week on which shops may remain open until 9 p.m.

The Home Secretary in March, 1928, announced the Government decision to make early closing a permanent part of the law of the land, and the Bill of Sir Park Goff, with Government support, passed second reading without division. This Bill was important as a new precedent in industrial legislation inasmuch as it seeks to regulate hours of employment by limiting the hours during which the employing industry can legally be carried on. In his announcement the Home Secretary opposed the clause exempting one-man businesses, in which he was strongly supported by the Labour party.

The administrative principle of the Shops Acts has remained the

---

[22] *Op. cit.*, p. 290.
[23] *Parl. Deb.*, 5 S. H.C., 1911, vol. 23, pp. 1685–1695 (Masterman); the Committee was allowed by a vote of 262—21; vol. 32, pp. 1773–1874, Committee Report, third reading and passing of the Shops Regulations Act, 1911; *ibid.*, pp. 2796–2808, consideration of Lords' amendments. In 1912 was passed the consolidating Shops Act, 1892–1912. Since the Select Committee of 1886 there have been others in 1892, 1895, 1901 and 1928.

same.[24] County and borough councils, and urban district councils in districts with a population over 20,000 can by order, confirmed by the central authority, fix the hours on the several days of the week at which all shops or shops of specified class are to be closed for serving customers. The Shops (House of Closing) Acts, 1912–1928, are administered by one body, namely, the local authority, which makes orders, appoints inspectors and attends to the details of administration: the Home Secretary is the central authority and his functions are confined to confirming and revoking orders, making regulations for procedure, holding inquiries, and the general supervision which results from his parliamentary responsibility for legislation. The Departmental Committee in 1928 considered the transfer of enforcement to the police, but recommended that no case had been made out for any change in the method of administration, and that in any new legislation the administration should be vested in the local authority.[25]

III
THE COAL MINES REGULATIONS ACTS

The general principle of industrial regulation can be well illustrated further in the Coal Mines Regulation Act, 1908, generally known as the Eight Hours Act, and the Coal Mines Act, 1911, comparable as an industrial code to the Factory Act of 1901. On the second reading debate of the first Coal Mines Regulation Bill in 1900, Sir Charles W. Dilke stated that the demand for the Bill was the demand of labour, and the one upon which labour was most agreed. Of all the suggested proposals put before Parliament by the trade unions in the ten years before, this was the one which had received the largest support from labour.[26] On the second reading debate in 1901 it was

[24] See section 1 of the 1904 Act, and sections 5 and 6 of the 1912 Act—"the principal Act"—and section 7 of 1928 Act, for procedure for closing orders. The Shops (Early Closing) Act 1920, continued the war-time regulations, and made them statutory, enforceable by the local authority. This Act was renewed in 1921, and annually until 1928.

[25] See *Departmental Committee Report on Shop Hours,* appointed March 1927, reported January 1928, Cmd. 3000. The terms of reference were: "To inquire into the working of the Shops (Early Closing) Acts, 1920 and 1921, and report whether it is desirable that those Acts should or should not be made permanent, and if made permanent whether with or without modifications."

[26] *Parl. Deb.,* 4 S.H.C., 1900, vol. LXXIX, p. 1329–1318 (Sir James Joicy, in opposition to Bill because the miners of Durham and Northumberland were opposed) ; and the footnotes give the references to the second readings of this Bill since 1892.

stated that the trade unions were turning more and more against strikes, and demanded the regulation of these things, wherever possible, by law.[27] It was very much better, it was said, that the public through their representatives legislate upon matters which affected the public at large than that a section of the population belonging to one particular trade, without conferring with others and without obeying what is the obvious desire of the public, should assert by voluntary effort what might be opposed to the interests of others. In other words, Parliament was a legislative machine for the purpose of giving effect to what was believed to be not merely for the interest of any particular class, but what was believed to be for the interest of the community at large.[28] The amount paid in wages in reference to the question of profit caused one member to say that the very same arguments which were used about the destruction of trade were used as far back as 1847, and if anyone would take up Hansard for that year he would find that practically he might be reading the very debate which was taking place in the House.[29]

Defeated on second reading in 1900 by 24 votes, in 1901 by 13 votes, the Miners' Eight Hours Bill continued each year to be introduced.[30] When it was presented in the 1906 session, the author, who had introduced the 1892 Bill, stated that it was drawn up on the example of the French Act dealing with that problem, that is, a gradual reduction of working hours extending over a number of years.[31] This was the seventh introduction of the Bill, it having been rejected four times and carried three times on second reading. The government asked for a Committee on Inquiry, promising if it were done to take care of the Bill.[32] The next year the Coal Mines (Eight

---

[27] *Parl. Deb.*, 4 S.H.C., 1901, vol. LXXXIX, p. 1365 (Yoxall).

[28] *Parl. Deb., op. cit.*, pp. 1380–1381 (Atherley-Jones). Mr. J. Keir Hardie used the Home Offices Report on the output of coal to answer attack of the opponents of the Bill on its unfair distribution cost (*op. cit.*, p. 1384).

[29] *Parl. Deb., op. cit.*, p. 1382 (Atherley-Jones).

[30] Two Dilke Bills of 1904 may be mentioned: the Coal Mines Regulation Bill (House Bill No. 42, 1904), to amend the law relating to coal miners, and the Coal Mines, (Employment) Bill (House Bill No. 57, 1904), to amend the Coal Mines Regulations Acts; and in 1905 the Coal Mines (Employment) Bill (House Bill No. 4, 1905), presented by Mr. Jacoby, reported before Committee and dropped.

[31] House Bill No. 11, 1906. *Parl. Deb.*, 4 S.H.C., 1906, vol. 157, pp. 41–45 (Brunner); pp. 41–95, debate.

[32] *Parl. Deb., op. cit.*, pp. 59–61 (Gladstone). The Coal Mines Regulation Bill (House Bill No. 16, 1906), introduced by Mr. Compton-Rickett, was

Hours) Bill [33] was introduced again by Mr. Walsh for the Labour Party and the Miners Federation. He referred to the Fact that for 19 years it had been presented as a distinct Bill for the limitation of the hours of labour in mines, coming from the House in that form in 1889 and for two years before that it took the form of the amendment of measures which were before the House. "There was a satisfaction in knowing that, after all," he said, "the matter has never been looked upon as a purely party question." [34] The Home Secretary, Mr. Gladstone, supported the Bill, asking that it go before the Committee on Trade; [35] and though the second reading of the Government Bill was not reached in the 1907 session, the Address of 1908 promised the Bill's introduction; it was presented [36] on June 21, and, by a vote of 204 to 89, became law that year.

The Coal Mines Regulation Act, 1908, prohibited a workman from being below ground in a mine for the purpose of his work, and of going to and from his work, for more than eight hours during any consecutive twenty-four hours. [37] The passing of this Act was the first definite statutory regulation of hours for adult male labour. The Factory and Workshop Act, 1901, did not directly interfere with the hours of adult male labour, but the same beneficial experience that Millerand sought in the limitation of hours of work for women and children—that it would by inspection and enforcement materially affect the working conditions of men—was true in England. But by the passing of the Act of 1908, Parliament began the interference

---

dropped; and in this year the Labour Bill on the Hours of Railway Servants (House Bill No. 211, 1906), was introduced by Mr. Crooks (see *Parl. Deb.,* 4 S.H.C., 1906, vol. 157, pp. 552–581, debate).

[33] House Bill No. 13, 1907; *Parl. Deb.,* 4 S.H.C., 1907, vol. 172, pp. 501–556, second reading debate.

[34] *Parl. Debate., op. cit.,* pp. 501–502.

[35] *Parl. Deb., op. cit.,* pp. 536–545 (Gladstone). The Walsh Bill provided that working hours below ground in coal mines be limited to nine in 1908, eight and one-half in 1909, and eight thenceforward. Dropped after report of Committee when Government Bill was prepared, Coal Mines (Eight Hours) Bill (No. 2), (House Bill No. 295, 1907).

[36] *Parl. Deb.,* 4 S.H.C., 1908, vol. 190, pp. 1343–1362 (Gladstone), pp. 1343–1456, debate, then vol. 191, pp. 1261–1344, further debate; note speeches of President of Board of Trade, pp. 1325–1354 (Churchill), and Hardie (1281–1288) Report stage: vol. 198, pp. 517–608, 779–907, 942–1098; third reading, pp. 1285–1361; consideration of Lords' amendments, pp. 2269–2294. For House of Lords: second reading, pp. 1418–1528; committee, pp. 2006–2040; third reading, pp. 2198–2205.

[37] Act of 1908, sect. 1.

with the right of a workman of full age to labour for any number of hours agreed upon between him and his employer. The contravention of this Act by the workman himself imposes a penalty upon him, and if the workman is below ground for a longer period during any consecutive twenty-four hours than the time fixed in the Act he shall be deemed to have been below ground in contravention of this Act unless the contrary is proved.[38] The passing of this Act made more certain the fact that the state was considered to be the protector of the life of the whole family, for legislation with regard to the adult male is in keeping with that faith. It was a long way from the Act of 1802. Post-War legislation is considered later, but it may be stated that the Coal Mines Act, 1919, a direct continuation of the Act of 1908, established the principle of a seven-hour day.[39] This was amended temporarily by the Coal Mines (Hours of Work) Act, 1926, which established the eight hour day. Besides the Coal Mines Act, 1919 establishing a seven-hour day, state action may be noted in the Coal Mines (Emergency) Act, 1920, the Price of Coal (Limitation) Act, 1920, and the Coal Mines (Decontrol) Act, 1921, which curtailed the duration and amended the Coal Mines (Emergency) Act, 1920.

COAL MINES ACT, 1911

In announcing the Government measure which became the Coal Mines Act, 1911, the Home Secretary said that it was based on the report of the Royal Commission appointed in 1906, with further provisions recommended by departmental experience and by recent colliery disasters. The legislation sought was essentially that of safety, it was said, and since 1887 there had been Acts dealing with specific points, but there was no further safety legislation.[40] The Bill as passed contained 127 sections,[41] being debated in committee for

[38] Act of 1908, sect. 7.
[39] Act of 1919, sect. 1.
[40] The beginning was the Coal Mines Regulations Act, 1887, then the Act of 1896 and the amending Act for 1887 of 1903. In connection should be taken the Coal Mines (Check Weighers) Act, 1894, the Coal Mines (Weighing of Minerals) Act, 1905 and the Check Weighing in Various Industries Act, 1919, providing protection for rights of the worker. Certain of the Factory Acts also applied.
[41] Part I, ss. 1–28, dealt with Management; Part II, ss. 28–75, with Safety; Part III, ss. 76–79, Provisions as to Health; Part IV, ss. 80–85, Provisions as to

thirty days, in contrast to the 1887 Act, which was discussed only four days in committee.[42] At the time the Act was passed the number of workers employed was 1,049,000, of whom 848,000 worked below ground, and their safety was the main consideration of the Government from first to last in the Bill.[43] The Home Department pointed out that in two recent mining disasters the loss of life had been more than in any battle fought in the South African War.

The administration of the Act again entrusted large powers to the central authority, for the Secretary of State was given the right to make general regulations and special regulations as well as power by Special Orders.[44] In the vote on Account, March 21, the Government promised 30 working class inspectors of mines in that year.[45] This fact together with the advance in protective provisions made the Act one of the most constructive passed by Parliament for the safety of the worker. It was no party question and it was passed without division. A minor amending Act was passed in 1914, and post-war legislation has only completed the comprehensive nature of the earlier Act. Post-war legislation has also increased the powers of the central authority; a good example of this tendency being the Check Weighing in Various Industries Act, 1919, an Act which applies primarily to the coal mining industry, but it is provided that the provisions of this Act may be extended by regulations made by the Secretary of State to any other industry where payment is made by weight.

A motion by a Labour member, Mr. George MacDonald, in the House of Commons on November 6, 1929, deploring the heavy loss of life and the large number of non-fatal accidents in coal-mines, was

---

Accidents; Part V, ss. 86–90, Regulations; Part VI, ss. 91–95, Employment (Boys, Girls and Women) ; Part VII, s. 96, Wages; Part VIII, ss. 97–100, Inspectors; Part IX, ss. 101–127, Supplemental.

[42] *Parl. Deb.*, H.C., 5 S., 1911, vol. 22, pp. 2646–2652 (Churchill), pp. 2646–2674, second reading debate entire; vol. 21, pp. 1392–1524, 1544–1629, consideration of Standing Committee's amendments; vol. 32, pp. 1233–1363, Report and third reading.

[43] *Parl. Deb., op. cit.,* pp. 1361–1362 (Masterman).

[44] See section 86 for procedure; also Schedule Second (Part I), for general regulations, and (Part II) special regulations. Cf. Section 19 of the Mining Industry Act, 1920.

[45] The factory inspectorate of 1912 included 205 inspectors and assistants, 18 of whom were women, administration costs being about £100,000. See *Annual Report of the Chief Inspector of Factories and Workshops for the Year 1912* (Cmd. 6852, 1913).

the occasion of a review of the Coal-Mines Regulation Act of 1911. The mover declared that mining life had changed since the regulations were made in 1911, and suggested an inquiry with the view to consolidating all the Statutory Orders issued since 1911 and getting an up-to-date Mines Regulation Act.[46] The Secretary for Mines, Mr. Ben Turner, stated that there were 106 inspectors, and the number of inspections of mines had increased from 18,941 in 1922 to 21,748 in 1928, and that every mine working was inspected once, and many of them more than once, in 1928. The Government spokesman did not promise new legislation, but urged co-operation of the workers with inspectors, and greater co-operation between the employers and the men to secure safety and comfort, and to assist in the economic restoration of the mining industry. This official statement indicates the emphasis today upon the voluntary aspects of labour law administration.

IV

The State and Compensation Legislation

The Workmen's Compensation Act of 1897, with which may be compared the French Act of April 9, 1898, introduced a new principle into English legislation, that an employer must, subject to certain limitations, insure his workmen against the risks of their employment. Until that time the employee had the same right to compensation when injured through the negligence of fellow workers as a stranger; but the law of that year provided that compensation for accidents should be paid without the application of the test for negligence. For proof of the employer's negligence there was substituted proof that personal injury by accident, arising out of and in the course of employment had been caused to the workman seeking compensation. This principle—comparable to French Act of June 30, 1899—was extended to include agricultural labourers in 1900, and was given wider application in the Workmen's Compensation Act, 1906, and the Health Insurance part of the National Insurance Act, 1911. The Act of 1900, unlike the Act of 1897, was not a Government measure, but it became law without serious opposition in either the House of Commons or the House of Lords. The Act was short, consisting of one operative section only: The Workmen's Compensation Act, 1897, shall apply to the employment of workmen in agriculture

[46] *Parl. Deb.*, 5 S.H.C., November 6, 1929, pp. 1083–1141, debate entire.

by an employer who habitually employs one or more workmen in such employment. This Bill was not a party question and was important in the 1900 session in extending the protective arm of legislation.[47]

It is well to note the administrative features of the Railway Employment (Prevention of Accidents) Act, 1900 before considering the important new principle which the Workmen's Compensation Act of 1906 introduced. This Act was passed on the recommendation of a Royal Commission and gave the Board of Trade extensive powers of making rules for the control of risks and the reducing of accidents in railway service. It was provided that the Board of Trade may, subject to the provisions of the Act, make such rules as they think fit with respect to any of the subjects mentioned in the schedule of this Act, with the object of reducing or removing the dangers and risks incidental to railway service. Where the Board of Trade consider that avoidable danger to persons employed on the railway arises from any operation of railway service (not being a matter in respect to which rules may be made under the foregoing provisions of the section), whether that danger arises from anything done or omitted to be done by the railway company or any of its officers or servants, or from any want of proper appliances or plant, they may, subject to the provisions of this Act, after communicating with the railway company, and giving them a reasonable opportunity of reducing or removing the danger of risk, make rules for that purpose.[48]

The schedule of the Act enumerated twelve subjects with respect to which the Board of Trade might make such rules as they saw fit and necessary. The first Rules under this Statute were made in 1902; in 1906 the Notice of Accidents Act substituted a much more stringent set of provisions as to notice of accidents, especially with regard to certain "dangerous occurrences," even though no bodily injury is caused by them; and later substantial change was made in the passing of new rules, known as the Prevention of Accident Rules, 1911.[49] When the original Bill came up for second reading Mr. Bryce

[47] Parl. Deb., 4 S., vol. LXXXII, 1900, pp. 490–493, and vol. LXXXIV, pp. 1211–1213, on extension of Act to naval and military workers.

[48] Sect. I, clauses 1 and 2 of the Act of 1900.

[49] S.R. and O., 1902, No. 616, and No. 1058, 1911. This Act of 1906 repealed Section 19 of the Act of 1901, and is one of the statutes which have come into force in the years after the Factory and Workshop Act, 1901, affecting the law relating to factories and workshops.

spoke of the gratifying unanimity with which it was received. "Everybody feels," he said, "that the state has now completely established its rights to intervene in matters of this kind, and we have scarcely heard any of the old arguments in favour of the *laissez-faire* attitude with which we used to be favoured." [50] This Act is one of the best examples of how far Parliament was willing to go in giving large administrative power to the central inspectorate of the Board of Trade. A new staff of inspectors were attached to the Board of Trade to carry out the provisions of the Act of 1900, which extended to the railway service the principles before recognized in the Mining Code administered by the Home Office and the mining inspectors.

There was constant legislative attempt to extend the Workmen's Compensation Act. The Address of 1905 [51] included three important proposals: the Trade Unions and Trade Disputes Bill, the Workmen's Compensation Bill, and the Unemployed Workmen Bill. The failure of the Government to pass the Workmen's Compensation Bill, a much-needed and non-controversial social measure, increased the outcry against the "legislative scandal of 1905." The Home Secretary, Mr. Akers-Douglas moving the second reading, [52] enumerated the additional classes of workmen whom it was now proposed to bring within the scope of the Act of 1897. They included workers in workshops where five persons or more were employed; persons employed in the care and management of horses and locomotives, including farriers; persons employed on buildings less than 30 feet in height and on which no machine or scaffolding was used; and persons employed on tramways and private railways and sidings. The aim of the Bill, the Government said, was to simplify and make less expensive its working, and also to remove so far as possible the temptation to litigation. The Bill would have introduced a great improvement in

[50] *Parl. Deb.*, 4 S., vol. LXXXI, 1900, pp. 1307–1308.
[51] *Parl. Deb.*, 4 S.H.C., 1905, vol. 141, pp. 1–5; see following speeches; the Prime Minister (Balfour), pp. 153–167 Campbell-Bannerman, pp. 120–121; Asquith, pp. 178–190; A. Chamberlain, pp. 190–209. They indicate the politics of the session. The Trade Union Workmen's Compensation Bill had been introduced in 1904 by Mr. R. Bell (House Bill No. 122, 1904); this was introduced by Mr. Shakelton (House Bill No. 84, 1905), and another by Lord Belper (House Bill No. 31, H.L.) *Parl. Deb.*, 4 S., 1905, vol. 144, pp. 263–284 for debate.
[52] *Parl. Deb.*, 4 S.H.C., 1905, vol. 144, pp. 263–284; the Bill (House Bill No. 31, 1905), was introduced in the Lords on April 4 and was disposed of by them on May 20; the second reading in House of Commons was moved by Home Secretary, Mr. Akers-Douglas, June 5.

the law of compensation, it was said, "and the failure to carry it through indicates a wanton disregard on behalf of the Government for the hopes and needs of Labour." [53] The attitude of the Trade Union Congress was indicated by the resolution passed, which called for the inclusion of all workmen, including every person who has entered into, or works, whether by way of manual labour or otherwise, under a contract of service anywhere in the United Kingdom. Also that the employer be compelled to register an agreement in the county court. The provision of some system of state compulsory insurance was demanded, to secure that employers should have paid the necessary funds to compensate for all accidents or injuries arising out of any employment. [54]

Workmen's Compensation Act, 1906

The most important development with regard to the law on accidents was the Workmen's Compensation Act, 1906, which corresponds to the French Act of April 12, 1906, introduced by the Government March 26, 1906. [55] The historical stages in the growth of the idea of compensation, noted by the Home Secretary, were the Employers' Liability Act of 1880 and the Workmen's Compensation Acts of 1897 and 1900. "The Government now think," he announced, "that the time has arrived for a wide extension of the Act of 1897 to every class of labour, and in the Bill a new principle is adopted which differentiates it from the Act of 1897. That Act excluded all classes of workmen who were not directly and expressly included; and it is now proposed to reverse this, and, subject to the definition of a workman in the Bill, all be included who are not expressly excluded." [56]

[53] *The Reformers' Year Book, 1906,* p. 66.

[54] See Report of the Parliamentary Committee at the Trade Union Congress, Leeds, 1904, *Trade Union Congress Report,* pp. 53–82, full survey; also pp. 47–53, the President's remarks on the Bill and the Labour amendments.

[55] The Act on 1906 was based on House Bills 1906, Nos. 123, 272, 365; see *Parl. Deb.* 4 S.H.C., vol. 154, 1906, pp. 886–895, for the Government exposé of their Bill; first reading debate, pp. 886–934; second reading debate, *ibid.,* vol. 155, pp. 523–578, and 1191–1219; third reading debate, *ibid.,* vol. 167, pp. 693–722. The Report stage of the Bill is interesting for which see vol. 166, pp. 321–392, 781–860, 974–1059, 1204–1271. The Bill referred to the Standing Committee on Law.

[56] *Parl. Deb.,* 4 S.H.C., vol. 154, 1906, pp. 886–887.

This Act thus began the series of Acts dealing with the protection of other than manual workers of all kinds, for under the inclusive clause a workman meant any person who has entered into or works under a contract of service or apprenticeship with an employer, whether by way of manual labour, clerical work or otherwise.[57] Almost equally important was the statement that while most of the proposals of the Bill were based fully or in part on the recommendations of the Departmental Committee over which Sir K. Digby presided, that the Government on its own initiative proposed to extend workmen's compensation to include industrial diseases. "That involves a new departure," the Home Secretary added.

This experiment was to extend to only six scheduled diseases, but the Home Secretary was authorized to extend the list by Order,[58] and as early as May, 1907, eighteen minor industrial diseases had been included. It was on this last feature that the former Home Secretary felt that there was any objection to the Bill; the principle had been firmly established and extension was a logical development of the experience gained by the preceding Acts.[59] Further legislation was foreshadowed by the statement of the Home Secretary that "the ultimate solution of the whole question is probably to be found in a scheme of compulsory insurance." [60] With this, Labour was in agreement,[61] believing with Sir Charles W. Dilke, that compulsory insurance in some form or other lay at the root of all improvement, and that France had given a good example of this regard, in her compulsory system.[62]

The third reading and the report stage of this Bill were indicative of the great interest in the principle of the measure. It was shown definitely that the new Labour Party was determined to use the Parliamentary machine for its full worth, and to profit by their influence at the time with the Government. Their faith too was fresh enough to keep them close to the dull detail of their duties, and their contribution to the success of the Bill was enough to cause them to

[57] Sect. 13, 1906 Act.
[58] See 1906 Act, sect. 8, for application to industrial diseases; compare French law of October 25, 1919.
[59] *Parl. Deb.*, 4 S.H.C., vol. 154, 1906, pp. 895–900; as Home Secretary he had introduced a similar Bill, not including industrial diseases, the year before.
[60] *Parl. Deb., Ibid.*, p. 889.
[61] *Parl. Deb., ibid.*, pp. 900–906 (Barnes).
[62] *Parl. Deb., Ibid.*, pp. 906–908; also *Parl. Deb.*, vol. 155, pp. 526–527.

credit this Act as one of the Labour Party's achievements. When introduced in 1906 the Government Bill was so limited in extent, wrote Hardie, that it only applied to about 2,000,000 workers. When it passed it applied to 6,000,000. The Government first of all excluded shop assistants, but after pressure from the Labour Party agreed to their inclusion when the number employed was more than three. The Party declined this compromise, and in the end the Government gave way. The Government proposed that compensation should not be payable until a week had elapsed from the date of accident. The Labour party carried an amendment in committee that it should begin in three days. At a later stage this was altered by agreement with the Party, so that if the incapacity of the injured workman lasted longer than two weeks, compensation should date from the day of accident. The Party also succeeded in carrying an amendment that an illegitimate child or the parent or grandparent of an illegitimate child, if dependent upon the workman, should rank as a dependent. The Labour party sought without success to add a clause providing that where an injured workman has sufficiently recovered to be able to perform some slight and less remunerative employment, reduced compensation shall not take place unless he is able to obtain such employment. The Government only proposed to schedule six "diseases of occupation" for the purpose of the Act, but the Labour party secured a pledge that this would be increased.[63]

From such testimony it is easily deduced that there was belief in England among the working class that Parliament could be responsive to the needs of the nation. The ideal of industrial legislation was including the whole nation's welfare, and the progressive extension of the Workmen's Compensation Act is a practical example. When the Act was first passed in 1897, protection was given to 6,000,000 workers, which in 1900 was granted to 1,000,000 more, and the Home Secretary in his concluding speech on the Bill pointed out that by its new provisions 6,000,000 additional workers would receive like benefits.[64] The Act besides extended the benefits of industrial legislation to a large number of non-manual workers, for the Act included all non-manual service, the remuneration of which did not

[63] J. Keir Hardie, *The Case for the Labour Party* (1909) p. 110; also pp. 111–113, for his summary of "Labour in Parliament, 1906–1908," by raising questions, Committee Work and Bills, being fuller than the Trade Union Congress Reports.

[64] *Parl. Deb.*, 4 S.H.C., vol. 167, 1906, pp. 693–695.

exceed £250 a year.[65] The contractual capacity of workmen and masters was cut down, and "in the background stands the state, determining in one most important aspect the terms of the labour contract." [66] Yet it was a principle given far wider effectiveness in the National Insurance Act, 1911. The principle was much more than compensation, for the Act gave a new and national status to the British worker—a status founded upon the recognition that, whether in public or private employment, he was playing a truly national part, and that his welfare and independence were a truly national concern.[67]

A natural consequence of the development of labour law dealing with workmen's compensation in France and England was the Workmen's Compensation (Anglo-French Convention) Act, 1909, granting to French citizens employed in the United Kingdom the same rights under the Act of 1906 that the English worker possessed. This Convention allowed to British subjects meeting with accidents arising out of their employment in France, and persons entitled to claim through or having rights derivable from them, the benefits of the compensation and guarantees secured to French citizens by the legislation in force in France.[68] The survey of the legislation of each nation shows a parallel development of legislation dealing with accidents and its extension to include non-manual workers and industrial diseases. The movement of thought was much the same in both countries, inspired by similar necessities which directed each to a common end. This treaty was an early illustration of what is, and will increasingly be, one of the most important developments of international labour protection.

POST-WAR LEGISLATION

It is necessary to note the passage of two Workmen's Compensation (War Addition) Acts, 1917–1919, which undertook to relieve the situation produced by changes in the value of currency and in the cost of living. The principle of professional diseases was further extended in the Workmen's Compensation (Silicosis) Act, 1918–

[65] Act of 1906, sect. 13.
[66] Dicey, *op cit.*, pp. 283–284.
[67] Cf. G. C. Cope, "Workmen's Compensation Act," in *Reformers' Year Book 1908*, p. 157.
[68] Article I of Convention.

1924; and the Workmen's Compensation (Illegal Employment) Act, 1918, allowed compensation even though the worker with or without his knowledge was illegally employed. An Act of 1923 amended the Workmen's Compensation Act, 1906, and the Acts amending that Act, and the law with respect to employers' liability insurance, the notification of accidents, first aid, and ambulance, bringing up to date the provisions of the principle Act. And this Act of 1923 in turn was superseded by the Act of 1925, amended in 1926, consolidating the law relating to compensation to workmen for injuries suffered in the course of their employment. The Acts of 1923 and 1925 provided for considerable increase in benefits, and extended the scope of the law with regard to salaried persons not engaged in manual labour, the wage limitation being raised from £250 to £350 thus permitting non-manual employees up to the higher range of salaries to receive the benefit of the law.[69] The number of persons employed and total compensation paid under the Workmen's Compensation Acts in 1926, were 7,143,440 persons, and £6,056,320.[70]

The Workmen's Compensation (Transfer of Funds) Act, 1927, gave effect to a resolution of the 1926 Imperial Conference relating to the transfer of funds to another part of the Empire when a beneficiary moves from one part to that other part of the Empire. This inter-empire principle of transfer with regard to social legislation was again confirmed in the Widows', Orphans' and Old Age Pensions' Act of 1929.[71] On November 29, 1929, a private members' Bill, introduced by Mr. George Hirst, was supported by the Government and received a second reading.[72] It was supported by all parties in the House. This Workmen's Compensation (Amendment) Bill sought to make plain the intent of the 1925 Act, for certain provisions had to be redrafted because of a legal decision of the House of Lords. The amending Bill provided that if a workman proved to the satisfaction of the Judge of the County Court that he had failed to obtain light employment, his incapacity should continue to be treated as a total incapacity, for such period and subject to such conditions as might be provided by the order of the Court.

An administrative feature of the Act of 1923, and continued in

[69] Section 3 of the Act of 1925.

[70] See *Nineteenth Abstract of Labour Statistics of the United Kingdom* (1928), pp. 158–159.

[71] Act of 1929, clause 3.

[72] *Parl. Deb.*, 5 S.H.C., vol. 232, pp. 1875–1890, debate entire.

the Act of 1925, is interesting, providing for reciprocity in matters relating to compensation to workmen for injuries by accident, by orders in council instead of by statute as formerly.[73] This is an extension of the principle of the Anglo-French Convention of 1909.[74] Also if the Secretary of State finds, from the number and nature of accidents in any factory or class of factories, that special safety provisions should be made, he may by order require such equipment or supervision to be made. In default of voluntary action on the part of the industries themselves, he may exercise compulsory powers which are conferred on him by section 29 of the Workmen's Compensation Act, 1923.[75] That section provides that "Where it appears to the Secretary of the State that, in view of the number and nature of accidents occurring in any factory or class of factories, special provision ought to be made at that factory or at factories of that class to secure the safety of persons employed therein, he may by order require the occupier to make such reasonable provision by arrangements for special supervision in regard to safety, investigation of the circumstances and causes of accidents, and otherwise as may be specified in the order. . . ."

The development and modification of the law with regard to industrial diseases have shown how effective is the responsibility vested in the Secretary of State. For he may make Orders for extending the provisions to other diseases and other processes, and to injuries due to the nature of any employment.[76] Orders have been made for particularly dangerous and unhealthy trades. The Workmen's Compensation (Industrial Diseases) Consolidation Order, 1929,[77] consolidating the previous orders from 1918 to 1927, listed 28 descriptions of disease or injury. These regulations are very carefully drawn up, and before they are made statutory, persons affected, both employers and workers, must be given an opportunity of raising objections to the draft provisions and an inquiry held if necessary.[78]

[73] Section 37 of the 1925 Act.
[74] A Convention respecting compensation to workmen for accidents arising out of their employment was signed at London, November 18, 1925, between the United Kingdom and Denmark. Ratifications were exchanged at London, April 5, 1927. (Treaty Series League of Nations, 1927, No. 12.)
[75] Section 29, clause 3.
[76] Section 3, Part II, Act of 1925.
[77] Statutory Rules and Orders, 1929, No. 2.
[78] Note *Appendix* to the *Annual Report of the Chief Inspector of Factories and Workshops for the year 1927* (Cmd. 3144, 1928), pp. 152–153.

The regulations must be laid before both Houses of Parliament, and may be annulled in whole or in part by resolution of either House. The law has thus combined the long experience of factory inspectors and the technical knowledge of experts, creating uniformity in the administration of its provisions and extending protection to an increasing number of workmen. In respect of industrial diseases the number of cases reported in 1925 were 17,256, in 1926, 14,752, and amount of payments £656,027 and £599,729 for compensation.[79]

In view of the fact that the liability to pay compensation is imposed by act of Parliament, the Government has always kept in mind the question whether or not a more economical system of insurance could be established. The Secretary of State for the Home Department appointed in May, 1919, a committee to inquire into the present system of the payment of workmen's compensation, to consider the desirability of establishing a system of insurance under the control or supervision of the state, and to recommend such alterations as might seem desirable to remedy defects which experience had disclosed or to give effect to their recommendations.[80] The matter of state control was considered under two general heads: First, whether or not a state fund should be established, either exclusive or competitive, or again by a system of mutual insurance; or, secondly, whether state control of commercial companies and supervision of mutual associations and self-insurers would afford sufficient security. Speaking generally, the witnesses representing the trade unions were in favour of a monopolistic state fund, mainly on the ground that the money which goes in profits to the insurance companies would be available for the workmen. On the other hand, the employers and their representatives were unanimous against a monopolistic state fund, urging that it would be more expensive than the present system and would not work so efficiently or satisfactorily in any respect. The 1923 Act, which came into effect January 1, 1924, was preceded by an agreement between the Government and the accident insurance companies, and while there will be no interference with the carrying on of the business by insurance officers, there has

---

[79] See *Nineteenth Abstract of Labour Statistics of the United Kingdom* (1928), pp. 162–163.

[80] See *Departmental Committee on Workmen's Compensation. Report to the Rt. Hon. the Secretary of State for the Home Department*, (1920).

been an agreement reached whereby the cost of insurance is materially reduced.

Apart from the exercise of the statutory powers, the Home Office has promoted the beneficial working of the Act through conference and negotiations. An annual report is compiled and published from the returns received from employers and from insurance companies. There are no inspectors or special officers appointed under the Act and the whole of the administrative work is done by the Industrial Division of the Home Office.

V

THE STATE AND LEGISLATION DEALING WITH YOUNG PERSONS AND CHILDREN

The conditions imposed by the state on the employment of young persons and children is a history of continuous progressive legislation. It is best to look at the provisions along with the general policy of intervention by the state in the industrial system. The effort of the community to secure conditions of health and opportunity for the young is unbroken from the Health and Morals of Apprentices Act, 1802, to the Acts passed in the early years of this century, and to the latest Education Acts. The important history of the Acts before 1900 affecting children, and their connection with the Factory Acts, has been given earlier in this study. It is clear that the Act of 1900, the Mines Prohibition of Child Labour Underground Act, was an extension of long established principles of state interference. It was enacted in section one that a boy under the age of thirteen should not be employed in or allowed to be for the purpose of employment in any mine below ground; that sections four and five of the Coal Mines Regulation Act, 1887, and section four of the Metalliferous Mines Regulation Act, 1872, should read and have effect as if for the word "twelve" the word "thirteen" were substituted. By 1900 the number of boys affected by the Act were only [81] 3000: and there were members of Parliament who wanted them to be allowed to work; but the number employed seemed sufficient to compel the state positively to say that it would see that they did not work underground.

---

[81] *Parl. Deb.*, 4 S.H.C., vol. LXXX, 1900, p. 463; also 4 S.H.C., vol. LXXXI, 1900, p. 148 (Sir Charles Dilke).

This same principle was invoked in the legislation for other small groups, especially for the three Bills and the Government measure in 1900 for the Inspection and Registration of Boilers. The mover of the second reading of this latter Bill said that "it may be and probably will be contended during the course of this debate that the loss of life and injury to persons from such a cause is very small compared with the number of steam boilers in use, but be the loss and injury small or great, if we can prove, as I believe we can, that such loss and suffering arise from preventable causes, then I contend we shall have made out a case for further intervention on the part of the legislature in the interests of the general community." [82]

The close connection between measures of social reform became more evident as the administration of industrial and social legislation was more adequately organized. Perhaps the most obvious example in the field of legislation is that dealing with young persons and children. The gradual raising of the age at which employment of young persons and children became legal went steadily on from the passing of the Education Act of 1870. This Act was the outcome of the Duke of Newcastle's Commission Report on Elementary Education, which had found in 1861 that only two-thirds of the children of the working classes attended any school at all, and that so small a proportion remained long enough to receive any permanent benefit that it could be said that only about one child in seven was getting satisfactory instruction. From the Education Act of 1870 to the Education Acts of 1918 and 1921 is over half of a century, but in that short time the conviction had expressed itself in Parliamentary Acts that the proper place for the child was in the school, and that the emphasis should not be on the number of hours spent in the factory and workshop. Education and factory legislation from 1857 were making comparatively quick strides and marching side by side, and both were profiting by their alliance in Parliament and in administration. It has often been pointed out that the lack of an effective Education Act kept back factory legislation with regard to children, and it is rather interesting to notice the mutual reaction of the two causes. Education was made the motive and object of restricting children's hours of work, and then the factory inspectors in their turn became promoters or furtherers of state education, because they realised that only thereby could the restriction of hours become

[82] *Parl. Deb.,* 4 S.H.C., vol. LXXX, 1900, pp. 266–267 (Fenwick).

effective.[83] From 1870 to 1921 some twenty-three Acts, exclusive of Acts incidentally affecting education, contributed to build up the public system in England. In 1921 the necessary consolidation of the law relating to education was undertaken. An experienced administrator declared it was a troublesome business, but profitable not only in that it brought together the provisions of many Education Acts, but also brought into relation with the provisions of the Education Acts proper a number of provisions from other Acts relevant to the service of education, especially those affecting the employment of children.[84]

The intervention of the state was much more drastic in the Employment of Children Act, 1903, which dealt with the whole question of child labour outside factories, workshops and places of public entertainment. The Education Act of 1921 codified the law as to the employment of children outside school hours, thus repealing this Act. The necessity of enforcing well-defined standards and making the laws responsive to changing industrial conditions with regard to children, account for the administrative provisions of this Act, which gave large powers to local authorities to make bye-laws for regulating the employment of children.[85] Any local authority was given power to make bye-laws prescribing for all children, or for boys and girls separately, and with respect to all occupations or to any specified occupation, (a) the age below which employment is illegal; and (b) the hours between which employment is legal; and (c) the number of daily and weekly hours beyond which employment is illegal. Further power was given to make bye-laws "prohibiting absolutely or permitting, subject to conditions, the employment of children in any specified occupation." Besides these special powers given to local authorities the general restrictions on employment of children were

[83] See Hutchins and Harrison, *op. cit.,* p. 79; Frank Tillyard, *The Worker and the State* (1923), p. 114; and *Report of the Departmental Committee on the Night Employment of Male Young Persons in Factories* (Cmd. 6533, 1912), *Minutes of Evidence* (Cmd. 6711, 1913).

[84] Sir Lewis Amherst Selby-Bigge, *The Board of Education* (1927), p. 21. Also Education Act of 1918, sections 13–16, on children's rights; sections 17–25, on the extension of powers and duties within the Act.

[85] See *Report of the Departmental Committee on the Hours and Conditions of Employment of Van Boys and Warehouse Boys* (Cmd. 6886, 1913) and, *Minutes of Evidence* (Cmd. 6887, 1913), for progress of administrative powers by bye-laws. The Committee recommended that powers should be given to local authorities to frame bye-laws regulating the employment of all van boys under 18.

comprehensive.[86] A child could not be employed between the hours of nine in the evening and six in the morning; a child under eleven could not be employed in street trading; and it was forbidden to employ a child in any occupation likely to be injurious to life, limb, health or education, regard being had to the physical condition of the child worker. The state went so far in its protection power of guardianship that both the parent and the employer of the child were held liable to a fine when the Act was contravened. It declared that society had rights in child life that only the state could adequately protect; and where a parent through carelessness or through necessity allowed these rights to be disregarded the duty of the state in its police power was to penalize. Bye-laws made under this Act could apply to either the whole of the area of the local authority or to any specified part thereof; and it was also provided that bye-laws made under the Prevention of Cruelty to Children Act, 1894, should be made by the same authority and confirmed in the same way as bye-laws under this Act. The Prevention of Cruelty to Children Act, 1904, practically re-enacted, with a few modifications, the Act of 1894; thus, as legislation was becoming uniform there were beneficial effects in unifying administration. This is to be noted in the Education Acts 1918–1921. Section 14 of the Education Act of 1918 and Part VIII of the Education Act 1921 deal with the provisions relating to the employment of children. Section 90 of the 1921 Act gives the power to a local education authority for elementary education to make bye-laws covering the whole employment of children outside school hours.

EDUCATION (PROVISION OF MEALS) ACT, 1906

The Acts of 1900 and 1903 and 1904 definitely confirmed the principle of state intervention for the welfare of children, and indicated also that the Government were prepared to place unusual powers in the hands of local authorities. The Education (Provision of Meals) Act, 1906, established a new principle of state action. Professor Dicey held that the statesmen who passed the Education Act of 1870 might not have passed the Act of 1891, relieving parents from the necessity of paying for any part of their children's elementary education, and it is certain that they would have opposed the Act of 1906.[87] The attitude of the Government toward the Bill was

---

[86] See Act of 1903, sections 1, 3, 5 and 6. Section 4, general provisions for bye-laws.

[87] Dicey, *op. cit., p. L, Introduction,* 1914 Edition.

given by the President of the Board of Education who stated that the Government considered that the Bill "was in the first place an education question." [88] It was significant that the Government had directed its Minister of Education to handle the Bill, an indication of the common bond of human interest which was an important part of social legislation. The source of the Bill was interesting, having been first introduced for the Labour Party by Mr. W. T. Wilson, February 22, 1906, but it had its real beginning in the steady policy of agitation which had been skilfully carried on in unsuccessful Bills, yet which gained in April, 1905, the Resolution by the Government on the feeding of school children.

The Bill provided that local education authorities might supply food for any children attending a public elementary school who might be unable through want of food to take full advantage of the education offered; it also proposed to sanction the provision of food for other children and enable the authorities to recover the cost from the parents or guardians. The provision of food was not to be deemed parochial relief, which meant that the father of a child who was fed by the state retained the right of voting for a member of Parliament.[89] This caused Professor Dicey to declare, "Why a man who first neglects his duty as a father and then defrauds the state should retain his full political rights is a question easier to ask than answer."

The debates on the second and third readings of this Bill indicated the main dividing issues which were constantly to appeal in the debates on the social measures of the Government. It was maintained by the Labour leaders "that the late Government recognized that there was an evil and a public responsibility for finding a remedy for that evil," and that "the principle had been admitted in past sessions of Parliament by all sections of the House." [90] Several of the speeches

[88] *Parl. Deb.*, 4 S.H.C., vol. 152, 1906, pp. 1440–1443.

[89] The Act of 1906 was based on House Bills Nos. 10, 331, and 366, 1906. Note sections 3 and 4, 1906 Act, for provisions cited.

[90] *Parl. Deb.*, 4 S.H.C., vol. 152, 1906, pp. 1394–1399 (A. Henderson). Two Education (Provision of Meals) Bills, based on the Report on Physical Deterioration, 1904, were introduced in 1905 by Mr. Henderson (House Bills of 1905), Nos. 132 and 196); and two Elementary Education (Feeding of Children) Bills (House Bills of 1905, Nos. 126 and 197), meet the same fate of being withdrawn or dropped. The tendency of legislation and the public interest were manifest. *Parl. Deb.*, 4 S.H.C., vol. 152, 1906, pp. 1390–1447, second reading debate; committee stage and the numerous amendments by opponents of the Bill, chiefly by Mr. Harold Cox and Sir H. (now Lord) Banbury, *Parl. Deb.*, 4 S.H.C., vol. 166, 1906, pp. 1315–1465. Note pp. 1440–1443, 1446–1447 for Government statement. *Parl. Deb.*, 4 S.H.C., vol. 152, 1906, p. 1435.

indicated the danger of socialism, but for the great majority of the members of Parliament the Act was a good step toward wider protective enactments which would include the whole interests of the child and the family. The Parliament of 1906 had very little sympathy for a doctrinaire individualism, especially when the victims of its logic were children; and it was alleged that the leader of the opposition "had put his opposition to the Bill on the peculiarly arid ground of individualistic dogmatism." [91] This feeling was not shared by any party in the House of Commons, for after the Government had accepted and sponsored the Bill the third reading was passed without division.[92] In the Select Committee the Government accepted another Labour measure, the Education (Provision of Meals) (Scotland) Bill,[93] yet when the Bill was given back to the lower House, Scotland was omitted from the working of the Act.[94] But among the first Bills of the 1907 session was the reintroduction of the Scottish Bill,[95] supported by the Parliamentary Secretary of the Local Government Board, Dr. MacNamara, who had given aid to the 1906 Bill. The opposition remained the same small minority. Though the question of party alignment was not present with regard to this Bill, which was not at all true of the contentious legislation of the following years, it is well to note that the same course was followed by the Government of accepting and sponsoring Labour Bills in the sessions of 1906 and 1907. There was a real effort on the part of the Government to keep the Labour party in full confidence of its friendship, for valuable concessions were made in accepting amendments and in making the provisions of Acts more comprehensive. The Education (Provision of Meals) Act is a good example. "This issue formed one of the chief demands of the Labour movement in 1906," wrote J. Keir Hardie, and "the political independence of the Party was thus justified in its very first attempt at industrial legislation." [96]

It would be difficult to place too much emphasis on the new principle of state action which the Education (Provision of Meals)

[91] *Parl. Deb.*, 4 S.H.C., vol. 152, 1906, p. 1435.
[92] *Parl. Deb.*, 4 S.H.C., vol. 167, 1906, pp. 722–780.
[93] House Bill No. 92, 1906, introduced by Mr. Barnes.
[94] For course of this Bill through the House of Lords, which caused longer debate, and apparently more interest, than the Trade Disputes Act, 1906, see *Parl. Deb.*, 4 S.H.L., vol. 167, pp. 1473–1482, pp. 1629–1670. Parts of two days were given for a discussion of all stages, which was unusual for a Bill in the House of Lords.
[95] House Bill, No. 14, 1907 (J. Ramsay MacDonald).
[96] J. Keir Hardie, *op. cit.*, p. 106.

Act implied, for in a nation jealous of individual rights and proud of its conservative instincts it was nothing less than a revolutionary principle. Thirty-six years after the passing of the Elementary Education Act, 1870, Parliament had declared that the same necessity which gave the state the duty of educating its children also demanded that there should be provision for the hungry and underfed. It was not the fault of the children that they were undernourished, and if the parents through force of circumstances were unable to feed them properly the state should see that they were fed. If the parents were unable to pay they should not be pauperised by accepting such assistance.[97]

The state believed it was the part of wisdom to meet the need through the agency of the educational authorities, though in some ways the Act was "industrial legislation," as the Labour leader suggested. This again proved that progress was slowly being made in social legislation toward the ideal of the common and inter-related life of the whole community as the aim of all enactments and their administration. The Act of 1906 was accepted by all parties. In 1912 Mr. Lansbury asked the Prime Minister if he would arrange for sufficient time being given to allow the House to pass the necessary amending Bill to the 1906 Act to enable feeding of the children during holiday time. Mr. Asquith's reply was: "I am not aware that any Bill for this purpose is before the House. The Government are, however, prepared to give favorable consideration to the principle." [98]

The Education (Provision of Meals) Act was only the beginning of legislation affecting children. The carrying out of the recommendations of the Report of the Interdepartmental Commission on Physical Deterioration, a large proportion of which dealt with child life, was demanded by public opinion stirred by a survey of the awful cost childhood was being called on to pay in both city and country.[99] There was an agreement by all parties with the Prime Minister who said in his Budget Speech, April 18, 1907, that "there is nothing that calls so loudly or so imperiously as the possibilities of Social reform." [100] The Education Act of that year reflected this sentiment, containing provisions for play centres, vacation schools and for free medical inspection of children. To decrease the alarming

[97] *Parl. Deb.*, 4 S.H.C., vol. 152, 1906, pp. 1390–1393.
[98] *Parl. Deb.*, 5 S.H.C., vol. 35, 1912, p. 379.
[99] Published July 28, 1904, Cmd. 2175, 2210, 2186. Contained fifty-three recommendations by which physical deterioration could be diminished.
[100] *Parl. Deb.*, 4 S.H.C., vol. 172, 1907, pp. 1189–1193 (Asquith).

infant mortality rate and secure proper medical care for young children, Lord Robert Cecil introduced a Bill on April 23, 1904,[101] which was eventually enacted as the Notification of Births Act. Just a year before Hardie said in the debate on the Address that "property was secured in England but life was a thing of no account." "Why was it," he asked, "that amongst the children of the poor in our great cities 66 per 1000 died before they reached one year of age, while only 18 per 1000 of the children of the class who sat in Parliament died before attaining one year?" [102] In France, only a year before, in the debate which caused the downfall of the Combes Ministry, M. Dejeante, answering the taunt of the Centre Party against the Socialists for supporting the Government, gave the death rate among children in France as the specific proof of a class struggle—6 per 100 among the rich, and 60–70 per 100 among the poor. "The world of labour," he said, "does not accept any more than you the theory of the class struggle, but protests on the contrary with the greatest energy against the practice of the class struggle carried on without scruple and without pity against the working class, a struggle which the bourgeois Republicans have only increased in alarming proportions." [103] It is evident then in the Labour movement of France and England that any legislative Act which would protect the child would help to decrease the bitterness of social outlook which the above typical quotations represent in a sober way. Herein lies the value of such legislation in a survey of legislation, for it tends to remove a peculiarly malignant source of class warfare and helps to free the energies of the community from futile hatreds.

The Government introduced February 10, 1908, the Children's Act, consolidating 38 previous Acts. This measure dealt with practically every phase of infant and child life, protection and treatment of children in reformatories and industrial schools, the question of juvenile crime, children's courts and probation officers.[104] The Housing and Town Planning Act, 1909, considered the health

---

[101] *Parl. Deb.*, 4 S.H.C., vol. 172, 1907, pp. 1572 seq. In this year the Probation of Offenders Act, was passed, dealing with juvenile offenders along reformatory rather than punitive lines. The first Act was extended by the Act of 1915, with which compare the Maternity and Child Welfare Act, 1918, and the Local Education Authorities (Medical Treatment) Act, 1909.

[102] *Parl. Deb.*, 4 S.H.C., vol. 152, 1906, p. 27; pp. 193–201 entire.

[103] *J.O.*, January 15, 1905, p. 27; pp. 27–31, entire.

[104] Amended by 1910 Act; *Parl. Deb.*, 4 S.H.C., vol. 183, 1908, pp. 1432 seq., for speech of the Under-Secretary of the Home Department, Mr. Herbert Samuel; this Bill passed third reading in the House of Commons, October 19,

and general welfare of child life,[105] in the nation as well as the adults ; the Labour Exchanges Act, 1909, made special provision for juvenile employment, and in addition the Ministry of Labour co-operates with committees appointed by various local education authorities in England and Wales in accordance with schemes approved by the Board of Education under the Education (Choice of Employment) Act, 1910,[106] and with Scotland under the Education (Scotland) Act, 1908. Local Employment Committees under the Employment Exchanges Act have established Juvenile Employment Committees, which have set up After-Care Committees in various areas for dealing with the problem of juvenile employment. Further recognition of the interdependent problem of the school-leaving age and the employment question is seen in the provision of the Unemployment Act of 1927, which gives the Minister of Labour, with the consent of the Treasury, power to authorize payments of the Unemployment Fund towards the cost of approved courses for boys and girls aged 16 to 18 who are insured persons under the scheme or are normally employed, or likely to be employed, in an insured occupation.[107] Mr. Sorensen, a Labour member, on November 29, 1929 introduced his Employment of Young Persons (Employment and Protection) Bill.[108] The Government could not accept the Bill because its provisions practically codified the whole law on child life, and cut across both the Factory Acts and the Education Acts. But there was effective support for the principles of the Bill, and the Government promised action.

---

and in the House of Lords, November 30. See the Carnegie Report on *The Physical Welfare of Mothers and Children, England and Wales,* vols. I and II (Liverpool, 1917), especially pp. 87–112, vol. I for abstract of legislative enactments in operation in England and Wales. This is a comprehensive survey of the legislation under discussion, showing the inter-relationship of the social legislation of this century and giving the pertinent provisions of the major Acts. Cf. *The Labour Year Book 1916,* pp. 297–302, on State interference, and Tillyard, *op. cit.,* section 3, chap. II, pp. 117–153.

[105] See speech of the President of the Local Government Board (Mr. Burns), on introducing the Bill of that year, May 12, 1908, *Parl. Deb.,* 4 S.H.C., vol. 188, pp. 947–968 and his remarks on the Bill of 1909 on second reading, *Parl. Deb.,* 5 S.H.C., vol. 9, pp. 733 seq.

[106] Cf. The Children (Employment Abroad) Act, 1913. See *Parl. Deb.* 5 S.H.L., 1911, vol. 7, pp. 780–807, and vol. 8, pp. 277–298, 831–834, for the committee discussion of the Employment of Children Act (1903) Amendment Bill, 1911; and Vol. 36, 1912, pp. 759–834, for second reading debate of same Bill, which passed without division.

[107] Section 8 of the Act of 1927.

[108] *Parl. Deb.,* 5 S.H.C., vol. 232, pp. 1805–1874.

The state has taken upon itself unusual responsibilities for young people until they reach the age of eighteen, and this legislation is not only important itself but often it provides the basis of the more advanced enactments dealing with adults. It is only a matter of time until bye-laws making powers of the local authorities will enable them to bring within their control all work of boys and girls up to 18 years of age. The rising generation has been seen from the national point of view, and when considered in their relationship to the future of British industry the view today is that the quality of industrial production rests first and last on the ability of the nation to give its children scope and freedom for the development of their natural endowments. From the Act of 1802 to the Education Act of 1918, and the accepted view today of the child's training as a factor in British security, is a period of progress. The London *Times* summed up this development in the statement that the "intimate connection between public health and education is perhaps the one indisputable fact upon which all progressive social legislation in every civilised country in the world has been based for nearly half a century." Sir George Newman, the Chief Medical Officer of the Board of Education, quoting this statement in his annual report on the school medical service in 1928 under the title of "The Health of the School Child", defined this service. A minimum national standard of health for all school children should first be conceived. "This minimum standard", says the report, "should be available for all school children, the cost entailed being adjusted as between the parent and the state." The general improvement in the conditions of child life and the social responsibility of the community towards these problems could not be better reflected than in the Annual Report in 1929 of the President of the Board of Health, *Education in 1928,* and in the Annual Report of the Chief Medical Officer of the Ministry of Health for the Year 1928.[109] The provisions today for maternity and child welfare, the insurance medical service, and the additional possibilities through the Local Government Act of 1929 in the Poor Law Services—all reflect a higher standard of civic responsibility as well as a determination that English life shall be of sounder quality.

[109] See *Britain's Industrial Future* (1928), chapter XXVII, "The Rising Generation, Its Education and Employment," for a thorough statement of this changed view and its implications in English life. Also Part I of *Education in 1928* (Cmd. 3307, 1929), and Parts I–IV, pp. 5–97, of the *Annual Report of the Chief Medical Officer of the Ministry of Health for the Year 1928* (1929).

One fact stands out very plain in the legislation dealing with children and young persons in England, and it is that Parliament has consistently used the educational authorities to carry out reforms which are directly industrial in their consequence. The Education Act of 1918 abolished the half-time system in factories and raised the school leaving age to fourteen years. The Education Act of 1921 codified the law as to the employment of children outside school hours. In the House of Commons, November 13, 1929, the President of the Board of Education, Sir Charles Trevelyan, announced the Labour Government's Education (School Attendance) Bill. He directly linked the school-leaving age with unemployment. In the present situation of the country, he said, 400,000 children went out at the age of 14 to join the crowd grabbing for a wage pittance in a labour market where there were more than 1,000,000 unemployed. "The folly of it", he reflected. The purpose of the Government measure was to amend the Education Act, 1921, in order to raise to 15 years the school-leaving age and to make provision for maintenance allowances in respect of children attending school up to that age who are over the age of 14 years. It is intended that the Act come into force on April 1, 1931.[110] The Minister of Education declared that there was no substantial objection to the Government proposal on the part of the working classes, whose children were going to benefit. The Act would mean a year more of school for over 400,000 children. It was so big a thing that it was worth "facing difficulties, spending money, and taking risks."

[110] *Parl. Deb.*, 5 S.H.C., November 13, 1929, pp. 2080–2087 (Trevelyan); pp. 2067–2125, debate entire.

CHAPTER IV

SOCIAL LEGISLATION IN ENGLAND: HOUSING AND TOWN PLANNING ACTS

Two important aspects of state action between 1900 and 1930 are dealt with in this section on the Housing of the Working Classes, and in the section which follows on Old Age Pensions. The state, in the first, has intervened after the breakdown of private enterprise to supply a public need; and in the second, the state has established the civil right of a citizen for a pension. A standard of life in each instance has been affirmed, for which the state stands as guardian for the whole community, and, with regard to certain classes, under-takes on its own responsibility to make possible. This standard of life is determined in national terms for the community and for the individual; the common bond between them is recognized in the statutes which aim to protect the nation and the individual from falling below a certain minimum. The constant re-interpretation of a satisfactory standard of life and the consequent effect on legislation is a remarkable feature of Housing and Old Age Pensions enact-ments. It is a reflection of a developing social and personal standard of life in the community as well as a test of how far the state will go in helping to promote that standard by laying down from time to time a progressive minimum of existence. Just as a higher standard of working class houses made private speculation insufficient and its failure a social menace, so a better security of a personal standard of living under modern conditions compelled the state to consider the needs of over half of its old age population.

I

THE HISTORY OF THE HOUSING ACTS

The Housing of the Working Classes Acts provide a continuous history of Parliamentary action on an important social problem. The debates of 1900 reviewed the history of the Acts passed the fifty preceding years, beginning with Lord Shaftesbury's Labouring Classes Lodging Houses Act, 1851, continuing with the Torrens Acts of 1868–1882, the Cross Acts of 1875–1882, the consolidated Housing of the Working Classes Act, 1885, and the Housing of the Working Classes Act, 1890, which repealed all previous legislation.[1] Lord Salisbury moved in the House of Lords in 1884 for a Royal Commission on Housing, and in that year Mr. Gladstone appointed the Commission whose Report, a Labour member believed, was responsible for Salisbury and his party being in power in 1880.[2] The Act of that year based on the Report represents the progress of public and legislative opinion.

The period included between the Labouring Classes Lodging Act, 1851, and the Housing of the Working Classes Act, 1900, marks the development of modern public administration in Great Britain.[3] The expansion of central and local authority is obvious in the Housing Acts. A growth of sentiment which made it possible for the Act of 1890 to empower local authorities to purchase—with right of compulsion—land on which they could build houses for sale to private individuals, was only another indication of the creation of administrative agencies to meet the necessary legislation which resulted from the spread of collectivist doctrine. Before 1890 the local authority had little power with regard to house building, but the Act of that year gave large powers of buying up insanitary areas, of demolishing insanitary dwellings, of letting out land to contractors under conditions as to the rebuilding of dwellings for the poor and of selling to private persons the houses erected. Municipalities were allowed to build additional houses on land not previously built upon, and to erect, furnish and manage lodging houses.

[1] A summary of the Acts repealed in 1890 follows: Dwelling Houses (Scotland) Act, 1855; Labouring Classes Dwelling Homes Act, 1866; Artizans' and Labourers' Dwelling Act, 1868; Labouring Classes' Lodging Houses and Dwellings (Ireland) Act, 1866; Artizans' and Labourers' Dwellings Improvement Act, 1875; for Scotland, 1875; Artizans' and Laborers' Dwellings Improvement Act, 1879; for Scotland, 1880; Artizans' and Labourers' Dwelling Act (1868) Amendment Act, 1879; and Amending Act same year, 1879; and finally, Artizans' Dwellings Act, 1882.

[2] *Parl. Deb.*, 4 S.H.C., 1900, vol. LXXXII, pp. 1274–1287 (Steadman).

[3] Cf. F. W. Maitland, *op. cit.* Period V. Sketch of Public Law at the Present Day, 1887–8, sect. H. "Social Affairs and Local Government," pp. 492–506. See Sidney Webb, *Socialism in England* (1890) and W. G. Towler, *Socialism in Local Government* (1908).

The advocates of Housing reform throughout the debates of 1900 sought to place foremost their contention that greater opportunities should be given to the local authorities to grapple with the areas for which they were responsible. The debates on Local Taxation that year were an interesting commentary in point,[4] and the fact was emphasized by Mr. Lloyd George that "during the course of the last 25 years there were 119 purposes for which local taxation had been authorized by Parliament." [5] The discussions on Municipal Trading which preceded the appointment of a Select Committee on that subject bear also upon the unusual growth of the powers of local authorities.[6] The large administrative powers given to district councils under the Housing of the Working Classes Acts and the Factory and Workshop Act, 1901, are proof of the progress made up to that time. Subsequent legislation down to 1914 carried forward very quickly and in a comprehensive manner this principle of state administration. "It should never be forgotten," Professor Dicey pointed out, "that powers given to local authorities are, no less than powers possessed by the central government, in reality powers exercised by the state." [7] Twenty-five years later Lord Hewart instanced the Housing Acts as examples of "The New Despotism." [8]

The Government in introducing in 1900 their Bill to amend Part III of the 1890 Act, made it plain that they had in mind not so much fresh legislation as a more effective administration of the existing laws.[9] The new principle they proposed to enact was that local

[4] *Parl. Deb.,* 4 S.H.C., 1900, vol. LXXXII, pp. 441–483. Cf. Debate on Amendment to 1911 Address on Burden of Local Rates, the official Opposition Amendment, *Parl. Deb.,* 5 S.H.C., 1911, vol. 21, pp. 700–818.

[5] *Parl. Deb., op. cit.,* p. 442.

[6] *Parl. Deb.,* 4 S.H.C., 1900, vol. LXXXI, pp. 757–776, 1343–1374.

[7] *Op. cit.,* p. 291 n 1. See *Final Report of the Royal Commission on Local Taxation,* 1900 (Cmd. 638, 1900) ; and *The Appendix to the Final Report (England and Wales) of the Royal Commission on Local Taxation,* 1902 (Cmd. 1221). Compare the *Final Report of the Departmental Committee on Local Taxation* (Cmd. 7315), 1914, considering "locally administered services of a national character." . . . "The characteristic of this intermediate class of semi-national services is that while they are administered by local authorities, the state has at the same time so marked an interest in their efficiency as to justify a claim to the supervision of their administration." The budget of 1914 (H.C. Papers No. 132) considers the changes affecting the relations of central and local taxation.

[8] *Op. cit.,* pp. 241 fp.

[9] *Parl. Deb.,* 4 S.H.C., 1900, vol. LXXIX, p. 839. The President of the Local Government Board introduced the Bill for the Government.

authorities should be empowered to go outside their districts for the purpose of establishing working men's dwellings for those who worked inside their areas. Any council, except a rural district council, which had already complied with the earlier law was to have the power of acquiring or building lodging houses for the working classes outside their districts.[10]

The debates [11] on Housing were perhaps the most illustrative for the purposes of this study in the 1900–1901 Parliament. It is often-times a difficult thing to judge how far members of any Parliament use the privileges of debate for party propaganda, the airing of personal bias and prejudice, and the bringing forward of controversial issues between parties which may be used for campaign purposes. In the speeches of party leaders or private members and in the programme of parties due allowances must be made for such considerations. But in the Parliamentary democracies of France and England responsibility can nearly always be brought home; for the Government necessarily must define a policy and the Opposition, having always before it the possibility of becoming the Government, must assume likewise on important questions an official attitude. Often too, debates are held for no other reason than to allow a subject to be discussed from all sides and leaders given a chance to interpret party wishes. With this in mind there is a fair basis of judging the conviction of the individual member and of ascertaining the general principles for which a party stands.

The partizan emphasis and the avowal of class interest were not lacking by any side in the first Housing debate in this century. One Labour member declared "I never knew yet when the time was opportune to discuss legislation that had for its object benefit for the working classes of this country. Working men may be deluded by some of your promises for a short time, but they find you out. The interest of my own class is paramount with me over the interests of all other classes." [12] The Government was able to find money to carry on the War, he said further, but for every measure of social reform there

[10] Act of 1900, sect. 1.
[11] *Parl. Deb.*, 4 S.H.C., 1900, vol. LXXXII, pp. 1260–1350, vol. LXXXIII, pp. 427–523, and vol. LXXXIV, pp. 923–1018, for debates which bring out full opposition to the policy of the Government because of its inadequate Bill to meet the Housing situation at beginning of century. The third reading was passed by 325 votes to 293: vol. LXXXV, pp. 1394–1422.
[12] *Parl. Deb.*, 4 S.H.C., 1900, vol. LXXXII, pp. 281–283 (Steadman).

was the denial because of the expense which such reforms entailed. A member representing a working class constituency said, "When we go into the homes of the people and speak with them across the table, and not from the platform, we learn that there are two questions that profoundly interest them. They ask, 'Can nothing be done to improve the housing of the working classes?' and 'When are the old age pensions coming into operation?' These questions are much more interesting to them than the abolition of the House of Lords. The social policy is what claims their attention." [13] Statements such as these provided good background for Sir Robert Reid's belief that some satisfactory way could be found, some proposal could be followed "unless the evil reaches such a stage that the people become desperate and lose their sense of justice." [14]

The Prime Minister, Mr. Balfour, stated that the proposals brought forward heretofore had "violated some fundamental principle of equity," [15] and, quoting Lord Salisbury, he said that "our friends are anxious to magnify the defects of our institutions in order to destroy them; we are anxious to remedy the defects of our institutions in order to preserve them." [16] But the proposal of the Government "whispers housing reform to the ear and breaks it to the hope of every poor workman," said Mr. John Burns, who was to be responsible in the next Government for a solution of the problem of housing.[17] The problem was such, one member believed, that "no work that we can undertake can be greater or more important, but it is not a work that should be undertaken for a moment as a party work; it is merely a work of justice to our working classes. There may be points of a party character suggested as solutions, but the real question we have at heart is not a question of party at all; it is a question of the country; it is a question of everyone living in the land." [18]

The housing of the working classes "struck at conditions which made decency impossible and morality a miracle," declared Sir Walter Foster, who deplored the fact that the Government Bill in

[13] *Parl. Deb.*, 4 S.H.C., 1900, vol. LXXXII, p. 431 (H. C. Richards).
[14] *Parl. Deb., ibid.*, p. 436.
[15] *Parl. Deb., ibid.*, p. 509.
[16] *Parl. Deb., ibid.*, p. 432.
[17] *Parl. Deb.*, 4 S.H.C., 1900, vol. LXXXV, p. 1417 (Burns).
[18] *Parl. Deb.*, 4, S.H.C., 1900, vol. LXXXII, pp. 1293-1294 (Sir Samuel Hoare); pp. 1287-1294, speech entire.

respect to rural districts did practically nothing and that it could not be looked upon as in any way an adequate method of meeting a great national emergency.[19] Any Bill which attempted to grapple with this problem, he said, ought to afford opportunities to the local authorities to reach the man who was fattening on the miseries of his fellow creatures. It should also give power to the local authorities to take over by a simpler and cheaper method all property declared to be insanitary at the bare price of land and materials; and it should further provide simple and inexpensive methods of taking land by purchase or by hire for this great public purpose in which the ordinary expense of taking land compulsorily should not be allowed. Power should also be vested in a central authority, to supervise local areas and to force local authorities to do their duty; and also means should be provided by which money should be granted at the lowest possible rate of interest for the longest period in order to enable local authorities to carry out the work of housing the people without unduly adding to the rates.[20]

It was successfully brought out in 1900 that one of the chief defects of the 1890 Act was failure to help solve the problem in rural communities, and in this connection the Small Holdings and Allotments Acts should be kept in mind. Legislation on this subject has extended over a long time; the Allotments Acts 1887–1890,[21] consolidating a long line of earlier Acts which had done comparatively small good; and in 1892 the first Small Holdings Act for England and Wales gave county councils the power to buy land and let it out in small holdings. In 1907 a new Small Holdings and Allotments Act was passed, and in 1908 a consolidating Act was passed which was amended in 1910.[22]

---

[19] One of the final Bills to be introduced in the session of 1904 was his Housing of the Working Classes (Rural Districts) Bill (House Bill No. 207, 1904). Also a Bill introduced by Mr. Nannetti, the Housing of the Working Classes, etc., Bill (House Bill No. 92, 1904), received much support; its purpose was to amend the law relating to housing of the working classes, amend the law of rating, and to establish fair rent courts. Both reintroduced in 1905 were dropped again. Also Mr. Hutton introduced in 1904 a Cottage Homes Bill (House Bill No. 195, 1905).

[20] *Parl Deb.*, 4 S.H.C., 1900, vol. LXIX, pp. 840–841.

[21] A rapid survey of earlier legislation can be had from consulting the repeal schedule of these two Acts, in the General Statutes of those years.

[22] The Small Landowners Act for Scotland, 1911, and the 1908–1910 Acts, consolidated enactments with respect to small holdings and allotments in England, Wales and Scotland. *Parl. Deb.*, 5 S.H.C., 1911, vol. 26, pp. 1355–1424, second reading debate on Small Landowners (Scotland) Bill; vol. 30, pp. 1285–

County councils were given the power in 1908 to obtain land for small holdings by compelling owners to sell it to them for this purpose. The same powers were given to local authorities under these Acts as were given under the Housing Acts. Their vital significance is that with regard to Land, definite principles of state interference and control had been established which were more comprehensively elaborated in later legislation. The various Irish Land Laws and the Land Valuation Acts have special social significance when the theory of state interference for the common good is considered.[23] People became accustomed to a state authority being exercised with regard to the Land without at all agreeing at other times to proposals which sought to apply the same principle in other activities. A minimum wage for agricultural labourers, considered later, again provided an illustration of the far reaching effects of the land question, the Government in 1914 definitely including this principle in their programme of land reform.[24]

The powers of the local authorities were being felt in many financial and administrative directions, and the effect was evident in the debates of the House of Commons.[25] The means of administration of the proposals for legislation demanded as much care and discussion

---

1434, Standing Committee; vol. 31, pp. 650–656, 675–788, further Committee and third reading. Progress in House of Lords: *Parl. Deb.*, H.L., vol. 10, pp. 293–360, second reading; pp. 487–648, Committee. On the Small Holdings and Allotments Bill, 1911, moved by the Secretary for Agriculture, see *Parl. Deb.*, 5 S.H.L., 1911, vol. 10, pp. 335–352, second reading; pp. 923–962, Committee, and pp. 1091–1115, third reading. In connection with this subject may be taken the Land Settlement (Facilities) Act, 1919, an Act to make further provision for the acquisition of land for the purpose of small holdings, amending the principal Act of 1908.

[23] The social significance of the Budget is a commonplace. For years in France and England the Treasury Ministers have remarked on this phase of their duty. The Budgets in England from 1909–1914 have special significance with regard to land taxes, and in both countries in the same period with regard to social legislation expense.

[24] Cf. The Report of the *Land Enquiry Committee* (2 vols. 1914), chap. I, Part I, vol. II (Urban) on ill housing; also a most significant study is *Property: Its Duties and Rights, Historically, Philosophically, and Religiously Regarded*. Essays by various writers with an Introduction by the Bishop of Oxford (1914, 2nd ed. 1915), note papers by Mr. A. D. Lindsay and Mr. L. T. Hobhouse. Cf. H. Seebohm Rowntree, *Land and Labour: Lessons from Belgium* (1910), and the *Liberal Land Inquiry Report* (2 vols., 1925).

[25] See *30th Annual Report of the Local Government Board, 1900–1901;* also *Economic Journal*, June, 1902, "The Financial Control of Local Authorities," pp. 182–191; *ibid.* "Local Authorities and the Housing Problem in 1901," by Lettice Fisher, pp. 263–271.

as the actual needs contained in a Bill. Often the argument was advanced that those whom an Act would affect were not in favour of it, as the Miners' Bill of 1900; or that the machinery of enforcement was inadequate and that administration would be a failure, as in the discussion of the Housing of the Working Classes Amendment of the same year. The other partner in administration—public opinion —had increasing recognition. This was suggested by Mr. Asquith in the debate on lead poisoning in potteries, when he said: "It is only by focusing public opinion in such cases that we can create the feeling of public sentiment which as everyone concerned in the administration of these laws knows is necessary for their vigilant enforcement." [26]

Public opinion has played an especially strong part in the Housing agitation. This is especially seen in the National Housing Reform Council, founded in 1900, and changed in 1910 to the National Housing and Town Planning Council. In organization and method this national council is a model of public service councils developed by individual efforts. The place of public opinion was accurately stated by a mover of an amendment to the 1900 Bill of the Government. He declared that "When people come to understand the magnitude of this evil this question will be put first in every political programme. It is a national danger in the very fullest sense. You may expand or consolidate your empire as much as you like; you may increase your defence forces; you may add to your wealth and excel in every external sign of national greatness; but if you let this question alone, if you leave it to be cured by Bills of this kind before us, you will allow the foundations of all national greatness to be sapped." [27]

Three years after the 1900 Act the Housing of the Working Classes Act, 1903, gave further powers of control and administration to the local authorities. This Act—a social commentary—defined "working class" to constitute mechanics and labourers working for wages; hawkers and others who did not employ anyone but their own family; and persons other than domestic servants whose income did not exceed 30 shillings a week. Regulations were made for the re-housing of the persons of the working class whose land was compulsorily taken, it being enacted that where houses occupied

[26] *Parl. Deb.,* 4 S.H.C., 1900, vol. LXIX, p. 988.
[27] *Parl. Deb.,* 4 S.H.C., 1900, vol. LXXXII, pp. 1266–1273 (Robson).

by 30 or more persons of the working class were taken, a re-housing scheme was required to be approved by the Local Government Board before any house was removed, under the penalty of a £500 fine. The Act also provided that in any letting of a working class house there should always be an implied condition that it was reasonably fit for human habitation, notwithstanding any agreement to the contrary. This Act and the Workmen's Compensation Act set up different rights than the common law recognized.

The progress of legislation dealing with overcrowded and insanitary living conditions had complementary aid from the Public Health Acts. The system of sanitary law can be stated to have started in 1848, the main stages being marked by Acts of 1848, 1858, and 1875; and in 1919 the Ministry of Health was established. The public sanitary code is represented chiefly by the Public Health Act, 1875, and its amending Acts of 1890 and 1907, and the Public Health (London) Act, 1891, which gave powers to local authorities for dealing with specific nuisances and isolated cases of overcrowding. These Acts were all administered by local authorities, with special powers often remaining in the hands of the Local Government Board; and the Acts enabled the local councils to deal with every problem of insanitary housing accommodation which affects the worker in either an urban or a rural area. The central authority is now of course the Ministry of Health, which often uses the Public Health Acts in cases of Orders affecting bad and insanitary housing.

II

THE HOUSING AND TOWN PLANNING ACT, 1909

The progress of Housing legislation since the Royal Commission under Sir Charles W. Dilke was appointed in 1884, was best indicated in the Government Bill of 1908,[28] introduced by the President

[28] Preceding this Bill were the Housing of the Working Classes Acts Amendment Bill (House Bill No. 9, 1906, presented by Mr. Mackarness), and the Bill of Mr. Steadman (House Bill No. 104, 1906, withdrawn). The mover of the first said the principle had been approved by all parties, and in the fifty years before 35 measures had been passed with a view to improving the condition of the rural population in this regard (*Parl. Deb.*, 4 S.H.C., 1906, vol. 156, pp. 131-144; pp. 131-180, and pp. 1274 ff. debate entire). The Government asked for a Select Committee, announcing that the debate had been "absolutely free from party recriminations" (*op. cit.*, p. 171, Burns).

of the Local Government Board, Mr. John Burns, who outlined the scope of the Bill and the policy of the Government.[29] "This is not a party matter," he said, "it is one in which partisanship of any kind ought not to find a place." [30] The Government purposed through the Bill to provide "a domestic condition for the people in which their physical health, their morals, their character, and their whole social condition can be improved by what we hope to secure in this Bill. The Bill aims in broad outline at, and hopes to secure, the home healthy, the house beautiful, the town pleasant, the city dignified, the suburbs salubrious." [31]

If one is inclined to wonder at the phrasing of the Government's purpose, one can be reminded of a judgment of the time, that this was a Parliament "optimistic and reforming" given a "Mephisto-phelian touch" by the leader of the Opposition, Mr. Balfour.[32] But the Government had seen to its facts. The responsible Minister showed that the population was becoming urban, overcrowding was bad in the cities, the industrial areas especially, and in the counties. In Glasgow 26 per cent of the population lived in one room, and in London 14 per cent. The Government in reintroducing the Bill in 1909 declared that "the majority of those for whose welfare this Act is designed have at present no home." [33] Class legislation; but a necessity had to be faced. By their declarations the Government was committed to a radical programme, justifying it on straightfor-ward collectivist doctrine, they intended for the state to do what had not been done or could not be done by private or individual effort.

The Act of 1909, "an Act to Amend the Law relating to the Housing of the Working Classes, to provide for the working of Town Planning Scheme, and to make further provision with respect to the appointment and duties of County Medical Officers of Health,

[29] The Bill was introduced March 26, 1908, and the second reading debate was May 12, for which see, *Parl. Deb.* 4 S.H.C., 1908, vol. 188, pp. 947–1063; failing to pass in that session it was re-introduced February 17, 1909, by the President of the Local Government Board, who said on second reading debate, April 5, that it was an almost exact reproduction of the Bill before the Grand Committee in 1908.

[30] *Parl. Deb.*, 4 S.H.C., 1908, vol. 188, pp. 968; pp. 947–968, speech entire.

[31] *Parl. Deb., ibid.,* p. 949.

[32] The *Nation* (London), August 31, 1907, p. 949.

[33] *Parl. Deb.*, H.C., 1909, vol. 3, p. 797 (Masterman) ; pp. 787–798, entire speech; pp. 733–742, entire speech of President of the Local Government Board in reintroducing Bill; and pp. 733–798, 849–871, complete second reading debate, 1909.

and to provide for the establishment of Public Health and Housing Committees of County Councils," set forth a new constructive principle, Town Planning. This Act extended the powers delegated to the local authority, broadly confirming this general administrative tendency which endowed with larger and more stringent powers the local government councils of England. This is made clear by the fact that the 1890 Act made it optional for the Council to build new houses in extreme instances, but the 1909 Act made it the duty of the Council to build new houses where needed. Part III of the Housing Act of 1890 was made universally applicable without adoption, so that local authorities might build new houses without getting leave from the County Council; and the Act allowed land to be acquired compulsorily on the terms of the Small Holdings and Allotments Act, 1907. The Public Works Loan Commissioners were empowered to grant loans to rural authorities for the purposes of the Bill for eighty years, the rate of interest not varying with the duration of the loan. The Act enabled the Local Government Board to authorize a "borough or urban District Council to prepare a town planning" scheme in or about the neighbourhood of their area; to facilitate such a programme various provisions were made for the exchange of land and for compulsory purchase.

This Act besides consolidating the previous Housing Acts, made a decided step in advance in dealing with the Housing situation by making the existing law obligatory which enabled local authorities to provide houses. The first part of the Act of 1909 dealt with the housing of the working classes, and the second part with town planning.[34] The Bill was subjected in the House of Lords to several amendments which were unsatisfactory to the Government.[35] The great objection to the Bill by the Lords was that it conferred too great powers on the Local Government Board, which was viewed as

[34] *Parl. Deb.*, H.C. 1909, vol. 6, pp. 833–906, for opening discussion on the allocation of time for Committee stage; vol. 10, pp. 28–150, for Committee debate on Part I Housing; pp. 187–324, for Part II, Town Planning; pp. 1635–1714, consideration and third reading.

[35] *Parl. Deb.*, H. L., 5 S., 1909, vol. 2, pp. 1140–1184, second reading debate in House of Lords; presented by Earl Beauchamp for Government (pp. 1140–1147), supported chiefly by the Bishop of Birmingham (pp. 1157–1161) and the Archbishop of Canterbury (pp. 1165–1168). Committee stage, *Parl. Deb.*, 5 S.H.L., 1909, vol. 3, pp. 25–126, pp. 130–359; third reading and passed, *op. cit.*, pp. 635–712, and p. 1007.

an increasing menace.[36] The Lords amendments when sent to the House were considered unsatisfactory, and the Bill was returned for further consideration.[37] At that time the debate centred about the increasing power which the Local Government Board might exercise, but the Marquess of Salisbury counselled patience and tact, for the country, he said, must be conciliated on the question of social reform and the House of Lords could not allow the impression to grow that they were opposed to measures of reform.[38] This has its significance in this study, wholly aside from the constitutional issue, because it was the same argument which had been used in 1906 by the Marquess of Lansdowne on the Trade Disputes Bill, when he counselled acceptance. It has never ceased to be heard when there is conflict between the two Houses of Parliament.

The importance of administration was emphasized in the strong objections that the House of Lords held to any extension of the powers of the Local Government Board. In 1919 the duties of the Local Government Board were taken over by the Ministry of Health, an interesting commentary on the growth of state departments and their functions in England, which the transfer clause of the Act suggests. Professor Maitland, years ago, observed that "every reform of local government has hitherto meant an addition to the powers of the central government. These two processes have been going on side by side; on the one hand we get new organs of local government, on the other hand we get new organs of central government." [39]

The Act of 1909 effectively laid down administrative discipline. It made compulsory the optional clauses of the 1890 Act with regard to inspection, and every County Council was required to appoint a medical officer of health with full powers over housing and inspec-

[36] *Parl. Deb.*, 5 S.H.L., 1909, vol. 2, pp. 1147–1157 (Earl of Onslow).

[37] *Parl. Deb.*, 5 S.H.C., 1909, vol. 2, pp. 1448–1627, reconsideration; Government reasons for refusal of amendments, pp. 1448–1450 (Burns); and final reconsideration, second time, after Lords consideration of Commons amendments, *Parl. Deb.*, 5 S.H.C., 1909, vol. 13, pp. 445–448.

[38] *Parl. Deb.*, 5 S.H.L., 1909, vol. 4, pp. 667–673; and pp. 667–728, entire debate on Commons amendments.

[39] *Op. cit.*, p. 498. Compare with this Lord Hewart's strictures on Sect. I of Town Planning Act of 1925. See also the First Report (Cmd. 2506, 1925) and the Final Report (Cmd. 3436, 1929) of the Royal Commission on Local Government, appointed in 1921.

tions.[40] Then as now the Council of every borough or urban or rural district must cause their district to be inspected in order to ascertain whether any dwelling-house is in a state so dangerous or injurious to health as to be unfit for human habitation. The regulations made by the old Local Government Board and later the Ministry of Health under the Act, have built up a system of inspection reports that show how effectively the Housings Acts are being carried out in every administrative area; and the exact condition of the housing situation of any district can be got from these reports. The detailed attention given to the work of inspection and the powers of the Council to act upon the reports of the Medical Officer of Health and the Inspector of Nuisances, together with the penal power contained in the closing Order of the Council, gave the Act of 1909 a comprehensiveness that no Act of social legislation had had up to that time. The drastic powers as to the closing and demolition of insanitary dwellings, the clearance and rehousing powers, together with the constructive duty of providing more houses, indicate how seriously the central government concerned itself with the housing of the people. By 1909 the state had definitely put forward the housing of the people as foremost public concern.[41]

THE DEVELOPMENT ACT OF 1909

Before considering post-war legislation on housing, the programme of national development, which the famous Budget speech of April 29, 1909, intimated would be introduced, may be considered.[42] The Chancellor of the Exchequer said the Development Bill which the Government had in mind would include such objects as the institution of schools of forestry, the purchase and preparation of land for afforestation, the setting up of a number of experimental forests on a large scale, expenditure upon scientific research in the

[40] Act of 1909, sect. 17.

[41] For debate on administration of Housing Act in the Supply vote for the Local Government Board, 1912, see *Parl. Deb.*, 5 S.H.C., 1912, vol. 39, pp. 137–216. See also the debate on the Housing of the Working Classes Bills (I and II) of Sir A. Griffith-Boscawen, based on the French State system, it was claimed, offered as amending measures to the 1909 Act: *Parl. Deb.*, 5 S.H.C., 1912, vol. 35, pp. 1413–1495, and vol. 41 (Bill No. 2), pp. 2973–2975.

[42] *Parl. Deb.*, H.C., 1909, vol. 4, pp. 472–548; social problems dealt with in pp. 481–494.

interests of agriculture, experimental farms, the improvement of
stock, the equipment of agencies for disseminating agricultural information, the encouragement and promotion of coöperation, the
improvement of rural transport so as to make markets more accessi-
ble, the facilitation of all well-considered schemes and measures for
attracting labour back to the land by small holdings or reclamation
of wastes. That was only one side of the problem which fully illustrates the essentially serious attitude of the leaders of the Government in making legislation an instrument of service in raising the
condition of the people of England. That there has been no new
legislation but what has been built on the achievement of those years
is proof of the constructive genius of a Parliament which passed
ameliorative and protective measures a nation has used in a long
struggle of war and in an equally difficult time of peace. But the
spirit of the Government is more important; it is the force which
gives validity to the passion for social betterment, interpreting the
indictment of countless bluebooks. One side of the problem was to
remake England—no less a task than seemed fit for Parliament's
endeavour then—and the other was to replenish the capital of human
material. "We have, more especially during the last sixty years,"
the Chancellor of the Exchequer continued, "in this country accumulated wealth to an extent which is almost unparalleled in the
history of the world, but we have done it at an appalling waste of
human material. We have drawn upon the robust vitality of the
rural areas of Great Britain, and especially of Ireland, and spent its
energies recklessly in the devitalizing atmosphere of urban factories
and workshops as if the supply were inexhaustible. We are now
beginning to realize that we have been spending our capital, and at
a disastrous rate, and it is time we should make a real, concerted,
national effort to replenish it. I put forward this proposal, not a
very extravagant one, as a beginning."

On the second reading of the Development Bill,[43] the success of
which had been linked with the Budget,[44] Lord Hugh Cecil, a strenuous opponent of the Bill, quoted the words of the Labour leader,
Hardie, who had just written that it was "the most revolutionary

[43] Introduced August 26, 1909, and read a second time on September 6,
Parl. Deb., 5 S.H.C., 1909, vol. 10, pp. 906–1046, second reading and passed by
a vote of 137 to 17, after closure applied, and after a defeat by 105 votes to 6
of an amendment limiting the grant to one year of £500,000.

[44] Part VII, clauses 87–91, of the Finance Act, 1909, are the provisions.

measure ever introduced into Parliament, and that it endorses one of the main principles of the Right to Work Bill." [45] Two years later, 1911, the mover of the Labour Right to Work Amendment Bill declared that: "That act (the Development Act, 1909) contains every proposal of the Labour and Socialist movement for the last 20 and 25 years, proposals about afforestation, erosion of the coast, building of light railways, and reclamation of land." [46]

There is no wonder that the chief objection in the House of Lords was that the Bill meant in the long run nationalization of land,[47] but the President on the Board of Agriculture in his explanation [48] of the six clauses on development and the other fourteen on road improvement gave no such interpretation. All efforts to amend the Bill failed,[49] which again called down condemnation from the leader of the Opposition in the House of Lords, Lord Lansdowne, on the policy of the Government. The Development and Road Improvements Funds Act (1909) Amendment Bill which was brought forward the next year,[50] supplementary to the 1909 Act, provided an opportunity for Lord Hugh Cecil to recall his opposition to the original Act because "it has always seemed to me," he said, "to fulfil the idea of a Socialist measure more completely than any Act which has been before Parliament." [51] The debate was interesting also because the Act was taken by Mr. Belloc as an opportunity of again showing, to his satisfaction, that the party system was the curse of Parliament, and to pay his respects to the author of the Act (Mr. Lloyd George) as the chief example of the evil which he condemned.[52] Criticism of Acts of Parliament on the grounds of their

[45] *Parl. Deb.,* 5 S.H.C., 1909, vol. 10, p. 1047.
[46] *Parl. Deb.,* 5 S.H.C., 1909, vol. 21, p. 590 (O'Grady).
[47] *Parl. Deb.,* 5 S.H.L., 1909, vol. 3, pp. 291–299.
[48] *Parl. Deb., ibid.,* pp. 1225–1233 (Earl Carrington) ; second reading debate, pp. 1225–1283—note speech of Marquess of Salisbury, pp. 1233–1242; Committee stage, *Parl. Deb.,* 5 S.H.L., 1909, vol. 4, pp. 200–311 ; amendments from Commons reported and third reading, *ibid.,* pp. 443–477.
[49] Committee stage in House of Commons, *Parl. Deb.,* 5 S.H.C., 1909, vol. 10, pp. 1047–1065, 1277–1279; further procedure, vol. II, pp. 1932–1966; report stage and third reading, *ibid.,* pp. 2204–2335, 2347–2454; consideration of Lords amendments, *ibid.,* pp. 445–448, and vol. 13, pp. 372–445.
[50] *Parl. Deb.,* 5 S.H.C., 1909, vol. 17, pp. 155–183, second reading debate entire; pp. 155–157 (Lloyd George), pp. 158–161 (Sir F. Banbury) ; Committee stage, *ibid.,* pp. 377–399, 535–536, 581–595. All stages in House of Lords, *Parl. Deb.,* 5 S.H.L., 1909, vol. 5, pp. 815–817.
[51] *Parl. Deb.,* 5 S.H.C., 1909, vol. 17, p. 166.
[52] *Parl. Deb., ibid.,* p. 385.

Socialistic nature, such as against the Development Act, read strangely now, when the legislation of 1909 is considered with post-war development, conditioned necessarily by the experience of the War and the needs when peace came. However, in 1914 a competent critic believed: [53] "State Socialism has been accepted in fact if not in name; and there is no influential body of political thought which repudiates the principles, though there is much controversy as to the extent and manner of its application."

III

POST-WAR LEGISLATION

Legislation after the war has extended the powers of the state with regard to Housing and Land; the policy of state aid and control has been directly pursued and new principles confirmed. Early in the War the Rent Restriction Act, 1915, gave Government protection against raised rents and evictions; and by the yearly extension of the Increase of Rent and Mortgage Interest (Restrictions) Act— millions of working class and middle class tenants have been granted since the war the protection of the earlier Act.[54] The Act of 1915, with its amendments, has been continued because it has not been possible for private or state aid to establish a normal housing situation. The principle already seems so securely fixed in the minds of the people, believes one observer, "that though these (Rent Restriction Acts) are at present classed as emergency legislation, the principle of no longer leaving rent to the higgling of the market, on which they are based, has in the opinion of many, come to stay.[55]

[53] Cf. Sir Sidney Low, *Governance of England* (1st ed. 1904), *Introduction* to 1914 edition.

[54] The Increase of Rent and Mortgage Interest (Restrictions) Act, 1920, re-pealed all previous rent restriction Acts, including the principal Act of 1915, the Court (Emergency Powers) Act, 1917, and its extension in 1919, the Increase of Rent and Mortgage Interest (Amendment) Act, 1918, the Increase of Rent (Amendment) Act, 1919. Important social principles of State control of prices and powers of investigation for "limiting the profit" were contained in the Act to Check Profiteering (Continuance) Act, and the Profiteering (Amendment) Act, 1920.

[55] E. F. Foa, *The Law of Landlord and Tenant* (6th ed. 1924), Preface, III–IV; pp. 911–966, for Rent Acts. Also debate on Rent Restriction Motion, July 15, 1929, *Parl. Deb.*, 5 S.H.C., vol. 230, pp. 177–186.

The Minister of Health refused on November 26, 1929 to exclude the Rent Restriction Act from the Expiring Laws Continuance Act, extending it through 1930.

THE HOUSING AND TOWN PLANNING ACT, 1919

The Minister of Reconstruction, Dr. Christopher Addison, was convinced that the state would have to assume the major burden of providing houses for the people,[56] and in 1919 the Government confirmed completely the Act of 1909 in passing the Housing, Town Planning, etc., Act "an Act to amend the enactments pertaining to the Housing of the Working Classes, Town Planning and the Acquisition of Small Holdings." The Act made it "the duty of every local authority to consider the needs of their area with respect to the provision of houses for the working classes, and within three months after the passing of this Act, and as often thereafter as occasion arises, or within three months after notice has been given to them by the Local Government Board, to prepare and submit to their Local Government Board a scheme for the exercise of their powers." [57] Under this section 1805 local authorities were required by the central authority to submit schemes for house building in their area; a special Department of Housing was set up by the Ministry of Health, subdivided into an administrative and a technical section. The new feature of this Act was the taking over by the state of the financial loss on any unsound investment of capital by the local authorities on any scheme approved under Parts I, II, III, of the principal Act; that is acquisition, clearance, development and rehousing; [58] and additional powers were given to alter, enlarge, repair and improve.[59] This Act was "a step which was indicated by the realization of the social necessity of house building." [60] This was further indicated in

---

[56] See *Memorandum by the Advisory Housing Panel on the Emergency Problem in Housing,* 1918: also *The Betrayal of the Slums,* by the Rt. Hon. Christopher Addison, M.D. (1922), Minister of Reconstruction and the first Minister of Health.

[57] Act of 1919, sect. 1. To be taken with comments below on Housing Act of 1929 and the Local Government Act of 1929.

[58] Act of 1919, Sect. 7. Cf. Part III of the Land Settlement (Facilities) Act, 1919, on recoupment of losses incurred by Councils.

[59] *Ibid.,* Sect. 12. Compare with Sect. I, Town Planning Act, 1925.

[60] *European Housing Problems Since the War, 1914–1923* (Geneva, 1924), p. 87, International Labour Office; pp. 71–110, survey of Great Britain.

the Housing (Additional Powers) Act, 1919, allowing the payment of a lump sum as a subsidy to private builders of working class houses, a completely new feature in English housing legislation. The first Act of 1919 allowed financial aid out of monies provided by Parliament to a Public Utility Society, registered under the Industrial and Provident Societies Act, 1893; and the second Act of that year permitted the Ministry of Health to authorize the local authority to issue bonds for house building, town planning and other purposes of the Act. Subsidization of loss and a subsidy to private capital were the features of these two Acts. The Housing Act of 1921 sought to revive the Small Dwellings Acquisition Act, 1899 (an Act rarely used by local authorities), and the same object of encouraging private enterprise was in the Housing, Town Planning, etc., Act, 1923, known as the Chamberlain Act. The essential fact of pre-war legislation and its extension remained in full force, for the Minister of Health was authorized to make contributions out of monies provided by Parliament toward any expense incurred by local authorities in promoting the building of houses by private enterprise or in providing houses itself.[61] The Act authorized the local authorities with the approval of the Minister of Health to assist private enterprise in building houses. The assistance to take the form of a lump-sum grant, the refund of rates for a specified period, or repayment of advances to a building society. The Act authorized the Metropolitan Borough Councils to provide houses themselves, instead of promoting their construction by others, and permitted the London County Council to supplement the state contribution in respect of such houses to an extent not exceeding £3 a house each year for a period not exceeding 20 years.

The Housing Act of 1924 of the Labour Government, the Wheatley Act, extended subsidies in the effort to get co-operation from the local authorities. This Act provided for a 15-year local programme, offering a state subsidy for houses completed before October, 1939. The principle of a state subsidy is here the important point. This same principle is in the Small Holdings and Allotments Act, 1926, amending 1908–1919 Acts, which requires County Councils to provide holdings (1) if they can do so without loss; and (2) if it appears that a loss will be incurred, the Council shall submit their proposals to the Minister of Agriculture, who may make a contribution not

[61] Act of 1923, Sect. 1, subsect. 1, 2 and 6.

exceeding 75 per cent of the estimated loss. On December 13, 1929 a second reading was given, with Government support, to the Small Landholders (Scotland) Acts (1886–1919) Amendment Bill. It was estimated the Bill would bring 10,000 additional cultivators within the Small Landholders Act, which were now about 50,000 small landholders in Scotland—something like two-thirds of the total number of agriculturalists—and with their families they formed about 250,000, and were the backbone of the country. It was proposed to widen the scope of the previous measures so as to bring in holdings up to a limit of 100 acres and £100 rental a year.

Housing Acts, 1925–1929

The law with regard to Housing was consolidated in the Act of 1925, bringing together all the permanent provisions of earlier legislation. The temporary provisions of the Acts of 1923 and 1924 were not included in the Act of 1925. The five parts of the 1925 Act are: Part I. Provision for securing the repair, maintenance and sanitary conditions of houses; Part II. Improvement and reconstruction schemes; Part III. Provision of houses for the working classes; Part IV. and Part V. Financial and General. The Ministry of Health, the central authority for the Housing Acts, broadly interprets the term "working classes". The Fifth Schedule of the Housing Act, 1925—contrasting to 1903 Act—includes in this term mechanics, citizens, labourers, and others working for wages, but working at some trade or handicraft without employing others, except members of their own family, and persons, other than domestic servants, whose income in any case does not exceed an average of *three pounds* a week, and the families of any such persons who may be residing with them. This very definition is significant of the social condition of England. Further provision for grants by the state for the housing of workers were given in the Housing (Rural Workers) Act, 1926, and the Housing Act of 1927 further confirmed the principle of a government subsidy. The former Act enables County or County Borough Councils to make grants or loans, with Government assistance, for the improvement of rural housing accommodation. The making of grants shall be subject to the conditions—likewise a reflection of social conditions—that the dwelling shall not be occupied except (a) by a person, whether owner or

tenant, whose income is, in the opinion of the local authority, such
that he would not ordinarily pay a rent in excess of that paid by
agricultural workers in the district, or (b) an agriculture worker
employed by the person who is rated in respect of the dwelling. No
assistance may be given where the value of the dwelling after the
completion of the works exceeds £400. This Act was contemptuously
described by the former Minister of Health in the Labour Government, Mr. Wheatley, as a bill "to provide stables for heroes". In
his annual review of his department, the Minister of Health in 1928,
Mr. Neville Chamberlain, declared the Act had not so far achieved
much result, which he attributed to the fact that the Act was unknown
in the country. The Minister of Health, Mr. Greenwood, stated in
the House of Commons November 14, 1929, that the number of
dwellings actually completed at September 20, 1929, in agricultural
parishes under the provisions of the Housing (Financial Provisions) Act. 1924, was 14,487. Up to the same date assistance had
been promised under the Housing (Rural Workers) Act in respect
to 2,200 dwellings.

The Labour Government in 1924 introduced a Bill to consolidate
the Town Planning Acts, and, though passing the House of Lords,
time was not sufficient for its completion by passage in the House of
Commons. Town-planning schemes in preparation in 1925 covered
considerably more than a million acres of land, and pending the
preparation and approval of the schemes, the development was
guided by the responsible Local Authorities over the whole of the
area under Interim Development Orders issued by the Minister of
Health, and subject to appeal. Thus all development was brought into
conformity by the Ministry of Health. The Town Planning Act of
1925, strongly condemned by Lord Hewart as an example of administrative despotism, consolidated the law on town-planning. The
Local Government Act, 1929, extended the date for submission of
obligatory schemes required by the 1919 Act for Boroughs and
Urban Districts with a population of over 20,000, to January 1, 1934,
with power of the Minister to extend the date further, but not beyond
December 31, 1938. The Tenth Report of the Minister of Health,
1929, recorded that during the year 1928, 64 preliminary town planning proposals, and 14 complete schemes had been submitted, and
20 statements and 4 schemes approved. The Local Government Act
of 1929 extended to County Councils the definite right to share in

the administration of town planning schemes, the purpose being, the Minister of Health says, to identify County Councils more closely with town planning functions and so overcome some of the legal and practical difficulties which have hitherto attended town-planning schemes. The real purpose of the intermixture of urban and rural development is plain in the Town Planning Acts.

It is significant of a spirit of co-operation that the Council for the Preservation of Rural England, in conjunction with the Royal Institute of British Architects, have established panels covering all parts of England and Wales, to advise and assist both owners and Local Authorities, without charge, in carrying out the provisions of the Housing (Rural Workers) Act, and also in connection with town-planning. There were at the beginning of 1930 in England and Wales 56 Joint Advisory and 17 Joint Executive Committees, the function of which was to increase the arrangements for carrying out concerted plans of town-planning. The National Housing and Town-Planning Council have a technical committee to consider what extensions and amendments of the Town-Planning Act, 1925, are desirable. The Ministry of Health can thus depend upon a voluntary and professional support of its Housing and Town Planning policies which can create effective public opinion. This is primarily a post-war development in England, so far as the larger national aspects of housing and town-planning are concerned.

The achievements of housing accomplished in England since the armistice can be described truthfully as remarkable.[62] The number of houses built from 1919 to 1928 was 1,275,000, of which 829,000 were built with state assistance. The exchequer subsidy since the war, 1919–1929, is the large sum of £84,874,607. The Estimates for the year 1929–1930 contained provision for £11,150,000 in respect of housing subsidies.

The extensive powers of the Home Secretary under the Factory and Workshops Acts are matched by the comprehensive powers under the Housing Acts given to the Minister of Health. Administrative powers are mainly exercised by Ministers, and the great majority of determinative powers are either exercised or controlled by the central government in London.[63] Under the Housing Acts,

[62] *Tenth Annual Report of Ministry of Health, 1929*, p. 67.

[63] See the study of Ernst Freund, *Administrative Powers Over Persons and Property* (1928), pp. 37–38, and the study of W. A. Robson, *Justice and Administrative Law* (1928), pp. 105–107. These two studies are important contributions to the whole field covered by this present study.

the Ministry of Health is the appellate body in regard to the important matters affecting the rights of owners of slum property and work-men's dwelling-houses. The Minister of Health determines the rules of appeals to the central department, and in regard to any matter brought before him on appeal "may make such order in the matter as he thinks equitable", and his decision is then binding and conclusive on all parties. Wide powers are given the Ministry of Health over the local authorities in the carrying out of the provisions of the Acts. The aim, of course, has been to create the conditions of co-operation between the central and local authority, which is necessary for the best use of the existing Acts, and this has been greatly helped by the intelligent lay interest in England in matters of housing. Perhaps no social problem, save unemployment, has been given such consistent study by voluntary agencies in England. The results of the studies of independent researches have often stirred official action, and have pointed the way to community co-operation.

The national housing emergency since 1919 has been partially met by the state spending money amounting to nearly ten million pounds a year. Parliament was informed by the Minister of Health in December, 1926, that he expected the subsidies would increase by nine hundred thousand pounds a year, so that in 1929–1930 the total figure would be eleven million pounds. His figures proved correct, as noted above. By order of the Ministry of Health in December, 1928, the subsidy under the Act of 1923 was withdrawn, and that under the Act of 1924 reduced, the Government subsidy going wholly to the building of houses to let, under the Act of 1924. The Housing (Revision of Contributions) Act, 1929, passed by the Labour Government, restored the subsidy paid in respect of houses built under the Act of 1924.

The housing situation has been relieved but a state of over-crowding exists which is appalling. The problem of the slums remains acute. There is, for instance, the statement from the Scottish Board of Health's report for 1926–1927, which says that "It is impossible to draw any picture which could adequately describe the conditions under which we found human beings living in practically the whole of the houses we inspected." The Report on the 1921 Census, issued in 1927, showed that in 1921 over 637,000 persons in England and Wales, as compared with 515,000 in 1911, were living three, four and more to one room, and 3,480,000, or six per cent. of the popula-tion were living at a density of more than two persons per room; in the county of London, in spite of some improvement since 1911, there were still 680,000 persons, or over 16 per cent of the county population, living more than two persons to a room; while in Northumberland and Durham the proportion rises to 30.8 per cent and 29.5 per cent respectively, and is even higher than in 1911.[64] The National Housing and Town Planning Council in 1929 issued without editorial comment extracts from the official Health and Medical reports of the United Kingdom, and these showed the terrible effects of overcrowding. So long as such conditions exist housing in England is a national problem.

In this long survey the overwhelming detail of Acts from 1851 to 1929 may obscure the important principle of state action which unifies them in aim and gives them great importance in this study of social legislation. The solution of the housing problem has demanded the best thought of Parliamentary leaders. It has not been a party issue. During the housing debate in December, 1925, raised by the Liberal party, the Prime Minister, Mr. Baldwin, made an announcement of the new state housing plan for Scotland. Mr. Baldwin stated that the Government's offer made to Scotland of a special subsidy of £40 a house had definitely failed in its object of encouraging local authorities to bestir themselves to deal with a national scandal. The offer, he announced, had lapsed, and the Government had decided to build, itself, 2,000 houses in Scotland. The Prime Minister said some persons expected the population that lives in the infamous conditions that have made the Clyde notorious to be patient and forbearing and to admire the civilization which in these places is represented by these conditions.[65] The Prime Minister was quoted by Mr. David Kirkwood, the irrepressible Labour member from the Clyde, as saying of the slums of Glasgow, "it is damnable". Mr. Baldwin looked on as he was quoted by Labour. The Report of the Liberal Industrial Inquiry, 1928, declared that housing conditions in the centres of too many towns today were a disgrace. "Room to live and room to play are the rights of every deserving citizen, and if these rights are ignored the price must be paid in ill-health and ill-will, in poor physique and poor production." [66]

[64] See the comments in *The Monthly Circular* of the Labour Research Department, August, 1927, "The Housing Problem," pp. 180–182.

[65] See *Report of the Committee on the Rent Restriction Acts, Edinburgh,* (1925 Cmd. 2423), for a full account of the problem.

[66] *Op. cit.,* p. 298.

The state determined before 1914 that a minimum standard of housing was necessary for reasons of public health and decency. This aim of a minimum standard has gradually become more insistent as the standards of community life have been raised. The state has considered housing as a public service, and while it has outlined large duties for local authorities, it has vastly increased the central authority's power of control. The Minister of Health on December 18, 1925, in one of the periodic debates on housing, hinted at new powers for local authorities to deal with slums, giving them powers compulsorily to buy slum property in preparation for future building schemes. In the meantime the property had to be more habitable. The purpose of this is plain. The Housing problem is a particular instance of the general principle elaborated by Professor Pigou that it is the duty of the civilized state to lay down certain minimum conditions in every department of life below which it refuses to allow its free citizens to fall. Any man or any family which fails to attain independence to any of these must be regarded as a proper subject for state action.[67]

This principle was recognized in the Report of the National House Building Committee in 1924, composed of building employers and employees, and a committee of manufacturers and dealers in building materials.[68] The report plainly stated that the high cost of producing houses was such that working-class houses could not be produced on an economically satisfactory basis such as would induce the investment of capital, unless a subsidy was provided by the state. The committee declared the subsidy provided in the Chamberlain Act of 1923 had proved inadequate, and for this reason the Wheatley Act of 1924 attempted to carry into effect the Committee's recommendations. When Mr. Neville Chamberlain again assumed charge of the national housing policy, after the first Labour Government, his problem in the Ministry of Health was not less serious than in 1923. He found it necessary to depend upon subsidies from the central and local authorities to stimulate the building of houses, and the provision by local authorities of new houses for the use of the working class population has not been less an important task of local governing authorities.

[67] *Economics of Welfare* (1924, new ed. 1929) Part II, chap. XIX.
[68] *National House Building Committee Report,* (Cmd. 2104, 1924) and also the Second and Third Interim Reports of that year (Cmd. 2310 and Cmd. 2334, 1924).

The housing problem is today more than ever a part of a larger problem—that of enabling society to control the expression and arrangements of its social life; and, for this purpose, as the Liberal Land Reports of 1925 declared, the interests of property may have to be put second to the needs of the nation. This same insistence on the rights of the community is found in the 1928 election manifesto of the Labour Party, where the housing and health of the people are joined together as a common problem in Labour's attack on the Conservative Government and its record.[69] The Labour Government have promised, through the Ministry of Health, to introduce in 1930 a comprehensive new Housing Bill which will contain broad powers for a determined attack by the national and local government upon the slums of England. Public opinion is prepared for such a policy by the national government.

[69] *Labour and the Nation*, p. 31.

CHAPTER V

SOCIAL LEGISLATION IN ENGLAND AND A NATIONAL PENSION POLICY

The numerous proposals before Parliament dealing with old age pensions indicated in England, as in France, the general trend of popular and legislative opinion. The principle was becoming clearer and more fully defined as each Parliamentary session passed. It had practically ceased to be a party question. The Government spokesman in 1900 said, "this question of old age pensions is one which should be placed above and beyond party politics"; and, giving broader endorsement, declared, "the elementary principle of honourable pensions for the deserving in their old age has been recognized by the community just as clearly as it has recognized the necessity for the education of our children." [1] The second reading of the Old Age Pensions Bill in that session meant an acceptance by the Government of the principle, but the matter of expense was the Government reason for not pursuing the question further at that time. The cost of Poor Law Relief was given for 1874 and 1897; in the former year there were 820,446 paupers in England and Wales, costing the state £7,664,959, or £9.5.0. per head; and in 1897 there were 814,887 paupers, kept at an expense of £10,432,189 or £12.16.0 each. The financial report on the Chaplin scheme, noted below, revealed the wide need of a great part of the population and yet compared with the 1919 Report to the Treasury, its underestimate is patent. The mover of one of the Aged Pensioners Bills in 1904 [2] had declared that in 1902 and 1903 a Bill similar to his had reached second reading, and that the Government by allowing each year a Bill of that nature to pass second reading was committed in principle to the passing of an old age pensions scheme. [3]

[1] *Parl. Deb.,* 4 S.H.C., 1900, vol. LXXX, p. 315.
[2] Public Bills of 1904, No. 17.
[3] *Parl. Deb.,* 4 S.H.C., 1904, vol. 134, pp. 696–699 (Tennant).

I

THE EARLY AGITATION FOR OLD AGE PENSIONS

Long continued agitation for the state to assume a duty toward the aged poor resulted in the Old Age Pensions Act, 1908, which provided that every person of British nationality who had resided within the United Kingdom for twelve years, and whose yearly means did not exceed £31.10.0, became entitled, as of right, on attaining the age of seventy to receive at the cost of the state a weekly pension of from one shilling to five shillings a week.[4] This large responsibility for the welfare of its citizens which the state accepted, definitely recognized that the aged poor had a claim against the community. The pensioner was not a pauper, and it was enacted that the receipt of an old age pension under this Act should not deprive the pensioner of any franchise, right or privilege, or subject him to any disability.[5] The problem of old age pensions was before Parliament between 1896 and 1905 in no less than 37 Bills,[6] and there was no part of the social programme of the Government which had received more general attention than the proposal for old age pensions.[7]

A Royal Commission on the Aged Poor appointed in 1893, presided over by Lord Aberdare, reported in 1895; the following year[8] by a Treasury Minute a Committee of nine, under Lord Rothschild, was set up "to consider any schemes that may be submitted to them for encouraging the industrial population, by state aid or otherwise, to make provision for old age." In June, 1898, the Committee reported that after careful examination of all the schemes which seemed worthy of attention, they were reluctantly forced to the conclusion that there was not one of them, whatever its particular merits, which would not ultimately injure rather than serve the best

[4] Act of 1908, sects. 1, 2 and Schedule.

[5] Act of 1908, sect. 1, subsect. 4.

[6] For a full survey of the early schemes see the *Report of the Old Age Pensions Committee,* (Cmd. 8911, 1898) pp. 159–183. The *Economic Journal,* March, 1909, in the article by Bertram Wilson, "Economic Legislation of 1908," pp. 130–151, gives the above number for the Old Age Pension Bills. Each year's debates in the House of Commons from 1900 on, provide the best running commentary on the history of the agitation.

[7] *Parl. Deb.,* 4 S.H.C., 1900 (Sir J. Fortescue Flannery) vol. LXXX, pp. 312–313.

[8] *Report of the Royal Commission on the Aged Poor* (Cmd. 7684), 1895.

interests of the industrial population.[9] The Report of the Select Committee in 1899 under the President of the Local Government Board,[10] Mr. Chaplin, stated that "if the state is to provide the means for the cost of pensions, the state, it seems to us, must necessarily administer the scheme, and that is a proposition which we are unable to support." [11]

The Chaplin Report of 1899 said that their scheme could be easily put into legislation subject to the difficulties of a financial kind being overcome.[12] The cost of the system was to be met two-thirds by Parliament and one-third out of the county rates; and the county councils were to administer the system. It was provided that members of the Friendly Societies were to have the right to a payment of five shillings a week at the age of 65, but that those in regular employment receiving more than that sum a week in wages or in receipt of an income of over £40 were excluded. "Let us experiment practically by some legislation," one of the Committee said, "and extend the application of the system afterwards. Make a beginning which would show the country that this House is in earnest, and which would be doing something to bring justice to the humbler workers, and remove what has been rightly described as one of the greatest scandals of the nineteenth century." [13]

The Trade Union Congress of 1900 declared in favour of the principle of old age pensions as a "civic right". But this was not the point of view of those who looked on the Report of the Select Committee as representing "the reaction in favour of the increased dependence of individuals on the state," and who saw in this reaction the main reason for the administrative failure of the poor law.[14] It had been argued by Mr. Charles Booth that the millions spent for pensions would be used as advantageously for the community in the

[9] *The Report of 1898* (Rothschild), p. 9.

[10] *The Report of the Select Committee on Aged Deserving Poor*, 1899 (Cmd. 296); also the *Report of the Departmental Committee on the Financial Aspects of the Proposals made by the Select Committee of the House of Commons of 1899 About the Aged Deserving Poor*, 1900 (Cmd. 67).

[11] The Report of 1899 (Chaplin), p. ix; pp. III–XIII for summary and proposals of their scheme.

[12] The 1899 Report (pp. iii–xiii) and the 1900 Report (p. iii).

[13] *Parl. Deb.*, 4 S.H.C., 1900, vol. LXXX, pp. 317–319 (Sir J. Fortescue Flannery).

[14] See *Economic Journal*, vol. IX, 1899, pp. 520–540, "Old Age Pensions," by C. S. Loch.

hands of the pensioners as in those of private persons.[15] For a great many people this was a revolutionary doctrine in relief and in state protection. "Such an argument implies socially and economically," wrote one recognized critic, "an entirely different theory from that of anti-corn days, and it cannot fail to influence sentiment, as similar theories have done in the past. That the individual member of society should be under a social obligation to maintain himself is the older view which the conditions under which the Poor Laws were enacted were plainly intended to enforce. The new view is that this obligation is of a very limited nature. The state and the municipality are to make grants to the individual and even to cater for his purely private and personal relief. The principal object of these grants is not to promote the growth of well-disciplined citizenship. They are largess. That they are reserved for old age makes in principle no difference. They are the result of the same change in sentiment as during the last years has weakened the administration of the poor law, and cannot but in time lower the estimation at which prudence and self-help are held by the people. Of this change, both in sentiment and in economic theory, a new system of state finance is a necessary corollary; and a state in which classes of citizens have the social protection of special grants and government aid, is necessarily in theory and temper, and, therefore ultimately in practice, protective in the interests of class against class, and also as against other countries. It is to protection or class legislation that his report (Chaplin's) taken as an indication of public sentiment, logically leads." [16]

The foreshadowing of the Minority Report of the Poor Law Commission could be plainly seen in the tendency of Bills before Parliament in the early years of this century. Three Outdoor Relief (Friendly Societies) Bills were introduced in the session of 1904,[17]

---

[15] See *Economic Journal*, vol. IX, 1899, pp. 212–223, "Poor Law Statistics as used in Connection with the Old Age Pension Question," by Charles Booth. It is hardly necessary to suggest the great influence of this author on the social problems of his time by his monumental survey of conditions among the poor. No study was cited nearly so often as his in Parliamentary debates.

[16] Loch, *op. cit.*, pp. 527–528. See also his *Old Age Pensions: A Collection of Short Papers* (1903). Mr. Loch was long Secretary of the London Charity Organization.

[17] The first (House Bill No. 5, 1904; *Parl. Deb.*, 4 S.H.C., 1904, vol. 129, p. 854), and the third (House Bill No. 188; *Parl. Deb.*, 4 S.H.C., 1904, vol. 134, p. 574), were withdrawn; but the second, introduced by Mr. Gretton (House Bill No. 106; *Parl. Deb.*, 4 S.H.C., 1904, vol. 130, p. 1493), became law.

the purpose of which was to do away with any discredit or "stigma of pauperism". The Outdoor Relief (Friendly Societies) Act, 1894, authorized boards of guardians, when granting outdoor relief, not to take into consideration any sum up to five shillings a week received by the applicant as member of a friendly society. The Outdoor Relief (Friendly Societies) Act of 1904 made a course of action which was optional imperative. "The board of guardians shall not take into consideration any sum received from friendly society as sick pay, except in so far as such sum shall exceed five shillings a week." [18] The propaganda of the years had done its work, and enactments made plain the results. In that same year, 1904, five Bills on the subject of Old Age Pensions marked the importance of that question before Parliament; [19] two Bills on Old Age Pensions were re-introduced in 1905,[20] and in the session of 1906, five such Bills were put before the House of Commons.[21]

The Labour Party in the session of 1907 followed its policy of moving for debate on a popular subject by submitting an amendment regretting the absence from the sessional programme of a measure making provision for an adequate pension for the aged poor. The Party, the mover said,[22] "approached the subject in no carping spirit of factious opposition to the Government," but that the time had been reached when the problem must be settled on "a universal plan, giving pensions not as a consequence of poverty or desert but

[18] Act of 1904, sect. 1, subsect. 1.

[19] Four were dropped, one withdrawn. The first two were presented by Mr. Remnant, with whom were associated several Labour and Liberal members; see *Parl. Deb.*, 4 S.H.C., 1904, vol. 134, pp. 669–699, for debate on the first (House Bill No. 17); and the Old Age Pensions Bill (No. 2), (House Bill No. 23), was the first Bill re-submitted. The three remaining sponsors for Bills were, Mr. Spear (House Bill No. 24, Old Age Pensions Bill); Mr. Channing (House Bill No. 37, Old Age Pensions Bill); and Sir James Rankin (House Bill No. 108); *Parl. Deb.*, 4 S.H.C., 1904, vol. 131, p. 85.

[20] Old Age Pensions Bill, House Bill No. 171, 1905 (Channing); and the Aged Pensions Bill, House Bill No. 1905 (Goulding).

[21] Aged Pensioners, House Bill No. 28, 1906 (Roberts), withdrawn; Aged Pensioners (No. 2) House Bill No. 152, 1906 (Roberts), dropped; Old Age Pensions, House Bill No. 18, 1906 (Wilson), withdrawn; Old Age Pensions (No. 2) House Bill No. 47, 1906 (Channing), withdrawn; Old Age Pensions (No. 3) House Bill No. 146, 1906 (Wilson) dropped.

[22] *Parl. Deb.,* 4 S.H.C., 1907, vol. 169, pp. 216–222 (Barnes); on this amendment see speeches of Mr. Harold Cox (pp. 227–233), Sir Howard Vincent (pp. 233–238), Mr. A. Chamberlain (pp. 261–265); for Labour, Mr. Hardie (pp. 265–268), and Mr. Shackelton (pp. 256–257).

as a civil right to every man and woman who had conformed to the laws of the country and was entitled by residential qualifications." The Chancellor of the Exchequer, Mr. Asquith, replying, said "the figure of a man or woman who, in old age, through no fault or default is compelled to beg bread or lodging, is an eyesore in our social system and a standing, and indeed, a crying reproach to our statesmanship." He believed that when the Government could invite the House to take effective steps toward the solution of the question, it would be with the universal good will of all the parties, and confidence that they were making substantial strides in advance on the path of true social reform; [23] and that any proposal to be brought forward by the Government or other parts of the House in regard to old age pensions should be discussed on its merits apart from all party feeling.[24]

The statement of the Chancellor of the Exchequer in the Budget speech, that financial plans were being laid for an old age pension system, had been forecasted by Mr. Asquith himself, and the President of the Local Government Board expressly pledged the Government to carry forward old age pensions so far as time, means and opportunity allowed.[25] The Budget statement of 1907 defined the policy of the Government on social reform, based especially on the duty of the State to the child and to the aged.[26] Taken together with the Budget statement of 1908,[27] made by the Prime Minister himself, it is a good introduction for the social finance features of the epochal Budget of 1909. With regard to old age pensions the belief became more insistent that the state should assume the financial burden. The Lever Old Age Pension Bill of 1907 [28] provided that one-tenth of the funds necessary should be supplied by local taxation funds and nine-tenths by the Exchequer. The object of this Bill was to provide pensions for persons of 65 upwards; in the first year of operation pensions would be paid to persons of 75 and upwards; in the second year to persons of 70 and upwards; and in the third year to persons 65 and upwards.

The temper of the Parliament of 1907 on the principle of old age

[23] *Parl. Deb., op. cit.,* pp. 222–227.
[24] *Op. cit.,* p. 227. The Barnes amendment, which Labour refused to support after the Government statement, forced to a vote, in which Labour abstained, was defeated by 231 votes to 61.
[25] *Parl. Deb., op. cit.,* pp. 257–261 (Burns).
[26] *Parl. Deb.,* 4 S.H.C., 1907, vol. 172, pp. 1175–1211; pp. 1189–1193, the section on social reform.
[27] *Parl. Deb.,* 4 S.H.C., 1908, vol. 188, pp. 445–480.
[28] House Bill No. 17, 1907.

pensions was indicated on the motion for second reading of the
Lever Bill, when a counter motion by Mr. Harold Cox, seconded by
Sir Frederick Banbury, declaring that the House declined to proceed
further with a measure which would enormously add to the national
expenditure until the country had an opportunity of saying whether
it was willing to bear the necessary burden of taxation, was defeated
by 232 votes to 19.[29] After the Government had said that all were
agreed that something should be done and that the Government
accepted the principle of the Bill, the second reading was passed, and
the Bill was referred to a Committee where it was finally dropped.

But the agitation for old age pensions went on unabated by the
failure of the Bill of 1907. The continued discussion that centred
about the Poor Law Commission helped to keep the major problems
of Poor Law relief and principles of state aid before the nation.
There was a determined conviction that the state should actively
interfere to redress what was considered a national scandal, the lot
of the aged poor.[30] At the annual conference of the Labour Party at
Hull in 1908, it was urged that the Labour Party not be "inveigled
into discussing Protection, or the abolition of the House of Lords, or
allowing them to be the battle cries next General Election when Old
Age Pensions and the Unemployed Problem need facing and dealing
with. Our Party must make the social poverty problem the election
cry of the future." [31] The Labour Party considered the question of
old age pensions in a special conference that year, together with a
conference on unemployment.

The Old Age Pensions Act of 1908

The inclusion in the Address [32] of 1908 of the promise that in
connection with the financial arrangements of the year a proposal
would be brought forward making better provisions for old age, fulfilled the Budget pledge of 1907, and was fully carried out in the
introduction by the Chancellor of the Exchequer of the Government

[29] *Parl. Deb.*, 4 S.H.C., 1907, vol. 174, pp. 470–530, second reading debate;
pp. 470–477, the author's speech; pp. 477–483, the seconder (Sir F. Channing);
pp. 483–495 (Cox); pp. 495–501 (Banbury); pp. 523–530 (Burns), who as the
President of the Local Government Board gave the Government statement.

[30] See the *Nation* (London), March 9, 1907, pp. 104–105, editorial, "Pensions and the Poor Law," for a characteristic point of view.

[31] *Annual Report of the Labour Conference, 1908*, p. 10; pp. 83–97, for Report of Conferences on Old Age Pensions and Unemployment.

[32] *Parl. Deb.*, 4 S.H.C., 1908, vol. 183, p. 4.

measure for old age pensions.[33] The principles on which the Government based their Bill were given by Mr. Lloyd George. It was non-contributory—in contradistinction to the French system—because "a workman who has contributed health and strength, vigor and skill, to the creation of wealth by which taxation is borne has made his contribution already to the fund which is to give him a pension when he is no longer fit to create that wealth." [34]

The Government had been attacked by the *Spectator* on the provisions of the Bill, and the interesting Ministerial reply gives added insight into the purpose of the Government. The weekly was referred to by Mr. Lloyd George as "the official organ of the new anarchist party which has appeared in this House. They are frankly and ruthlessly individual." [35] But the Government were not unmindful of the task before it, of legislation for a nation "with its thronging millions, with its rooted complexities; and everyone who has been engaged in any kind of reform knows how difficult it is to make way through the inextricable tangle of an old society like ours." The Government in their Bill were asking the House, continued Mr. Lloyd George, "to sanction not merely its principle, but also its finance, having regard to the fact that we are anxious to utilize the resources of the state to make provision for undeserved poverty and destitution in all its branches." [36] The attitude of Labour was again plainly stated. They wanted it to be "perfectly clearly understood that the claim put forward from these benches was that old age pensions should be given as a social right without respect to any qualifications." [37]

[33] *Parl. Deb.*, 4 S.H.C., 1908, vol. 189, pp. 564–586, speech moving second reading.

[34] *Op. cit.*, p. 563.

[35] *Parl. Deb., op. cit.*, p. 584. The reference was to Mr. Harold Cox and Sir Frederick Banbury, who consistently gave similar arguments against social reform measures. For an interesting French point of view on this period and the men mentioned, as well as the typical attitude of the editor of the *Journal des Economistes,* see *Politique parlementaire et politique atavique,* M. Yves-Guyot (1924) Book VI.

[36] *Parl. Deb., op. cit.*, pp. 585–586; note also the two Government speeches, the Prime Minister (pp. 823–832) and the Secretary of State for War, Mr. Haldane (pp. 660–672). For varying points of view in opposition to the Bill of the Government see speeches of Mr. Balfour (pp. 812–823), Lord Robert Cecil (pp. 613–618), and Mr. Harold Cox (pp. 596–613).

[37] *Parl. Deb.*, 4 S.H.C., 1908, vol. 189, p. 620, and pp. 618–626, entire speech; see also for Labour Mr. Barnes (pp. 804–812).

The Committee stage of the Old Age Pensions Act, 1908, is especially interesting now in the light of subsequent legislation which has extended the financial provisions of the original Act.[38] The amendments moved by Lord Cecil and Mr. Bowles, altering the wording of the first clause so as to stamp the measure as experimental. were rejected respectively by 293 votes to 55, and 341 votes to 103. An amendment by Viscount Castlereagh, embodying the principle of a sliding scale according to means, was opposed by Labour members, though they would accept a scale ranging from ten to fifteen shillings a week. Lord Robert Cecil proposed another amendment, providing that the scheme should be contributory under regulations made by the Treasury, but this was rejected by 346 votes to 86, after the Government had repeated its objections to the contributory principle. These decisive votes together with the passing of the third reading by 315 votes to 10, sufficiently attest to the general acceptance of the principle. The leader of the Opposition defending his action and that of his party through Committee, announced that he would vote for the Bill.[39] This was a signal for Labour bitterly to attack the policy of the Opposition,[40] but the Parliamentary Secretary to the Local Government Board and the Chancellor of the Exchequer were both willing to end the debate for the Government, convinced that a measure was passed which had met with almost unanimous assent.[41]

On the second reading [42] of the Bill in the House of Lords it was

[38] The opening struggle on this Bill was the Old Age Pensions (Expenses) Motion, which was leave asked to bring in the Bill; for this see *Parl. Deb.*, 4 S.H.C., 1908, vol. 189, pp. 1126–1145, 1389–1395. The second reading debate, *Parl. Deb.*, 4 S.H.C., 1908, vol. 190, pp. 564–676, pp. 725–836, and pp. 889–992; Committee stage, June 23–24, *op. cit.*, pp. 1530–1636, and pp. 1737–1836; and for Committee July 6–7, *Parl. Deb.*, 4 S.H.C., 1908, vol. 191, pp. 1343–1415, and pp. 1489–1592. For consideration in Committee on Supply of the vote for £910,000 for payment of old age pensions and administrative expenses in 1909, see *Parl. Deb.*, 5 S.H.C., 1909, vol. 1, pp. 1136–1217; pp. 1279–1312 (Resolution reported); vol. 2, pp. 2027–2033; vol. 3, pp. 1209–1216; for Old Age Pensions (Ireland), vol. 4, pp. 2026–2096, pp. 2103–2131. These extended debates provide full commentary on the first year's working of the system.

[39] *Parl. Deb.*, 4 S.H.C., 1908, vol. 192, pp. 175–187 (Balfour).

[40] *Op. cit.*, pp. 193–202 (Crooks); pp. 148–158 (Snowden), also for Labour.

[41] *Op. cit.*, pp. 139–148 (Masterman); pp. 187–193 (Lloyd George). The Bill was fought to the end by Mr. Harold Cox and Sir Henry Craik, for whose final speeches see pp. 106–123.

[42] *Parl. Deb.*, 4 S.H.C., 1908, vol. 192, pp. 1335–1432, complete debate on second reading. Introduced in the House of Lords July 10, the Bill came up

moved by the Earl of Wemyss that such legislation was unwise pending the Report of the Poor Law Commission.[43] Lord Rosebery, while profoundly disquieted as to the effects of the Bill,[44] urged the House of Lords not to incur the risk of a dispute with the House of Commons by rejecting a measure that was largely fiscal.[45] The leader of the Opposition, Lord Lansdowne, declared that he was opposed to the Bill, but counselled its adoption as good party tactics. So for a third time since 1906 almost identical advice had been given by two leaders, which certainly has its interest in the social politics of the period of constitutional turmoil. The rejection by the House of Lords of a Bill very dear to the Government, and upon which a great deal of the legislative year had been spent, the 1908 Licensing Bill, was alleged to be responsible for this last caution. At any rate the House of Commons refused to accept any of the Lords amendments to the Old Age Pensions Bill,[46] and on January 1, 1909, the Government Act became operative. Approval of the Act was evident in the policy of the Government.[47]

The Act, far from being "a mortal blow to the Empire," as the Chancellor of the Exchequer quoted from the debate in the House of Lords, was used as an argument for the national insurance programme of the Government.[48] Administrative improvements were made by the amending Act of 1911,[49] and continuous efforts were

for second reading July 20. For all stages of this Bill following second reading, July 28–30, see *Parl. Deb.*, 4 S.H.L., 1908, vol. 193, pp. 1073–1164, 1438–1444, and p. 1637.

[43] *Parl. Deb.*, 4 S.H.L., 1908, vol. 192, pp. 1335 ff.

[44] *Op. cit.*, pp. 1379 ff. It may be noted that the Archbishop of Canterbury and the Bishop of Ripon defended the Bill, see *ibid.*, pp. 1389 ff.

[45] For the expression of this view from the Labour Party, see remarks of Mr. Shackelton on the Budget and Old Age Pensions, *Parl. Deb.*, 4 S.H.C., 1907, vol. 169, pp. 256–257.

[46] *Parl. Deb.*, 4 S.H.C., 1908, vol. 193, pp. 1970–2000.

[47] See *Report of the Local Government Board, 1912–1913*, Part I. *Administration of the Poor Law, the Unemployed Workmen Act, and the Old Age Pensions Act* (Cmd. 6980), 1913. The number of pensioners in the United Kingdom, March 28, 1913, was 967,921, made up of 363,811 men and 604,110 women. An increase from 1911–1912 of 4 per cent in England and 2.7 per cent in the United Kingdom. Cf. H. J. Hoare, *Old Age Pensions* (1915), chap. IX, pp. 163–184, a practical study.

[48] D. Lloyd George, *The People's Insurance* (1911), p. 221.

[49] *Parl. Deb.*, 5 S.H.C., 1911, vol. 25, pp. 2284–2354, second reading debate entire, moved by Hayes-Fisher (pp. 2286–2294) ; see speeches of Barnes, pp. 2302–2307, A. Henderson, pp. 2317–2321, and Lloyd George, pp. 2338–2339. No division on Bill *(Parl. Deb.*, 5 S.H.C., 1911, vol. 27, pp. 103–117) ; also vol. 29, pp. 2261–2263, agreement of Lords amendments.

being made to reduce the age at which pensions were payable from 70 to 65. Besides this provision the Labour Party's Bill introduced in 1913 by Mr. Barnes, sought to provide that small pensions from friendly societies and trade unions, as well as the pensions of soldiers and sailors, should not be included in calculations of income.

At the beginning of 1914 there were 982,292 old age pensioners in the United Kingdom, and throughout the War the problem of administration became increasingly, difficult.[50] A Departmental Committee reported in 1919.[51] It had been charged "to consider what alterations if any, as regards rates of pension or qualifications shall be made in the existing statutory scheme of Old Age Pensions." Reviewing the statistical history of the state system, the fact was pointed out that 56 per cent of the estimated total septuagenarian population were in receipt of Old Age Pensions, and that approximately nine-tenths of the persons were in receipt of the maximum rate. "The result is," the Report says, "that hopes of state assistance are now entertained by large sections of the community to a much greater degree than ever previously known." But the inference drawn is the commentary that is significant. "The final object which we have in view is a system under which complete and adequate public assistance would be available in all cases in which it is required, whether the need arises from old age in particular, or from invalidity, unemployment or other forms of disability, and whether or not the need extends to destitution. Such a system would cover the field occupied by Old Age Pensions and National Insurance on the one side, and the Poor Law, regenerated as welfare, on the other." [52] This is a significant expression of early post-war opinion.

II

POST-WAR LEGISLATION

Post-war legislation on old age pensions is represented by the Old Age Pensions Act, 1919, the Old Age Pensions Act, 1924, and

[50] Cf. *Administrative Concessions Made to Old Age Pensioners Since the Commencement of the War* (Cmd. No. 8320, 1916).

[51] *Report of the Departmental Committee on Old Age Pensions,* (Cmd. No. 410, 1919), and *The Appendix to the Report of the Departmental Committee on Old Age Pensions* (Cmd. No. 411, 1919), contain complete statistical and financial history of the system.

[52] *Report of the Departmental Committee on Old Age Pensions,* 1919, p. 7.

the Widows', Orphans' and Old Age Contributory Pensions Acts, 1925–1929. The first Act increased the rate to 10s. a week for those whose means do not exceed £26.5.0 a year, and so proportionately up to the means limit of £49.17.6. The Act of 1924 provided that "a person will not in future be disqualified for receiving or continuing to receive an old age pension by reason of the receipt of outdoor relief," and exempted from consideration in the pension scale all yearly income up to £38 or £79 for man and wife.[53] The Widows', Orphans', and Old Age Contributory Pensions Act, 1925, amended by the 1929 Act, created the right of a pension at 10s. a week to all persons who have attained the age of 65 and were insured under the National Health Insurance Act or were the wives of persons so insured, the conditions as to means, residence or nationality enjoined by the Old Age Pensions Acts 1908–1924 not being taken into account. In March, 1927, there were 1,245,887 old age pensioners in the United Kingdom and the total value of orders and allowances paid in the year was £31,152,000.[54] The Blind Persons Act, 1920, may be considered with these Old Age Pensions Acts, 1908 to 1924, for the administrative regulations are from the same central authority. This Act provided that every blind person who has attained the age of fifty shall be entitled to receive such pension as, under the Old Age Pensions Acts, he would be entitled to receive if he had attained the age of seventy.

THE WIDOWS', ORPHANS' AND OLD AGE CONTRIBUTORY PENSIONS ACTS, 1925 AND 1929

1. *The 1925 Act.*

The place of old age pensions in the national social insurance system of England has long been of significant importance. This fact was well expressed by the Minister of Health in the Conservative Government, Mr. Neville Chamberlain, in moving the second reading of the Widows', Orphans', and Old Age Contributory Pensions Bill, in the House of Commons, May 18, 1925. This Bill was passed and received royal assent on August 7, 1925, coming into operation

[53] Cf. S.R. & O., 1921, No. 2001, *Old Age Pensions Consolidated Regulations, and, Circular No. 521, Ministry of Health, August, 1924.*
[54] See *Nineteenth Abstract of Labour Statistics of the United Kingdom,* pp. 200–203.

January 4, 1926. This Act and the debates in Parliament about it are noticed at length because they offer a commentary on post-war social policy in England. It was an opportunity for a full review of the national policy of social insurance. The Minister said he did not think that any Bill which he had introduced could be compared with the Bill which was before the House for the width of its range or for the permanence of the mark which it was likely to leave on the life of the nation or for the intensity of its human interest. The Bill, the Minister of Health continued, was in the direct succession of a long line of measures, all of which had been passed within the last 30 years and all of which had been founded on the recognition of the fact that there existed a state of society in which a large part of the population no longer themselves produced the necessaries of life, but depended upon continuous employment in other occupations to obtain the means of purchasing. A state of society of that kind involved constant menace and risk to the security of the worker, and involved, therefore a corresponding need for providing against that risk. The first step toward that provision was taken by the Workmen's Compensation Act which was passed in 1897, and which provided for the dependents of a man who was injured or killed by accident in the course of his trade. Then, in 1908 came the first Old Age Pensions Act, which, at any rate, attempted to make some provision for the decline of earning power as old age came upon the worker, and in 1911, three years later, there came the great Insurance Act—an even more important measure, because, for the first time, it established the principle of contributions from the employer, from the worker, and from the state. Every one of those Acts had been extended and expanded, and in particular the 1920 Unemployment Insurance Act, which very greatly increased the number of workers coming within the unemployment provision of the previous Act, so that at the time (1925) it covered something like 12,000,000 workers. Taking all these measures together, it might be said that they had effected in that short space of time "a profound and almost revolutionary change in the status of the workers of the country." [55]

[55] Second reading debate, *Parl. Deb.*, 5 S.H.C., vol. 184, May 18, 1925, pp. 73–193, May 19, pp. 267–325, passing second reading vote by 401—125 votes, Committee, May 20–21, pp. 441–511, 839–847. Note Chamberlain, N., pp. 73–92, Wheatley, 93–108, Lloyd George, pp. 109–121, Marriott, pp. 121–128, Lansbury, pp. 128–135, Pethick-Lawrence, pp. 158–164, Miss Wilkinson, pp. 181–185, Duff Cooper, pp. 187–193.

The object of the Bill, it was explained,[56] was to add to the existing schemes of health insurance, unemployment insurance, and workmen's compensation a scheme of pensions for widows and dependent children, and for old age pensions commencing at the age of 65 instead of 70, and passing, on the attainment of 70, into pensions under the Old Age Pensions Act, freed from the restrictions and disqualifications at present applied to such pensions. With regard to administration the Government considered whether they should set up a new machine to administer the scheme or attempt to link it up with one of the existing systems of insurance. For reasons of economy it was obviously undesirable to set up a new machine, and they chose to link their scheme up with health insurance, chiefly on the ground that health insurance covered so much wider a field than unemployment insurance, including something like 15,000,000 workers, against 12,000,000 workers covered by unemployment insurance. So the scheme was interlocked with the National Health Act, and was compulsory upon all workers who came under the terms of that Act.

The provisions as to pensions to widows and orphans commenced from January 4, 1926. The Act provided that the widow of a man who died at any time after that date and who had satisfied the conditions in the Act should be entitled to a pension of 10s. a week until she reached the age of 70, when she came into the old age pension, or until she remarried. If she had young children dependent upon her she received an additional allowance of 5s. in respect of the eldest and 3s. each in respect of the others, including those under the age of 14. If the mother died, orphan allowances were allowed at a higher scale. The provisions as to unrestricted old age pensions (i.e., pensions freed from the restrictions and disqualifications existing under the then Old Age Pensions Act), awarded to or in respect of persons over 70 on July 2, 1926, or who attain the age of 70 between July 2, 1926, and January 2, 1928, commenced from July 2, 1926. The provisions as to other old age pensions commenced January 2, 1928.[57] The Government's intent was expressed by Mr. Neville Chamberlain, the Minister of Health, declaring that "it is not the function of any system of state insurance to supersede every other

---

[56] See *Memorandum of Ministry of Health,* explanatory of the Bill (Bill No. 164, 1925), Cmd. 2405, p. 2.

[57] See *Report of the Government Actuary on the Financial Provisions of the Bill* (Cmd. 2406, 1925).

kind of thrift. We regard the function of a state scheme as being to provide a basis so substantial that it will encourage people to try and add to it and thus achieve complete independence for themselves."

The Minister of Health linked this Bill of the Government with the Rating and Valuation Bill of the Government. Different as the two Bills were in character, scope, and purpose, each of them, he said, filled its allotted place in the scheme of social reform which the Government had set before themselves and which they meant to pursue so long as they had the power and the opportunity. The policy of the Government was to use the great resources of the state not for the distribution of an indiscriminate largess, but to help those who had the will and the desire to raise themselves to higher and better things. They could find that policy, Mr. Chamberlain affirmed, in the Housing Act of 1923, and in the Rating and Valuation Bill, where for the first time, they were trying to set up a standard by which they could measure the ability of the local authorities to bear their burdens, and the need they might have of assistance from the central authority. They would find it again, in the measure which he hoped to introduce next year (1926) for the reformation of the Poor Law, and for the more scientific and equitable distribution of public assistance. Preeminently they would find it in the present Bill, which, following on the two great schemes of insurance, combined with workmen's compensation and old age pensions under existing Acts, completed the circle of security for the worker.

On the second reading of the Bill, the Minister of Health in the MacDonald cabinet, Mr. John Wheatley, one of the most vigorous debaters that Labour commands, offered the Labour party amendment: "That this House, while it would welcome a just and generous scheme of widowed mothers' and orphans' pensions with a reduction of the age of qualification for old age pensions and the removal of the means limit, declines to give a second reading to a Bill which exacts contributions from wage earners and imposes an additional burden on industry, makes no provision for a large number of widows and orphans and families where the father is incapacitated, and, in the case of those qualified to become recipients, provides allowances which are wholly inadequate." It was quite true, Mr. Wheatley said, that today every party in the House was in favour of the principle of widows' pensions. The Labour Party were the pioneers of this policy. In 1908, the annual conference of the Women's Labour League passed a resolution in favour of a widows' pension scheme, and at various times since conferences of trade unions and of the Labour Party had passed similar resolutions. But Mr. Lloyd George, in his speech of "helpful criticism", wisely remarked that Mr. Wheatley's quotations of Labour Party resolutions would have been more effective if the Labour Government had taken the first opportunity to carry it into effect. Yet he admitted that Mr. Wheatley had made out a strong case against a contributory scheme. He declared, however, "you have to educate people very gradually to their taxable capacity." The chief complaint of the militant Labour leader was that the Bill would not benefit more than a small fraction of the population. It would do nothing for widows, dependent children, or orphans, and he questioned whether it would do anything in the matter of old age pensions. Its benefits were not equal to the burden that it was placing on the mass of the population and, particularly, on the struggling industries of the country. He was amazed that those who claimed to represent the capitalists should make such a great gamble on the future industrial prosperity of the country. He could only suppose that a few die-hard economists among Conservative members felt it was worth taking the risk, knowing that the wages and incomes of the very poorest to a large extent determined the rate of wages, and thinking that if they were to have fuller control of the fixing of wages they must have greater control of the fixing of incomes. The only consolation he found in the whole miserable scheme was that any scheme of the kind based on the poverty of 70 per cent of the population, "stereotyping in poverty" a people, brought the country nearer to the end of the capitalist system. Four years later he was to give hard battle against the Bill his own Labour colleagues introduced, the Widows', Orphans' and Old Age Pensions Act, 1929.

Nor could Mr. George Lansbury, the veteran Labour member from Bow and Bromley, allow to pass the opportunity of the 1925 debate for a characteristic assault. He said that the Bill just gave sufficient for people to starve upon. It was a disgrace to the British Parliament that such a paltry allowance as 10s. a week should be proposed, and if he was told that there was not sufficient money to pay more he would reply that, in spite of all the taxes that had been put on, the rich were still rich and getting richer, and that profits and dividends instead of failing, were in many industries going up.

He would never allow the statement to go through without protest that the expense could not be afforded at a time when the state paid an ex-Queen £80,000 without any contribution from her, £10,000 a year for Princesses, and £6,000 for others, and hundreds of thousands of pounds to well-to-do people who never paid a halfpenny or did any really useful work for it. Sir John A. R. Marriott, Unionist, regarded the Bill as a really courageous, honest, and laudable attempt to advance another step toward that system of better co-ordination and more comprehensive insurance which would do something to mitigate that sense of instability and insecurity which was eating into the vitals of English industrial life. Labour again expressed objection to the contributory principle, Mr. Pethick-Lawrence saying that the fundamental objection was that it picked and chose quite improperly: and Miss Wilkinson believed that the scheme bore very hardly on the single women in industry. There were from 1,500,000 to 2,000,000 women who would in the normal course of things never marry and would remain in industry all their lives. The debate was ended by the Unionist member from Oldham, Mr. Duff Cooper, quoting Mr. Wheatley as saying that as a result of the capitalist system widows had to be pensioned. Socialism was to abolish a great many things, but how or when was it to abolish widows? Widows would always be widows until a scheme was devised for the simultaneous destruction of spouses. Despite Labour opposition on second reading and in Committee the Labour Party did not divide against the third reading.

In a report by the Government actuary on the financial provisions of the Bill, it was stated that the estimated number of employed persons under the age of 65 coming into insurance at the beginning of the scheme would be 10,170,000 men and 4,595,000 women. These numbers would increase until about the year 1960, when the estimated numbers are 11,671,000 men and 4,842,000 women. From that time onwards some reduction in the insured population between the ages of 16 and 65 is indicated by the actuary's calculations. In addition it was estimated that there would be 275,000 men and 50,000 women employed contributors between the ages of 65 and 70 in January, 1926, in respect of whom contributions would be payable between the years 1926 and 1927, so long as they were in insurable employment and still under 70. This made a total of 15,090,000 employed persons (10,445,000 men and 4,645,000 women) brought in as contributors at the outset. No wonder that the Act was regarded as a landmark in the history of social legislation, for by this Act every person in Great Britan already insured under the National Health Insurance scheme was guaranteed further state protection against want and suffering, to an extent which would have been thought quite impossible a generation ago.

The central pension authority for the Widows', Orphans' and Old Age Contributory Pensions Acts, 1925–1929, is the Ministry of Health, and the necessary forms of application and the payment are provided through the Post Office. The general administration of the Old Age Pensions Acts 1908–1924 is vested in the department of Customs and Excise. The local pension authorities are the local Pension Committees. Under the Act of 1908 all claims for pension and all questions whether a person was qualified in law to receive a pension were to stand referred to the local Pension Committees which were set up throughout the country; and the Committee were to obtain a report from the local pension officer, an official appointed by the Treasury, and then give their decision on the claim. An appeal could be taken from the Local Pension Committee to the central pension authority, which was at first the Local Government Board, and now the Ministry of Health. The decision of that department is final and conclusive. The Act of 1925 for Widows', and Orphans' Pensions provided that all claims for pensions must be made direct to the Minister of Health, who makes a decision. The award of the Minister may be appealed and referred to one or more referees selected from a panel of referees; and their decision is final and conclusive.[58]

Administrative provisions for the Act of 1925 follow closely the previous Old Age Pensions Act of 1908, and the more recent National Health Insurance Acts. The Ministry of Health, in conjunction with the Treasury so far as relates to matters with respect to which the Treasury so direct, and in conjunction with the Postmaster-General so far as relates to the Post Office, may make regulations generally for carrying this Act into effect,[59] and "for prescribing anything under this Act to be prescribed." [60] Regulations made under

[58] See Old Age Pensions Act, 1908, section 7, and Widows', Orphans', and Old Age Contributory Pensions Act, 1925, section 29; and note Robson, *op. cit.*, pp. 137–139, and Clarke, *op. cit.*, Chapters XXIV and XXIX.

[59] Section 30 of the Act of 1925, with which compare Act of 1908, Section 10.

[60] Section 30, clause (h).

this section shall be laid before both Houses of Parliament as soon as may be after they are made and shall have effect as if enacted in this Act; "Provided that, if an address is presented to his Majesty by either House within the next subsequent twenty-one days on which that House has set next after the regulation is laid before, praying that the regulation may be annulled. His Majesty may by Order in Council annul the regulation, but without prejudice to the validity of anything previously done thereunder." [61] The Act of 1925 provided that the National Health Insurance Committee shall exercise and perform such powers and duties of the Minister of Health and the Scottish Board of Health under this Act, either alone or jointly with either of them, as may be prescribed by regulations of the Joint Committee.[62] The Minister was given the power, with the consent of the Treasury, by order to "do anything which appears to be necessary or expedient for bringing this Act into operation," provided that the powers conferred by this section ended December 31, 1926.[63] This is an interesting example of Parliament allowing official discretion.

One source of satisfaction with regard to the Act of 1925, the London *Times* in an editorial on December 31, 1925, said, was that the Act was not a mere partisan measure, but was the product of the united wisdom of Parliament, since it was the outcome of the deliberations of Parliaments wherein first Conservatives, then Labourites and then again Conservatives predominated. It further declared that the new pension scheme for the relief and assistance of widows and orphans and old age, was a notable landmark in British social history. The Prime Minister, the Government and Parliament as a whole could justly be proud of the results of their exertions. The Act as it stood was the coping stone on all the various measures of social insurance which had been carried on by successive Parliaments. The essence of it was that it was compulsory and contributory. It called employers, employed and the state into co-operation as three partners in the great human work of caring for those of the employed wage earners and their dependents who are less able to fend for themselves.

The most encouraging thing about the new Government insurance scheme of 1925 and its development has been the fact that sound dis-

[61] Section 30, part (3), with which compare Act of 1908, Section 10 (3).
[62] Act of 1925, Section 32.
[63] Act of 1925, Section 36.

cussion of state policy has been encouraged, and there is a clearer understanding today of what is demanded from the social system with regard to the minimum of security for the worker. Yet criticism has been direct and penetrating. How significant is this indictment, written in the year the Bill was passed: [64] "The most terrible thing about the Widows' Bill is that the Government appear to envisage a permanent state of civilisation in this country in which those who have lived a life of toil and industry are unable to lay aside any adequate maintenance for their old age, and are compelled to live not on the fruits of their labour, but from the alien hands of the state. The Bill assumes that there are at present fifteen millions of persons in that condition, and the Government Actuary contemplates that in the year 1960 the number will have risen to sixteen and a half millions. It is scarcely surprising that the Socialists are not satisfied with civilisation as it exists at present if this is all it has to offer. The Conservatives appear to envisage a permanent future in which the vast majority of the population are workers at a weekly wage so insufficient that they cannot make provision for their subsistence in old age and for the maintenance of their dependents. They live in rows of houses, within convenient reach of the nearest factories, built with the aid of public money, and as expensive as they look cheap. They are mulcted weekly of a part of their scanty earnings in order to provide for an entirely insufficient maintenance for an old age they may never enjoy and dependents who may never be attached to them. Their outings are to Blackpool and even Wembley, but not to Paris or Venice. They ride in trains, but not, as in the United States, in motor cars. Their amusements are the cinema (American) and the fringe of the football field. For intellectual recreation they can rely on the growing provision of public libraries and University tutorial classes; for outside society, on the health visitor, the school attendance officer, and the panel doctor. . . . It is a dingy prospect."

There is much to be gained from such taunts against social legislation, for it means that it is impossible to go back to the dreary argument of early Parliamentary debate and the stale cries of a meaningless Individualism. State action and state aid have done a great deal if they have helped to bring the conscience and intelligence

[64] The *Nineteenth Century and After*, No. 581, vol. XCVIII, July, 1925, "The Widows' and Old Age Contributory Pensions Bill," W. R. Barker, pp. 19–31.

of the community to know wherein the present organization of society has failed to create the conditions which make possible the living of the good life. The reaction to schemes of social insurance is thus a healthy condition of revolt. It will be even stronger when the organised Labour movement gains a firm economic position in England.

2. *The Act of 1929.*

It was early seen that the original Act of 1925 would have to be amended by subsequent legislation. The Labour party on February 22, 1928, in their motion, presented by Mr. Cove, alleged that the Pensions Acts encouraged wage reductions, imposed conditions for the receipt of benefit which many persons were unable to fulfil, failed to pension many women of 65, and gave inadequate old age pensions. The motion called for "immediate legislation to make the benefits of the Act more appropriate to human needs." This motion was rejected by the Government, after the Minister of Health had replied that the Act ought to be improved as experience suggested, but that no fundamental defect had been shown to exist in it. However, in 1929, of the 24 clauses of the Bill, the author of the 1925 Act, Mr. Neville Chamberlain, pointed out that 14 clauses dealt with necessary changes.

The introduction by the Labour Government of the Widows', Orphans' and Old Age Contributory Pensions Bill in 1929 was the opportunity of reviewing the national policy of social insurance, just as the earlier 1925 debates had proved to be. The Address, when the second Labour Government met Parliament in July, 1929, had promised "a general survey of the various National Insurance and Pensions schemes." [65] This promise was dealt with by the Minister of Health, Mr. Arthur Greenwood, in moving the second reading of the Government Bill on October 31, 1929 to amend the Act of 1925.[66] He emphasized the fact that the national system of social insurance was being studied by the Government. "There are three

---

[65] *Parl. Deb.,* 5 S.H.C., vol. 229, July 2, 1929, pp. 47–49.

[66] *Parl. Deb.,* 5 S.H.C., vol. 231, October 31, 1929, pp. 365–471, second reading debate; pp. 365–382, Greenwood, pp. 382–394, Chamberlain (N.), pp. 401–417, three men who had headed the Ministry of Health; pp. 455–462, Sir Kingsley Wood, pp. 462–470, Miss Lawrence, Parliamentary Secretary to Ministry of Health. Committee stage, November 1, 4, 7, 11, 12, 14, *ibid.,* pp. 495–571, 770–791, 1340–1410, 1567–1688, 1769–2006, 2271–2402; vol. 232, 18–19, December, Committee and third reading, and December 5, disagreement with Lords amendments, pp. 72–237, 325–450, 2722–2732.

major problems," he said, "to which the Government at present is giving its attention. The first is the problem of the inclusion of persons who today are either wholly or partially excluded from the existing schemes. The second is the problem of extending the existing services. The third is the very large question of the financial aspects of social insurance." The whole nation was concerned because "people are realizing increasingly the cumulative advantages which have accrued to the workers by association in schemes of insurance supplemented by the financial intervention of the state." And then the Labour Minister of Health made the statement which was taken as a text in argument against him, for he said that "broadly speaking, whether a nation can afford a thing or not depends upon how much it wants it." But the proposals of the Government were not satisfactory to the leader of the "Labour Fourth Party", Mr. Wheatley, who reminded the Government that "these poor whom we are discussing are now the rulers of the country," and that the country was prepared to back the Government in abolishing poverty.

Mr. Greenwood on the third reading of the Bill, having successfully with Miss Lawrence, Parliamentary Secretary to the Ministry of Health, seen the Bill through Parliament, declared that the Bill did not profess to be final. He had worked with the tools at his disposal when the Government took office, and, whatever might be the inperfections of the proposals, he might claim that it removed many injustices and would bring comfort and hope to more than half a million people. So long as there was in the country sufficient wealth to enable the well-to-do out of their surplus to assist the poor, every Government must do its utmost to help. If they were all poor together there would be no injustice, but the problem they had to face was the contrast between unmerited riches and unmerited poverty, and the Government had tried in the Bill to do a little to redress the balance. The Bill, he said, was the beginning of a series of measures which must continue until every citizen of the country received his full opportunities to "a decent and honourable and dignified existence." The Bill was read a third time and passed without a division, just as in the case of the 1925 Act. The Government majorities on this Bill were remarkably high for a minority Government, reaching, for example, 197, 192, 177. But to some observers, as the House of Lords debates revealed on second reading, November 26, 1929, this only meant that Socialists and Liberals and Conservatives were competitors in an auction for votes. This is an echo of far-off debates.

The general provisions of the Amending Act, 1929,[67] which came into force January 2, 1930, included the payment of pensions from July, 1930 to widows at the age of 60, whose husbands died or attained the age of 70 before January, 1926, and to certain other widows at age 60; and from January 1, 1931, the payment of pensions to widows at age 55, whose husbands died or attained age 70 before January 4, 1926, and to certain other widows at age 55. The other benefits remained, with several minor changes affecting conditions, the same. There was no means test to the Act, and it was estimated that the grand total of widows who would receive pensions would be somewhere about 729,000. The amount payable by Parliament began with £9,000,000 in 1930 and was estimated at £21,000,000 for 1945.

The Old Age Pensions Acts 1908–1924, which give pensions at various rates to persons who have attained the age of 70, and who comply with certain stipulated conditions as to means, residence and nationality, as given above, is founded entirely upon a non-contributory basis, the cost being borne by monies provided by Parliament. The 1925 and 1929 Widows', Orphans' and Old Age Contributory Pensions Acts have affected the administration of the Old Age Pensions Acts, 1908–1924 by giving to persons after 70, who receive pensions under the Acts of 1925 and 1929, a pension under the Old Age Pensions Acts 1908–1924, without regard to the conditions as to means, residence and nationality imposed by those Acts. This is an important change in the conceptions of pensions, and brings nearer the idea of what may be termed a retirement pension.

The working of the Old Age Pensions Acts 1908–1924 and the Widows', Orphans' and Old Age Pensions Contributory Acts 1925 and 1929 may be seen from the following tables: [68]

---

[67] See *Memorandum* on the Widows', Orphans' and Old Age Contributory Pensions Bill, 1929 (Cmd. 3412, 1929).

[68] *Twentieth Report of the Commissioners of H.M. Customs and Excise for the Year ending 31st March, 1929* (Cmd. 3435, 1929), pp. 133–135.

Old Age Pensions under 1908–1924 Acts, in March each year:

Year	Pensioners
1908–9	463,994
*1910–11	705,678
1921–22	858,497
1922–23	895,924
1923–24	916,771
1924–25	1,010,684
1925–26	1,071,093
1927–28	995,978
1928–29	950,978

1925 Widows', Orphans' and Old Age Pensions Contributory Act:

Year	Pensioners
1926–27	166,132
1927–28	289,681
1928–29	366,584

Plainly, then, from this survey it is seen that the state has extended the principles which were established in the Act of 1908, and has already embodied nearly all of the advanced proposals submitted at that time. Beset by untoward necessities Governments have been forced to first consider a way to safety—ordinary maintenance—for the population. There has been little latitude for reconstruction. The Parliamentary debates of 1919–1930 contain no such defence of individualism nor no such hope from collective action as those of 1906–1912. It is enough that there is an Act to amend or continue; but the large hopes of pre-war legislation are expressed rarely in the Parliaments of today. Men are more uncertain of what to do, also less willing to make unusual and experimental effort. Necessity for action has largely taken the place in the England of today of any theory of state action. Each Government is confronted with an appalling need, and its duty is to administer the legislation of relief and protection. It is well that there were years in this century when great constructive programmes of social reform could be discussed by Parliament and a basis made for the

* Poor Law disqualification removed January 1, 1911.

legislation of the future. There are signs that another period of creative thought about social legislation may not be far away. The fight against poverty is now, however, upon a different basis. The legislation surveyed in this chapter, by raising the standard of human existence in England for many homes, has made it possible to plan more securely for welfare of the whole of the nation.

CHAPTER VI

SOCIAL LEGISLATION IN ENGLAND AND THE DEVELOPMENT OF A NATIONAL STANDARD OF LIFE

I

THE STATE AND A LIVING WAGE

THE effort of the state to enable the working class to establish a satisfactory standard of life is studied in the legislation which this chapter and the following chapter survey. The Acts of Parliament which are considered are taken primarily for the purpose of illustrating the progressive development in legislation of a national standard of life. The early agitation against the sweated industries is the beginning of the long struggle for a living wage. State policy has been defined in the Trade Boards Act, 1908–1918, the Fair Wages Clause, and the ideal of a living wage is implicit in the terms of reference of many of the committees and commissions which the Governments since 1900 have set up. The oft-heard demand of organized labour for a general minimum wage, the recognition by the state of the demand in the agricultural industry and the mining industry, are part of the evidence of the twentieth century. It will be seen that since the war this ideal of a living wage has been extended into the whole field of industrial relationships by the place that it has held in the disastrous wage disputes since 1918. The long conflict between the coal-miners and the coal-owners is the symbol of the British industrial discord, and it is evidence of the determined will of the miners to obtain a standard of life as the first charge upon industry. The Industrial Court Act, 1919 and the national wages agreements are referred to briefly for the confirmation which they offer of the broad acceptance of a national minimum in the industrial life of England.

The conditions under which the working class lived became known by the commissions studying old age pensions, and by the enforcement of the Housing Act, the Factory and Workshop Acts, and the Public Health Laws. Year by year departmental reports supplemented by competent private investigation such as that of Booth and Rowntree, made it possible for a larger number of people to become acquainted with the "condition of England" question, and to be aware of the "startling probability" that from 25 to 30 per cent of the town population of the United Kingdom were living in poverty. The low earnings in sweated trades had for many years been the subject of public discussion. The evil of cheap labour had been denounced in a sound economic argument by John Stuart Mill in a chapter "On Popular Remedies for Low Wages," in his *Political Economy;* and as early as 1889 a Select Committee under Lord Dunraven had made a report recommending better inspection and registration of outworkers in industries that depended largely upon sweated labours.[1] In 1900 a Wages Board Bill was introduced. "to provide for the establishment of Wages Boards." [2] Dr. MacNamara introduced in 1902 the Bill for the Workmen's National Housing Council which would have excluded outwork and sweating as allowed under the Factory Acts.[3]

The first introduction of such a Wages Board scheme in the House of Commons was in 1898, by Sir Charles W. Dilke, who reintroduced a Bill for this purpose in 1904 and 1905.[4] The Board of Trade in 1906 began a remarkable survey and census of Earnings and Hours of Employment of Workpeople in the United Kingdom. The first two volumes of this series dealt with the textile trades and the clothing trades, containing appalling evidence of the industrial degradation of the nation, particularly with reference to women and

[1] Cmd. No. 62, 1890.
[2] House Bill No. 102, 1900.
[3] See *Report of the Trade Union Congress, 1902,* pp. 81–82.
[4] House Bill No. 47, 1904; A Home Industries Bill (House Bill No. 64, 1904), was also introduced. House Bill No. 33, 1905; supported by Bell, Burns and Trevelyan.

girl workers.[5] The Home Office in 1907 sent Mr. Ernest Aves to study the system of work in Austrialia and New Zealand.[6] That year a Sweated Industries Bill was introduced by Mr. Arthur Henderson;[7] a Wages Boards Bill by Mr. E. Lamb;[8] a Home Bill by Mr. Barnes;[9] and a Home Work Regulation Bill by Mr. J. Ramsay MacDonald.[10] The principle that the first two Bills proposed to establish was that of the minimum wage, determined by Wages Boards composed of equal numbers of employers and employees in the trades where the conditions were notoriously bad; and the last two Bills were intended to protect the home worker. The four Bills were dropped.

The Sweated Industries Bill was reintroduced, February 21, 1908, and had for its purpose the establishment of wages boards with power to fix the minimum wage for workers in certain scheduled trades; the Home Secretary having power to add to the schedule, and payment of the minimum wage to be enforced through the factory inspectors.[11] Sir Frederick Banbury again saw "the thin edge of a Socialist wedge," but it was accepted by the Government, the Home Secretary asking that it be referred to a Select Committee on Home Work. The Government prepared their Bill on the recommendations of this Committee, under Sir Thomas Whittaker, which issued its report in June, 1908.[12] Two Bills dealing with the problem of sweating were introduced independently in 1909. Mr. H. Marks,

[5] See *Report of an Enquiry by the Board of Trade into the Earnings and Hours of Employment of Workpeople in the United Kingdom in 1906;* No. I. *Textile Trades,* Cmd. 5445 (1909); No. II. *Clothing Trades,* Cmd. 4844 (1909); No. III. *Building and Woodmaking,* Cmd. 5086 (1910); No. IV. *Public Utility Service,* Cmd. 5196 (1910); No. V. *Agriculture,* Cmd. 5460 (1910); No. VI. *Metal, Engineering and Shipbuilding Trades,* Cmd. 5814 (1911); No. VII. *Railway Service,* Cmd. 6053 (1912); No. VIII. *Paper, Printing and Miscellaneous Trades,* Cmd. 6556 (1913). The date refers to the year the Report was published; there was a similar survey in 1886, and the final Report of that study was in 1893. A summary of each Report can be found in pp. iii–iv of each volume, except Nos. II and VII. With these should be compared the equally important Census of Production Reports.

[6] See *Report of the Wages Board and Industrial Conciliation and Arbitration Acts of Australia and New Zealand* (Cmd. 4167, 1908).

[7] Public Bills 1907, No. 27.

[8] Public Bills 1907, No. 20.

[9] Public Bills 1907, No. 158.

[10] Public Bills 1907, No. 60.

[11] Public Bills 1908, No. 2 (Toulmin).

[12] Cmd. 1908, No. 246.

a Conservative and protectionist, unsuccessfully moved on March 23 for leave to bring in a Bill providing that when a minimum rate of wages in any trade had been established by law or custom, it should be protected from the competition of goods produced abroad by sweated or lower paid labour.[13] On March 26, Mr. Hills, a Conservative, moved the second reading of the Dilke Wages Boards Bill, which was designed to create wage boards of employers and employed to fix a minimum wage for tailoring, dressmaking, and shirt-making, and certain other trades to be designated by the Home Secretary.[14] The debate on this Bill was adjourned pending the second reading of the Government Bill, which was introduced by the President of the Board of Trade, Mr. Churchill, on March 24, 1909.

THE TRADE BOARDS ACT, 1909

The central principle of the Trade Boards Bill the Government declared, was the establishment of a minimum standard of wages, and the enforcement by those Trade Boards of that minimum when fixed. The Trade Boards set up under this Bill would exercise other functions besides their particular statutory functions of fixing a minimum rate of wages. They were to be a centre of information, and become the foci of organization. As centres of information they would in time be charged with some other aspects of the administration of the work of the trades, with the question of the training of workers, and also they would be able to afford information upon the subject of unemployment. They would generally be not merely boards for the purpose of fixing the minimum rate of wages, for that was their primary purpose, but boards designated to nourish, so far as possible, the interests of the worker, the health, and the state of industry of each particular trade in which they operated.[15]

The Government statement was immediately attacked by Sir Frederick Banbury, who declared the right honourable gentleman, Mr. Churchill, might have saved the time of the House, and made his position more clear if he had said that the principles which actuated His Majesty's Government were to be found in a complete surrender to the Socialist party.[16] His opinion was that the Bill

[13] *Parl. Deb.*, 5 S.H.C., 1909, vol. 2, pp. 1642–1644.
[14] *Parl. Deb.*, 5 S.H.C., 1909, vol. 2, 2061–2129.
[15] *Parl. Deb.*, 5 S.H.C., 1909, vol. 2, pp. 1787–1792 (Churchill).
[16] *Parl. Deb.*, *op. cit.*, pp. 1792–1793.

would put the final nail in the coffin of what was left of the trade of the country. The Parliamentary Secretary to the Board of Trade, Mr. H. J. Tennant, moved on April 23, the second reading of the Government Bill. "Our remedy," he said, "proceeds upon lines parallel with those which have led the state to interfere with the control of the hours of labour, and the conditions of safety and sanitation. Our proposals are very limited in their application, they are limited to those plague spots of industry where, without drastic treatment, they will continue, as they have continued for three-quarters of a century, feeding upon the national wealth, supplying recruits to our hospitals, asylums, and workhouses, and swelling the ranks of the unemployable. When I am told that this legislation will subvert the foundations upon which the commercial supremacy of this country is based, I decline to believe that the commercial supremacy of this or any other country rests upon sweated labour. If I am told Capital will not stand it, I answer there is another and a greater capital with greater claims upon us. It is against the drain upon this capital that we protest—I mean the life capital of the nation." [17]

The Home Secretary, Mr. Winston Churchill, believed that the passing of the Bill would have a good influence on the progress of similar legislation in Europe. (So Professor Pic agreed in France.) He thought Parliament would not only be dealing manfully with a grave social evil, but would also take another step upon that path of social organization on which they had fully entered, and along which the Parliaments of this generation of whatever complexion, willingly or unwillingly, would have to march. [18]

The second reading of the Bill was passed without division. In Committee the Labour leaders fought to provide for the inclusion of other trades besides those scheduled, [19] but on this point had to be

---

[17] *Parl. Deb.*, 5 S.H.C., 1909, vol. 4, p. 351; pp. 342–351, speech entire.

[18] *Parl. Deb., ibid.*, p. 393; pp. 385–393, speech entire (Churchill); pp. 341–411, second reading debate entire. The Bill went to a standing committee, and was reported to the House and read a third time July 16: *Parl. Deb.*, 5 S.H.C., 1909, vol. 5, pp. 961–966, 1551–1562, for finance motion; and for Committee and third reading, vol. 7, H.C., pp. 2429–2481. The Bill was introduced in the House of Lords by Lord Hamilton, who moved the second reading on August 30: *Parl. Deb.*, 5 S.H.L., 1909, vol. 2, pp. 974–980; the Bill was opposed by the Marquess of Salisbury: *Parl. Deb., ibid.*, pp. 979 ff.; for entire debate, pp. 974–1015; Committee and third reading, pp. 1076–1117, September 13.

[19] See *Report of the Trade Union Congress, 1909*, p. 72.

satisfied with the granting to the Board of Trade of the power to extend the Act, by a provisional order, when they were satisfied (a) that the rate of wages in certain trades or in parts of them are "exceptionally low," as compared with other employments; and (b) that the other circumstances of the trade are such as render the application of this Act to the trade expedient.[20] As early as 1913 four new trades were included within the provisions of the Act, through the Trade Boards Provisional Orders Confirmation Acts, 1913.

The Trade Boards Act, 1909, is important because it indicates plainly how far Parliament interference had been carried into the actual control of the industrial system. The wide powers of the Trade Boards for the establishment of minimum rates of wages meant a definite decision by Parliament that below a certain standard it was not possible for a worker to be legally employed.[21] How that principle has been modified and extended will be later considered. The Board of Trade were only empowered to apply the Act to specified trades, and, by Order, which had to be confirmed by Parliament, to extend the Act to other trades. The trades that were in mind were notoriously underpaid ones, the sweated and unorganized ones. It was estimated that the six Boards in the four originally scheduled trades covered 200,000 workers, of whom about 70,000 were women. The Secretary of the General Federation of Trade Unions wrote in 1910, the year the Act became operative, that "the results of the Act are not reassuring. The Trade Boards have served one useful purpose; they have assisted the Labour Exchanges to demonstrate the futility of attempting the millennium from mere Acts of Parliament."

However useful the Act would have been from that point of view alone, it was the beginning of a movement that has become increasingly important in legislation and has achieved great administrative changes in English labour organization. In the beginning it united the sympathies of great numbers of people, directing attention specifically to the social question of housing and the better enforce-

[20] Act of 1909, Sect. 1, subsect. 2.
[21] Act of 1909, Sects. 1 and 4. Cf. *Memoranda in reference to the Working of the Trade Boards Act* (H.C. Papers 134), 1913; also the *Special Report from the Select Committee on the Trade Boards Act, Provisional Orders Bill,* etc. (H.C. Papers No. 209), 1913. These two reports provide a full account of the administration and extension of the Act of 1909.

ment of the laws of public health, and gave prominence to the investigations of the Parliamentary Committees and the National Anti-Sweating League.[22] By 1909 the Government were compelled to introduce legislation on this important point of wages control, passing an Act which was "blessed by everyone, and became an Act without any vote on principle having been registered against it." [23] But it was the conviction, Professor Dicey declared, of English economists and social reformers up until the last quarter of the nineteenth century, "that any attempt to fix by law the rate of wages was an antiquated folly. This belief is no longer entertained by our Parliamentary statesman." [24] The conviction had become widespread that "when the conditions of the workman's life are settled, without interference by law or trade unionism, by absolutely free contact between man and man, the workman's freedom is delusive"; and the "growing consciousness of the weakness of the wage earner in his bargaining with the great capitalist employer is to bring us, at the opening of the 20th century, to the threshold of the Legal Minimum Wage for every branch of industry." [25] Public opinion

---

[22] See Stephen W. Gwynn and Gertrude M. Tuckwell, *The Life of Sir Charles W. Dilke*, 2 vols. (1917), vol. II, pp. 342–367; Emmeline Pethick Lawrence, "The Sweating Exhibition," the *Reformers' Year Book, 1907*, pp. 160–161.

[23] *The Labour Year Book, 1916*, p. 214. The following Government Reports give a comprehensive account of the industrial situation in the period of 1909–1913; taken together with the eight Reports noted above: (1) *Report of an Enquiry by the Board of Trade into Working Class Rents and Retail Prices, together with the Rate of Wages in Certain Occupations in the Principal Towns of the United Kingdom* (Cmd. 6955, 1913). A similar *Report* was made in 1905, and the two *Reports* on 88 towns, London treated separately, are compared. *Board of Trade Report on Changes in Rate and Hours of Labour in the United Kingdom in 1912* (Cmd. 7080, 1913); and (3) a similar *Report* for 1913 (Cmd. 7635) gives comparative statistics and a chart of wages, 1895–1913. In 1909 a *Report* (Cmd. 4512) on France was made, of working class rents, housing and retail prices, together with the rate of wages in certain occupations, with introductory memoranda and comparison of the conditions in France and England.

[24] *Op cit.*, p. xlix.

[25] Cf. Sidney and Beatrice Webb, *Introduction to their Problems of Modern Industry* (1902); also *Industrial Democracy, Part III*, chap. II–III, and *The Case for the Factory Acts* (1902), and *The Industrial Unrest and the Living Wage: Lectures Given at the Interdenominational Summer School at Swanwick, July 1913* (1913), on significance of the progress of the ideal of a Living Wage as a revolt due to social progress, and not to abject misery; it was an

had come to defend quickly any serious attack on the Standard of Life. It was necessary to get back as a community what had been lost by individuals. On this basis the proposals that a minimum wage should be fixed by authority of Government, below which no one might work, had a wide collective appeal, which was reflected in the belief of Professor Marshall that the minimum wage should be in many cases adjusted to the family, instead of the individual.[26] Before the Act of 1909 was passed the Cambridge economist declared in the Economic Society Address of 1907, that he had been steadily growing a more convinced supporter of social reform by state agency. The ideal of escape from the degradation caused by the waste in the human cost of the industrial system, providing remedies against the dangers of modern industrialism, has inspired a large part of the efforts of legislative enactments in modern democracies. To safeguard genuine freedom has been an increasing concern, and the Act of 1909 committed the state to far-reaching powers of control over the wage contract.

The Act of 1909 helped to stir the conscience of the "aristocratic" and prosperous trade unions, convincing them of the necessity of organization in all the ranks of Labour.[27] Four years after the passing of the Trade Boards Act a careful student, Mr. R. H. Tawney, who knew at first hand the working of this Act, said that the most important results of the Trade Boards were the spread of organization in the trades affected, which brought in for the first time the principle of collective bargaining between the employers and the work-people in the trades scheduled in the Act. Immediate extensions of Trade Union membership and improvements in Trade Union organization in the industries concerned have followed the Trade Disputes Act of 1906, the Trade Boards Act of 1908, the Coal Mines Regulation (Eight Hours) Act, 1908, the National Insurance Act, 1911, the Trade Union Act, 1913, the Corn Production Act, 1917, and the Trade Boards Extension Act, 1918.[28]

---

achievement of the workers, creating the conditions for the good life. Also J. Ramsay MacDonald, *The Social Unrest, Its Cause and Solution* (1913).

[26] *Principles of Economics* (8th ed. 1920), p. 715.

[27] See *Report of the Trade Union Congress, 1909*, pp. 47–53, presidential address of Mr. D. J. Shackelton. Cf. Rt. Hon. Charles Booth, *Industrial Unrest and Trade Union Policy*, 1913.

[28] Cf. Sidney and Beatrice Webb, *History of Trade Unionism*, pp. 474–475; also G. D. H. Cole, *Organized Labour* (1924), pp. 144–147.

II

THE MINERS' MINIMUM WAGE STRUGGLE

The power of organized Labour during 1911–12 was seen in the demand of one of the most effectively organized and comparatively higher paid trades, the Miners' Federation of Great Britain, for the establishment of a legal minimum wage for coal and iron mines. The Federation backed the demand, after negotiations between coal owners and workers had failed, by calling a general strike. Before this the Government had given to representatives of the coal owners and workers proposals which embodied the principles of the Coal Mines (Minimum Wage) Act, 1912, "An Act to provide a Minimum Wage in the case of Workmen employed underground in Coal Mines." The Government statement was:

(1) His Majesty's Government are satisfied, after careful consideration, that there are cases in which underground employees cannot earn a reasonable minimum wage, from causes over which they have no control.

(2) They are further satisfied that the power to earn such a wage should be secured by arrangements suitable to the special circumstances of each district. Adequate safeguards to be provided to protect the employer from abuse.

(3) His Majesty's Government are prepared to confer with the parties as to the best method of giving practical effect to the conclusions, by means of district conferences between the parties, a representative appointed by the Government being present.

(4) In the event of any of the Conferences failing to arrive at a complete settlement within a reasonable time, the representatives appointed by his Majesty's Government to decide jointly any outstanding points for the purpose of giving effect in that district to the above principles.[29]

The proposals of the Government were accepted by coal owners representing 60 per cent of the coal trade of the country as measured by output. The Miners' Federation answered the proposals with the following resolution: "That we agree to re-affirm the resolution

[29] The statement was made by Mr. Lloyd George on February 28 in the House of Commons, but the Government proposals were given on February 17: see *Parl. Deb.*, 5 S.H.C., 1912, vol. 34, pp. 1492–1415.

passed by the Executive Committee and the 17 additional representatives from districts, and we repeat that there can be no settlement
of the present dispute unless the principle of an individual minimum wage for all underground workers is agreed to by the coal
owners. We are still willing to meet the coal owners at any time they
desire to discuss the minimum rates of each district, as passed at
special conferences of this Federation." [30]

The *impasse* was pointedly put by the Prime Minister, Mr.
Asquith, when he stated at the end of the conferences with the
Ministers' Executive Committee, on February 28, that the Government had made itself responsible for putting forward proposals to
insure that a reasonable minimum wage should be secured for underground workers, and that these proposals had been accepted by a
majority of coal owners, but that it was impossible, without discussion and negotiations between the parties, as proposed by the
Government, to determine the amount of the minimum wage suitable
to each district. On the other hand, the representatives of the men
stated that they were not prepared to regard the amount of the
minimum wage for coal getters, as revised and finally adopted on
the second of February, 1912, as open to negotiations.[31] Four days
later the Prime Minister made his statement on the Coal Strike and
the Minimum Wage, prefacing it by saying that the Government had
taken it as a duty to intervene in the coal dispute, issuing invitations
to both the interests concerned to confer separately with the Government. "We have unanimously come to certain conclusions," he
stated. "The first was that there are cases in which underground
workers in the coal industry are prevented by causes over which
they have no control, and for which they are not responsible, from
earning a minimum wage. We came further to the conclusion, in
which we were equally unanimous, that such cases ought to be met,
and must be met, by the recognition and application of what, if I
may use a compendious expression, I may call district minimum
wages." [32]

The Government proposals had been accepted by practically all

[30] *Parl. Deb.*, 5 S.H.C., 1912, vol. 34, p. 1494.
[31] *Ibid.*, p. 1495.
[32] *Parl. Deb.*, 5 S.H.C., 1912, vol. 34, pp. 39–48 (Asquith), including quotations below.

of the coal owners of England and North Wales, but rejected by those who represented South Wales and Scotland. The miners were satisfied—they had every reason to be satisfied, said the Prime Minister, adding that the Government had recognized, and that 65 per cent of the owners had recognized, the principle of a minimum wage for which they had been contending. But Mr. Asquith was anxious to make clear that he did not regard the grant of the minimum wage in the coal industry as the first step to the attainment, apparently by legislation, at any rate by some form of compulsion, of a minimum wage in all the industries of the country. "I am not in the habit," he declared, "of engaging in sly flirtations of this kind with Socialism and then trying to conceal from the public the manner in which I have been employing my time." Yet he reminded the Miners and the Labour party that "you are now, today, in a position which a year ago, six months ago, six weeks ago, you would have thought it would be impossible to be placed in. What have you got? You have 65 per cent of the coal owners of the country agreeing that a reasonable minimum wage must be established in your industry. You have got further than that, the representatives of the responsible Government of the country declaring they are convinced of the reasonableness and justice of that principle, and that they will take whatever means are necessary, notwithstanding the reluctance or even the resistance of what we hope and believe is a dwindling minority of owners who still take the other view, to carry out that principle throughout the coalfields of this country. You have got the principle for which you have been fighting and contending recognized practically by the employers and recognized in terms by the Government of the country." That the situation was considered most grave by the Government was evident in the closing words of the Prime Minister. He said that "the responsibility of those, who having it in their power to take any step to minimize and shorten this terrible national calamity, do not use it to the full is a responsibility which history will not measure."

THE COAL MINES (MINIMUM WAGE) ACT, 1912

When he announced, on March 18, that the next day he would ask leave to introduce a Bill to provide for the payment of a minimum

wage for persons employed underground in coal mines, he stated
that not only the introduction, but the passing of the Bill at the
earliest possible moment was very serious, and indeed, imperative.[33]
The Government had left the matter until the last possible moment,
Lord Hugh Cecil declared, "until the crisis is so acute and the situation so terrible that all considerations of ordinary Parliamentary
procedure must be of secondary importance." [34] The consequences
were not overlooked by another member who thought the Government Bill "one of the most important measures that had ever been
submitted to this House during the last twenty years—a measure
changing the whole economic conditions of labour and employment
in this country." [35]

The Prime Minister stated that the introduction of such a Bill
by the Government, and its passing by Parliament promptly and
within a very short period of time, was absolutely imperative in the
best interests of the country. "I say with perfect confidence every
effort was made to bridge or circumvent, by persuasion and by
argument, the chasm which divided them. As time went on it became
clear at last that, by such means, that chasm was impossible. The
injury not only to the actual combatants, but to the country at large,
is increasing every day, both in the width of its area and the gravity
of its character. In these circumstances His Majesty's Government
came without hesitation to the conclusion that Parliament must be
asked to intervene, and that if the parties could not agree to a settlement, the State must provide a settlement for them."

The Bill was emergency legislation, a temporary measure, for
according to its final clause it was to continue in force for three
years, unless Parliament chose to prolong it. "It starts with this,"
the Prime Minister said, "that *prima facie* it is to be a statutory
term of every contract for the employment of workmen underground in a coal mine, that the employer shall pay to the working-
man wages of not less than the minimum rate settled under the Act
and applicable to that workman. Any contract to the contrary will
be void."

The administration of the Act was an advanced step toward a

---

[33] *Parl. Deb.*, 5 S.H.C., 1912, vol. 34, p. 1544; pp. 1544–1549, entire.
[34] *Ibid.*, vol. 35, p. 1720.
[35] *Ibid.*, p. 1720 (Sir Frederick Banbury).

share in control for the worker and for the public.[36] It was defended as such by the Prime Minister. "We propose," Mr. Asquith said, "that both the rate of the minimum wage, and what I call the district rules—that is to say the rules for securing efficiency and regularity of work—should be settled by Joint District Boards, recognized as to each district, by the Board of Trade. These Joint Boards will be the existing Boards of Conciliation, or such other Boards as may be constituted and are considered by the Board of Trade to fairly and adequately represent the employers and workmen in the various districts. There will be practically equal and even representation of both parties. Each Board will have an independent chairman, who will be appointed between the two sides of the Board, or, in default of agreement, by the Board of Trade. The chairman shall have a casting vote in any case or difference of opinion between the two sides of the Board, and if it is thought desirable, three persons may be appointed to act as chairman instead of one. The Joint Boards will settle the general minimum rate for the district and the general district rules."

The Bill was to have no penal provisions, but what the Bill says —Mr. Asquith declared—is this: "A coal mine is opened for work by the employer, and if a man descends the pit to work underground, it is to work, so far as the minimum wage is concerned, upon these statutory terms—the employer is liable to pay the underground worker a wage of not less than the wage fixed in the manner provided by this Bill. Owing to the special conditions of a particular trade, and the special emergency affecting the whole community in almost all its interests, the state by this Bill steps in, and with the state, after this Bill has become an Act of Parliament, both interests will have to reckon. We are asking Parliament here to make a legislative

[36] On April 10, 1912, the following Resolution was moved: "That this House having regard to the vital importance to the nation of economic power production, and recognizing that the United Kingdom has a special relative advantage in regard to coal which needs to be carefully conserved, calls for the public control of the coal-mining industry and the establishment of a permanent Power Commission charged with the conservation, development, control, and distribution of power." The Government spokesman replying to Sir Leo Chiozza Money, said: "I have indicated my general assent to the line of reasoning, and taken his survey and summary as a kind of step in the evolution of society and of the world." (p. 1384) *Parl. Deb.* 5 S.H.C., 1912, vol. 36, pp. 1367-1384, debate entire; pp. 1367-1380, Chiozza Money; pp. 1381-1384, J. M. Robertson, Under Secretary.

declaration of the principle of a statutory minimum wage. We are asking Parliament by this Bill to set up as a necessary accompaniment and corollary of that legislative declaration a perfectly fair, independent, and impartial machinery for the ascertainment of that wage and the conditions under which it shall be enjoyed in all the special areas of the country.[37]

The leader of the Conservative Opposition declared immediately that Society had been held up. "It is one of the greatest evils which can possibly happen to any society. It has been forced in many countries by many Governments, some of them even Socialistic Governments; but there never has been any Government which forced it in the way in which this Government does." [38]

This statement caused the leader of the Labour Party to inquire from Mr. Bonar Law, "Does he mean to destroy collective bargaining, with all its consequences, or does he mean to establish paternal Government which will be Socialism in its very worst form?" [39] He added, "I regret the Bill, I suppose we all regret the Bill"; his objection being primarily to any feature of compulsory arbitration. Lord Hugh Cecil declared that it was absurd to treat this as a mere, ordinary labour dispute. It was really ridiculous to treat it that way. It was unquestionably an attempt to obtain control of the industries of this country by a band of men with revolutionary and anarchical theories which they recommend.[40] The Labour spokesman had anticipated such a view and had said that syndicalism and those sort of things are not matters which emanate only from two or three gentlemen who have gone to Ruskin College, Oxford. They are created because owners, more particularly in South Wales, have taken up in these negotiations, and in what preceded these negotiations, an attitude which no body of self-respecting workmen would tolerate for a single instant. "After all, men have got to be treated as human beings and not as beasts of burden or as mere profit-making machines." [41] But

---

[37] *Parl. Deb., cit.,* pp. 1723–1733, Prime Minister's (Asquith) speech introducing the Bill, March 19, 1912; pp. 1723–1797, first reading debate entire.

[38] *Parl. Deb., cit.,* p. 1739; pp. 1733–1742, speech entire (Bonar Law).

[39] *Parl. Deb., cit.,* p. 1743; pp. 1742–1750, speech entire (MacDonald).

[40] *Parl. Deb., cit.,* p. 1767; pp. 1764–1773, speech entire. The September, 1910, *The Industrial Syndicalist* and the September, 1911, *Socialist Review* were the sources quoted by Lord Hugh Cecil supporting this view. They did not include Trade Union Congress Reports.

[41] *Parl. Deb., cit.,* p. 1749 (MacDonald).

Lord Cecil declared he looked to causes that were deeper, saying that, "The root cause of the whole difficulty is that there is growing up, and has grown up in the past, a measure of class hostility which is a profound danger to civilization. I do not deny there are secondary causes. There are the speeches of the right honourable gentleman (Mr. Lloyd George) the Chancellor of the Exchequer, speeches which could not have been better designed if their purpose had been to stir up hatred between class and class, to encourage the rich in the oppression of the poor, and to influence the poor into resentment against the rich. Though these causes have undoubtedly increased the difficulty, I do feel that the fundamental difficulty is not due to the hostility between classes. The chief offender, in my judgment, is the wages system. (Cheers from Labour benches.) I submit that the system by which you buy the labour of a fellow creature, without any other element in it than the mere transaction of bargain and sale of another man's labour, is a thoroughly bad system. If you are going to put an end to the growing hostility which at present exists you must devise some new system of industry which shall recognize that the working man is something more than a mere labour machine, and that doles and gifts are perfectly useless and do not touch even the fringe of the question. What you want to do is to give every man a genuine living interest in the industry in which he is engaged. I dismiss State Socialism, which has succumbed to the Syndicalist parasite which has grown upon it. It is absolutely intolerable to have the tyranny of any class—I care not whether it is the working class or the landowning class or any other class. If the result of the transactions which have led up to this Bill, and if this Bill brings us appreciably nearer to the tyranny of the organized working classes, the trade unions organized and directed by men who are moved by the wildest economic and political theories, I am certain that that is absolutely intolerable. If you are to pass legislation in obedience or in deference to mere agitation, you must take care that it is of such a character that it will not hand over this country entirely to the domination of these Syndicalist people." [42]

The Government point of view was given by Mr. Lloyd George, the Chancellor of the Exchequer, who did not believe Syndicalism was a real peril. "I cannot see," he said, "men of very great weight

[42] *Parl. Deb., cit.*, pp. 1772–1773; see also speech of Mr. Stephen Walsh for the Miners, pp. 1758–1764.

in the Labour movement who have committed themselves to it. No men of real influence or power have committed themselves to Syndicalism. Syndicalism and Socialism are, of course, two totally different things. They are mutually destructive. As a matter of fact the Socialist would prefer to deal with the capitalist rather than the Syndicalist, for the simple reason that it is much more easy to deal with the Capitalist than the Syndicalist, because when once you hand over the whole profits of an industry merely to that industry, without any regard to the interests of the community, you raise a very formidable obstacle in the way of Socialism which is not in existence now, so that I can understand the Syndicalist as the bitterest enemy of the Socialist. Let the Noble Lord take this comfort, that the best policeman for the Syndicalist is the Socialist."

To which statement, the member referred to said that, "the best policeman for the thief is the lunatic." The Chancellor replied that, "I do not think the Noble Lord will consider that very fair, for the greatest intellects in Europe have been the greatest believers in Socialism." Adding, "I have seen the strikers; I have seen the leaders of the strike, but their position has not been the Syndicalist position. After all, the demand for the minimum wage is not a Syndicalist demand." [43]

Opposition to the Bill continued on the second reading; [44] at which time Mr. Balfour, moving the reading this day six months, which automatically would have destroyed the Bill, asked: "Has any feudal baron ever exercised his powers in the manner which the leaders of this great trade union are now using theirs? This is the first formidable exhibition or display of a policy and a power, which if it be allowed unlimited sway will be absolutely destructive of society." [45]

But a Labour member declared [46] that "as a result of the Strike Syndicalism will have its death blow"; and the veteran Keir Hardie stated that he was prepared to go farther in denunciation of the Syndicalist position. [47] The second reading of the Bill was passed

[43] *Parl. Deb., cit.,* pp. 1773–1783, speech entire (Lloyd George).

[44] Public House Bills of 1912, No. 92. Second reading debate, March 21, pp. 2077–2202 entire debate; note Prime Minister's speech, pp. 2089–2097.

[45] *Parl. Deb., cit.,* p. 2088; pp. 2077–2089, entire speech.

[46] *Parl. Deb., cit.,* p. 2121; pp. 2120–2128, entire speech (Brace).

[47] *Parl. Deb., cit.,* p. 2163; see p. 2164 (Lansbury). Note speeches of the Secretary of Foreign Affairs (2179–2187), Sir Edward Grey; pp. 2171–2179, Mr. A. Chamberlain.

by 348 votes to 225. Following Committee [48] stage, during which the Labour party failed to secure the including of the miners' list of minimum rates as a schedule to the Bill, the Bill was passed on third reading,[49] Labour opposing, by 213 votes to 48. The close connection of the Labour party and the Miners' Federation in the dispute was evident; and throughout the varying course of the dispute the Parliamentary party was in constant touch with the officials of the Miners' Federation, and all actions taken on the floor of the House were the subject of joint consultation.[50] One writer has observed that organized Labour in a trade upon which the whole industrial life of the United Kingdom was dependent had forced Parliament in the interests of industrial peace, to pass an Act which was more or less contrary to the opinion of the country as a whole. This Act he gave as a typical example of direct action.[51]

Though Parliament by passing this Act plainly established the principle "that wages can rightly be fixed by law and not by mere haggling of the market." [52] the fact remained, one observed, that in the social life of England there was nothing better than a state of economic war.[53] The Coal Mines (Minimum Wage) Act, 1912 has been continued from year to year by the Expiring Laws Continuance Act.

The developments in this problem of the nation and the coal mines are given below when wage disputes and governmental investigations are considered. The 1912 debates have been given in detail here because they plainly indicate the temper of the times and illustrate fully the changing attitude of organized Labour in politics and industrial organization. This was the prelude of the long

[48] *Parl. Deb., cit.,* pp. 2229–2427, complete; Bill reported as amended, House Bill No. 103.

[49] *Parl. Deb.,* H.C. 5 S., vol. 36, pp. 223–385 (Report), and pp. 385–400, third reading: Banbury (385–386); MacDonald (386–388); Lloyd George (389–391); Hardie (391–393); and S. Walsh (396–398).

[50] *Labour Year Book, 1916,* p. 330, "The Parliamentary Labour Party."

[51] B. G. De Montgomery, *British and Continental Labour Policy* (1922), p. 361.

[52] Dicey, *op. cit.,* p. xlix.

[53] Cf. A. J. Carlyle, *Wages (1912),* chap. IX–X, pp. 104–125. See *Political Quarterly,* January 1930, G. D. H. Cole, "The Problem of the Coal Mines," for comment on this Act and the coal crisis. He says, "If the Act of 1912 had been so drafted as to concede an effective minimum apart from agreement between owners and miners much subsequent trouble might have been avoided." It is difficult to see how this could have been done at the time.

post-war years of dispute between the miners and the coal-owners, with a whole nation as a battle-ground.

GOVERNMENT INTERFERENCE BEFORE 1914 AND THE INDUSTRIAL COUNCIL

Before briefly bringing the survey of minimum wage legislation down to date, as affected by emergency enactments in the war-time and post-war conditions, the Report of the Industrial Council may well be outlined for it belongs to the period in which the whole tendency of Labour legislation was toward approving the principle of the minimum wage. This was less true in France than in England, but there was a persistent demand in both countries for a Living Wage, and the all-round protection of the family as a working-unit, as well as the protection of the individual worker. The Industrial Council was appointed in 1911 by the Government in order to aid in the settlement of important trade disputes, its formation resulting directly from the railway strike of that year. The widespread industrial unrest of 1911–12, a period in which more persons had been involved in strikes than in the previous ten years put together (and the number of days lost were far greater) forced the Government to act. The disorganization of the industry and trade of the country was a menacing and recurrent problem.[54] The railway world, the coal trade and the transport industry, the fundamental trade organizations, had been the first to indicate that a new spirit on the part of the Government and the leaders of the organized workmen was imperatively demanded. During 1911, Mr. Asquith, the Prime Minister, and M. Sidney Buxton, President of the Board of Trade, consulted with leading employers and workers with a view to strengthening the official machinery for dealing with labour questions. The Government resolved to establish an Industrial Council, which consisted of thirteen representatives of employers and thirteen representatives of workers, with Sir George (now Lord) Askwith as chairman. Meetings were held in 1911, and 1912 and 1913.

The Industrial Council members were appointed for the period of one year, and the appointments were renewed once and on their expiration there was no further renewal. But it is interesting to

[54] See *Board of Trade Report on Strikes and Lockouts and on Conciliation and Arbitration Boards in the United Kingdom in 1913* (Cmd. 1914, 7658.

note this experiment, both because it reflects in its Report the disturbed period of 1911–1913 and because it was a forerunner of the National Advisory Economic Committee appointed in 1930 by Mr. MacDonald.[55] The Royal Commission on Labour, appointed in 1891, had considered the advisability of recommending the creation of a "Higher Council of Labour"—(the French Superior Labour Council perhaps suggested the idea, for it was set up in 1891)—which would enable a common view to be formed and expressed regarding labour matters. The Commission reported, however, that "regard being had to the number, magnitude and complexity of industries in this country, we think that it would be difficult by any system of nomination or election to compose a body of employers, workmen and others which would give general satisfaction as a central council, thoroughly representative of all the interests concerned." [56]

The Prime Minister stated the view of the Government in the House of Commons, in June, 1912, when he instructed the Industrial Council on the work of inquiry it was intended they should carry out. Taken together with the Government statements on the Port of London Strike, the attitude of the responsible Ministers was known. The Prime Minister declared that:

In the experience derived from the industrial disputes which have lately occurred, it had become evident that one of the chief difficulties in the way of peaceful and friendly relations between employers and men was the want of effective measures for securing the due observance of industrial agreements by both sides. Further, in agreements between employers and workmen in regard to conditions of employment the agreement, though binding on those who are parties to it, it was not binding on the whole of the trade of the district. These matters affected the employers and workmen alike, and it seemed essential to ascertain (1) What was the best method of securing the due fulfilment of industrial agreements? (2) How far industrial agreements, which were made between representative

[55] See *Economic Advisory Council,* Copy of Treasury Minute, dated 27th January, 1930 (Cmd. 3478).

[56] Quoted by Lord Amulree (Sir William MacKenzie) *Industrial Arbitration in Great Britain* (1929), p. 114. The Royal Commission issued its final report in May, 1894 *(Fifth and Final Report of Royal Commission on Labour).* Cmd. No. 7421. Report, Minutes of Evidence, etc., are given in their 67 publications.

bodies of employers and workmen should be enforced throughout the particular trade or district? The Government, he declared, were anxious to have inquiry made into the matter, and to receive advice from those best qualified to give it. In these circumstances, they proposed to refer the above questions to the Industrial Council, which was representative of the employers and the men in the great industries of the country; to request the Council carefully to consider the matter, to take such evidence as they thought fit, and to report to the Government any conclusions to which they might come. The view of the Government had been strengthened by the following resolution of the Industrial Council, which had considered the matter: "The question of the maintenance of industrial agreements having come before the Industrial Council, that Council are of the opinion that this subject is of the highest importance to employers and Trade Unions, and work people generally, and would welcome an immediate inquiry into the matter." The resolution was agreed to unanimously. The Government in requesting the Industrial Council to undertake the inquiry, pledged the most earnest attention to any recommendation which the Council might be able to make.

The Report of the Industrial Council was presented to Parliament in July, 1913.[57] The Council expressed themselves in favour of the continued maintenance of voluntary conciliation and arbitration boards, and against compulsion, or against "any alternative based upon principles other than mutual consent." They considered that the machinery for the voluntary settlement of disputes should be strengthened by the right of appeal to some independent body or impartial individual. The Council strongly emphasized the importance of efficient organization on the part of employers and work people as one method of securing the due fulfilment of agreement. The value of "moral obligation" was a strong factor, the report argued, and the pressure of moral influence should be brought to bear upon all parties in the settlement of disputes. The consideration of the second part of the reference of the Government, relating to the extension of industrial agreements, formed a large section of the Report. Where Trade Union organization was strong, it was

---

[57] *The Industrial Council: Report on Enquiry into Industrial Agreements (Cmd. 6952)* 1913. Also Ninth and Tenth Reports of Proceedings under the Conciliation Act, 1896, March 29, 1912, and November 28, 1913; and Lord Amulree, *op. cit.,* pp. 114–118.

often possible to exert sufficient pressure on non-associated employers to induce them to observe agreements with the masters'
associations. When, however, organization was imperfect, the effective maintenance of agreements was jeopardized by the existence
of a section (perhaps only a minority) which was not party to, and
therefore not in any sense bound by whatever agreement may be
arrived at by the rest of the trade.[58] It was suggested that the Board
of Trade should have power to extend agreements made by trade
unions and employers' associations to the whole industry of a district,
on application to the central authority by either of the parties in the
agreement, provided that the Board of Trade was satisfied that the
associations represented by the signatories to the agreement constitute a substantial body of the employers and workmen in the
trade or district, and that the agreement is a proper agreement and
one that might suitably be extended.

This proposal of the Industrial Council would have virtually
amounted therefore, to the establishment of a legal minimum wage
by trades, or sections of trades, for the agreements made by voluntarily constituted Trade Boards would be officially ratified.[59] This
report indicated the extent of common agreement between the employers and the representatives of Labour with regard to state
intervention. It cannot be said to have done anything more than interpret the sentiment of the time, proving that there was no strong
tendency toward compulsory arbitration; but, on the other hand,
there was complete willingness for the state to continue to act as a
mediator, furthering the work of industrial agreement by official
machinery. The year that the Parliamentary Committee made its
report on systems of conciliation and arbitration, at the 1911 Congress, a Bill [60] was introduced in the House of Commons by Mr. W.
Crooks, which attempted to guarantee a settlement of trade disputes.
It was supported by several of the leading Labour members, in-

---

[58] In the Parliamentary Committee's Report on the General Federation of
Trade Unions at the Bristol Congress, it was declared as one of the reasons
for the value of the Federation that "complete organization means industrial
peace to the nation," *The Report of the Trade Union Congress, Bristol,* 1904,
p. 77. The Reports of the General Federation of Trade Unions fully discuss
this point. Cf. *Fifth Report of the General Federation of Trade Unions, 1904,*
and *Ministry of Labour Report for the year 1928,* chap. I.

[59] Cf. Arthur Greenwood, article in *Economic Journal,* September 1913, pp.
449–451; also not Supplement on Minimum Wage in the *Crusade,* June, 1912.

[60] Public Bills, 1911, No. 360.

cluding Mr. Arthur Henderson. The provisions of the Bill were such that it could not be successful. Each workman should be liable to a fine of not less than two pounds and not more than ten pounds for each day or part of a day that he was on strike contrary to the provisions of the Bill; and the employer declaring or causing a lockout contrary to the provisions of the Bill should be liable to a fine of not less than twenty pounds and not more than two hundred pounds a day. The failure of this Bill made more evident the wisdom of building up a strong sentiment for making voluntary agreements more effective, and the Government had done this in supplementing the Conciliation Act, 1896, by the Government Memorandum of September 1, 1908. This Memorandum was sent to all employers' and workmen's associations and Chambers of Commerce. It provided for the establishment of a Court of Arbitration composed of three to five members, according to the wishes of the parties. The members of the Court were to be appointed by the Board of Trade, employers and workmen to be represented in equal number. The arbitration by the Court was of a purely voluntary character.

In the Port of London (Transport) Strike the attitude of Labour was manifest in the Industrial Agreements Bill.[61] introduced June 25, 1912, "to make agreements come to voluntarily between employers and workers in the Port of London legally enforceable on the whole trade." In the Bill there was no clause relating to the legal enforcement of the agreement.[62] From the standpoint of the Labour party the chief value of the Parliamentary discussions on the Port of London Authority Dispute was to bring pressure to bear upon the Board of Trade.[63] Earlier in the long dispute the Chancellor of the Exchequer, Mr. Lloyd George, in reply to a question raised by a Labour member,[64] declared that, "I do not suppose anyone in the House will accept the view laid down by the Hon. Baronet (Sir

---

[61] Public Bills of 1912, No. 253; introduced by Mr. J. Ramsay MacDonald. See *Parl. Deb.*, H.C., 5 S., 1912, vol. 39, pp. 220–222.

[62] This was true of the Millerand decrees. For a full treatment see *Industrial Negotiations and Agreements,* Foreword by J. R. Clynes, published by the Trade Union Congress and Labour Party (1923).

[63] *Labour Year Book,* 1916, pp. 330–331.

[64] *Parl. Deb.,* H. C., 5 S., 1912, vol. 39, pp. 216–224 (O'Grady); pp. 216–257, debate entire. See Lloyd George (pp. 235–243); Bonar Law (pp. 244–248); MacDonald (pp. 248–255). June 6: 422–428; June 12: pp. 872–996, very important debate; June 17: pp. 1316–1323; June 24: pp. 30–37, vol. 40; June 25–26, vol. 40, pp. 212–215, 326–330.

Frederick Banbury)[65] that it is the business of the Government to stand aside and let the parties fight it out. That has been abandoned long ago." [66]

In this long drawn out dispute Labour brought forward several pronouncements; and on July 1, a motion by Mr. O'Grady was passed by 254 votes to 188. It was "That, in the opinion of this House it is expedient that the representatives of the employers' and the workmen's organizations involved in the present dispute should meet, with the view of arriving at a settlement." [67] The Labour motion was based on the belief that "the events of the last 12 months have surely taught us that the era of *laissez-faire* has definitely passed away, and that Governments in future must be prepared to take a regular though not necessarily an arbitrary part in all important industrial conflicts. For in every industrial conflict the general interests of the community are directly and vitally engaged, alike in the conflict itself and in its sequel. . . . Whenever an industrial dispute takes place in which the weaker party is forced into accepting terms degrading and injurious to its standard of life, it is the manifest duty of the state to intervene." [68]

The Government too were convinced that the time had come for the reconsideration of the whole problem of the settlement of trade disputes. "I do not believe it is possible to deal with them without some form of legislative sanction," Mr. Lloyd George said, "because you always come up against some employer or some union who will listen to no appeal, and who are perfectly indifferent to public opinion, and there mere methods of conciliation must be a failure. In a case of that kind there must necessarily be legislation, the sanction of some legislation which can be enforced. The Government have come to the conclusion that it will be necessary to deal with this problem. The weapon with which the Executive is armed is absolutely futile beyond a certain point. I am not criticising the Act of 1896, because I do not think public opinion would

[65] *Parl. Deb.,* H.C., 5 S., vol. 39, pp. 224–230.
[66] *Parl. Deb., cit.,* p. 236.
[67] *Parl. Deb.,* 5 S.H.C., 1912, vol. 40, p. 849; pp. 849–902, debate entire on O'Grady motion; note Bonar Law (pp. 862–871); MacDonald (pp. 871–877); the Prime Minister (pp. 859–862); Barnes (pp. 882–885).
[68] *Parl. Deb., cit.,* p. 854. In 1904 Mr. R. Bell introduced for Labour a Conciliation and Arbitration Act (1896) Amendment Bill (House Bill No. 122, 1904).

have justified the Government of the day going beyond legislation at that stage. But since then a great deal has happened. Therefore the Government have come to the conclusion that it will be necessary to deal with the whole problem, and to deal with it in the immediate future." [69]

It is well to bear in mind that upon the question of arbitration and conciliation the Government had always to be very cautious in bringing forward any measure, for the Trade Unions and the employers' associations have at no time been in agreement among themselves or between each other on what is a workable solution of the industrial disputes that are continually arising. There are many sides to this question and it is bound up with a number of other important social questions. The Bill of Mr. Crooks, while supported by some of the Labour Party, was more usually denounced; and the Trade Union Congresses of 1912 and 1913 defeated resolutions that embodied to some extent the principle of Mr. MacDonald's Bill of 1912.[70] The Report of Lord Askwith (then Sir George), Chief Industrial Commissioner of the Industrial Council, avoided making any definite recommendations, limiting its observations to the possibility of the application of the conciliatory features of the Canadian Arbitration and Conciliation Law to England.[71] The Social Reform Committee of the Conservative and Unionist Party issued a report in 1914 which gave its solution of industrial unrest.[72] It recommended that officially appointed Boards should in case of industrial disputes, publish definite recommendations for a settlement. The Boards should have compulsory powers, but the recommendations were to be published for the guidance of public opinion. The second recommendation was the gradual extension

[69] *Parl. Deb.*, 5 S.H.C., 1912, vol. 41, pp. 1111–1120, speech entire; note appeal for settlement by Messrs. Crooks and O'Grady, July 9 and July 11, pp. 1843–1847, pp. 2222–2225, vol. 40. Note also on July 23, together with the speech of the Chancellor of the Exchequer, the following: O'Grady (pp. 1079–1090); Lansbury (1090–1097); MacDonald (1104–1108); Bonar Law (pp. 1120–1123); all of which are in vol. 41, the debate entire being in pp. 1079–1130.

[70] Cf. Parliamentary Committee's Report, *Report of the Trade Union Congress, 1913*, pp. 77–170.

[71] Cf. *Report to the Board of Trade on the Industrial Disputes Investigation Act of Canada, 1907*, by Sir George Askwith, Chief Industrial Commissioner, Cmd. 6603, 1913.

[72] *Industrial Unrest, A Practical Solution: The Report of the Unionist Social Reform Committee*, Introduction by F. E. Smith (1914).

of the principle of the minimum wage; and the third, a reorganization of the Board of Trade, and the improvement of its usefulness for all of industry and trade.

The three recommendations of the Social Reform Committee of the Unionist Party represented phases of a tendency in all the political parties since 1890, to round out a social programme which would be self-consistent. From the miners' strike in 1893 when the cry for "a living wage" was heard, to 1914 was hardly over twenty years, yet by that time in the House of Commons there was something like a real unanimity in facing the question of the minimum wage and in adjusting the disputes of industry in a peaceful fashion. The Bill introduced by Mr. Bell in 1904 and Mr. MacDonald in 1912 have a good deal in common with the first recommendation of the Unionist Committee, however long the fight might be carried on over certain interpretations in the execution of the provisions of a law. The third point, the reorganization of the Board of Trade, had been dealt with by the Labour and Conservative parties. When the Board of Trade Amendment of the Conservative Party in 1908 was given, the Labour Party promptly offered its Amendment to the Address on a Ministry of Labour.[73] The Leicester Trade Union Congress of 1903 had also passed a resolution on the extension of the Labour department and asking for the appointment of a Minister of Labour.

The Labour motion stated that, "the era of *laissez-faire*" had definitely passed away, and it was believed then that the abandonment of the *laissez-faire* policy by the Government in regard to industrial disputes would one day come to be recognized as the most important development in economic matters in the last fifty years. While part of a more complex industrial problem—the control of industry—this agitation had direct bearing upon the question of the better standard of living, which, to bring about, organized labour had determined to use its complete economic and political power. Brief mention of the Fair Wages Clause debate of 1909 and the General Minimum Wage Resolution of 1911, may well conclude this survey of the problem in its Parliamentary history, down to 1914. It is a very significant commentary both on the social condition of England and the organized trade union movement, that

[73] Cf. Parliamentary Committees' Report, *Report of the Trade Union Congress, 1909*, p. 25.

before 1914 so much attention had to be given by the Government and the industrial Labour movement to the gaining of a minimum standard of living.

FAIR WAGES CLAUSE AND THE GENERAL MINIMUM WAGE

The most important motion brought forward by the Labour party in the 1909 Parliament dealt with the administration of the Fair Wages Clause.[74] "We are recognizing in prospective legislation," it was stated, "that the Government has a right to see to it that every willing worker has a living wage in return for the labour he performs." [75] The new Clause agreed to in 1909 indicates the progress of a standard of "the fair wage" which the Government recognizes: [76] "The contractor shall, under the penalty of a fine or otherwise pay rates of wages and observe hours of labour not less favourable than those commonly recognized by employers and trade societies (or, in the absence of such recognized wages and hours, those which in practice prevail amongst good employers) in the trade in the district where the work is carried out. Where there are no such wages or hours recognized or prevailing in the district, those recognized or prevailing in the nearest district in which the general industrial circumstances are similar shall be adopted. Further, the conditions of employment generally accepted in the district in the trade concerned shall be taken into account in considering how far the terms of the fair wages clauses are being observed. The contractor shall be prohibited from transferring or assigning directly or indirectly, to any person or persons whatever, any portion of his contract without the written permission of the department. Subletting, other than that which may be customary in the trade concerned, shall be prohibited. The contractor shall be responsible for the observance of the Fair Wages Clauses by the sub-contractor." [77]

---

[74] *Parl. Deb.*, 5 S.H.C., 1909, vol. 2, pp. 415–420, pp. 415–458, debate entire.

[75] *Parl. Deb., cit.*, p. 424; pp. 420–425, entire speech (Roberts); motion moved by Mr. J. Hodge.

[76] Cf. *Report of the Fair Wages Committee* (Cmd. 4422, 1908) appointed in August, 1907, by the Treasury to consider the working of the Fair Wages Resolution of the House of Commons of February 13, 1891.

[77] Compare with the Millerand Decrees of August 10, 1899, given below. From 1894 measures had been before the Chamber of Deputies, but M. Millerand did not wish to risk the fate of any Act on wages of employees in public works before the Senate, so his end was gained through Departmental Decrees.

In the agenda of the Trade Union Congress each year the Fair Wages Clause had a place, and continual deputations kept the matter before the Government. The Prime Minister in 1905, replying to a deputation, said that the Government were determined to be model employers.[78] During the debate on the motion in 1909 the Government policy was outlined by the Postmaster General,[79] whose personal responsibility for the Fair Wages Clause gave his testimony of the progress made since 1891 added weight. The Fair Wages Resolution applied, he said, as a legal obligation, only to workers engaged on the Government contract in question. It would, however, not be the practice of Government departments to keep on their lists of contractors firms who obeyed the letter of the Clause by paying recognized rates on Government contracts, but who were proved to be notoriously bad employers in other directions. Still less would a department give work to a firm who took advantage of the fair wages paid in Government work, to employ those same workers at a rate even below the normal in the output of non-Government articles—a practice that had been known to exist in sweating trades. The real security in regard to this matter was that contracts were renewable from time to time, and this gave the power and the opportunity to review the conditions of labour under any contract. The Local Government Board had issued to all local authorities a Circular urging them to adopt the Fair Wages Clause as adopted by the Government in its contracts.[80] The London County Council provisions with regard to Fair Wages cover about twenty pages of the Standing Orders; Liverpool, Glasgow and other cities have adopted strict forms of contract to fully protect Trade Union and Labour rates and standards.[81] This is a field where Trade Unions have very effectively put pressure on the local authorities, as the Report of the Committee in 1908 pointed out.

[78] Parliamentary Committee's Report to the Trade Union Congress of 1905, *Annual Trade Union Congress Report, 1905,* pp. 67–68.

[79] *Parl. Deb.,* 5 S.H.C., 1909, vol. 2, pp. 425–435.

[80] Cf. A. Millerand, *Politique de Realisations,* p. 188, "the State as a model employer"; the entire debate in the Chamber of Deputies, December 15, 1910, on the railway strike, is valuable for the survey that M. Millrand gave of the State and its attitude toward the workers, *op. cit.,* pp. 163–190.

[81] *Labour Year Book 1916,* pp. 633–641, for extracts from Fair Wages Clauses in London and other cities, and charts dealing with wages and conditions of municipal employees. See London County Council Standing Orders Nos. 281, 286, 287.

The resolution moved for a General Minimum Wage, on April 26, 1911, declared: "That the right of every family of the country to an income sufficient to enable it to maintain its members in decency and comfort should be recognized; and this House is therefore of the opinion that a general minimum wage of thirty shillings per week for every adult worker should be established by law, and also declares that the Government should set an example by adopting this standard in their own workshops." [82]

The mover declared, "You do not and never will employ men for the love of God. You employ them for what you can make out of them." He effectively portrayed the tragic fact that the study of the family budgets in England revealed a destitution and poverty which were degrading, and made right living almost impossible. It was emphasized in the debate that the share of capital in the product had increased much more than that of labour.[83] The Parliamentary Secretary for the Board of Trade replied for the Government, stating that it was impossible to accept the motion; of the 3,600,000 workers of whom there were statistics 60 per cent received a wage less than 30s. a week. The Fair Wages Clause of 1909 and the increased wages in Government departments, together with the Trade Boards Act, 1908, were pointed out by the Government as efforts toward raising the standards of life and work.[84] State action had shown that the nation was alive to the peril of the unfit and the underpaid. This view found expression in the national minimum wage motion brought forward in Parliament, March 4, 1924, and adopted without division. This motion is given later.

III

POST-WAR LEGISLATION

The extension of the principles embodied in the Coal Mines (Minimum Wage) Act, 1912, to apply to the emergency of war-time conditions is indicated in the Munitions of War Act, 1915,

[82] *Parl. Deb.*, 5 S.H.C., 1911, vol. 24, pp. 1881–1924, debate entire; pp. 1881–1882, the Resolution, moved by Mr. Crooks (pp. 1881–1892); seconded by Mr. Will Thorne (pp. 1892–1895). *Parl. Deb.*, 5 S.H.C., 1911, vol. 26, pp. 1136–1155, pp. 1459–1498, debate on Fair Wages Clause in Government works.

[83] *Parl. Deb., cit.*, pp. 1907–1914 (Chiozza-Money); also note Steel-Maitland (pp. 1895–1907).

[84] *Parl. Deb., cit.*, pp. 1919–1924 (Tennant).

the Amending Act of 1916, and the Munitions of War Act, 1917. The Wages (Temporary Regulation) Act, 1918, an effort to aid in restoring stable conditions in the labour market, prescribed a minimum wage,[85] and the Amending Act of 1919 continued its provisions for six months longer (Part I relating to the settlement of labour differences and prohibition of strikes and lockouts). The Corn Production Acts, 1917–1920 (the latter being Part I of the Agricultural Act, 1920), extended the principle of a minimum wage to the key industry of agriculture,[86] establishing Wages Boards and District Wages Committees.[87] The Corn Production Acts (Repeal) Act, 1921, abolished the Agricultural Wages Board for England and Wales, established by the Act of 1917, creating in place voluntary joint councils of employers and workmen in agriculture.[88] But the Agricultural Wages (Regulation) Act, 1924, provided for the establishment of an Agricultural Wages Board and Agricultural Wages Committees, with powers and duties with respect to minimum rates of wages for agricultural workers.[89] The two points most strongly debated were whether the Bill should include a legal minimum below which no district might go, and whether the local committees should have full power, or be subordinate to a central board. The Act provided that the County Committees, which consist of equal numbers of workers and employers, together with two appointed members and a chairman, have the duty of fixing statutory minimum rates of wages for agricultural workers.[90] The Agricultural Wages Board consists of equal numbers of workers and employers together with a number of appointed members not exceeding one-fourth of the total numbers of the Board. The Board has the power to fix, cancel, or vary the rates fixed by the County Committees, if a County Committee does not within two months of its establishment notify the Board a minimum rate which it has fixed; if a County Committee fails to substitute a new rate for one which has ceased to operate; and if a resolution of the representative

[85] Act of 1918, Section I. The second section provides arbitration through the Ministry of Labour.

[86] Act of 1917, Part II, Sections 4–7, 11–13 and 17 of 1909 Trade Boards Act were applicable.

[87] Act of 1917, Part IV.

[88] Act of 1921, Section 4.

[89] Act of 1924, Sections I and II, and see First Schedule.

[90] Compare Section 4 of the Corn Production Acts (Repeal) Act, 1921.

members of a County Committee requests the Board to fix, cancel, or vary a minimum rate. The Minister of Agriculture has power also to direct County Committees to reconsider their rates. The Act requires that the Minister of Agriculture establish an agricultural wages committee for each county, or for a group of counties, in England and Wales, and the Agricultural Wages Board for all England and Wales. Labour has advocated greater powers for these Central Wages Boards and stricter enforcement of the Act by adequate inspection.

The Minister of Agriculture, in addition to any special power to make regulations given to him under this Act, has the power to make regulations dealing with inspection and the powers of the officers he appoints for the purpose of investigating complaints. Through these regulations the Minister has general administrative control of the Agricultural Wages Boards and the wages committees.[91] Any regulations made under this Act shall be laid before both Houses of Parliament forthwith; and, if an address to His Majesty is agreed to by either House of Parliament within the next subsequent twenty-eight days on which that House has sat after any such regulation is laid before it praying that the regulation may be annulled, it shall henceforth be void, but without prejudice to the validity of anything previously done thereunder or the making of a new regulation.

While no minimum rate was fixed by the Act of 1924 itself, the Act directed that a committee shall, so far as practicable, secure for able-bodied men such wages as are adequate to promote efficiency, and to enable a man to maintain himself and his family in accordance with a reasonable standard of comfort. By January, 1925, a great majority of the County Committees had already agreed upon minimum rates for their areas.[92] Minimum rates of wages fixed by orders of The Agricultural Wages Board for ordinary adult male labourers and for females employed in agriculture in England and Wales at January 1, 1928, obtained in 45 areas.[93] In a reply to a question in the House of Commons on July 15, 1929, Mr. Noel Buxton, the Minister of Agriculture, said that with regard to observance of the Agricul-

---

[91] Act of 1924, Section 8 for power to make regulations and procedure.

[92] *Parl. Deb.*, 5 S.H.C., December 15, 1924, pp. 603–608, for first decisions as to minimum rates reached by the County Committees.

[93] See *Nineteenth Abstract of Labour Statistics*, pp. 94–96.

tural Wages (Regulation) Act, 1924, he was satisfied that in far too many cases wages below the minimum rates authorized for the different districts were being paid. He proposed therefore to increase the number of inspectors engaged on that work.

In the report of Mr. Lloyd George's Liberal Land Committee, 1923–25, a minimum wage condition for agricultural workers is laid down.[94] The suggestion is there made that before the fair rents are fixed in any area a minimum wage for agricultural workers shall be fixed for that area. When the fair rent is fixed for any holding, the cultivating tenant shall have a right of appeal against it on the ground that he cannot pay the minimum wage to labour at the rate fixed.

TRADE BOARDS ACT, 1918

The Trade Boards Act, 1918, which may be applied "if no adequate machinery exists for the effective regulation of wages throughout the trade," gave the Minister of Labour power to make a Special Order applying the principal Act to that trade.[95] If at any time he is of the opinion that the conditions of employment in any trade to which it is applied have so altered as to render the application of the principal Act to the trade unnecessary, then the Minister of Labour may make a Special Order withdrawing that trade from the operation of the Act.

When the Trade Boards Act of 1909 was passed the Minister— the Ministry concerned being the Board of Trade at the time—was not empowered to extend the scope of the Acts. The procedure followed was that the Minister issued a Provisional Order to establish trade boards for any additional industries, and these Orders could not become effective until ratified by Act of Parliament, duly passed through all stages in House of Commons and House of Lords. But by 1918 the administration of the Act had been so successful that Parliament gave to the Minister of Labour by the amending Act of 1918 the power to extend the Act to additional trades by Special Order. The procedure of a Special Order thus replaced the Provisional Order, which meant that the Minister of Labour could extend the Act, after considering objections, and if necessary holding

---

[94] *The Land and the Nation,* published in October, 1925, is the Rural Report; *Towns and Land* (1925) is the Urban Report.
[95] Act of 1918, Section II and First Schedule.

an enquiry, by means of a Special Order. Such a Special Order does not need confirmation by Act of Parliament, but it must be laid before Parliament immediately it is issued and may be challenged within 40 days by a motion requesting its amendment. Each trade is exactly defined in the Order establishing its Trade Board, and in some cases there are several Boards set up for what are in fact branches of one industry. The Trade Board Acts are administered by the Ministry of Labour, whose officers have power to enter workshops and inspect wage sheets, and have the same power to conduct proceedings as is possessed by Factory Inspectors. At the end of 1928 the total number of officers engaged on Trade Board Inspection was 60.

Trade Boards are constituted in accordance with regulations made under these Acts, for any trade to which this Act applies. They consist of representatives of employers and workers in equal numbers, together with members appointed by the Ministry of Labour. These must at no time exceed the whole of the representative members in number. Women are eligible both as appointed and as representative members.

Since the passing of the Trade Boards Act, 1918, a Trade Board has power to fix a general minimum trade rate of wages for time work. It may also fix (a) a general minimum piece rate of wages for piece work; (b) a minimum time rate to apply in the case of workers employed on piece work; (c) a guaranteed time rate (whether a time rate or a piece rate) to apply in substitution for a minimum rate which would otherwise be applicable; and, (d) an overtime rate. The Trade Boards are authorized to apply such rates universally to the trade, or to any special process, or to any class of workers, or to any special area. They may establish District Trade Committees, and refer to them any matter which they think expedient, other than special minimum piece rates. The Trade Boards are empowered to announce to employers the making of an Order affecting their trade, and to furnish them with particulars. They are also empowered to consider matters referred to them by Government Departments, and to make recommendations to any Government Department with reference to the industrial conditions of the trade. The Trade Boards Orders are confirmed by the Minister of Labour within one month from the date which the notification from the Trade Board is received. It is obligatory on all persons employing labour, or employed. Any minimum rate or the cancellation or variation of any such rate then becomes effective as from the date specified in the Order. The central supervision of the Act is under the Ministry of Labour, appointed officers investigating complaints and securing the observance of the Act.

The details of the 1918 Act, completing earlier legislation, have been given for this Act is an interesting example of the development of administrative organization.[96] A Trade Board rate, it is plain, is an instance of self-government in industry, and the co-operation of other bodies is necessary to the functioning of the Act. There are many Trade Boards and they are limited industrial legislatures. The administration of the Act demands co-operation and co-ordination of effort of these groups, and the principle has gained the recognition of all the groups concerned. The Minister of Labour in his annual report, May 1929, recorded that in 1928 the usual practice of obtaining nominations for the Trade Boards from organizations of employers and workers was followed. Of 1,021 employers' representatives and the same number of workers' representatives on all Boards and District Trade Committees, only 134 and 264 representatives respectively were unconnected with an organization.[97]

The expansion of the Trade Boards Act of 1909 in 1918 made permanent some of the wage machinery in operation during the war, and in the working of this Act Labour has taken a great interest. The progress since the original Act in 1909 is nothing less than phenomenal, and the history of the administration of the Act is a tribute to the Ministry of Labour and the staff of inspectors. The great strain that prolonged industrial depression has put upon the system has been recognized, and the fact that today over 3,000,000 workers in about forty trades are protected by the Act is significant proof of the will of the state to protect the worker. The trade boards system, as it has developed, is bipartite. Legislative power is vested in the Trade Boards, administrative and executive functions rest with the Ministry of Labour and have in practice involved four distinct features: (1) setting up of Boards, (2) confirmation of rates, (3) enforcement of legal rates, (4) decision on questions of

[96] Cf. C. Delisle Burns, *Government and Industry* (1921), pp. 111–112.
[97] See *Nineteenth Abstract of Labour Statistics,* pp. 92–93; and *Report of the Ministry of Labour for 1928,* pp. 74–83, for administration of Trade Boards Acts.

demarcation and scope. The Liberal Industry Inquiry taking into account the immense difficulty of wage regulation since the War, considered the Trade Board Acts to have been surprisingly successful and to be among the most beneficent measures of social reform ever introduced.[98] Labour declares that the Act must be extended to include within its scope classes of workers who are at present defenceless, and the machinery of inspection through which the payment of the rates fixed is enforced, must be enlarged.[99]

The principle of 1909 has become completely confirmed by postwar enactment. There has been further confirmation in the Coal Industry Commission Act, 1919, prescribing for the Commissioners that all investigation into the industry must take into consideration the acceptance of a "reasonable standard of living amongst the colliery workers." [100] The Act provided that a commission should be constituted to inquire into the position of and conditions prevailing in the industry with special reference *inter alia* to wages, hours of work, cost of production and distribution, selling prices and profits, and the social condition of colliery workers. The Coal Mines Act, 1919, and the Mining Industry Act, 1920, the provisions of which are noted herein, carried out recommendations of the commission. A similar provision was contained in the terms of reference for the Agricultural Tribunal of Investigation, 1922, their findings having regard to "the employment of labour at a living wage." The Mining Industry Act, 1920,[101] established a new principle in industrial welfare legislation, providing a fund for "social improvement," a Mines Department of the Board of Trade, an Advisory Committee on Coal and Coal Industry, and for Pit Committees. The Mining Industry (Welfare Fund) Act, 1925, and the Mining Industry Act, 1926 (Part III) confirmed and extended this principle. A national standard of life is implicit in all these Acts.

A return to the principle of the 1909 Act was suggested by the Departmental Committee appointed in September, 1921, under the presidency of Viscount Cave, "to inquire into the working of the Trade Boards Acts, and to report what changes, if any, are re-

[98] *Britain's Industrial Future,* p. 171.
[99] *Labour and the Nation,* p. 17, and see *Labour Year Book 1928,* pp. 84–89.
[100] Act of 1919, Section 1; full duties of investigation are set forth.
[101] Act of 1920, Part I, Sections 1–6, deals with Administration; Part II, with Regulation of Coal Mines.

quired." [102] On the other hand there are the Whitley Reports,[103] (1917-1918) and the Memorandum of the Labour representatives of the Joint Industrial Council (1919) attesting to the power behind the continuing agitation for a higher standard of living among the people.[104] There is the certainty, moreover, that the ideal of a Living Wage will find expression in legislative and administrative measures based on the experience gained by the state in attempting to insure a decent minimum of existence for the workers. The state itself will be increasingly concerned to sanction by legislation the advancing standards which the community conscience both demands and makes possible. The national minimum wage motion brought forward in Parliament on March 4, 1924, and adopted without division is one of the recent indications of the strength of the movement in England. The following is the motion: "That in view of the practically universal acceptance of the principle that a living wage for all workers should be the first charge upon industry, and in view of the large measure of agreement with respect to the advisability of fixing minimum time rates of wages reached at the national industrial conference, this House urges the Government to proceed without delay with the Bill introduced by the Government of the day of 1919, constituting a Commission to inquire into and report upon legal minimum time rates and wages."

A Consumers' Food Council

In bringing to a close the problem of a living wage and official sanction of the Government to the principle, it is well to note that on July 28, 1925, a committee of twelve was announced to serve as the Food Council recommended by the Royal Commission on Food Prices in its Report.[105] The Council was authorized to investigate and report on the supply and prices of food in general, and of the staples in particular. It is to undertake investigations when called

[102] The Report of the Committee was issued in April, 1922. Cmd. 1645. Cf. *Trade Boards Acts, 1909-1918. Statement of the Government's Policy in the Administration of the Acts Pending Legislation* (Cmd. 1712), 1922.

[103] Cmd. 8606, Cmd. 9001, Cmd. 9002, Cmd. 9085, Cmd. 9099, and Cmd. 9153.

[104] *Report of the Provisional Joint Committee to the meeting of the Industrial Conference,* April 4, 1919 (Cmd. 139). See Dorothy Sells, *The British Trade Boards System* (1923), for a careful survey and estimate of the system.

[105] *Royal Commission on Food Prices, First Report,* (vol. I, 1925, Cmd. 2390).

upon to do so by the President of the Board of Trade, or when in its judgment the interests of consumers or traders require such action. Its powers are somewhat limited, but according to a statement made by the chairman these may be enlarged if necessary. One of the interesting developments of the future will be the extension of the powers and activities of this Food Council. What it is likely to become was intimated by Sir Charles Fielding, in his evidence before the Royal Commission on Food Prices. Sir Charles, who was Director of Food Production in 1918, suggested that the first Board be appointed in the same manner as the Metropolitan Water Board and the Port of London Authority, the former composed of representatives nominated by public authorities in the water area, while the Port of London Authority consists of both elected and appointed members. Sir Charles proposed that the Board should control and organize the import of wheat, the price of bread to the consumer over the baker's counter, the import of meat, and the yearly price to be paid by a municipality or Food Board Centre to the farmer for milk. The Board, he also proposed, should have power to erect flour mills, bakeries, bacon factories, and to establish a minimum guarantee for certain farm products. Whatever the future may hold with regard to the place of the state in control of the standard of living, it is proved that the state is to be more than a co-ordinating agency.

This fact was emphasized by the President of the Board of Trade, Mr. William Graham, in the House of Commons on November 5, 1929, in announcing the Labour Government's determination to create a Consumers' Council. He declared the Government recognised the value of the work done by the Food Council notwithstanding that since its inception in 1925 it had had no statutory basis and had been without power to compel the observance of the Food Council's recommendations. In fact in August 1928 the London Milk distributors refused to conform to the Council's recommendations as to the retail price of milk. The Government, Mr. Graham said, intended to ask Parliament to set up a Consumers' Council which would have power to obtain compulsorily any information that it might require for the purpose of its inquiries. The Government intended also to submit proposals enabling them to deal with trading interests which refuse to accept the views which the Government might reach after considering the recommendations of the Consumers' Council.

THE INDEPENDENT LABOUR PARTY'S LIVING WAGE PROGRAMME

The ideal of a living wage has been shown to be one of the most persistent ideals of social politics in the twentieth century. All parties within the state have recognized it in their programme of action. It is significant that the National Council of the Independent Labour Party put this demand first in their policy, outlined at the annual conference at Whitley Bay, Easter, 1926. The object the party sets before itself is "winning Socialism in our time" by a "conscious and resolute Socialist policy planned deliberately to carry us rapidly through the period of transition from the old to the new civilization." The key to the programme is a "national living wage," in which the "I.L.P. sees a first demand for justice, with the power, if we follow its logic with courage, to carry us rapidly towards the realization of a Socialist State." The demand necessitates the establishment of a national banking system, with the control of credit and currency for national purposes; the nationalization of the importation of food and raw materials; the nationalization, as co-ordinated services, of railways, mines, and electrical generation; the reorganization and development of agriculture and the public ownership of land, and the national organization of the building industry and of the production of building materials. This series of measures, it is declared, "would lay the foundation of the new Socialist State." It was proposed that "the whole Labour movement should at once set up a commission of its own to fix a living wage, representing the minimum standard of civilized existence which should be tolerated. It should then make the demand for this standard the key of its policy, both politically and industrially."

The party programme as outlined by the National Council demanded that the Labour Party in Parliament should not be satisfied with opposing the actions of the Government, but should seek any and every opportunity of asserting the demand for a living wage and of advocating the broad Socialist programme through which it alone can be realized. The I.L.P. considered that the Labour Party should make it clear that it would introduce this programme whenever the opportunity to take office recurs. Immediate steps should be taken to prepare measures for the necessary economic reorganization, so that Labour may be ready to introduce them without delay. The fact that it had only a minority behind it should not deter a Labour Government from this purpose. The responsibility should be placed upon Labour's opponents of rejecting the Socialist measures proposed. By this means the issue of the poverty of the people and the proposals of constructive Socialism would be thrust into the forefront of practical politics. The Independent Labour Party programme was urged with great insistence—even to the point of voting against the Labour Government when the second MacDonald Government began the task of revising national schemes of social insurance.

The proposal of the Independent Labour Party that the whole Labour movement should set up a commission of its own was carried out in the joint inquiry into the question of the living wage conducted in Great Britain by the General Council of the Trades Union Congress and the Independent Labour Party. The scope of the inquiry plainly indicated that the general conception of the problem of a living wage has undergone a substantial change since the early debates on the Fair Wages Clause. England's industrial life is seen in its world-wide relationships and Labour has a broader view of the conditions of national prosperity. The scope of the inquiry begun early in 1928, was outlined as follows:

(1) General conception of the living wage.

(2) Present productivity in relation to the wage standard aimed at.

(3) Present distribution of the product of industry.

(4) Defects of the present system of production, distribution, and finance, and the problem of foreign markets and international competition.

(5) Immediate improvements in the level of wage rates: (i) changes in organization, technique, etc.; (ii) the high wage policy and maintenance of consuming power; (iii) family allowances; (iv) social insurance and the extension of socially provided income, etc.

(6) The present tendencies of capitalism and transitional forms of industrial organization.

(7) Socialisation: (i) general considerations; (ii) specific industries.

There is yet another significant post-war development with regard to the minimum wage standard. Agreement is general that there is a *minimum* below which no worker should fall, and yet it is recognised that the fixing of a universal national minimum is impracticable. The problem has been seen as one demanding the co-operation of the properly constituted negotiating bodies and the industries affected, and here voluntary action must carry forward the principle set forth by state enactment. The importance of an elastic system with regard to control of wages is evident when the subject of family allowances is joined to the study of the minimum wage industry. It has been urged in both England and France since the War that some system of family allowances would provide a means of meeting more adequately the needs of the workers. The Liberal Industrial Inquiry recommended that every negotiating body should be urged to consider whether and how such a system could be applied in its industry. The Labour movement in both England and France have not seen in any system of family allowances a hopeful advance for the working man. The French General Confederation of Labour voted in 1923 against the acceptance of any scheme for a "family wage," on the grounds that it was only a new form of "wage slavery," and contrary to the principles of trade unionism. The British Trade Union Congress has resolutely taken this attitude, and the annual Labour party conferences have opposed the proposals of the Independent Labour party for family allowances.

The question of family allowances was considered in 1930 by a special joint committee appointed by the Trades Union Congress and the National Executive of the Labour Party. A majority report signed by nine members of the committee, and a minority report of three of the members of the committee were given to the Trades Union Congress in their 1930 meeting. The Trades Union Congress accepted the minority report against family allowances. Mr. Cramp, who has been always a strong opponent of the policy, estimated the cost of family allowances at £70,000,000, which added to the proposed £250,000,000 for pensions at 60 would bring the total to half the total of the present British budget.

The general conception of a minimum wage has been often debated in Parliament in both England and France. The state has accepted the responsibility of intervention, and has since the War faced the emergency of national industrial disputes. Yet it is increasingly clear that there is a limited sphere of action for the agencies of government, and the more lasting results will come from the joint co-operative action of the negotiating bodies and industry and labour. The parties within the state have before them the duty of organizing the agencies of control and co-operation, for within the industries themselves and through the accredited bargaining bodies for management and workers the most effective administration will be achieved.

xxxxxxxxxxxx. xxxxxxxxxxxxxx xxxxxxxx xxxxxxxxxxxx xxx
xxxxx xx xxxxxxxxxxx xxx xxxxxxxxxxxx xx xxxxxxx xxx xxxxxxxx xx xxx
xxxxxx xxx xxxxxxxxx xxxxxxxx, xxx xxxxxxx xxx xxxxxxxxx xxx
xxxxxxx xxxxxx xx xxxxxxxxxx xxx xxxxxxx xxx xxxx xxxxxxxx
xxxxxxxxxxxx xxxx xx xxxxxxxxx

CHAPTER VII

SOCIAL LEGISLATION IN ENGLAND AND THE EXTENSION OF THE PROBLEM OF A NATIONAL MINIMUM IN WAGE DISPUTES

THE STATE AND WAGE DISPUTES

The requirements of the War necessitated new powers for dealing with labour disputes with regard to wages, and Parliament did not hesitate to take the most drastic measures of control during the War period to speed up production and insure a minimum amount of stoppage of work owing to trade disputes. The "Treasury Agreement" of March, 1915, entered into by the Government and the principal trade unions, proposed to limit profits and prevent strikes, and this principle was extended effectively to the Munitions of War Acts, 1915–18.[1] Yet in the years after the War the Government is continually faced with the problem of avoiding a great national crisis in the coal or the railway industry by the breakdown of the wage agreements in these important public services. It is no exaggeration to say that a war condition has often obtained in these national wage disputes.

It is necessary to record the fact that the intervention of the state since 1918 in wage disputes has been in the well organized and powerful unions. For instance, the railway workers and the miners are among the most highly organized workers in Great Britain. The intervention of the state in these services has forced upon the nation the importance of responsible trade union organization and also the need for permanent machinery to conduct joint negotiations. The government has not failed in its duty of pointing the

[1] See the *Ministry of Labour Report* (Cmd. 185, 1919), which is the Twelfth Report under the Conciliation Act, 1896, and reports on arbitration under the Munitions of War Acts. Together with particulars of (1) Proceedings under the Wages (Temporary Regulation) Act, 1918, and (2) Settlements arrived at under the Coal Mines (Minimum Wage) Act, 1912. General Report 1914–1918.

way to common agreements reached by the industries affected, and supported by government action following their decisions.

For the well-organized trades it was felt that the Whitley Councils introduced in 1918 would meet the needs. There were formed 73 Joint Industrial Councils and 19 Interim Industrial Reconstruction Committees; however the active bodies are 63 in number, 55 being Joint Industrial Councils. It is estimated that some 3,000,000 workers are now covered by Joint Industrial Councils or Interim Industrial Reconstruction Committees. The principal groups of workers outside the scope of such organizations are the miners, the iron and steel workers and the cotton workers, all of whom are well-organized groups with elaborate negotiating machinery of their own already in existence. In addition to the National and District Councils there are estimated to be over 1,000 Works Committees in existence. It is important to note that the single item which has bulked most largely in the activities of the Joint Industrial Councils has been wage negotiations. The attitude of Labour has been sceptical, and the Trade Union Congress in 1923 voted decisively against legislation of voluntary agreements. Labour has been of the opinion that employers have no intention of handing over to the workers any share in control, and the continued trade depression in England has made many workers thoroughly dissatisfied with Whitleyism. Labour distrust was thus expressed in 1924: "One good result followed: "Organization of the workers was greatly encouraged, and joint consultation and action between, and even amalgamation of, Unions in the same industry were stimulated by the joint activity on Whitley Councils. Otherwise Whitleyism merely typified the optimism and superficial harmony which prevailed during the period immediately following the Armistice, just as its results showed how empty and hollow these sentiments really were when brought to the test of practical application." [2] This statement would certainly have to be revised now that the Trade Union Congress is committed to a policy of joint consultation with the employers' associations of Great Britain.

The Whitley scheme contemplated organization by industries, each established of a given industry to have Works Committees, formed of representatives of employers and workers, for handling the problems of the individual plant. Above these were to be District

[2] *Labour Year Book, 1924,* p. 51.

Councils, uniting the plants of a given district, and, for the industry as a whole, a National Joint Industrial Council to pass upon general questions.[3]

The Minister of Labour in his annual report in May, 1929 said of the Joint Industrial Councils that "It is satisfactory to record that the activities of the Councils in existence have in no way diminished." The main subject of consideration by most of the Councils in 1928, as in the past, was wages and working conditions. But the Minister pointed out that much other useful work was accomplished by many Councils, particularly with regard to the Printing Joint Industrial Council and the effort to improve the status of that industry. The Pottery Council gave much attention to research work in regard both to the facts concerning the financial position of the industry and to such matters as the problem of the collection of dust, ventilation, etc. Many Councils, the Minister affirmed, rendered valuable assistance by consultation with Government Departments on action affecting such matters as health and safety. Much attention was also given to educational work. At a time when industrial co-operation is offering new opportunities of workers and employers understanding each others problems, and both together aiding the government in social policies, the work of the Joint Industrial Councils can create a body of informed opinion which will help to resolve the necessary difficulties in reaching common agreement. Looking back upon his work as President of the Industrial Court, Lord Amulree (Sir William MacKenzie) in his preface to his study, *Industrial Arbitration in Great Britain,* attests to the value of just such opinion as the Joint Industrial Councils may help to create. "One conclusion," he wrote, "stands out prominently from the mere narrative (of arbitration history), namely that the settlement of industrial differences otherwise than by means of a trial of strength between employers and work-people is primarily not a matter of administrative machinery or legislative provision, but of goodwill and common-sense."

[3] See *Ministry of Labour Report, 1923,* on the establishment and progress of Joint Industrial Councils, 1917–1922. In all 73 Joint Industrial Councils were formed, 20 in 1918, 32 in 1919, 16 in 1920, 5 in 1921, and none in 1922. In 1928 the Artificial Stone Interim Industrial Reconstruction Committee assumed the status of a Joint Industrial Council. Cf. G. D. H. Cole, *Workshop Organization* (1923), chap. XIII, and *Appendices* for survey of work shop organization under the Whitley Report, also *Ministry of Labour Report, 1928,* pp. 9–10.

THE INDUSTRIAL COURTS ACT, 1919

The termination of the Wages (Temporary Regulation) Act, 1918, made it necessary for Parliament to legislate into existence permanent machinery for the voluntary arbitration of trade disputes. This was done by what is known as the Industrial Courts Act, which became a law November 20, 1919. Under the terms of the 1918 Act wages had, since the Armistice, been maintained at a level not lower than that prevailing at that time, unless modified by agreement of the parties concerned or by awards made by the Interim Court of Arbitration, and thus there had been prevented a sudden drop in wages while industry was passing from a war to a peace basis. The Interim Court of Arbitration, established upon the passing of the Act of 1918, continued the work of the Committee on Production which was created in February, 1915, and which fixed wage awards during the War. With the establishment of the Ministry of Munitions in 1915, the functions of the Committee in regard to production were absorbed by the Ministry. The Committee then became an arbitration body and quickly developed into the principal arbitration tribunal for the settlement of labour disputes.[4] So successful had their work been that it seemed advisable to form a permanent body to which disputes could in all cases of necessity be referred for settlement. The Act provided first, Part I, a permanent court of arbitration, to which industrial disputes may be referred; secondly, Part II, the Act provided for the appointment of a Court of Inquiry which shall make immediate investigation of any existing or apprehended dispute and give an impartial report of its merits to the public; and thirdly, Part III, the Wages (Temporary Regulation) Act, 1918, was continued to September, 1920. The Court functions in an advisory and consultative capacity as well as judicially, and while voluntary it depends upon the honour and civic sense of the disputants to carry out the awards. The elimination of any provisions dealing with compulsory arbitration won Trade Union support.

The Minister of Labour in Part IV of the Act, is given wide latitude in the establishment of the Industrial Court and of the Courts of Inquiry. For the purpose of the settlement of trade disputes in manner provided by this Act, it is provided, in section one, that

---

[4] See Munitions of War Act, 1916, Section 8.

there shall be a standing Industrial Court, consisting of persons to be appointed by the Minister of Labour, of whom some shall be independent persons, some shall be persons representing employers, and some shall be persons representing workmen, and in addition one or more women.

For the purposes of this Act the expression "trade dispute" is broadly defined, in section eight, as any dispute or difference between employers and workmen, or between workmen and workmen connected with the employment or non-employment, or the terms of the employment or with the conditions of labour of any person. The Act provides that any trade dispute, whether existing or apprehended, may be reported to the Minister by or on behalf of either of the parties to the dispute, and the Minister shall thereupon take the matter into his consideration and take such steps as seem to him expedient for promoting a settlement thereof. Where a trade dispute exists or is apprehended, the Minister may, if he thinks fit and if both parties consent, either refer the matter for settlement to the Industrial Court or refer the matter for settlement to the arbitration of one or more persons appointed by him; or refer the matter for settlement to a board of arbitration consisting of one or more persons nominated by or on behalf of the employers concerned and an equal number of persons nominated by or on behalf of the workmen concerned, and an independent chairman nominated by the Minister, and, for the purpose of facilitating the nomination of persons to act as members of a board of arbitration, the Minister of Labour shall constitute panels of persons, appearing to him suitable so to act, and women shall be included in the panels. The Minister may refer to the Industrial Court for advice any matter relating to or arising out of a trade dispute, or trade disputes in general or trade disputes of any class, or any other matter which in his opinion ought to be so referred.[5]

The Minister of Labour is responsible for the administration of the Act and he is given the power to make, or may authorize the Industrial Court to make, rules regulating the procedure of that Court. He may also make rules regulating the procedure to be followed in cases where matters are referred for settlement to the arbitration of one or more persons appointed by the Minister.[6] It

[5] See section 2 of the Act of 1920.
[6] See section 3 of Act of 1920, and Industrial Court (Procedure) Rules, 1920.

has been usual to appoint representatives of employing and Trade union interests and an independent chairman to form a Court of Inquiry. But early in January, 1930, the Minister of Labour, Miss Bondfield, appointed Mr. H. P. Macmillan to be a Court of Inquiry, acting alone, in the Wool Trade Dispute.

The first president of the Industrial Court of Great Britain, Sir William MacKenzie (now Lord Amulree), while believing that industrial arbitration is "a plant of slow growth," considers however that the Industrial Court may reasonably be expected to shape and express the increasing sense of industrial good will and to "establish a recognized body of principles by which industrial questions can be judged." He warns, however, "that ambition may easily overreach itself in this matter," and concludes that all law is the result of a process of crystallizing the good sense of mankind into definite rules. But what has been so slow in the matter of common and criminal law can not be effected by hasty generalizations in the sphere of industrial relationships, where the matters at issue often represent a tangle in which law, ethics, economics, and politics are inextricably woven.[7]

In all wage disputes before the Industrial Court and in all investigations by the Courts of Inquiry due weight has been given to the necessity of preventing wages from falling below the level necessary for an adequate standard of living. The operation of this Act has had to be carried on in a period during which there has been a downward trend of wages. There have been important strikes over wage disputes since 1918; and there have been many disputes; but the fact is well stated by Labour that the extent to which some of the disputes might have developed had the Government not taken steps to see "fair play" can better be imagined than recorded in cold print. "By availing themselves of the powers afforded by the Industrial Courts Act, and appointing Courts of Inquiry to investigate in public the merits of the various claims they were able to ensure the facts being impartially placed before the public, and to call upon the employers to refute the workers' claims by logical argument instead of by brute force. It was this fact that brought many of the big disputes to an end in a comparatively short time, the employers' case being shattered so soon as the workers' representatives

[7] See article by Sir William MacKenzie in the *International Labour Review*, Geneva, July–August, 1921.

had an opportunity of submitting their opponents' witnesses to cross-examination." [8]

Important Courts of Inquiry have been the Dockers' Court of Inquiry early in 1920; coal tippers and their employers concerning hours of labour (1920); engineering workers and the Engineering and National Employers' Federation concerning wages (1920); shipbuilding workers and employers concerning wages (1920); engineering workers and the Engineering and National Employers' Federation (1922); printing workers and employers (1922); and in 1924 seven important wage disputes were under Inquiry, including the Dockers' Strike, the Building Trade Strike and the Coal Mines Dispute. In 1925 there was the important Coalmining Industry Inquiry, and in 1930 the Court of Inquiry into the Wool Trade Dispute and the Cotton Trade Inquiry.

The emphasis put by Mr. Baldwin upon the spirit of industry and labour being one of mutual forbearance, and the effort of trade union leaders to find a working plan for co-operation with industry, together with the general determination in Great Britain that the standard of living of the workers must not be lowered, have all contributed to making a serious national problem less bitter. Justice will be done because nothing less can satisfy the nation. Consultation and conference have been used much more as means of conciliation since 1918 than before 1914. The usefulness of this new diplomacy in industry will increase. During 1928 there were issued 52 awards on cases referred to the Industrial Court, making a total of 1,406 awards since the establishment of the Court. Sir Harold Morris succeeded Sir William MacKenzie as President of the Industrial Court, and the cases have in the main been heard in London, but the Court has also sat in Glasgow, Manchester, Leeds and Barnsley. Slowly the Industrial Court is building up a body of law governing industrial relationships, but more important than this is the increasing desire of employers and workers to raise the level of their relationships to the basis where common agreement is possible.

CONTROL OF RAILWAY WAGES

The state has been forced to consider the wage scale in three great national services, in agriculture, in the coal mines, and in the rail-

[8] *Labour Year Book, 1925,* p. 78.

way system of Great Britain. The state made the epochal step with regard to the coal industry of granting a subsidy, and this was even urged with regard to the wages of railway workers. In November, 1925, the National Wages Board had before it the petition of the workers on the railways for wage increase, and at the same time the owners were asking for reductions. The *Manchester Guardian Weekly's* comment at the time was that "a decision against the unions may easily lead to trouble, and Mr. Baldwin may yet be asked to give still another subsidy." [9] In these two instances, coal mines and the railways, the movement toward nationalization is often joined with the problem of the wage scale. It is urged that only by taking over the mines and the railways can the state fulfil its duty to the workers. Between the industrial and political Labour movement the chief difficulty seems to be the agreement with regard to compensation to be offered the owners of the mines and the railways. The whole subject however is not in any form now for practical political discussion, so far as Parliament is concerned.

The Ministry of Transport Act, 1919, provided for the unified governmental control of all railways and other means of transportation. The Ministry was given power to improve existing lines or to construct additional facilities. Control was temporary, the law lapsing after two years, but in that time the Minister of Transport was given authority to fix railway tariffs and wages. The Act also set up an advisory panel or committee, consisting of 16 members; and the first consisted of 12 railroad managers and four representatives of the workers. [10] In 1920 the organizations of employees whose members were concerned in the negotiations with the Government for the standardization of railway wages made arrangements with the Government for dealing with questions of wages and conditions of employment during the period when the railways were under the control of the Ministry of Transport. [11] A central

[9] November 20, 1925.
[10] Section 23 of the Act of 1919.
[11] A very able study by Mr. Edward Cleveland-Stevens, *English Railways, Their Development and Their Relation to the State (1915)* gives a detailed historical account of the control by Parliament of the railways in the interests of the public. His conclusion (p. 324) is interesting: "Whatever the future may bring, a strong, continuous, certain and comprehensive policy of state control must be evolved, and the outstanding lesson to be drawn from the history of English railways is the danger of entrusting control to the Legislature. The central problem, whether the railways remain in private hands or be taken over

wage board was constituted consisting of five railway managers and five representatives of the trade unions and each side had the power to add a sixth member. Failing agreement by this central board, matters of dispute were referred to a national wages board consisting of four railway managers, four railway workers (or their representatives), and four users of the railways, of whom one was to be nominated by the Parliamentary Committee of the Trade Union Congress, one by the Co-operative Union, one by the Federation of British Industries, and one by the Associated Chambers of Commerce. An independent chairman was appointed by the Government. The Unions agreed that no strike would take place on account of a dispute arising on wage matters until one month after the question in dispute had been referred to the National Wages Board. Local committees were to look after the details of wage agreements.

The reorganization and the regulation of the British railways after the expiration in August, 1921, of the period of Government control was provided for in the British Railways Act, 1921. This Act provided for the amalgamation of the existing railway companies into six groups and the establishment of a tribunal to deal with the question of railway charges. The tribunal consists of three members, an experienced lawyer to act as chairman, and two members having experience, one in commercial affairs, and the other in railway business. The Minister of Transport has authority when it is considered necessary in any particular case to add two other members, one from a "railway panel" and one from a "general panel" of 36 persons, 22 of whom are nominated by the President of the Board of Trade to represent business interests, 12 by the Minister of Labour after consultation with bodies representing the interests of labour and the passengers on the railways, and two by the Minister of Agriculture and Fisheries to represent agricultural interests. The Act further provided that the Central and National Wages Boards, as outlined above, were to continue at least until January 1, 1924, during which time all questions relating to rates of pay, hours of work, etc., should in default of agreement, be referred to the Central Wages Board, or upon appeal, to the National Wages Board. The railway companies and the workers may

by the state, is the creation of a permanent Board of Control, and one as far removed as is possible from the interference of Parliament." It is well to note how this has been carried out with regard to the settlement of the wage contract.

either accept or reject the recommendations of the National Railway Wages Board, for it does not render binding decisions. This provision is yet in force in 1930. The Act also provided for the constitution of one or more counsels for each of the railway companies consisting of officers of the railway companies and elected representatives of the workers. Each railway company may also establish a similar conference for the police force of the company to which all questions of wages, hours, and conditions of service shall be referred which may be appealed to the central conference composed of representatives of the conference of the separate railways. In case of disagreement an independent chairman shall be appointed who has the power to give binding decisions. There is thus established a Council of railway companies. The highly organised condition of the railwaymen and the amalgamated railway companies makes joint discussion essentially a competent deliberative process.

It is interesting to record that the Labour Government's Coal Mines Bill, introduced by the President of the Board of Trade, December 12, 1929, creating a Coal Mines National Industrial Board, follows in respect of powers as well as composition the model of the National Railway Wages Board. But one important fact with regard to the National Railway Wages Board is the support which it is possible for the closely knit railwaymen's Trade Unions to give to their leaders, who over a long period of years have won for them an enviable bargaining position with the railway companies. These leaders have never failed to urge an increasing standard of life for the workers they represent.

The Nation and the Coal Mines

The first great inquiry after the War was not conducted under the Industrial Courts Act, which had not then been passed, but under the special Act of Parliament which set up the Coal Industry Commission, on which Mr. Justice Sankey was chairman. This Commission consisted of six representatives of labour (three of whom directly represented miners), six representatives of employers (three of whom represented mining interests) and the chairman. The proposals of this Commission, and those of the miners themselves as embodied in their Nationalization of the Mines and Minerals Bill, remain today the chief issues of this great national controversy. The chairman's Interim Report advocated either nationalization or unification of the industry, and recommended that the workers should have an effective voice in the direction of the mines. The chairman's final Report advocated immediate state ownership of coal royalties; the principle of the state ownership of mines, and a scheme for acquiring the mines for the state in three years' time together with a scheme for administration.[12] Mr. Justice Sankey declared that there was "fair reason to expect that the relationship between Labour and the community will be an improvement upon the relationship between Labour and Capital in the coal fields." The main difference between the Report of the Chairman, which has overshadowed the other three Reports presented by the different members and groups of the Commission, and the Labour Report,[13] is that the Labour representatives claimed more power for the miners over the administration of the mines. Throughout the whole discussion of the relation of the state to the coal industry the problem of a decent standard of living has been kept to the front, and the emphasis has been placed at times on the question of housing and the hours of work. The Sankey Commission Reports rank among the most valuable social documents of this century, and the Commission made a contribution to the statement of the problem of industry and labour in modern civilization. They have often been referred to in the debates in Parliament. The very topics they discussed indicate what changes have come about in the world of capital and labour. The fact that they did discuss them indicates that the effort is being made to understand what are the conditions of justice for workers.

1. *Post-War Chaos in Coal Mines Negotiations*

This principle is further made plain in the effort to get at a fair wage scale for the mine workers, as well as in the effort to make

---

[12] *Interim Report of the Commission,* 1919, Cmd. 84; *Final Report,* 1919, Cmd. 210.

[13] *Cmd. 201, 1919.* Two Appendices of importance are attached to Mr. Cole's *Chaos and Order in Industry,* (1920) the first is a *Memorandum* on the causes of and remedies for labour unrest, presented by the trade union representatives on the joint committee appointed at the National Industrial Conference, London, February 27, 1919, signed by Arthur Henderson and G. D. H. Cole; and the second is the Mines Nationalization Bill mentioned above. Chapter V, pp. 62–85, is an interesting comment on the Coal Commission and the political situation in England during the period from 1918–1920.

the coal industry of Great Britain a factor in national and industrial well being. The Miners' Federation in 1921 objected to the Government Coal Mines (Decontrol) Act, 1921, which terminated Government control of the mines. The miners and the mine owners could not agree upon a scheme for regulating wages, and in 1921 a lockout occurred in the coal industry which resulted in the pits being closed from April 1 to July 4 throughout the country. The question of the future regulation of the wage contract was definitely made one of the major points of the workers' programme. By the agreement of July 1, 1921, known as the National Wages Agreement, the state affirmed most emphatically the right of the worker to a decent standard of living. That standard was to be the first charge on industry, a principle that is nothing less than a landmark in the development of social theory. Moreover the Government allocated £10,000,000 to prevent the immediate reduction of wages in certain districts, and National and District Wages Boards were set up for the industry. Wages were to be regulated on a "collective profit-sharing" principle, the first charge on the industry being standard wages at the district rates prevailing in 1914 plus 20 per cent. It was also provided that wages were to be fixed by the District Wages Board for low-paid workers. Thus in 1921 the miners failed to obtain the principle of the financial unification of the industry with the pooling of profits, and wages fixed upon a national basis. But the nation knew the acute situation in which the workers, and the owners, of a vital industry were placed, and the best brains of the country have tried to work out a national programme for the mining industry. It is a step in advance to have the problems of the owners and the workers and the public placed on a national basis.

This was proved in 1924, when on January 17, the Miners' Federation of Great Britain gave three months' notice to the Mining Association of Great Britain to terminate the National Wages Agreement of July 1, 1921. Proposals were offered by both the miners and the mine owners. On the recommendation of the Executive of the Miners' Federation of Great Britain the Minister of Labour set up a Court of Inquiry under the Industrial Courts Act, to investigate the matters at issue between the parties. Lord Buckmaster was chairman of the Court, before whom the miners put the claim of "a living wage, which should not be less than the rates obtaining in 1914." The Court of Inquiry, after the public hearings, recommended that it should be possible for the two parties to come to a new agreement. The terms of settlement finally accepted by the miners provided that the standard profits item was to be 15 per cent of the standard wages item, instead of 17 per cent. Of the surplus proceeds 88 per cent was to be allocated to wages instead of 83 per cent. The minimum percentage payable on basis rates was increased from 20 per cent to 33⅓ per cent above standard wages. Subsistence wages already granted in certain districts were increased one-eighth and the proviso was added that no wage was to fall below an amount equal to 40 per cent on the standard wage of the lowest-paid class in the district. This agreement remained in force from May 1, 1924, to May 1, 1925, thereafter being terminated by a month's notice on either side. It was recognized on all sides that the year's agreement would provide little more than a truce, and that during the year the coal owners and the miners would spend much time upon the propaganda phases of the struggle between the operators and the workers. The year 1925 began with a warning from Mr. A. J. Cook, Secretary of the Miners' Federation of Great Britain, who said that there was no doubt whatever that the purpose of the coal owners in suggesting a joint inquiry was to press the necessity for a reversion to the eight-hour day, and, probably, a revision of wage rates. It was no use blinking at the facts. "The year 1925 will test the courage and solidarity of the Miners' Federation to the utmost. . . . By virtue of their dangerous calling and its importance to the community, the public should long ago have recognized the right of the miners to a living wage, and not allowed them to struggle and suffer for the smallest improvement in their miserable lot." [14]

So it was not at all surprising that the miners unanimously rejected the terms of the operators, which involved a complete change in the existing methods of wage fixing. The General Council of the Trades Union Congress clearly stated the important issue for the workers, and the significance of the principle of the minimum wage was stressed. The terms put forward by the mining associa-

[14] *Daily Herald,* January 3, 1925, p. 6, from article, "Mine Owners to Attack Hours and Wages." See the Secretary's article in the *Daily Herald,* January 5, 1925, in which he discusses his proposal for a minimum wage of twelve shillings a day.

tion for a revised agreement proposed drastic reductions in the already meagre wages paid to the miners, abolished the principle of the minimum wage, destroyed the principle of national agreement, making the national unification of industry an impossibility, and would, if carried to their logical conclusions, eventually lead to settlements between individual companies and their workers and cause chaos within the industry. It was an unnecessary backward step.

The principle of the minimum wage was again put to the front when Labour, refusing to appear before the Court of Inquiry, declared they would not enter any discussion in which the principle of a guaranteed minimum wage should be called into question. It was also pointed out that for the fourth time in six years the British Coal industry found itself facing the prospect of a disastrous struggle between employers and employees, and that within the six years several Courts of Inquiry had been set up, the latest only a year before, and that they saw no good to be served by another of the same kind. However the Court of Inquiry was appointed on July 13, and presented its Report on July 28, 1925.[15] It is very important to record, though the miners refused to appear before it at all, that the Report of the Macmillan Inquiry of 1925 gave official sanction to the view that "wages at some agreed minimum rate must in practice be a charge before profits are taken." "We are satisfied on one point," the Report continued, "that the workers are justified in claiming that any wages agreement which they can be asked to accept should provide for a minimum wage. What that minimum should be is a matter for negotiation between the parties. We do not think that a method of finding wages which allows of their indefinite diminution can be regarded as satisfactory."

Also it is well to note that the Court of Inquiry considered that there were other means than a reduction of wages for improving the condition of the industry. Good-will, it was held, was an important matter in the industry, and the organization of the industry must take that factor into consideration. The Court of Inquiry could do nothing to stem the tide of high feelings, and the Government were forced to avert a national stoppage in the mining industry. The coal crisis brought to a head the tremendous feeling of insecu-

[15] *Court of Inquiry Concerning the Coal Mines Dispute, 1925. Report.* (1925, Cmd. 2478.)

rity with regard to the wage contract that was common among the highly organized industries of Great Britain. At the time the railwaymen and the engineers were threatened with lower wages or longer hours, and it was felt that the defeat of the miners would be a blow to their own resistance, and would be the first victory in a general campaign against wages and hours in other industries. The fight of the miners was taken up, and the railwaymen and the transport workers pledged themselves not to move coal, if a stoppage came, by land or water, for domestic or any other use. The Alliance of Unions was not perfected, but the conduct of affairs was placed in the hands of the Trade Union Congress, which was authorized to call strikes if necessary. The Trade Union Congress represented at the time a membership of over 4,000,000; and in a period of industrial depression and widespread unrest, the Government decided that at any cost a general strike must be prevented. There was in the country something of the tense feeling of 1911 and 1913, and the National Minority Movement had helped to give a "militancy" to the workers in certain districts. The miners had in their fiery secretary, Mr. A. J. "Emperor" Cook, a militant leader, and the Left Wing of the Labour Party added its influence to the industrial section. Parliamentary action appeared to be indecisive.

On July 31, the Prime Minister, Mr. Baldwin, announced in Parliament that an arrangement had been made with the owners, under which the notices they had given were to be withdrawn for a fortnight, during which time a permanent agreement was to be drawn up. The withdrawal was made after the Government had promised aid to the coal industry in the form of a subsidy, extending over nine months, from August 1, 1925, to May 1, 1926. During this wages to be paid on the basis of the 1924 agreement. The Treasury Memorandum issued to the House of Commons before the vote asked the House to make provision for a temporary subvention to enable the coal mining industry to continue the payment of wages at rates not less than those obtaining in July, 1925.

The explanatory memorandum of the settlement issued on August 5, 1925, as a Parliamentary Paper,[16] simply announced the continuation of the 1924 National Wages Agreement. When the subsidy was granted it was thought that £9,000,000 would be sufficient, but

[16] *Coal-mining Industry: Explanatory Memorandum of the Terms of Settlement of the Dispute in the Coal-mining Industry,* (1925. Cmd. 2488).

in December, 1925, Mr. Churchill, the Chancellor of the Exchequer, asked the House of Commons for nine additional millions. By May, 1926, the coal subsidy cost the country between twenty and twenty-one million pounds, far more than the official estimate. It was a disquieting situation.

It can be fairly said that the settlement of the coal dispute in 1925 was not regarded with entire favour by anyone, the Government, the Labour Party, the mine owners, the workers, the general public. It was avowedly a makeshift, but what else could have been done by the Government? The comment of the leader of the Opposition, the ex-Labour Prime Minister, Mr. J. Ramsey MacDonald, was that the settlement was "an interesting chapter in the revolutionary effects of reactionary governments." [17] The vigorous old leader of many battles, Mr. Robert Smillie, told the House of Commons that it was not the threat of a general strike, but the answer of the House to the humanitarian appeal of the miners that prompted the subvention. Whatever the result, it was now certain that the state had carefully to consider every proposal brought forward that offered a solution to one of the most important industrial problems of Great Britain.

2. The 1925 Coal Commission.

There is support for this view in the fact that as part of the settlement a Government Commission was appointed in September, 1925, to inquire into the whole situation in the industry, with a view to seeing whether it could not be put into a better economic position. The terms of reference of the Coal Commission were the widest possible terms: "To inquire into and report upon the economic position of the coal industry and the condition affecting it and to make any recommendations for the improvement thereon." This was the fourth tribunal of investigation set to work to study the problem of the coal mines since the War. It is well worth while to record certain expressed opinions given at the time. The Government anxiously awaited the final Report of the Royal Commission. A former member of the MacDonald Ministry believed that the subsidy had come to stay, and that the inevitable outcome was com-

[17] See his article, "British Constitutionalism and the Coal Settlement," in the *Nation* (New York), August 26, 1925, No. 3138, p. 226.

plete state ownership. He said the issue before the British people was one of principle and doctrine. "We are really fighting out at home an ancient fight; the echoes of 1893, the last occasion when the miners of Great Britian fought for a living wage, are in our ears." [18]

An observer of the contemporary political and industrial struggle in Great Britain recorded his impressions of what was going on in the dispute. He wrote: "One sees something, I believe, of what is amiss in the present position by attending a session or two of the Coal Commission. Sir Herbert Samuel is as able a chairman as one could wish to find—quick, courteous, incisive, and supremely intelligent. Sir William Beveridge is as fine a master of the art of cross-examination as I have ever seen on a Royal Commission. If attention to the economic aspect of the problem could solve it, it would, for sheer ability at getting at facts, have been solved already. But, with all the good will possible, I do not feel that the Commission realizes that its issue is at least as much moral as it is economic. One feels that as one watches the antagonism of miner and mine owner over each minute point that arises. One grasps it even more clearly in listening to the entire inability of a great technical expert like Sir Richard Redmayne to understand why the miner seeks nationalization as a solution. And one detects, I think, a certain impatience in the Commission itself when the issue is moved from purely economic considerations. The Sankey Commission had great defects; but its chairman grasped early and never lost sight of, the root fact that there is a reserve of moral energy in the miners which the present system of ownership can never bring into play." [19]

In the light of these criticisms it is well to note the proposals that were put before the Coal Commission. The owners proposed that

[18] See "British Industrial Crisis," an article by Brigadier General the Rt. Hon. Lord Thomson, in *Proceedings of the Academy of Political Science,* vol. XI (January, 1926), No. 4, pp. 163–168. Cf. *Coal & Power,* the Report of an Inquiry presided over by the Rt. Hon. D. Lloyd George, 1924, with appendix on "Housing Conditions in Mining Areas," by R. A. Scot-Jones. This Report indicates the major problems and the solution of a recognized group. This Report and the 1928 Liberal Yellow Book should be taken together.

[19] See article of Mr. Harold J. Laski, "Great Britain and the Communists," in the *Nation* (New York), January 6, 1926, vol. XLV, no. 579, pp. 183–184, and his article in the same weekly, December 16, 1925, "Mr. Baldwin's First Year," for the quotation above (p. 104). Cf. *Labour Year Book, 1927,* pp. 200–204, and *Labour Year Book, 1928,* pp. 196–197, 200–202.

the industry should be left alone to seek its own salvation with the help of longer working hours, drastically reduced wages, and a large reduction in railway rates at the expense of railwaymen's wages. It has been well said that this plan that holds out no prospect of peace for the industry, and its economic wisdom is equally questionable. Sir Herbert Samuel, the chairman, said that the scheme meant that even if all the coal owners' expectations were fulfilled, the industry would still be unprofitable, and that it would be producing a greatly increased output of coal, which, if it were not taken up, could only bring prices down still more ruinously or throw 100,000 men out of work. The miners denounced the scheme as a wage-lowering device, and they refused to be a party to an attack on the wages of their fellow workers in more "sheltered" trades.

The miners, backed by the industrial and political Labour movement, put forward a scheme of nationalization. The scheme was considered of such importance that it was worked out as the joint policy of the whole Labour movement—that is by the Executive of the Miners' Federation, the Labour Party Executive, the Executive of the Parliamentary Labour party (members in Parliament), and the General Council of the Trade Union Congress. General agreement was quickly reached on the general principles of the scheme, which was a bold plan for combining public control with the scientific development of the industry. Difference of opinion arose on the question of compensation to royalty owners, and this has been a thorny question for several years between the industrial and political Labour movement. By the Labour programme put before the Coal Commission, the coal industry was to become an organization for mining coal, manufacturing electrical power on a very large scale, making both coke and smokeless fuel, and producing, in addition, a large range of by-products. The transformed industry was to be nationally owned. It was to be administered by a statutory body—a power and transport commission to replace the present Electricity Commission. Below this supreme body was a national coal and power production council of technicians and workers, and below that provincial councils, pit and works committees. A consumers' council was also to be set up. Exports were to be dealt with by a coal export commission. Political interference was sought to be eliminated by the statutory character of the main commission. It was also intended that the industry should be self-supporting without Parliamentary subsidy. It was said that in principle the scheme adopted the main outlines of the Liberal "coal and power" scheme, but carried them very much farther, to the point of elimination of private enterprise. "Whatever its political future, the scheme marks an important development in modern Socialist thought," [20] was a contemporary reflection. This is an interesting comment, especially in the light of what has been written since 1918 by the leaders of the Labour party with regard to the reorganization of national industries. The chief argument of British Socialism today is that the state must be directly concerned within the area of production upon which public welfare depends.[21] This principle was defined in the *Memorandum* of the Government wherein it was stated that the "Government have recognized that the coalmining industry as a whole is under existing conditions financially unable to continue either to give employment or to produce coal on a scale which the interests of the country demand." Agreement on this general principle has been affirmed by every party in Parliament.

This Government *Memorandum* of 1925 simply accepted the situation. When the Samuel Commission Report was submitted early in March, 1926, it was evident that the solution of the coal problem was unachieved. The miners were not satisfied and the owners were not. Again the Government were faced with the bitterest labour struggle in England, and behind all the negotiations was the pledge of the Trades Union Congress in 1925, that its support would be given to the Miners' Federation even to the calling of a general sympathetic strike. The Samuel Report, while opposing nationalization, proposed the nationalization of royalties, organization of research, and encouragement of colliery amalgamations, which were to be accomplished by compulsory powers if voluntary efforts failed. The wage problem was dealt with by the Commission declaring that "if the present hours are to be retained, we think a revision of the 'minimum percentage addition to standard rates of wages' fixed in 1924 at a time of temporary prosperity is indispen-

---

[20] *Manchester Guardian Weekly,* January 15, 1926, p. 41.

[21] Cf. H. J. Laski, *A Grammar of Politics* (1925), chap. 9, "Economic Institutions," pp. 433–540, a suggestive treatment of the whole problem. A volume published by the Fabian Research Department in 1916, edited by Sidney Webb, is interesting, *How to Pay for the War,* especially chapters II and III. See G. D. H. Cole, *The Next Ten Years in British Social and Economic Policy* (1929) chapter VII, "Socialisation," pp. 130–157.

sable." It was declared that disaster impeded over the industry and immediate reductions in working costs were essential to save it. The reductions in wages set forth by the Commission were less than the owners asked, but the miners' representatives were not prepared to accept a reduction in wages as a preliminary to the reorganization of the industry. The Commission did not favour an increase of working hours, unless the miners preferred this to the wage reductions proposed in the Report. The coal subsidy from the Government had never been considered satisfactory by anyone, and the Commission, as was expected, recommended that it be discontinued. No permanent economic reconstruction could be based on the principle of Government subsidies.

Following the submission of the Samuel Report the miners appealed to the Trade Union Congress for their support, and this was given through the Special Industrial Committee of the Trade Union Congress. The miners based their policy upon the necessity of wages not being reduced, of no increase in hours, and no interference with the principle of national agreements. The miners' programme was met by the owners' attitude of resistance to the fixation of a national minimum percentage, and they demanded that wages be determined by districts. The Government attempted negotiations with the view of reaching some sort of working settlement. It was not possible. The negotiations failed. On April 30, 1926, the Government subsidy to the coal industry ceased, and on that date the miners were locked out. In the House of Commons on May 3, the Prime Minister made a full statement of the negotiations, declaring the Government's efforts had failed to bring about a settlement. The sympathetic strike, the "General Strike of 1926," began on May 4, and was terminated by the General Council of the Trade Union Congress on May 12. The whole nation was stirred by the General Strike. Its effects were and will be far reaching on the political and industrial labour movement. This is not the place to discuss the effects of that unprecedented event, but the action of the Government and the attitude of Labour may best be given in the sections dealing with industrial unrest and the Trade Union Act of 1927.

The collapse of the General Strike did not bring to an end the struggle of the miners against the owners. Government and owners' proposals were rejected by the miners, and the dispute continued until November, 1926, when the miners accepted terms which called for the settlement of wages by districts. This meant that no national agreement could be made. The struggle from 1921—even from 1911 —has been uninterrupted. The post-war labour anarchy in the coal mines has been taken as the symbolic issue of the industrial conflict going on in Great Britain. The Government Reports have been submitted, Labour has set forth its policy and the owners have given their side of the case. The nation has tried to make up its mind as to what can be done. At best it is certain that the suffering of men and women and children has not gone unnoticed, for the whole nation has refused to let the unsettled coal policy keep back the hand of charity. But that is not a solution, nor is chaotic disorganization a situation that can long continue. But it may be that the desperate events since 1921 in the coal mines, the long days of Commission hearings, and the studies of individuals and political parties, may suggest a way out of the deadlock which the nation will finally break compulsorily if men do not voluntarily find a basis of settlement.

3.   *The Coal Mines Bill of the Labour Government.*

The Coal Mines Bill of the Labour Government was one more compromise effort between compulsory and voluntary agreement. It was certain that when a Labour Government went into office that they would be obligated to redeem their pledges to the mine workers to reduce the hours of work and to support a policy of a minimum wage. Soon after the second Labour Government was formed in June, 1929 the Government were in consultation with representatives of the Mining Association, speaking for the great bulk of the colliery proprietors of Great Britain, and the representatives of the miners. The Labour Government took an increasing interest in the international aspects of the British coal situation, even taking their problem to Geneva, and succeeding in having the International Labour Office call a conference early in 1930 to consider the problems of the European coal market. This was not an unenlightened policy of British Labour dealing with a great industrial question.

The complexity of the problem is not necessary to suggest, for it has baffled the successive Governments of England since 1918. A Labour Government could not hope to escape it. On December 17, 1929, the President of the Board of Trade, Mr. Graham, moved the second reading of the Government's Coal Mines Bill, a measure described as one "to provide for regulating and facilitating the production, supply, and sale of coal by owners of coal-mines; for the temporary amendment of section three of the Coal Mines Regulation Act, 1908; for the constitution and functions of a Coal Mines National Industrial Board; and for purposes connected with the matters aforesaid." The Bill was in four parts. Part I, consisting of eight clauses, proposed to regulate the production, supply, and sale of coal by means of a central co-ordinating scheme for the whole of Great Britain and district schemes for all colliery districts, and these schemes, when approved or made by the Board of Trade, were to have statutory effect. The Memorandum explanatory of the Bill gave the complicated detail of the scheme. The reduction of hours was the intent of Part II of the Bill, a single clause, which proposed that during the continuance of the Coal Mines Act, 1926, the extra hour which it allowed over the 1908 Act, be reduced to half an hour. Part III, likewise of one clause, would authorize the Board of Trade to set up a Coal Mines National Industrial Board with powers to investigate and report upon any disputes to the terms of a proposed agreement for the regulation of the wages or other conditions of colliery workers in any district where there has been a failure to settle the dispute in accordance with any arrangements in force in the district. Part IV of the Bill dealt with general provisions. The Bill which is now (February, 1930) before Parliament can of course be sketched here only under correction of Parliament's final action.

The significance of the Government measure for this study is that it marked another effort to establish a great national industry on a firm basis, and to protect the rights of the workers, the owners and the nation. The Government did not fulfil in the Bill the pledge of a seven hour day for the miners, but the wage standard was not molested, and provision for a Coal Mines National Industrial Board was included to aid in regulation of "the wages or other conditions of colliery workers." The President of the Board of Trade in his long explanation of the Bill before Parliament included this in his defence of the measure. He urged that the half-hour reduction time could be secured without any inroad on the level of wages, which, he said, "I have never heard a single soul defend, and which runs down to something like 35s., 39s., and £2 a week, or very little more than that, except in certain classes of coal production, and which is bound up with distress and humiliation in these colliery districts which no words of mine this afternoon could properly describe." The coal-owners have never lacked a human appeal in their distress.

The importance of the Labour Government's Coal Mines Bill is again in the confirmation that it gives to the established policy of the English method of intervention in the settlement of trade disputes affecting wages. Slowly the determined intent of social control takes form, and the British method of compromise is made plain. The compromise by the Labour party in bringing forward a Bill which was not what they had promised indicated a Parliamentary sense which their Left wing cannot share. It is again a vindication of the principle by which Sir William Beveridge has summarized the change in the wage contract from an unconditioned to a conditioned contract. This began when the government legalized the action of Trade Unions, and was officially sanctioned in the Fair Wages Clause in the public contracts. The intervention of state action in the twentieth century has been plainly marked, as the legislation surveyed in the last two chapters proves. The Trade Boards Acts, 1909–1918, the Miners' Minimum Wage Act, 1912, the Corn Production and Agricultural Wages Acts, 1917–1924 have been far-reaching in their settlement of wages. Professor Clay has classified the whole of British effort in his statement that actual fixing of wages is left always to a joint body representative of the parties of the wage contract.[22] "Thus, the state policy may be said to have been to encourage, assist, supplement, and, if necessary, compel collective bargaining, but always to avoid the responsibility of directly settling the value of any kind of labour by Act of Parliament or Departmental action. The regulative aspects offers fewest problems, because this country has the longest experience of state regulation of industrial conditions and has done most to devise a technique of regulation. Careful drafting of detailed regulations after consultation with trade representatives, and adequate inspection by a specialized inspectorate are the chief requirements." Such a policy makes it possible also for the workers and the employers to develop a common responsibility for their own wage policy, and as both workers' and employers' organizations become better equipped to adjust their differences among themselves, the gain to the whole community will

[22] See *Public Administration*, vol. IV. No. 3 (July 1926), Professor Clay surveys state policy with regard to wages in England.

be manifest. The established standards today of effectively organized Trade Unions indicate the progress of the social ideal of a satisfactory standard of life. It has been necessary, as this survey has shown, to bring to the support of the workers the power of the national government. The future may reveal less need of Parliamentary action, for the very forces which create a better standard of life help to establish the secure strength for its maintenance.

CHAPTER VIII

THE REACTION TO SOCIAL LEGISLATION: THE CONSTITUTIONAL CRISIS AND THE BUDGET OF 1909 WITH REFERENCE TO SOCIAL LEGISLATION

There is much discussion today of the cost of social services through state agencies, and especially is there criticism of the extension of the national insurance system. State policy with regard to unemployment has particularly been condemned. A good deal of this criticism is reminiscent of the years in which the national insurance system of England was being put upon the statute book for the first time. Before taking up the final phase of the comprehensive Liberal programme of social legislation as represented in the national insurance system inaugurated in 1911, it is well to record the struggle in Parliament over the Budget of 1909. This historic Parliamentary battle sharply separates the period of the early development of England's public social services from the expanding era of social legislation when the framers of Budgets became the dictators of social policy. This period of 1909–1911 which is given supplies the necessary background for the introduction of the national system of social insurance as it was originally set up, and the final chapter on social legislation will make it possible to indicate the changes in the law and in the administration. The Budget debates of 1909 and the discussion they aroused are the best Parliamentary commentary on English social policy up to that time.

The financial policy of the state as affected by the costs of social legislation will now be briefly considered before further details of pre-war Liberal social reform and the post-war development of social legislation can be adequately presented. The Budget of 1909 marks an epoch in the history of social reform and the state. The conflict centering about the constitutional question of the powers of the House of Lords must also be briefly outlined, in so far as it, like the Budget, provides any material for the purpose of this study.

Financial and constitutional theories are outside the scope of this survey, but the controversies about the Budget and the Upper House may help to illustrate important tendencies of the time. In retrospect one writer has said, "In the scale in which we now measure public finance, the Budget of 1909 looks trivial and the passions which it aroused seem to belong to another world." [1] Things were different in 1909.

I

THE INTERLUDE BETWEEN 1907 AND 1909

The 1907 Parliament opened with the certainty that the conflict between the House of Lords and the House of Commons would be one of the outstanding considerations of the year. The clause in the King's Speech dealing with the House of Lords was most important, though Bills were announced for regulating the hours of labour in mines and for the better housing of the people. [2] The Government had gone through the hard year of 1906; already had set in the first ebb-tide of popular feeling from a united party and Labour. Above all the Lords veto of the Education Bill of Mr. Birrell, the Licensing Bill and the Plural Voting Bill provided the Liberal party with the necessary determination to make sure the rights and powers of the Commons. "Serious questions affecting the working of our Parliamentary system" it was said in the Speech, "have arisen from unfortunate differences between the two Houses. My Ministers have this important subject under consideration with a view to a solution of the difficulty."

This announcement was enough for the Opposition to allege that the Liberal party was repeating its mistakes, and that social reform would be neglected while the Government engaged in an effort that was contrary to the Constitution and the history of the nation. [3] The Prime Minister, openly declaring that Mr. Balfour was directing and controlling the course of Bills in the House of Lords, said, "I would have him remember what is the essential and inherent nature

[1] J. A. Spender, *Life, Journalism and Politics* (2 vols.) 1927 vol. I, p. 230.
[2] *Parl. Deb.*, 4 S.H.C., 1907, vol. 169, pp. 1–3.
[3] *Parl. Deb., ibid.*, pp. 18–31, for speech of the Marquess of Lansdowne, leader of Opposition in House of Lords, on conflict between the two Houses; pp. 62–78, for Mr. Balfour's speech, Opposition leader in House of Commons.

of the constitution of this country. It is that it is representative. But ours ceases to be a representative system if the leader of a party who has been overwhelmingly defeated by the popular voice at the polls is to remain, directly or indirectly, in supreme control of the legislation of the country." He added further that, "the present state of things is discreditable; it is dangerous; it is demoralizing. It is demoralizing to this House." [4]

The leader of the Labour party in his speech gave attention to the problem of social reform.[5] He regretted the omission of any reference to old age pensions and to the unemployed. He disputed the proposition that a certain amount of unemployment must exist in order to give fluidity to the industrial system. If the industrial system could only be carried on by such demoralizing means it must be so reconstructed that everybody should be given work, and poverty should be driven from the shores. He appealed to "the honourable members opposite and to the Government," before proceeding with highly contentious legislation, to call a truce of God in regard to all social reform touching the common people. They would go on with their fight with the Lords, they would enjoy it, and in the end they would triumph, but let them not forget those who had no share in that fight. Let them think of the suffering children, the aged poor, and see to it that the claims of our common humanity were met before entering into a conflict of that kind.

The debate on the Address was given fresh life by the principle attack of the Opposition, the amendment moved by Earl Percy deploring that the social legislation declared by Ministers to be urgent should be postponed in order to effect revolutionary changes in Parliamentary control over the affairs of the United Kingdom, and in the constitutional relations between the Houses.[6] The Chancellor of the Exchequer, Mr. Asquith, made the principle speech for the Government on this amendment.[7] It was his belief that the House of Lords did not really fulfil the function of a second chamber, but that it was primarily concerned with protecting the vested interests from progressive social reform. "The deliberate opinion of His Majesty's Government," was, he declared, "that we are face to face

[4] *Parl. Deb., ibid.,* pp. 78–89 (Campbell-Bannerman).
[5] *Parl. Deb., ibid.,* pp. 104–111 (Hardie).
[6] *Parl. Deb.,* 4 S.H.C., 1907, vol. 169, pp. 571–587, for remarks of Earl Percy; for debate amendment, pp. 571–667.
[7] *Parl. Deb., ibid.,* pp. 587–597.

with a caricature and a mockery of representative government." [8]
Labour, through Mr. Henderson, believed that the House of Lords
needed ending not mending.[9] Mr. F. E. Smith, (Lord Birkenhead)
whose remarks on the Trade Disputes Bill in 1906 had caused a
member to wish "that there was a little more of Christian charity
and less brilliancy,[10] warned the Government against confounding
the Liberal party with the people, and asked what signs there were
in the country of public indignation against the Lords. The leader
of the Opposition, Mr. Balfour, believed that it would be utter folly
to intrust legislation to a single Chamber working under closure
rules. The controversy over the Lords, he said would postpone indefinitely all social reforms. Mr. Birrell, whose illfated Education
Bills were consuming time and Government patience, ended the
debate for the Government.[11] Parliament had listened to the chief
speakers on all sides on this important question: the problem had
been fully set forth. The amendment of Earl Percy was rejected by
374 votes to 111.

The Prime Minister introduced on June 24, 1907, the Resolution
dealing with the relations between the two Houses of Parliament.
He moved, "That in order to give effect to the will of the people, as
expressed by their elected representatives, it is necessary that the
power of the other House to alter or reject Bills passed by this
House should be so restricted by law as to secure that within the
limits of a single Parliament the final decision of the Commons shall
prevail." [12] The moving of this Resolution formally began the fight
for the curbing of the power of the House of Lords which was to
continue until the passing of the Parliament Act, 1911.

The motion affirmed the predominence of the House of Commons
as the representative House of Parliament, and the Prime Minister
submitted that in spirit and in fact that was the strictly true constitutional point of view. He affirmed that "the second Chamber was
being utilized as a mere annex of the Unionist party", and if the
authority to speak for the nation was not to remain in the House
of Commons, if that authority was to be usurped by the non-elective
House, it followed that representative institutions must take a

[8] *Parl. Deb., ibid.*, p. 597.
[9] *Parl. Deb., ibid.*, pp. 638–643.
[10] *Parl. Deb.*, 4 S.H.C., vol. 155, 1906, p. 33.
[11] *Parl. Deb.*, 4 S.H.C., vol. 169, 1907, pp. 661–668.
[12] *Parl. Deb.*, 4 S.H.C., 1907, vol. 176, pp. 909–926.

secondary place. It was proposed that if a Bill was sent up to the other House, and the two Houses found agreement impossible, a conference should be held between members appointed in equal numbers by the two Houses. The conference would be of small dimensions, its proceedings private, and its object would be to enable each party to negotiate and to seek for a common means of agreement which the Government might find itself able to adopt. The Prime Minister stated that the policy he had sketched would have to receive statutory definition, that is, be defined in an Act of Parliament.

It is worth while noting the trend that the Government policy was taking, and what problems affecting the life of the whole people were thrown into relief by this great political struggle. This is found on one hand in the attitude of the Labour party, and on the other, in the rather remarkable speeches of the Ministers. Mr. Arthur Henderson moved the Labour amendment, which stated that "the Upper House, being an irresponsible part of the legislature, and of necessity representative only of interests opposed to the general well-being, is a hindrance to national progress and ought to be abolished." [13]

The Under-Secretary of State for the Colonies, Mr. Winston Churchill, expressed in somewhat colourful manner one point of view in the debate. He stated that "in the main the lines of difference between the two parties are social and economic—in the main the lines of difference are increasingly becoming the lines of cleavage between the rich and the poor. Let that animate us in the great struggle which we are now undertaking, and in which we shall without rest press forward, confident of this, that, if we persevere we shall wrest from the hands of privilege and wealth the evil and sinister weapon of the Peers' veto which they have used so ill and so long." [14]

The speech of Mr. Lloyd George was peculiarly a setting for the struggles that he entered into two years later, for his taxation programme could be deduced from the remarks that he made on property and capital.[15] The resolution was carried by 432 votes

---

[13] *Parl. Deb.*, 4 S.H.C., 1907, vol. 176, pp. 1193–1202 (Henderson) ; pp. 941–947 (Shackelton).

[14] *Parl. Deb., ibid.*, pp. 1240–1254.

[15] *Parl. Deb., ibid.*, pp. 1420–1435.

against 147.[16] From that time the controversy was carried forward with increasing bitterness and recrimination. Out of the political turmoil which it occasioned there will be found some contribution made of the problems with which this study is concerned.

II

THE BUDGET OF 1909

The Budget of 1909 was introduced on April 29, 1909, by the Chancellor of the Exchequer, Mr. Lloyd George.[17] The Financial proposals submitted were under discussion in all seventy-two Parliamentary days, including several all-night sittings. On November 4 the Budget was passed by a majority of 230 votes. The Budget proposals were based on the common ground between the parties that the state urgently needed sixteen additional millions of money for the year. Tax expenditure on the Navy and Old Age Pensions were the major cause of the increased expenditure. The increased expenditure under both these heads, the Chancellor stated in his address— and this is an important point—was substantially incurred with the unanimous assent of all political parties in Parliament. What is more this "War Budget", as Mr. Lloyd George called it, against poverty, and social degradation, sought to make provision for old age pensions, general elementary education, labour exchanges, town planning and rural development. It had to provide for the maintenance of the whole machinery of administration set up by the social measures of the century, especially since 1905. It was this necessity that faced the Chancellor of the Exchequer. His closing words, after four and a half hours, were typical of the man and reveal the purpose of the Budget: "This, Mr. Emmot, is a War Budget. It is for raising money to wage implacable warfare against poverty and squalidness. I cannot help hoping and believing that before this

[16] *Parl. Deb., ibid.,* for the whole discussion on the Resolution: pp. 909–1011; 1157–1254; and, 1409–1524. Note especially the speeches of Lord Robert Cecil (1176–1184); Sir William Anson (997–1003); Mr. F. E. Smith (1435–1443); and Mr. Asquith (1506–1514).

[17] *Parl. Deb.,* 5 S.H.C., 1909, vol. 4, pp. 472–548. The speeches made by Mr. Lloyd George on the Land Question in 1925–1926 and in the Liberal Party campaign of 1928–1929 were reminiscent of the Budget speeches of 1909 and 1910.

generation has passed away we shall have advanced a great step towards that good time when poverty, and the wretchedness and human degradation which always follow in its camp will be as remote to the people of this country as the wolves which once infested its forests."

Old Age Pensions came first as the social measure which bore heaviest on the exchequer. For this, Mr. Lloyd George declared, "we simply honoured a cheque drawn years ago in favour of the aged poor, which bore at its foot the signature of all the leaders of political parties in this country." It was only one of the pressing social problems. "What the Government have to ask themselves is this: Can the whole subject of further social reform be postponed until the increasing demands made upon the National Exchequer by the growth of armaments have ceased? Not merely *can* it be postponed, but ought it to be postponed? Is there the slightest hope that if we deferred consideration of the matter, we are likely within a generation to find any more favourable moment for attending to it? And we have to ask ourselves this further question: If we put off dealing with these social sores, are the evils which arise from them not likely to grow and to fester, until finally the loss which the country sustains will be infinitely greater than anything it would have to bear in paying the cost of an immediate remedy?" [18]

That was a principle on which "the first democratic Budget" was based. No one can mistake the humanity of the further appeal of the Chancellor: "There are hundreds of thousands of men, women and children in this country now enduring hardships for which the sternest judge would not hold them responsible; hardships entirely due to circumstances over which they have not the slightest command; the fluctuations and changes of trade, even of fashions; ill-health and the premature breakdown or death of the breadwinner. Owing to events of this kind, all of them beyond human control—at any rate beyond the control of the victims—thousands, and I am not sure millions, are precipitated into a condition of acute distress and poverty. How many people there are of this kind in this wealthy land the figures as to the Old Age Pensions have thrown a very unpleasant light upon. Is it fair, is it just, is it humane, is it honourable, is it safe to subject such a multitude of our poor fellow-countrymen

---

[18] *Parl. Deb., ibid.,* pp. 481–494, for the social reform sections.

and countrywomen to continued endurance of these miseries until
nations have learnt wisdom not to squander their resources on these
huge machines for destruction of human life? I have no doubt as to
the answer which will be given to the question by a nation as rich in
humanity as it is in store."

Provision had to be made for those out of work through no fault
of their own; any pauper disqualifications from Old Age Pensions
must be removed; voluntary and compulsory systems of insurance
had to be considered; the Government pledge to deal on a comprehensive scale with unemployment had to be carried out through insurance against unemployment and a national system of labour exchanges. Mr. Lloyd George saw only one way to meet the financial
demands of reform; a radical application of the principle of direct
taxation—graduated income tax, super-tax, tax on the unearned
increment, and tax on undeveloped property. There was also to be
a readjustment of the indirect taxes, especially the licensing duties,
with a view to equalizing the financial burden among the various
classes in the community.

The Chancellor of the Exchequer believed that the greatest provision of all for unemployment was contained in the land clauses of
the Budget,[19] the provisions of which "must have the effect eventually
of destroying the selfish and stupid monopoly which now so egre-
giously mismanages the land." [20] It was this phase of the Budget
with its graduation of real estate duties and income tax, its distinction between earned and unearned income, which most successfully aroused the Opposition. One student has said, "Old Age
Pensions, Trade Boards, Labour Exchanges, Small Holdings,
Housing and Town Planning, all these measures might have been
overlooked, but the policy which places the control of industry in
the hands of the people and provides equal opportunity for self-
development, which asserts the claims of the state to a share of the
unearned increment, is a policy which had aroused the Opposition,
finally culminating in the revolt of the Lords and an attempt to
assert their supremacy. The famous Budget of Mr. Lloyd George

[19] Clauses 1-42, Part 1, the Finance Bill, 1909.
[20] D. Lloyd George, Preface, p. xi, to *The People's Budget*, a collection of
the speeches explaining and defending the provisions of the Budget. On this
point see also C. F. G. Masterman, *The Condition of England* (1909), the parts
dealing with rural conditions and agricultural labourers.

disciminated between income that is earned and income that is unearned." [21]

It was no wonder that Sir Frederick Banbury denounced it as "the maddest Budget ever introduced in the House of Commons," [22] saying that "for two hours we have listened to every Radical fad which I have ever heard enumerated, but which had nothing to do with the Budget Question." [23] The debate immediately after the Budget statement revealed the stunned condition of a good number of the members of Parliament. Mr. Austen Chamberlain and Mr. Balfour expressed the views of the Opposition, the latter dealing especially with the land values tax.[24] For the Labour Party Mr. Barnes declared, "we of the Labour Party will give a steady and consistent support to the Government in all the steps necessary to carry this Budget into effect." [25] The Postmaster General,[26] Mr. Buxton, spoke after Mr. Balfour, and in ending the discussion the Government was represented by Mr. Churchill. How inextricably the Budget was joined with a definite purpose and programme for social reorganization was expressed in his closing words: "We believe that if Great Britain is to remain great and famous in the world we cannot allow the present social and industrial disorders, with their profound physical and moral reaction, to continue unabated and unchecked. We propose to you a financial system; we also unfold a policy of social reorganization which will demand sacrifice from all classes but which will give security to all classes. By its means we shall be able notably to control some of the most wasteful processes at work in our social life; and without it let the Committee be sure that our country will remain exposed to some fatal dangers against which fleets and armies are of no avail." [27]

---

[21] Percy Alden, *Democratic England* (1910) p. 7. See also J. A. Hobson's *Industrial System* (1909), for a discussion of the relation of unearned increment and unemployment and the right of the state to the unearned surplus. Note speech of Mr. Churchill at Leicester on September 4, *Times,* September 6, 1909, p. 5.

[22] *Parl. Deb.,* 5 S., 1909, 4 H.C., p. 589.

[23] *Parl. Deb., ibid.,* p. 583, entire speech, pp. 583–589.

[24] *Parl. Deb.,* 5 S., 1909, 4 H.C., pp. 549–566 (Chamberlain); pp. 749–773 (Balfour).

[25] *Parl. Deb., ibid.,* p. 795; pp. 794–806, complete speech; pp. 579–583, for speech of the Irish Nationalist leader Mr. Redmond.

[26] *Parl. Deb., ibid.,* pp. 773–794.

[27] *Parl. Deb., ibid.,* p. 854; pp. 843–854; complete discussion on presentation of Budget, pp. 472–604, and pp. 749–854.

The general principles of the Budget were debated for three days, May 3–5, at which time the major tendencies of social politics between 1900–1909 were discussed.[28] "It is Socialism and nothing else which is the foundation of this Budget," one speaker declared;[29] while Lord Hugh Cecil said he could not believe "it is right to use taxation for the purpose of advancing the morality of temperance faddists or the prejudice of Radical politicians."[30] The speech of Mr. Snowden on May 5 was one of the strongest defences of the Budget, containing a wealth of detail relating to the social aspects of English life that the Budget touched upon.[31] It was this character of the Budget that appealed most strongly to Labour, for it presaged an increasing emphasis on social reform legislation. "There has never been a democratic government in the history of the world," Mr. Snowden said, "and we are just beginning to evolve a democratic government in this country. We are beginning to see what democracy is going to do to right wrong and set things right." He illustrated his attack on the social system by referring to the speech of the Home Secretary (Mr. Churchill) before the National Liberal Club, at which place he said "the condition of the poor in our great cities is much worse than that of naked savages in some parts of Africa." The Prime Minister gave for one of his defences of the tax on unearned increment, that it might relieve congestion in such places as Glasgow, where 120,000 people were living in one-room tenements.[32]

Budget resolutions were considered from May 3 to May 21. The progress of the Budget through to Report stage, May 24–26, was marked by repeated clashes of the partizans of the Budget and their opponents. The debates revealed the intense interest that was taken by the nation at large. The days on which the land values duties and the income tax and death duties were discussed are especially important for an understanding of the attitude of the Opposition to the

[28] Parl. Deb., 5 S., 1909, 4 H.C., whole debate, May 4, pp. 907–1008, May 5, pp. 1056–1124. Main speeches besides those referred to above were: for the Government, the Attorney-General, Sir W. Robson (pp. 941–951); Masterman (pp. 1116–1123); Lloyd George (pp. 987–1005); Opposition: Austen Chamberlain (1096–1115) and Chaplin (1057–1072); see also speech of Sir Charles W. Dilke (pp. 951–960).

[29] Parl. Deb., ibid., p. 908, E. G. Pretyman; pp. 929–941 entire.

[30] Parl. Deb., ibid., p. 950; pp. 941–951, entire.

[31] Parl. Deb., ibid., pp. 1072–1084.

[32] Parl. Deb., 1096–1115.

Government's plan of direct taxation. Perhaps no one better defined issues and made the differences clearer than Mr. F. E. Smith (now Lord Birkenhead). In his Parliamentary speeches quotations from party propaganda and party leaders were always apt. In one of the debates, May 10, he quoted the *New Age* on the Budget, illustrating the Socialistic nature of the Government's proposals: "Mr Lloyd George's Budget is splendid, almost as much as we should have expected from a Socialist Chancellor in his first year of office. We cannot deny that the author of the present Budget is good enough statesman for Socialist support, during the next five years at any rate. The Budget is not merely a Budget, but a programme; consequently it is to be regarded as Mr. Lloyd George's bid for the premiership." [33]

On the second reading [34] the Chancellor of the Exchequer referred to the taxes in France as compared with those in Britain.[35] It had been stated [36] that there was no income tax in France and no death duties. Mr. Lloyd George replied that in France their death duties run up from one per cent to 20½ per cent, and that in France the equivalent of the Government Income Tax was to be found in taxes on dividends, taxes on land—equivalent of Schedule A in England —and on trade.[37]

The third reading [38] passed by a majority of 230 on November 5.

[33] *Parl. Deb.*, 5 S., 1909, 10 H.C., p. 1573.

[34] On May 26 the Finance Bill was introduced and read for the first time, and on June 7 the four days' debate on the second reading began. From June 21 to October 7, the Finance Bill was considered in Committee, forty-two days in all, and from October 19 to 29 in report stage. Three days, Nov. 2-4, were taken for third reading. A review of the 1909 Budget can be found in *British Budgets, 1887-88 to 1912-13*, Bernard Mallet (1913), pp. 289-313; also pp. 313-323 for the 1910 Budget. See Mr. Lloyd George's summary in *Nation*, October 30, 1909.

[35] *Parl. Deb.*, 5 S., 1909, 6 H.C., pp. 333-349.

[36] *Parl. Deb., ibid.*, pp. 19-42 (A. Chamberlain).

[37] An authoritative opinion on the crisis of 1909-1910 from the French point of view may be found in *Le Budget*, Gaston Jeze, p. 501 *et seq.;* also his *Cours de science des finances et de legislation financiere française* (6th ed. 1922), pp. 45-56, on the Budget from the political point of view, with reference to the 1909-10 controversy in England. A more extended comment can be found in *Le régime parlementaire*, by Professor Robert Redslob (1924), pp. 68-86. The Leader of the Opposition in the House of Lords on the second reading debate, November 22, quoted approvingly from the adverse criticism on the Budget by M. Leroy-Beaulieu, who can fairly be taken as representing the economic Liberalism of his school. *(Parl. Deb.*, 5 S., 1909, 4 H.L., p. 739.)

[38] *Parl. Deb.*, 5 S., 1909, 12 H.C., pp. 1655-1666, Lloyd George's final speech and summary of Budget. See also the speech of Attorney General (Robson)

The final words of the Chancellor of the Exchequer were that the Budget made adequate provision, ample and adequate, for objects which make for the security of the state and the well-being of its people. On November 22 the Earl of Crewe moved the second reading in the House of Lords without a speech. The Marquis of Lansdowne moved his resolution that the House was not justified in giving its consent to the Bill until it had been submitted to the judgment of the country.[39] The Lord Chancellor, Lord Loreburn, replied for the Government, intimating the one resource the Government possessed—the power to create peers—and declared that the attitude of the Opposition was "a step toward constitutional revolution."[40] The Earl of Halsbury intimated that the Liberal idea of the House of Lords as an "appanage of Carlton Club" was at the basis of the Ministerial action,[41] and Lord Willoughby de Broke stated that the party, "they and their Cabinet have surrendered to the forces of revolution and to the forces of Socialism."[42]

The Earl of Camperdown on November 23 quoted from the speech of Mr. J. Kier Hardie in the House of Commons on September 20, when he said, "we are supporting this Budget well knowing that it is the first step towards the ideal which we have in mind—the absorption by the community for the use of the community of unearned incomes whether derived from land or from other sources."[43] The Prime Minister at Birmingham, on September 17, had made one of his strongest speeches on this point, in reply largely to Lord Rosebery who thought the Budget "the end of all," representing Socialism which meant the negation of faith, of family, of property, of monarchy, of Empire.[44] Mr. Asquith declared the Budget "pursued strictly and straightly into new territory the lines of historic Liberalism in the past. The equipoise of relations between the individual

---

pp. 1666–1673, and Mr. Snowden, p. 1681 seq., both the latter speeches dealing with Socialism and the Budget.

[39] *Parl. Deb.*, 5 S., 1909, 4 H.L., pp. 731–750. The complete debate in House of Lords, November 22, pp. 730–820; November 23, pp. 821–923; November 24, 925–1025; November 25, pp. 1023–1116; and November 30, pp. 1233–1342.

[40] *Parl. Deb.*, 5 S., 1909, 4 H.L., p. 755–760 entire.

[41] *Parl. Deb., ibid.*, 750–767.

[42] *Parl. Deb., ibid.*, p. 783; pp. 775–785 entire. Note speeches of Lord Bishop of Bristol (pp. 767–770) against, and the Lord Bishop of Birmingham (pp. 799–806) in favour of the Budget on grounds of social needs and social reforms; and Lord Sheffield (pp. 770–774) in support.

[43] *Parl. Deb., ibid.*, p. 855; pp. 852–861 entire.

[44] London *Times*, September 11, 1909, pp. 7–8, the Glasgow speech, note editorial, p. 11.

and the state could not be expressed in any scientific formula; it could be reconciled in practice." [45] The speech of Earl Camperdown was followed by Earl Russell who said, "your Lordships have inaugurated a revolution. We live nominally, and your Lordships will find we live really, under the control of the democracy of this country, and I think your Lordships will find that democracy intends to have the expression of its will obeyed and observed." [46]

When Lord Rosebery spoke on November 24 he stated he spoke with a sense of the "awful gravity of the situation, by far the gravest that has occurred in my lifetime or in the lifetime of any man who has been born since 1832." [47] "The Budget threatens," he continued, "to poison the very sources of our national supremacy." Of the Government and the Lords he said, "the menaces addressed to you now come from a wholly different school of opinion (referring to former Governments' pressure on House of Lords) who wish for a single chamber and who set no value on the controlling and revising forces of a second chamber—a school of opinion which, if you like it and do not dread the word, is eminently revolutionary in essence, if not in fact." [48] His hope was for a change which would bring a new Government; "we should then have an anti-Socialist Government, a luxury which I cannot say we possess now."

The Lord Bishop of Hereford allied himself with the Lord Bishop of Birmingham, and in his remarks stated that "you cannot expect an educated democracy and their leaders to remain content with the survivals which represent the present constitution of our society." [49] Such sentiments were constantly being expressed all over the country revealing underneath the great political forces of the day a conviction on English life and thought which was profoundly significant. Viscount Morley stated this phase of the question in his speech of November 25 when he charged the Lords with changing representative supremacy into oligarchic and non-representative supremacy. "The people of this country," he said, "are either of the predatory species or they are not. If they are, it is quite certain that the success of this Parliamentary operation of your Lordships will not set up any dam or rampart of barriers

[45] London *Times,* September 18, 1909, p. 7; note editorial, p. 11.
[46] *Parl. Deb.,* 5 S., 1909, 4 H.L., pp. 869–870; 861–871 entire.
[47] See also his Preface to the pamphlet edition of his Glasgow speech, and the *Times* editorial, "Lord Rosebery's Preface," September 17, 1909, p. 7.
[48] *Parl. Deb.,* 5 S., 1909, 4 H.L., pp. 942–954.
[49] *Parl. Deb., ibid.,* p. 1082; pp. 1080–1086 entire.

against the destructive flood such as would then arise. Anyone who tells you that by passing this Amendment you are obstructing Socialism is as foolish as the courtiers of King Canute. My own view about the present aspects of Socialism is that there is a great feeling pervading quite beyond the lines of Party in this country at present of pity, of sympathy, and of horror at the miseries which our industrial system entails."

The effect of the Budget on the Continent was in Lord Morley's mind, and he made the point with an opposite intention than that with which Lord Lansdowne began the debate in the House of Lords. "For many glorious generations," Lord Morley said, "England has been a stable and far-shining model of reform, and any clouding of her position in either fiscal or constitutional policy will be a gain, and a heavy gain, on the Continent of Europe to the parties of reaction." [50]

The final day of debate in the House of Lords was enlivened by the remarks of the Lord Archbishop of York who announced that he was going to vote for the Bill. He did not agree that the Bill was revolutionary. The supposed revolutionary tendency behind the Bill, found in the speeches of Mr. Lloyd George, he attributed to "the tendency of the Celtic temperament to respond to environment," a tendency promoted by the mysterious Celtic *huel*, "which makes the speaker say he knows not what, and excites the audience they know not why." He said further, "the Marxian Socialist is logical, the full-blown Protectionist is logical, we may thank Providence the English people is not logical." [51] With that observation the danger of Socialism was dismissed by him. Lord Curzon declared he welcomed the coming struggle,[52] and the Earl of Crewe closed the debate for the Government.[53] The Bill was defeated by 350 votes to 75.

[50] *Parl. Deb.*, 5 S., 1909, 4 H.L., pp. 1137–1153. He had earlier written of Gladstone's financial policy and the Continent in his *Life*. Lord Morley's account of the struggle is characteristically given in Book VI, chap. 1, of his *Recollections*. He seemed to see in the conflict a stage of the revolution from 1832, undermining steadily the old territorial aristocracy: "Today (1910) the particular stages did not matter. What was pulling them down was the revolt of general social conscience against both the spirit and the obstinate actual working of the institution." (p. 357.)

[51] *Parl. Deb.*, 5 S., 1909, 4 H.L., pp. 1234–1243.

[52] *Parl. Deb.*, *ibid.*, pp. 1243–1264.

[53] *Parl. Deb.*, *ibid.*, pp. 1324–1342. Note two earlier articles in the *Times*, "The Deadlock," No. 1, September 9, p. 6; No. 2, September 9, p. 8. Also the editorial, September 6, "The Unionists and the Budget," p. 7.

After the rejection Mr. Asquith gave notice that he would move the next day a resolution, "That the action of the House of Lords in refusing to pass into law the financial provision made by the House for the Service of the year is a breach of the Constitution and a usurpation of the rights of the Commons." After reading the Lords debates, the Prime Minister said, "I came to the conclusion that there was not a single one of our proposed new taxes, except perhaps the duty on motor spirit, in which the keen scent of one or another of the Tory spokesmen could not detect the fatal and poisonous taint of Socialism. We are living," he added, "under a system of false balances and loaded dice." Believing as the Ministry did that the first principles of representative government were at stake, they would ask the electorate to declare that the organ and voice of the free people of the country was to be found in the elected representatives of the people.[54] Mr. Balfour defended the action of the Lords and ridiculed the resolution as an abstract motion, and held that the Lords were within their rights in rejecting the Budget.[55]

The word "revolution" was perhaps the most used word of all in the debates of this period. A Labour member spoke to that point. He declared that "the Lords' action establishes an uncontrolled force, antagonistic to democratic thought and tendency. They are not only prepared to aid and abet revolution; they are actually daring to precipitate it. Many people in recent years have been afraid lest the demonstrations on Tower Hill and those great processions of the workless army on the Embankment might lead the people to revolt. No, the revolt is not coming from that direction. It is not the voices of the multitude of unemployed into whose souls the iron of want and suffering has eaten that has initiated this revolution. It has come from the representatives of privilege and vested interests." [56]

Parliament was prorogued on December 3, 1909, and subsequently dissolved. From then until January 15, 1910, the political controversy was the dominant thing. The rejection of the Budget had opened wide the whole question of social reform, constitutional reform and Government policy. The King's Speech at the end of the

[54] *Parl. Deb.*, 5 S., 1909, 13 H.C., pp. 546–558, Asquith; for the whole debate on resolution, pp. 546–578.

[55] *Parl. Deb., ibid.*, pp. 558–571.

[56] *Parl. Deb., ibid.*, p. 574; pp. 571–574 entire. (A. Henderson.)

1909 session expressed regret that provision for social reform had proved unavailing. The Government were determined to put that issue to the front as its most popular appeal. On the day Parliament adjourned the Chancellor addressed a meeting at the National Liberal Club, dealing thoroughly with the rejection, declaring that "every grain of freedom is more precious than radium."

There was, and is great divergence of opinion among constitutional authorities on the action of the House of Lords.[57] Sir Frederick Pollock considered the rejection of the Budget "the most audacious attempt to subvert the foundations of Parliamentary Government made since the Revolution of 1688," while other authorities of equal distinction, such as Professor Dicey and Sir William Anson, held that rejection to be perfectly legitimate.[58] Professor Dicey thought as a result of the Parliament Act of 1911 that the direct appeal from the House of Commons to the electorate by a sudden dissolution may henceforward become in England almost absolete,[59] and that with the increase of party power in the hands of political leaders the Parliament Act enabled a majority of the House of Commons to resist or overrule the will of the electors, or, in other words, the nation. "No impartial observer can therefore deny," he wrote, "the possibility that a fundamental change in our constitution may be carried out against the will of nation." [60]

Whatever the consequences, the Government had set out to settle the conflict between the House of Commons and the House of Lords. There was really no turning back from the day that Sir Henry Campbell-Bannerman put his Resolution to the House in 1907. The Prime Minister's resolution had passed by a vote of 349 to 134 on December 2. There was no mistaking the temper of the Liberal

[57] See *Annual Register 1909*, p. 258.

[58] Cf. May-Holland, *The Constitutional History of England* (ed. 1912, 3 vols.), vol. III, p. 358; pp. 355 ff.

[59] A. V. Dicey, *Law of the Constitution* (8th ed. 1915), p. liii. This has not been true since 1918.

[60] A. V. Dicey, *Law of the Constitution* (8th ed. 1915), p. liii. The *Introduction* to the last edition, written in 1914, is most valuable for the judgment of one who could compare critically the constitution as it stood in 1884 with the constitution as it stood in 1914. Dicey says, "It is thus possible to take a general view of the development of the constitution during a period filled with many changes both of law and of opinion." (pp. xvii–xviii.) He suggests comparison with the *Introduction* to the second edition of *Law and Public Opinion in England during the Nineteenth Century* (1914).

and Labour parties, and the four years of the 1906 Parliament had convinced them, to their own satisfaction, that the veto of the House of Lords must go. "During the four years of the Parliament of 1906 no Government measure against the third reading of which the official Opposition voted in the House of Commons passed into law." [61]

At the general election in January, 1910, the Government lost over one hundred seats, the Labour Party losing five and the Liberals ninety-nine seats. So far as Labour was concerned it had fewer numbers, yet relatively to the Government forces was more of a potent force, as Mr. Hardie declared in the presidential address at the Labour Party Conference at Newport in 1910.[62] Nor was the attitude of the Party such as to cause the Liberals to be alarmed over its desertion on the question of the Lords and their powers. For the first time in the history of the Labour Party, Labour went into the election under one banner,[63] and, while there were dissentient voices on the part that Labour should take in supporting the Government on the political issue, the support was given. This attitude was evident in the Labour reply to the King's Speech at the opening of the 1910 Parliament given by Mr. Barnes. "Of course we know democracy sometimes goes mad," he said, "but the House of Lords always goes mad with it. Democracy, or at all events Governments sent to represent democracy, sometimes do things in a hurry and repent them at leisure, but the House of Lords never has saved the democracy from itself." [64]

Labour was beginning to grow restive because it was not certain just what the policy of the Government would be in dealing with the House of Lords.[65] The King's Speech promised "Proposals, with all convenient speed, to define the relations between the Houses of Parliament, so as to secure the undivided authority of the House of Commons over Finance, and its predominance in legislation." On

---

[61] May-Holland, *op. cit.*, vol. III, p. 343. Mr. Francis Holland gives an account of the struggle over the Parliament Bill in the final chapter of his new edition. Compare Lowell, *op. cit.*, vol. I, chap. XXII, A, pp. 423–436, on the House of Lords and the Act of 1911.

[62] *Report of the 10th Annual Conference of the Labour Party, 1910*, p. 55.

[63] *Ibid.* "Report of the Executive for 1909," pp. 3–15.

[64] *Parl. Deb.*, 5 S., 1910, 14 H.C., p. 89; pp. 83–95 entire; note also Hardie, pp. 175–182.

[65] See William Stewart, *op. cit.*, pp. 290–325, on Labour and two general elections of 1910; also on the House of Lords, see J. Ramsay MacDonald, *Socialism and Government* (3rd ed. 1910), pp. 46–73.

February 28 the Prime Minister announced that the Government would deal with the matter at first by putting before the House Resolutions which would be the basis of the Bill which would be introduced at a later time.[66]

The Prime Minister's resolutions on the relation between the two Houses were put on the paper of the House of Commons on March 21. These resolutions declared "that the House of Lords be disabled by law from rejecting or amending a Money Bill, and that the powers of the House of Lords as respects Bills, other than Money Bills, be restricted by Law so that any such Bill which has passed the House of Commons in three successive sessions . . . shall become Law without the consent of the House of Lords on the Royal Assent being declared; provided that at least two years shall have elapsed between the date of the first introduction of the Bill in the House of Commons and the date on which it passes the House of Commons for the third time." A final resolution added, "that it is expedient to limit the duration of Parliament to five years." "We put them forward," Mr. Asquith said on March 29, "as the first and indispensable step to the emancipation of the House of Commons, and to preserve from something like paralysis the principles of popular government. . . . The absolute veto of the Lords must follow the veto of the Crown before the road can be clear for the advent of full-grown and unfettered democracy." [67]

The meaning of the constitutional question was expressed the next day, March 30, by Mr. J. Ramsay MacDonald, for Labour. "The simple truth is this," he said, "that in the social class and in the social interests represented exclusively by the House of Lords, is the source of much of the evils which necessitate social reform at the present moment. So far as we are concerned this is no mere barren political issue. It is a great economic issue." [68]

---

[66] *Parl. Deb.,* 5 S., 1910, 14 H.C., pp. 591–595, Asquith; Balfour, pp. 596–603; Lloyd George, pp. 632–637; Barnes, pp. 644–647; Belloc, on Party again, pp. 654–656.

[67] *Parl. Deb.,* 5 S., 1910, 15 H.C., pp. 1180–1182; pp. 1162–1182, entire; and pp. 1162–1278, complete debate on March 29, pp. 1303–1386, March 30; pp. 1471–1583, March 31, on Findlay resolution. Note speeches of Balfour, pp. 1182–1198; Barnes, pp. 1213–1222; F. E. Smith, pp. 1303–1318; Lord Hugh Cecil, pp. 1327–1342. On the Findlay motion, note speeches of Sir W. Robson, Attorney General, pp. 1491–1506; and Lloyd George, pp. 147–160, *Parl. Deb.,* 5 S., 1910, 16 H.C. The Government resolutions were carried by 357 votes against 251.

[68] *Parl. Deb.,* 5 S., 1910, 15 H.C., p. 1375; pp. 1363–1375 entire.

The Unionists the next day put forward their resolution through Sir R. Findlay who moved an amendment to the effect that the House was willing to consider proposals for the reform of the existing Second Chamber, but declined to proceed with proposals which would destroy the usefulness of any Second Chamber, and would remove the safeguard against changes by a Government without the consent, and against the wishes of the electorate.[69] This resolution called forth one of the most spirited of the Ministerial defences, Mr. Churchill claiming that the Conservatives would reduce the Liberal Party to impotency by their control of the House of Lords. He gave justification of the party system, which had been the favourite theme of attack for Mr. Belloc and Mr. Harold Cox.[70] When the Conservative object had been attained, Mr. Churchill said, "do not suppose, do not let honourable gentlemen opposite suppose, that thereby they will have escaped from the democratic movement. Those who are now grouped under the standard of party will re-form themselves under the standards of class. The class line must become, if the party system is shattered, the line of demarcation." [71]

The Prime Minister on April 5 moved the resolution for allocation of time on the resolutions which the Government had put before the House.[72] The first resolution was introduced by Mr. Haldane.[73] From April 11–14, the Committee considered the rights of the House of Lords on Bills other than Money Bills, the duration of Parliament and votes on general legislation.[74] On April 14 the Parliament Bill, 1910, based on the resolutions, was introduced by the Prime Minister, who declared that if the Lords refused to

[69] *Parl. Deb.*, 5 S., 1910, 15 H.C., pp. 1471–1494. The mover declared that "the new Liberalism was intellectually bankrupt." Mr. Lloyd George, *Parl. Deb.*, 5 S., 1910, pp. 147–160, gave a full summary of the action of the House of Lords since 1900 on legislation passed by the Commons.

[70] The day after Parliament met, 1910, Lord Rosebery presided at a dinner given to Mr. Cox, by the British Constitutional Association. In reply to his speech Mr. Cox attacked the tyranny of the two-party system and urged the rescue of the country from the growing despotism of the State. (*Annual Register, 1910*, p. 18.)

[71] *Parl. Deb.*, 5 S., 1910 15 H.C., p. 1582; pp. 1567–1683 entire.

[72] *Parl. Deb.*, 5 S., 1910, 16 H.C., pp. 229–382, entire discussion.

[73] *Parl. Deb., ibid.*, pp. 449–515, April 6; pp. 611–724, April 7.

[74] *Parl. Deb.*, 5 S., 1910, 16 H.C., April 11, pp. 895–1007; April 12, pp. 1082–1196; April 13, pp. 1251–1321; April 14, pp. 1425–1493; and pp. 1493–1531, on duration of Parliament, and pp. 1531–1547 votes on general legislation.

accept the plan, the Government would either resign or dissolve.[75]

The death of King Edward VII on May 6 made necessary a political truce between the parties. On the reassembling of Parliament, June 8, 1910, it was announced that the Ministry were ready to propose a small private conference between themselves and the Opposition leaders. This suggestion hardly met with approval from either side, but on June 16 the Conference was formally decided upon by the leaders on both sides and the next day the first meeting was held in the Prime Minister's rooms. The Government was represented by Mr. Asquith, Mr. Lloyd George, the Earl of Crewe and Mr. A. Birrell; Mr. Balfour, (A. J.), the Marquess of Lansdowne, Earl Cawdor and Mr. Austen Chamberlain represented the Opposition. On November 10, after twenty-one meetings of the conference, the Prime Minister announced the failure and stated that the Government had decided that after passing the Finance Bill for the year and a few other necessary measures, Parliament would be dissolved on November 28. The Prime Minister announced that it was useless to submit to the Lords the Parliament Bill which they were certain to reject.[76]

Lord Rosebery in 1907 had succeeded in having a Select Committee appointed to consider a reform in the composition of the House of Lords, following the first attack by Sir Henry Campbell-Bannerman. The Committee Report, published December 3, 1908,[77] proposed to distinguish between Peers and Lords of Parliament, or members of the House of Lords; and recommend that, except in case of a peer of the blood royal a peerage should not entitle one to a seat in that House. No action was taken upon that report. When Mr. Asquith met Parliament in 1910 he declared that the passing of the Budget would be insisted upon and a definite settlement of the constitutional question along the lines laid down by the Commons Resolution of 1907.[78] Lord Rosebery sought to anticipate the action of the Government and on February 24, 1910, gave notice that on

---

[75] Parl. Deb., 5 S., 1910, 16 H.C., pp. 1547–1548; pp. 1549–1551, Balfour's statement.

[76] Parl. Deb., 5 S., 1910, 20 H.C., pp. 82–87. See also, ibid., speeches of Balfour, pp. 87–93; Barnes, pp. 117–124, who introduced the subject of the Osborne judgment at this time; and Lloyd George, pp. 124–128.

[77] Annual Register 1908, p. 240 for summary.

[78] Parl. Deb., 4 S., 1907, 176 H.C., pp. 909–926, statement of Campbell-Bannerman; whole debate, pp. 909–1011, 1157–1254, 1409–1524.

March 14 he would move that the House of Lords resolve itself into Committee to consider the best means for so reforming its organization as to constitute it a strong and efficient Second Chamber. On March 12 a report was published of the public service of Peers.[79] This report showed that in 1909, 81 out of a total of 589 Peers, including minors and Peers kept away by their official duties or ill-health, did not attend the House of Lords, and 168 attended less than ten times.

The resolutions of Lord Rosebery were debated from March 14–25, at which time the old ground was gone over again, principally by Lord Morley for the Government, who differed diametrically from Lord Rosebery in the belief that the House of Lords could be reformed from the inside.[80] Lord Rosebery referred to his proposals in 1888 and to Lord Newton's Report in 1908, as indicating what could come about from within the House itself.[81] The Marquess of Salisbury took the opportunity to say that he thought the character and reputation and the independence of the House of Commons had decayed, believing that only in the House of Lords there was perfect independence.[82] This point is interesting with regard to similar expressions by the Earl of Rosebery, Mr. Belloc and Mr. Cox, men differing widely. The first two statesmen bridged the period of the old and the new in nineteenth century and twentieth century politics, and "possessed the greatest influence with the people," [83] wrote Mr. Lowell, at the beginning of the century; while in 1909–1910, Mr. Cox and Mr. Belloc were conspicuous, if minor figures, in the revolt against parliamentarianism and political democracy.[84]

The resolutions of Lord Rosebery were passed without division,[85] for the Government were centring their interest on the Parliament Bill and cared very little to become entangled in the efforts of the House of Lords to solve the controversy. On November 16 the

[79] *Parl. Deb.*, 5 S., 1910, 5 H.L., pp. 114–119.
[80] *Parl. Deb.*, 5 S., 1910, 5 H.L., pp. 140–169, Rosebery; pp. 169–189, Morley; whole debate; pp. 140–228, March 14.
[81] *Annual Register, 1888*, p. 58.
[82] *Parl. Deb.*, 5 S., 1910, 5 H.L., pp. 240–250.
[83] Lowell, *op. cit.*, p. 240.
[84] Cf. Beer, *op. cit.*, vol. I, p. 360.
[85] *Parl. Deb.*, 5 S., 1910, 6 H.L., pp. 232–276, March 15; pp. 277–366, March 16; pp. 371–410, March 17; pp. 413–450, March 21; pp. 459–494, March 22; pp. 683–694, March 25, cover the debate in the Lords on the Rosebery resolutions.

leader of the Opposition asked for the Government to bring in their Parliament Bill,[86] and at that time the Earl of Crewe introduced the Government measure in the House of Lords.[87] Further debate on the reform of the House of Lords took place on the 17th of November when Lord Rosebery brought forward his resolutions again,[88] and the question of dissolution gave further opportunity for party politics, and at that time the leaders again stated the issues before the House of Lords.[89]

The Earl of Crewe, Lord Privy Seal and Secretary of State for India, on November 21, moved the second reading of the Parliament Bill in the House of Lords. He thoroughly reviewed the political situation from 1906 when the House of Lords vetoed the Education Bill of that year, and set forth the provisions of the Parliament Bill.[90] The Marquess of Lansdowne vigorously opposed,[91] and the Earl of Rosebery complained that the House was regarded simply as a condemned criminal without the usual indulgences.[92] The Lord Chancellor, Lord Loreburn, declared it was futile to expect the House of Lords to reform itself from within.[93] But the Opposition had to face the country with a programme of their own, so the Marquess of Lansdowne presented to the House of Lords the scheme in the form of resolutions, November 23, and in his speech of that day he commented largely upon the value of the principle of Referendum.[94] These resolutions were passed at once, and the deadlock between the Houses and the Parties was now complete.

Parliament was prorogued preparatory to its dissolution on November 28, and from then until the election the controversy was carried on unabatingly. The result was much the same as in the January election, the Ministerialists with a possible 398 votes to

---

[86] *Parl. Deb.*, 5 S., 1910, 6 H.L., pp. 684–691.

[87] *Parl. Deb., ibid.*, pp. 691–697; entire debate, pp. 684–706. House of Lords Bill No. 167.

[88] *Parl. Deb., ibid.*, pp. 714–758, entire debate.

[89] *Parl. Deb., ibid.*, pp. 760–764, Crewe; pp. 764–769, Lansdowne; pp. 760–776 entire.

[90] *Parl. Deb., ibid.*, pp. 777–788; entire second reading debate, pp. 777–810, November 21; pp. 838–916, November 23; and pp. 924–1012, November 24.

[91] *Parl. Deb.*, 5 S., 1910, 6 H.L., pp. 788–797; see also speech of Marquess of Salisbury, pp. 798–799.

[92] *Parl. Deb., ibid.*, pp. 800 seq.

[93] *Parl. Deb., ibid.*, pp. 801 seq.

[94] *Parl. Deb., ibid.*, pp. 838–849; for reply to the Earl of Crewe, pp. 849–857.

271 Opposition. On February 21, 1911, the Prime Minister asked leave to introduce the Parliament Bill and the next day it passed first reading by 351 votes to 227.[95] The Prime Minister made his special indictment against the Referendum and Unionist support of the principle; it was Jacobin and Napoleonic, and showed the extreme to which Toryism had come. To apply the Referendum to British conditions was infinitely more revolutionary than anything in the Bill. It would reduce a general election to a sham parade, and degrade the House of Commons to the level of a talking Club. He had faith in the representative system with all its imperfections, and the Parliament Bill was only another expression of making the will of the people effective. The Labour Party leader, Mr. Mac-Donald, stated, "we regard the present Second Chamber purely as an economic expression," and expressed the opposition of his party to the Referendum because it was only a negative thing.[96] The Referendum was condemned by Mr. Churchill who ended the second day's debate for the Government; it led to anarchy, Jacobinism and Caesarism. "We believe in democracy," he said, "we believe in representative institutions, we believe in democracy acting through representative institutions." [97]

The debate on the second reading of the Parliament Bill began on February 27, and four days of debate were allowed before the vote was taken and the second reading passed by 368 votes to 243.[98] The Bill was in Committee thirteen days, three days were given for consideration of amendments, and on May 15 the third reading was passed by 362 votes against 241. The opinion of the Opposition

[95] *Parl. Deb.*, 5 S., 1911, 21 H.C., pp. 1742–1851, debate February 21, and pp. 1923–2042, February 22; and pp. 1742–1752, the Prime Minister's speech.
[96] *Parl. Deb.*, 5 S., 1911, 21 H.C., pp. 1765–1773.
[97] *Parl. Deb., ibid.*, pp. 2023–2038. Note the speeches of Mr. Balfour (pp. 1752–1765) and Mr. F. E. Smith (pp. 1926–1945).
[98] *Parl. Deb.*, 5 S., 1911, 22 H.C., 1st day, pp. 45–153; and pp. 218–289, 305–331; 3rd, pp. 389–502; 4th, pp. 565–686. Note especially speeches of Mr. Austen Chamberlain (pp. 45–57); Mr. Snowden (pp. 447–456); and Mr. Balfour (pp. 565–581). Committee debates, with Labour and Opposition Amendments, are found in *Parl. Deb.*, 5 S., 1911, 23 H.C., pp. 1815–1939, pp. 2016–2130, 2219–2350; 24 H.C., pp. 47–176, 252–392, 673–840, 1054–1241, 1369–1550, 1607–1759, 1808–1882 (on Referendum especially); 25 H.C., May 1–3, pp. 47–166, 219–397, 445–558 (Barnes Amendment). Prime Minister's speech on presenting motion for allocation of time, pp. 861–866; entire debate, pp. 861–916. Amendments considered, May 8–10, 25 H.C., pp. 915–983, 1045–1176, 1220–1340. *Parl. Deb.*, 5 S., 1911, 25 H.C., Third Reading, May 15, entire debate, pp. 1658–1786. Note speeches of Mr. F. E. Smith (pp. 1658–1674); Asquith (pp. 1691–1699); Balfour (pp. 1699–1709); Churchill (pp. 1768–1776).

on this Bill was stated by the Marquess of Lansdowne during debate on the King's Speech in the House of Lords. "It is a Bill," he said, "for breaking down the barriers and admitting the full flood tide of revolution into our institutions." [99] So it was expected that attempts would be made to again put obstacles in the way of the Government, or at least offer a satisfactory alternative to their measure. The first effort was the Bill introduced by Lord Balfour of Burleigh, on March 2, at which time the Government reply was given by the Earl of Crewe. [100] The second reading of this Bill, March 28–29, was again only an opportunity for the Marquess of Lansdowne to plead the cause of the Referendum as the necessity for the will of the people to be known, to which Lord Morley replied that it would corrupt the electorate. The debate on this Bill was adjourned indefinitely.

The Marquess of Lansdowne on May 8 introduced the House of Lords Reconstruction Bill. [101] Again Lord Morley [102] and Lord Loreburn brought out the now oft-told tale of what the Government position was on the Referendum, and on May 23 Lord Morley moved the second reading of the Parliament Bill. [103] The amendments that the Lords attached to the Bill were considered unsatisfactory by the Government, and on July 24 the Prime Minister announced the intention of the Government to advise the creation of enough Peers to pass the Bill, the assent of the King having been secured before the general election to the creation of peers in case of necessity. [104]

[99] Parl. Deb., 5 S., 1911, 7 H.L., p. 28; pp. 14–29 entire speech of Lansdowne; see reply of the Earl of Crewe, pp. 29–40.

[100] Public Bills 1911, House of Lords, No. 26; Parl. Deb., 5 S., 1911, 7 H.L., pp. 253–266; pp. 266–275 (Crewe); pp. 680–693 (Lansdowne); pp. 667–680 (Morley); note speech of Earl Beauchamp for Government, pp. 711–726; pp. 253–288, and pp. 657–718, the entire debate on this Bill.

[101] Public Bills, 1911, House of Lords, No. 75.

[102] Parl. Deb., 5 S., 1911, 8 H.L., pp. 236–242, and pp. 376–383, his two speeches on this Bill; pp. 215–236 and 369–376, and two speeches of the Marquess of Lansdowne. For complete debate on Bill: first reading, pp. 215–242; second reading, pp. 369–434, 444–486, 489–574, 635–694 (May 8, 15, 16, 17, 22, respectively).

[103] Parl. Deb., 5 S., 1911, 8 H.L., pp. 698–708, Morley; debate May 23, pp. 698–746; May 24, pp. 748–828; May 25, 839–908; May 29, 911–967. Committee stage, ibid., pp. 1031–1118, June 28; pp. 1122–1204, June 29, Parl. Deb., 5 S., 1911, 9 H.L., Committee stage, July 3–6, pp. 6–96, 100–192, 196–280, 283–386; Report and Third Reading, pp. 441–492, 572–620.

[104] Parl. Deb., 5 S., 1911, 28 H.C., pp. 1467–1484, consideration of Lords amendments; pp. 1470–1473, the Prime Minister's statement, and pp. 1473–1482, Balfour's reply. See also Parl. Deb., 5 S., 1911, 29 H.C., pp. 967–1116, for further consideration and final vote on Lords amendments.

Lord Lansdowne advised his followers to abstain from voting on the Bill. The fear that "puppet peers" might be created was sufficient however for a small number of Unionists to join with the Liberals, the two Archbishops and eleven Bishops making up a majority of 131 to 114 for the Bill. A vote of censure against the Government on the policy followed (the threat of the creation of peers) was introduced in the House of Lords by Lord Curzon,[105] passing by 281 votes to 68. Introduced in the House of Commons by Mr. Balfour, this resolution failed to pass by a vote of 365 to 246.[106] The passing of the Parliament Bill into law marked the end of the bitter struggle the consequences of which cannot yet be told. It served in a great measure to point out the fact that social and economic forces are making constantly for changes in the State and in the powers which the State exercises.

The Budget of 1909 and its rejection by the Lords was the challenge which brought to a head the constitutional crisis. The Government at all times declared that it was a Budget intended to meet the expenses of social reform legislation for which all parties in the state were responsible. It sets a precedent for the use of taxation for the promotion of political or social ends, Professor Dicey believed, and such taxation may easily become the instrument of tyranny. Revolution was not the more entitled to respect because it was carried through not by violence, but under the specious though delusive appearance of taxation imposed to meet the financial needs of the state.[107]

That was the principle on which the Finance (1909–10) Act 1910 was based.[108] When the Budget of 1910 was presented the

---

[105] *Parl. Deb.*, 5 S., 1911, 9 H.L., pp. 815–878, entire debate; pp. 815–832, Curzon; pp. 832–843, reply of the Earl of Crewe. See also pp. 833–982, 987–1077, August 9–10, the Lords consideration of the Commons reasons for disagreeing with Lords amendments.

[106] *Parl. Deb.*, 5S., 1911, 29 H.C., pp. 795–922, entire debate; see especially speeches of Balfour (795–807), Asquith (807–817), F. E. Smith (817–830), and Churchill (904–912).

[107] Dicey, *Law and Opinion in England,* pp. lii–liii; cf. Bernard Mallet, *op. cit.* the Preface, gives a more friendly view to the Budget and the principles on which the Chancellor of the Exchequer had to formulate his financial proposals. The needs of the state in 1845 could hardly be compared with the vast expenditure required in 1909. Professor Dicey underestimated this fact of hard necessity.

[108] The 1910 Bill, changed very little from 1909, was introduced April 20; *Parl. Deb.,* 16 H.C., pp. 1725–1838, 1903–2008, 2102–2200; second reading April

Chancellor of the Exchequer introduced at the same time the wider and more comprehensive programme of unemployment and in-validity insurance, nothing less than a national insurance scheme.[109] The state was fully pledged by these Budgets to financial responsibility for social legislation which the Parliaments of the century had passed.

Second Chamber Reform, as the phrase is now used, is a problem of first rate importance for English statesmen. The Government of Mr. Baldwin were early pledged to its consideration, and yet the subject is one that no leader of the Conservative party approaches without great caution. The Labour Party in 1918 stood for the complete abolition of the House of Lords and for a most strenuous opposition to any machinery for revision of legislation taking the form of a new Second Chamber, whether elected or not, having in it any element of heredity or privilege or of the control of the House of Commons by any party or class; [110] and the Webbs in their *Constitution for the Socialist Commonwealth of Great Britain* (1920) bluntly said, "there is, of course, in the Socialist Commonwealth no place for the House of Lords." This point of view is modified in the 1928 Labour Party programme as noted below. But so long as there are believers "that the Parliament Act has put into the hands of extremists a weapon of deadly potentiality, which will render it a simple matter to destroy the constitution, bring the country to ruin, and the Empire to dismemberment—by parliamentary procedure," [111] there will be efforts toward reform. There can be little of dispute that such a condition as exists today, an upper house within what is virtually a Single Chamber Government, is not conducive to a sound parliamentary system.

25, *Parl. Deb.*, 17 H. C., pp. 41–154, entire debate. Committee Stage and third reading, April 26–27, pp. 267–377, 461–530; passed by 324 votes to 231. Note speeches of Mr. A. Chamberlain (pp. 41–42) and Mr. Asquith (pp. 522–530). In the House of Lords, all stages, *Parl. Deb.*, 5 S., 1910, 5 H.L., pp. 775–815; note speech of Lord Chencellor, Lord Loreburn, pp. 810–815.

[109] *Parl. Deb.* 5 S., 1910, 18. H. C., pp. 1123–1143, Lloyd George's Budget statement; note the speeches of Mr. A. Chamberlain (pp. 1143–1153) and Mr. Barnes (pp. 1160–1164).

[110] *Labour and the New Social Order* (1918), the General Election manifesto.

[111] See the article in the *Ninteenth Century* vol. XCVIII, No. 585 (November, 1925), by Brigadier-General F. G. Stone, "The Parliament Act and Second Chamber Reform," and "Second Chamber Reform," published by National Union of Conservative and Unionist Associations.

The future reform of the House of Lords was clearly declared in the preamble of the Parliament Act of 1911, wherein it was stated that "it is intended to substitute for the House of Lords as it at present exists a Second Chamber constituted on a popular instead of hereditary basis." Mr. Lloyd George on August 25, 1917—he was then Prime Minister—appointed a Conference under the chairmanship of Viscount Bryce to examine the question of a Second Chamber. The outstanding proposal of the Bryce Report was for a Joint Committee on Financial Bills to be set up consisting of seven members from and appointed by each House.[112] Mr. Lloyd George and Mr. Bonar Law in the Coalition joint manifesto issued at the General Election in 1918 pledged themselves "to create a Second Chamber which will be based upon direct contact with the people, and will, therefore, be representative enough adequately to perform its functions." A Cabinet Committee was set up, and their report, after examination by the Cabinet, was announced in the House of Lords on July 18, 1922.[113] The defeat in 1922 of the Coalition Government ended the Lloyd George Cabinet proposals. However a Cabinet Committee of Mr. Baldwin's Government announced further proposals by the Lord Chancellor, Viscount Cave, in the House of Lords on June 20, 1927, and the proposals were similar to those put forward in 1918 and 1922. Labour and Liberal, and even Conservative, opposition was at once aroused. The Government of Mr. Baldwin carried the proposals nowhere, although they are the only definite basis of the Conservative party's policy toward second chamber reform. However, Mr. Baldwin in 1925 declared in the House of Commons that he would not announce a Government policy with regard to the Parliament Act.[114]

There was objection to the lessened power of the House of Commons on Money Bills, to the power of hereditary peers, and to the provision that the consent of the House of Lords was necessary for any change in the constitution or powers of that body. The chief objection of Labour has been that a Labour Government could not secure a majority in the House of Lords for many years, and then only with the greatest difficulty and by the creation of many peers; until that time when a majority was achieved their policies would

[112] *Cmd. 9038 of 1918.*
[113] *Cmd. 1715 of 1922.*
[114] *Parl. Deb.,* 5 S.H.C., vol. 184, p. 30.

be balked. The Labour Party is committed to the maintenance of the unquestioned supremacy of the House of Commons and an uncompromising resistance "to the establishment of a second chamber with authority over finance and power to hamper the House of Commons and defeat democratic decisions." [115] Socialist opposition to the Senate in France on such grounds has been party propaganda for years.

The lack of any definite programme of reform of the House of Lords accounts in part for the seeming impossibility of a change; yet when this is taken into account, there remains the more formidable reason of fear and suspicion on the part of many, that increase in the power of the House of Lords would be an obstacle in the way of progressive social legislation. This is seen in the popular agitation which accompanies every proposal of change in the House of Lords. At least the problem is always used for electoral purposes by Labour, which is significant for this study. Any disagreement between the two Houses is likewise a popular ground of Labour protest. It is not likely to decrease with a Labour Government in power.

[115] See *Labour and The Nation,* p. 50; also *The Labour Year Book, 1928,* pp. 214–224.

CHAPTER IX

SOCIAL LEGISLATION IN ENGLAND: THE NATIONAL SOCIAL INSURANCE SYSTEM AND ITS ADMINISTRATION

The policy of the state in dealing with the aged poor and the housing of the people developed no less a general principle of a decent standard of life, for the maintenance of which collective action became increasingly necessary, than resulted from the extended history of unemployment before the Parliament of England. The bitterness at times of the controversy has revealed the importance of the subject to many, and the long continuance of unemployment with its cumulative effect upon *morale* of the labouring classes and the efficiency of industry has constituted a menace to the nation's well-being. It is impossible to read debates in the House of Commons on the unemployment problem and not feel the intense social significance that it possesses for all parties. From the earliest debates on unemployment to the scientific discussions in post-war Britain of trade cycles and rationalization, the argument against social and economic waste has been insistently made against an industrial system which tolerates chronic unemployment. The background to today's debates can be found in many volumes of Hansard.

I

PARLIAMENT AND UNEMPLOYMENT

On the fourteenth day of the debate on the Address in 1904, the Labour leader, Hardie, introduced a resolution,[1] regretting that in view of the distress arising from lack of employment His Majesty's

[1] *Parl. Deb.,* 4 S.H.C., 1904, vol. 130, pp. 451–506, debate entire on Hardie Amendment; Hardie (pp. 451–466), seconded by Mr. W. Crooks (pp. 466–474). The amendment was lost by 231 votes to 151.

advisers had not seen fit to recommend the creation of a Department and Minister of Labour fully empowered, *inter alia,* to deal effectively, acting in conjunction with local authorities, with such lack of employment, mainly by the execution of necessary public works, and further by encouraging an increase in the number of those employed in agricultural pursuits.

This amendment was supported by the Liberal party, and the debate served to bring light to bear on the administrative side of governmental departments with regard to unemployment.[2] Mr. Hardie, in common with the well-informed Labour members of Parliament, was especially conversant with the powers and possibilities of local government authorities, and in this debate he quoted from a document issued by a Secretary of State in 1694 on the duties of local authorities. Their importance had been stressed in the series of conferences held between 1902–1904 on unemployment, and their cooperation with the central authority was specifically a part of the Unemployed Workmen Act, 1905, the one Government proposal on labour questions which was passed in the 1905 session.[3]

1. *The Unemployed Workmen Act, 1905.*

The Government altered in Committee stage the original Bill, so that the 1905 Act, while it provided certain machinery for dealing with the unemployed did not sanction wages being paid to them out of the rates under any circumstances whatever. The Act created throughout England and Wales a local body in each metropolitan borough and a central body for the whole of the London area dealing with the unemployed. The central authority had general supervision over the local bodies, and could establish labour exchanges and employment registries.[4] While it would be the duty of the local authorities to endeavour to obtain employment for applicants, they were not empowered to provide work, nor could they under certain conditions and limitations, which the original Bill outlined, allow for the payment of wages to the unemployed out of the rates. The powers

---

[2] *Parl. Deb., ibid.,* pp. 502–505, speech of Mr. Asquith, and pp. 481–483, of Mr. S. Buxton.

[3] Introduced by the President of the Local Government Board, Mr. Gerald Balfour, April 18, 1905; second reading June 20, and passed into law August 11. *Parl Deb.,* 4 S.H.C., 1905, vol. 145, pp. 459–461, speech of President of the Local Government Board; also pp. 461–463 (S. Buxton), opposition to Bill.

[4] Act of 1905, Sect. 1, subsect. 4.

granted the Local Government Board for making regulations for carrying into effect the Act provided the most hope for those who had long been fighting to bring the unemployment problem before the House of Commons.[5] But most of the powers were made discretionary rather than obligatory, and the amendment limiting the Act to three years tended to make the Act of less value than might otherwise have been the case. It has been renewed from time to time under the annual Expiring Laws Continuance Act. The Act was renewed during the industrial depression following the War but not acted upon.

The outstanding value of the Act of 1905 was that it put the problem of unemployment on a national basis, recognizing that the nation must concern itself seriously with the peril of the unemployed and the unemployable.[6] Parliament set up an additional authority to cope with the needs, and for this reason Labour leaders accepted the Act, giving their energies to enlarging and making effective its provisions.[7] The wisdom of the continued agitation on the unemployed problem was quickly manifest, for the chaotic condition of the Poor Law was constantly brought out in the debates in Parliament and in the propaganda literature on the subject. It was no surprise when on August 2, 1905, the Prime Minister was asked whether he would consider the advisability of the appointment at an early date of a Royal Commission to inquire into the workings of the Poor Law, and the results of the borough councils in finding work for the unemployed in pursuance of orders from the Local Government Board, in order to ascertain to what extent, if any, the existing powers of the Poor Law authorities were insufficient to meet modern industrial needs and conditions. Mr. Balfour replied that the Government were of the opinion that the time had come when a full in-

[5] Act of 1905, Sect. 3, subsects. a-m, for powers and provisions. *Report to the Board of Trade on Agencies and Methods for Dealing with the Unemployed in Certain Foreign Countries (Cmd. 2304, 1904)* by D. F. Schloss.

[6] See Percy Alden, *The Unemployed, A National Question (1905)*, with Preface by Sir John Gorst, for a convenient summary and interpretation of the two blue books on unemployment issued by the Board of Trade in 1893 and 1904 and their bearing on the life of the people: And Sir William Beveridge, *Unemployment, a Problem of Industry (1909)* for authoritative statement.

[7] See J. Keir Hardie, *John Bull and His Unemployed (1905)*, after the Local Government Board Orders were issued, an interpretation of the law; the Independent Labour Party issued in 1905 a pamphlet, *Unemployed Bill: What It Does and Does Not Do, but Should Be Made to Do,* and two other pamphlets dealing with the question.

quiry into subjects referred to in the question ought to be undertaken. There had been no inquiry since the great investigation of the
"thirties." So late in 1905 the Government appointed a Royal Commission to "consider how far the present powers of the Poor Law
Authorities are adequate to modern conditions." The scope of the
inquiry was to include "everything that pertains to the problem of
the Poor," whether "poor through their own fault or through lack
of employment." The very terms of reference for the work of the
Commission indicate how far public opinion and legislative thought
were removed from the Report of 1834.[8] The Unemployed Workmen Act, 1905, though unsatisfactory to Labour and the Trade
Union groups, who continued agitation within and outside Parliament, had made the important distinction that unemployment-relief
was not poor-relief, and that unemployment did not come under
the Poor Law. Mr. Lloyd George stated the matter succinctly when
he said that the Act would do very little good, but "it recognized the
right of a man to call upon the state to provide him with work, to
which the state replied by recognizing the right but refusing to provide the work."[9]

From the passing of the Act Labour's aim was to gain the acceptance of the principle that the state would provide the work or
provide the maintenance. This fact runs through the long years of
unemployment debates. The Prime Minister, Mr. Balfour, objected
to this principle, declaring it was one which he did not believe,[10]
the Government had put forth their policy with regard to unemployment in the passing of the Act which authorized the creation of Labour Bureaux in London,[11] the expenses of which were to be borne
out of the general rates, and in the Aliens Act, 1905, which had
caused in the House of Commons bitter controversy on unemployment. The session of 1906 continued the debate of the Aliens Act
and the Unemployed Workmen Act; the Labour amendment to the
Address being moved in 1906 by Mr. Hay and in 1907 by Mr.
Thorne, and in both years Mr. Hardie brought forward the question
on the motion for the Easter recess. The mover in 1907, regretting

[8] See vol. I, p. 109, of the *Majority Report of Poor Law Commission.*
[9] *Parl. Deb.,* 4 S.H.C., 1905, vol. 151, p. 432.
[10] *Ibid.,* p. 434.
[11] The Labour Bureaux (London) Act, 1902 allowed the Council of any
London Borough to establish such unemployment offices. See *Poor Law Report,
1909,* vol. I, pp. 509–510, on failure of this Act.

the absence from the Speech of any proposal for dealing with unemployment,[12] stated that 5 per cent of the most highly skilled artisans were out of work and that the Unemployed Workmen Act had proved inadequate.[13] The debates on unemployment 1904–1907, on the Address, show that Parliament necessarily had to concern itself with a problem which Labour and the workers in organized trades were especially bent upon keeping to the front of the discussion, and upon which every party had made important declarations. Unemployment gave a full opportunity for discussion of the fundamental questions of state responsibility, industrial organization and the social evils of the day; all of which brought the "condition of England question" to a place of great Parliamentary significance, especially in the new Parliament of 1906 which showed by positive enactment in what ways the state had accepted a share of the burden under modern conditions.

The Labour party introduced in 1907 their Unemployed Workmen Bill, but the Bill did not reach second reading.[14] It provided for the constitution of local and central unemployment authorities with powers and duties to form schemes to provide (a) reasonable public work, and, in default, (b) public maintenance for genuine and willing workers when in need through unemployment. The Bill conferred on all authorities large powers for the compulsory acquisition of land, and definitely directed the Local Government Board to draw up schemes for employment on works of national utility and to carry them out in times of exceptional distress. Unemployment was first brought to the attention of the House of Commons in the 1908 session by the newly elected leader of the Labour party, Mr. Arthur Henderson, in his reply to the Address; and the Unemployment Amendment was moved by Mr. J. Ramsay MacDonald, who deprecated waiting until the Poor Law Commission report because the Local Government Board already had sufficient information. Labour continued to agitate for the "right to work" principle. The President of the Local Government Board declared that the Act of 1905 would be continued pending the Poor Law Commission Report, and

[12] *Parl. Deb.*, 4 S.H.C., 1907, vol. 169, pp. 923–972, debate entire on the Labour unemployment amendment, which was rejected by 207 votes to 47.

[13] See *Poor Law Report, 1909*, vol. I, pp. 490–504, and vol. III, p. 544–546, on the failure of the Unemployed Workman Act, 1905.

[14] House Bill No. 273, 1907.

that the Government would continue supplying funds to districts where unemployment was most distressing. The Government would do nothing, he added, that would tend to pauperize the workers who were unemployed. In the division on the Labour Unemployment Amendment the Government majority fell to 49, the lowest it had experienced since it took office in 1905.[15]

This tactical advantage was followed by the reintroduction of the Unemployed Workmen Bill,[16] the Labour party being responsible for the "right to work clause," which they considered essential to the Bill,[17] though Mr. Wilson, who introduced the Bill for them, was willing to have that amended or deferred.[18] The Chancellor of the Exchequer, Mr. Asquith, announced that the Government were awaiting the Poor Law Commission Report before formulating their plans on state aid for the unemployed, and the House was asked not to sanction the principle that it was the duty of the state to provide work until the results of the Report were known. He held that the recognition of the right to work would ultimately necessitate the assumption by the state of complete control of the whole machinery of production.[19] The resolution against the Bill was carried by 241 votes to 95; however, 13 Liberals abstained from voting; "While ready to consider any practical proposal," the resolution read, "for dealing with the evil of unemployment, this House cannot entertain a measure which, by wasting the resources of the nation would throw out of work more persons than it could assist, and would destroy the power of organized labour, but hopes that the Government will give immediate consideration to the recommendations as to the unemployed in the forthcoming report on the Poor Law Commission."

[15] *Parl. Deb.*, 4 S.H.C., 1908, vol. 183, pp. 164–171 (Henderson); pp. 247–254 (MacDonald); pp. 254–259 (Curran), seconder's speech; pp. 247–359, debate entire on Amendment.

[16] House Bill No. 5, 1908. The Bill was reintroduced by Mr. P. W. Wilson, a Liberal, who moved its second reading, and seconded by Mr. J. Ramsay MacDonald. It was rejected by 265 votes to 116.

[17] *Parl. Deb.*, 4 S.H.C., 1908, vol. 186, pp. 19–28 (MacDonald). See also *Report of the Annual Conference of the Labour Party, 1908,* the Parliamentary Committee's Report on the activity of the Labour members on the unemployed question, and Appendix I, pp. 91–101, for the *Memorandum* of the Executive Committee on Unemployment.

[18] *Parl. Deb., ibid.,* pp. 10–19 (Wilson); pp. 10–100 entire debate on Bill.

[19] *Parl. Deb.*, 4 S.H.C., 1908, vol. 186, pp. 85–88 (Asquith). This is an interesting forecast of later developments.

2. Government Policy and the Labour Exchanges Act, 1909

The Government the next year set forth its constructive programme for the distribution of labour and employment in the Labour Exchange Bill. But the Government was forced throughout 1908 constantly to consider unemployment. On the 21st of October, Mr. Asquith, who was now Prime Minister, after a Cabinet Committee had considered the problem, made a statement in the House in reply to the formal question of the Labour leader.[20] This was of importance because he stated that in 1909 the Government would make a beginning with legislation dealing with the permanent causes of unemployment; and following a day of discussion of the statement, the official resolution, moved by Mr. Alden, welcomed the recognition of the national importance of unemployment and approved the Ministerial proposals. The Labour Amendment, moved by Hardie, brought again the doctrine of the "right to work" to the attention of the House. In the debate were seen the bitter feelings of Labour toward the President of the Local Government Board, Mr. John Burns, who appeared to be moving more and more toward the Right.[21] The first "Labour" Minister of England when compared with M. Millerand had not done "for the English workers what the other Socialist Minister of our generation achieved for French industrial law."[22] The Labour party brought forward again in 1908 their Right to Work Bill, which was defeated by 265 votes to 116, after which the Alden Resolution, supporting the Government unemployment policy, passed by 196 to 35 votes. Another most interesting thing in the unemployment debates was the attention with which all parties awaited the Report of the Poor Law Commission. The Government time and again stated that their policy would have to be carried out with reference to that Report.

The Labour party introduced again in 1909 their Unemployed Workmen or Right to Work Bill. The Bill proposed to require county and borough councils to provide work or maintenance for unemployed persons qualified by six months' residence, and pro-

[20] *Parl. Deb.*, 4 S.H.C., 1908, vol. 194, pp. 1160–1173 (Asquith); pp. 1631–1646 (Alden); pp. 1631–1778, entire debate on the Government Resolution and the Labour Amendment; pp. 1662–1679 (Burns); pp. 1646–1656 (Hardie); pp. 1656–1662 (Crooks); and pp. 1695–1707 (MacDonald).

[21] See S. D. Shallard, *"Has Liberalism a Future,"* The Present Ministers *and their Records (1909),* chap. 8, pp. 94–96, *"The Man with the Red Flag."*

[22] The *Nation* (London), August 31, 1907, p. 950.

vided that when the registered unemployed in a locality exceeded four per cent of the wage earners, the schemes for their benefit should be financed by monies voted by Parliament.[23] The mover of the second reading, Mr. John Hodges, stated in the debate that the permanent proportion of unemployed trade unionists averaged five per cent, or 250,000; this rate applied to the whole body of workers gave a total of 750,000 continually unemployed.[24] The Government's reply to the Labour Bill was that every workman who came under it would be pauperized, and Right to Work that its own proposals were dealing with the subject in better ways. The 1909 Bill was rejected by 228 to 115 votes. The debate on the supplementary vote of £100,000 for unemployment aid, under the 1905 Act, in this same year, was seized by Labour to put forward their attack on that Act and to urge active measures through administrative reform and new legislation.[25]

The debate on the Address at the opening of the Parliament of 1909 gave the President of the Board of Trade an opportunity to outline the Government policy on unemployment, based upon the Poor Law Commission Report.[26] The Labour unemployment amendment had again been moved,[27] and on May 19, Mr. Pickersgill, a Liberal, calling attention to the Minority Report of the Poor Law Commission, moved a resolution declaring the urgency of steps for the decasualization of casual labour and the absorption of the surplus labour thereby thrown out of employment; also to regularize the demand for labour, to develop trade union insurance against unemployment, and to establish training colonies and detention colonies.[28]

---

[23] *Parl. Deb.*, H.C., 5 S., 1909, vol. 4, pp. 633–700, second reading debate: pp. 633–638 (Hodge), pp. 685–691 (MacDonald), pp. 691–700 (Burns).

[24] See Report of the Parliamentary Committee of the Labour Party to the Newport Congress of 1910, *Annual Report of the Labour Party Conference*, pp. 16–22.

[25] *Parl. Deb.*, H.C., 5 S., 1909, vol. I, pp. 1217–1223, 1312–1346, and pp. 1441–1498.

[26] *Report of the Royal Commission on the Poor Laws and Relief of Distress*, vol. I (being Parts 1–6 of the Majority Report), Part VI, chap. 4, pp. 505–565; for Minority Report statement on unemployment, see vol. III, Part II, chap. 5, pp. 635–716.

[27] *Parl. Deb.*, H.C., 5 S., 1909, vol. I, pp. 98–108 (Barnes); and the Labour Party leader had made unemployment the main attack on the sessional programme, for which see *Parl. Deb. cit.*, pp. 50–56 (Henderson).

[28] *Parl. Deb.*, H.C., 5 S., 1909, vol. 5, pp. 484–490 (Pickersgill); the motion was seconded by Mr. Percy Alden (pp. 490–494), and supported by the Labour party (pp. 494–499) (MacDonald); pp. 484–525, debate entire; pp. 499–512 (Churchill); pp. 512–515 (F. E. Smith); pp. 515–518 (Henderson).

This all foreshadowed Government policy. At this time the President of the Board of Trade, Mr. Churchill, set forth the Government scheme of Labour exchanges and unemployment insurance. The principle of the first was accepted heartily by the Opposition, which did not commit itself on the question of universal compulsory insurance, but both principles affirmed by the Government were supported by Labour. The Pickersgill Resolution was withdrawn, and the next day the Government Labour Exchanges Bill was introduced.[29] The failure of the Acts of 1902 and 1905 was recognized, and the Labour Exchanges Act, 1909, gave the Board of Trade power to take over such exchanges as had been set up under these Acts. Further delegated authority was given by Parliament in this Act, which provided that the work of the Exchanges was to be conducted under general regulations made by the Board of Trade.[30] Legislation directly to be considered with the whole problem of unemployment and compulsory insurance will indicate more fully the powers of the state departments in this regard.

The problem of unemployment from the passing of the Labour Exchanges Act of 1909 has been seen increasingly as a national—even international—concern and the provisions against its ravages have been established on this basis. It is significant that the Government announced in 1916 that in the future the Labour Exchanges would be termed "Employment Exchanges," which has been taken to mean that the function of the state had obviously been thought of in a new way since 1910.[31] A further change was the transfer of the Exchanges in 1917 from the Board of Trade to the Ministry of Labour, which now administers the Act and may establish and maintain Exchanges in such places as it thinks fit, or assist Exchanges maintained by other authorities and persons, and may take over Employment Exchanges by agreement with the authority or person by whom any such Employment Exchange is maintained. By such other means as it thinks fit, it may collect and furnish in-

[29] *Parl. Deb., cit.,* pp. 579–582. *Parl. Deb.,* H.C., 5 S., 1909, vol. 6, pp. 994–1063, second reading debate entire; vol. 7 H.C., pp. 747–762, 1169–1171, Committee stage; vol. 8 H.C., pp. 1432–1437, third reading and passed. Progress in House of Lords: *Parl. Deb.,* 5 S.H.L., vol. 2, 1909, pp. 876–898, second reading; note the speeches of the Bishop of Birmingham (pp. 883–886), and the Marquess of Salisbury (pp. 886–892); Committee and third reading, pp. 951–955.

[30] Act of 1909, sect. 2.

[31] See C. Delisle Burns, *Government and Industry,* pp. 130–151, and Sir Alfred Mond, *Industry and Politics* (1927) pp. 83–108.

formation as to employers requiring work-people and work-people seeking engagement or employment. The phenomena of unemployment is studied in a new way by the Government, and this is indicated in the important feature of the work connected with the Employment Exchanges in the establishment of Local Employment Committees consisting of equal number of representatives of employers and trade unionists, nominated as a rule by associations in the various localities. The Minister of Labour adds to these additional members not exceeding one-third of the total membership. Regulations are made by the Ministry of Labour for the management of Employment Exchanges, which include regulations providing that no one shall be disqualified or prejudiced for refusing to accept employment found through an Employment Exchange where the ground for refusal is either that a dispute which affects his trade exists, or that the wages offered are lower than those current in the trade in the district where the employment is found. The Regulations require to be laid before Parliament for 40 days. The Employment Exchanges are also responsible for the administration of the Unemployment Insurance Act, described later.

The total number of applicants for employment registered at Employment Exchanges and branch offices between 1924 and 1927 were never less for any week than one million workers.[32] The peak was reached in the first two weeks of July, 1926, when the number was 1,704,534, and 1,715,939 respectively. It is believed that increasing efficiency and co-ordination are being achieved by the officials of the Employment Exchanges, and that the Exchanges are making an important contribution along with voluntary and co-operative agencies of trade and industry, toward an understanding of the unemployment crisis in Great Britain.

II

INSURANCE A NATIONAL PROBLEM

The Poor Law Commission Report of 1909 directed a great deal of attention to the administrative side of Poor Law Reform, and it was generally agreed that the first and most important consideration in all questions of Poor Law Reform related to the machinery cre-

[32] See *Nineteenth Abstract of Labour Statistics of the United Kingdom*, pp. 74–75.

ated to carry out the new principles of administration. There had been a change of public opinion between the Reports of the Poor Law Commissions of the nineteenth and the twentieth century. The Amendment offered during the Poor Law debate was proof of this. "This House," it read, "endorses the unanimous condemnation of the administration of the Poor Law contained in the Majority and Minority Reports of the recent Royal Commission, and is of opinion that the present administration of the Poor Law does not meet modern requirements and demands the immediate attention of His Majesty's Government." [33] The state was administering a sum of £60,000,000 in education, in Poor Law Relief and in public health services; and in Poor Law Relief was dealing with 1,700,000 people.[34]

The fact that the Minority Report of the Commission treated under Unemployment what was known as able-bodied pauperism in 1834, suggests an entirely different method of administering state aid. This no doubt was in the mind of one member of Parliament when he described the signers of the Report "as people suffering from soft hearts and soft heads, who are willing to dispose of the property of other people for the purpose of relieving distress whether the distress is owing to the fault of the distressed or not.[35] But the Parliamentary Committee of the 1909 Trade Union Congress reported that "if this Majority Report were carried out, the present Poor Law would merely be set up again, under a new name, without democratic control." [36]

But the temper of the time made it possible to conceive great

[33] Debate on Poor Law administration and reform in debate on supply, April 27, 1911: *Parl. Deb.*, H.C., 5 S., 1911, vol. 24, pp. 1980–2082, entire; Resolution, p. 1080; pp. 2024–2039, Secretary of Local Government Board; pp. 1997–2004 (Lansbury), pp. 2010–2015 (Addison). The vote on the official Gladstone motion for the Government fell to 107–48. Also note debate on the Prevention of Destitution Bill, 1910: *Parl. Deb.*, 5 S., 1910, vol. 16, pp. 780–852; and debate on the London Poor Bill, 1911: *Parl. Deb.*, 5 S., 1911, vol. 25, p. 2015 (Lord Thyme); second reading H.C. debate, vol. 26, pp. 593–670; see pp. 658–669 (Burns). Also 1912 debate on Poor Law administration: *Parl. Deb.*, H.C., 5 S., 1912, vol. 35, pp. 823–890, 903–912.

[34] Cf. *Comparative Statement of Pauperism and Cost of Relief of the Poor in Certain Years from 1848–49 to 1911–12* (Cmd. 6675, 1913); and, the scope of the problem is suggested by the *General Consolidated Index of the Royal Commission on the Poor Laws and Relief of Distress* (vol. XXXVII, Cmd. 5443, 1913), running to 1,086 double-column folio pages.

[35] *Parl. Deb.*, H.C., 5 S., 1911, vol. 26, p. 611. (Banbury).

[36] *Report of the 42nd Trade Union Congress, Ipswich, 1909*, p. 92.

changes and with large hopes plan far-reaching improvements. In
his appeal to constituents in September, 1909, Sir Charles W. Dilke
said that the Government "commanded a confident and an enthusiastic support on the part of a wider majority of people than any
other movement of modern times." [37] The Government seemed almost pleased to accept the taunt that they were planning a new
heaven and a new earth, a phrase Mr. Lloyd George inspired. The
Government programme outlined in the King's Speech in 1911
promised proposals for carrying out and extending the policy initiated in previous Parliaments, by securing the permanent provision
of old age pensions to persons previously disqualified by reason
of the receipt of poor relief; and by providing for the insurance of
the industrial population against sickness and invalidity, and for
the insurance against unemployment of those engaged in trades
specially liable to it. [38] In moving the formal address the Government spokesman said that "Old Age Pensions have almost passed beyond the range of controversy," [39] and on this subject the leader of
the Opposition replied that there was "no vital difference of opinion
between the two sides of the House." [40] It was hoped that in the
larger and more comprehensive reform which the Government had
on several occasions intimated it would introduce, and which had
been announced in the Budget Speech of 1910, there would be something of the same spirit of common purpose. For three years committees and experts had been considering the many problems involved in a scheme of national insurance; a revolutionary departure
in social legislation by which England was to assume an unquestioned leadership in pointing the way to state action.

THE NATIONAL INSURANCE BILL

The National Insurance Bill was introduced by the Chancellor
of the Exchequer on May 4, 1911, being the last important measure
of social reform enacted by Parliament in the decade preceding the
War. The Poor Law Commission Report had made necessary important legislation on new lines; even before its completed report
the influence of the inquiry was evident. The Government in 1908

[37] Quoted in Gwynn and Tuckwell, *op. cit.*, vol. II, p. 525.
[38] *Parl. Deb.*, H.C., 5 S., 1911, vol. 31, pp. 44–46.
[39] *Parl. Deb., cit.*, p. 49, pp. 46–50 entire.
[40] *Parl. Deb., cit.*, p. 62, pp. 52–64 entire (Balfour).

sought to find a remedy for the tragedy of the industrial worker who falls in service by the Old Age Pension Act, and thus dealt with one of the causes of pauperism.[41] Drink was a major cause,[42] and the Government attempted to deal with this evil in the Licensing Bill of 1908, adopted by a large vote in the House of Commons, but rejected in the upper House. Bad housing conditions and bad sanitation produced and aggravated certain of the causes which made for pauperism, the Commission reported; [43] the Government applied a remedy in the Housing and Town Planning Act, 1909. Another cause to which was assigned a distinct degree of pauperism in certain occupations was "earnings habitually below what are required for healthy subsistence"; [44] an evil the Trade Boards Act, 1909, sought to prevent.

Yet considering all of these causes the Poor Law Commission were of the opinion that the foremost industrial cause of pauperism was irregularity of employment. Their major recommendations were labour exchanges, vocational guidance and unemployment insurance.[45] The Labour Exchanges Act, 1909, was an effort to rid the nation of that evil, and in 1911 this effort was increased by the National Insurance Act, Part II, dealing with unemployment; and Part I dealt with another major cause of pauperism,[46] sickness. The Government had taken to the House of Commons the conclusions of the Poor Law Commission: "Notwithstanding our assumed moral and material progress," the report stated, "and notwithstanding the enormous annual expenditure, amounting to nearly sixty millions a year, upon relief, education and public health, we still

[41] Cf. *Poor Law Commission Report, 1909*, vol. I, pp. 284–286.

[42] *Ibid.*, pp. 286–287.

[43] *Ibid.*, pp. 288–289; also the special report of the *Relation of Industrial and Sanitary Conditions to Pauperism*, made by Mr. Steel-Maitland and Miss Squire.

[44] *Poor Law Commission Report, 1909*, vol. I, p. 291.

[45] *Ibid.*, Part VI; also vol. III (Minority Report), Part II, chaps. IV and V.

[46] *Poor Law Commission Report, 1909*, vol. I, Part V; Vol. III, Part I, chap. V. A convenient summary of the Commission is in *The Poor Law Report of 1909*, pp. 24–42, by Mrs. Bernard Bosanquet, a member of the Commission; *English Poor Law Policy* (1910), Sidney and Beatrice Webb, fully presents the view of the Minority Report of the four dissenting members of the Commission. On September 15, 1909, the Lord Archbishop of Canterbury reviewed the Report of the Poor Law Commission in the House of Lords; *Parl. Deb.*, H.C., 5 S., 1911, vol. 2, pp. 1195–1211; the two other speakers were the Earl of Crewe (pp. 1211–1217), and the Lord Bishop of Southwark (pp. 1217–1222).

have a vast army of persons quartered upon us unable to support themselves and an army which in numbers has recently shown signs of increase rather than decrease."

With this report as a background the Chancellor of the Exchequer, Mr. Lloyd George, brought in the National Insurance Bill,[47] turning "from controversial questions for a moment to a question which, at any rate, has never been the subject of controversy between the parties in the state." In presenting the Bill he said that 30 per cent of pauperism was attributable to sickness. A considerable percentage would have to be added to that for unemployment. The administration of the Old Age Pensions Act had revealed the fact that there was a mass of poverty and destitution in the country which was too proud to wear the badge of pauperism, and which declined to pin that badge to its children. They would rather suffer from deprivation than do so. He was perfectly certain, Mr. Lloyd George said, if that was the fact with regard to persons of seventy years of age, there must be a multitude of people of that kind before they reach that age. That was basis enough to bring forward a scheme that would attempt to remedy the major troubles which beset the working man and woman and young person. Against death, with which the Bill did not attempt to deal, there were, the Chancellor stated, 42,000,000 industrial policies where the payments were weekly, monthly or quarterly; in the Friendly Societies there were 6,000,000 people who had made provisions against sickness; and in the trade unions there were about 700,000 members insured for sick benefits. So far as unemployment went not one-tenth of the working classes had made any provision at all, only 1,400,000 being insured against that contingency.

That was the provision made in 1909 by the working classes: 42,000,000 policies against death, about 6,100,000 with some kind of provision against sickness, and 1,400,000 who had made some provision for unemployment. The decision of the Government to take action, the Chancellor of the Exchequer said, was due to that fact. It was not because the working classes did not consider it necessary to make provision against sickness and unemployment, but it was certain that those who stood most in need of it made up the bulk of the uninsured. "Why?" the Government asked. Because

[47] *Parl. Deb.*, H.C., 5 S., 1911, vol. 25, pp. 609–644 (Lloyd George); complete debate on first reading, pp. 609–677, 700–720.

very few could afford to pay the premiums, and pay them continuously, which enabled a man to provide against those three contingencies. As a matter of fact, you could not provide against all those three contingencies anything which would be worth a workman's while, without paying at any rate 1s.6d. or 2s. per week at the very lowest. There were a multitude of the working classes who could not spare that, and ought not to be asked to spare it, because it involved the deprivation of children of the necessities of life. Under the Government scheme 15,000,000 people would be insured; compulsory unemployment insurance would apply to the precarious trades which were liable to very considerable fluctuations and in which one-sixth of the industrial population were employed. It was a major task for the Government to institute a system whereby 15,000,000 people would be insured against the acute distress which darkened the homes of the workmen wherever there was sickness and unemployment.

The Government did not pretend that the Bill was a complete remedy. "Before you get a complete remedy," Mr. Lloyd George said, "for these social evils, you will have to cut deeper. But I think it is partly a remedy. I think it does more. It lays bare a good many of those social evils, and forces the state as a state, to pay attention to them. It does more than that. Meanwhile, till the advent of a complete remedy, this scheme does alleviate an immense mass of human suffering, and I am going to appeal, not merely to those who support the Government in this House, but to the House as a whole, to the men of all parties to assist us to carry through a measure that will relieve untold misery in myriads of homes—misery that is undeserved; that will help to prevent a good deal of wretchedness, and which will arm the nation to fight until it conquers 'the pestilence that walkest in darkness, and the destruction that wasteth at noonday'."

It is well to note this introductory speech. As the controversy over the Bill progressed the Chancellor of the Exchequer carried his plea to the Nation—a remarkable incident in modern social politics —and in his fighting speeches gave some of the most penetrating criticism of the social legislation of the first decade of this century. Of course it was impossible on the first reading of the Bill for any member to express a mature judgment on the Government's proposals, which had been under closest consideration for three years, but the Opposition, through Mr. Chamberlain, gave its opinion on the effort "to set the foundation-stone of a work which every party desires to see carried to a successful conclusion." [48] This responsible spokesman added, "We feel that a subject so vast, so difficult, and touching such complicated matters requires the good will and assistance of all sections without regard to party, and this ought not to be made the subject of party strife." [49] The attitude of Labour was very favourable, and the opportunity was taken to stress again the principle of the Right to Work Bill.[50] The Leicester Labour Congress of 1911 directed the party to bring a Bill in "That the State should take the responsibility directly of providing employment or maintenance for the unemployed." The Labour Amendment regretted "that no promise had been made of a Bill establishing the right to work by placing upon the State the responsibility of directly providing employment or maintenance for the genuine unemployed." [51] One Labour speaker stated that "this problem of unemployment is very much a problem of the State organization of industry, and not necessarily organization of industry by the State itself, but by the State taking such action that all industry shall be regulated in such a manner as to secure work for all citizens willing to work." [52]

The President of the Board of Trade, Mr. Sidney Buxton, on May 24, moved the second reading of the Bill.[53] "The idea on which it is based," he said, "is that under existing conditions the whole burden of sickness, invalidity, and unemployment over which the working man has no control, falls directly with crushing force on the individual whether he be provident or improvident, and I think the House is generally agreed that it is time that the employer and the State should enter into partnership, with the working man in order

---

[48] *Parl. Deb., cit.,* p. 645 (Chamberlain) ; pp. 644–651, entire.

[49] *Parl. Deb.,* p. 651

[50] *Parl. Deb.,* pp. 654–657 (MacDonald), also vol. 21, pp. 101–103, on the King's Speech (pp. 44–46), the principle set forth; pp. 586–659, the Labour Amendment on Right to Work or full maintenance by State.

[51] *Parl. Deb.,* p. 586.

[52] *Parl. Deb.,* p. 639 (Lansbury) ; pp. 639–649, entire. Cf. speeches of President of Local Government Board, pp. 627–638, and Chiozza-Money, pp. 606–614, and Clynes, pp. 591–600. The O'Grady Amendment was defeated by 225 votes to 39.

[53] *Parl. Deb.,* H.C., 5 S., 1911, vol. 26, pp. 270–387 (May 24) ; pp. 451–571 (May 25) ; pp. 718–832 (May 29) ; pp. 270–287 (Buxton).

so far as possible to mitigate the severity of the burden which falls upon him."

It would be difficult to find a second reading debate between 1900 and 1914 which contained more explicitly a definite acceptance of the State as a leader, even a pioneer, in social reform. This philosophy behind legislation was in all of the Government speeches, and the Labour members followed their discursive example. The first Labour member to speak remarked that with the advent of democracy to power new views regarding the duty of the State towards its individual members had come into being and found expression in Parliament. The Insurance Bill, he said, was the latest of a series of efforts made in the last generation to cope with the evils and miseries which have been produced by generations of class legislation in the interests of the rich.[54] Mr. Barnes, for Labour, declared that the divergences of opinion from the Government on the Bill which Labour had put forward, were not in any factious spirit. "We are very glad the Bill has been introduced. We think it marks a great step forward, because it brings many millions of workmen into direct contact with the State, and is therefore going to be of immense educational value. We believe people have been too much inclined to look upon the State simply as a big policeman and this Bill will enable a great many of them to realize that the State, after all, is what they like to make it. We welcome this Bill from that point of view." [55]

The members of the Cabinet were hardly less enthusiastic in praise of the Bill than the Chancellor of the Exchequer. The Attorney General, Sir Isaac Rufus, in a very carefully planned survey of the German social insurance system, said "this House has now the opportunity of placing the nation at the head of the world in social reform." [56] The Secretary of the Home Department, Mr. Churchill, had the duty of explaining the unemployment insurance features of the Bill, and the First Lord of the Admiralty, Mr. McKenna, outlined the invalidity sections. The former believed that no one could measure the futile, unnecessary loss which the State incurred. "Un-

[54] *Parl. Deb.*, H.C., 5S., 1911, vol. 26, p. 300; pp. 299–303, entire (Clancy).
[55] *Parl. Dab.*, H.C., 5 S., 1911, vol. 26, p. 303–314, entire (Barnes).
[56] *Parl. Deb., ibid.*, p. 458, pp. 368–387, entire; pp. 493–510 (Churchill); pp. 566–571 (McKenna). Cf. A brief study by Anne Ashley *The Social Policy of Bismarck: A Critical Study with a Comparison of German and English Insurance Legislation (1912)*, Section 12.

employment and sickness will return to the cottage of the working man, but they will not return alone. We are going to send him by this Bill other visitors to his home, visitors who will guard his fortunes and strengthen his right arm against every foe." Mr. Churchill between 1909 and 1911 shared with Mr. Lloyd George the duty of seeing social legislation through Parliament. His vigour was tremendous.

A speech such as this by Mr. Churchill would most likely convince Professor Dicey that the free discretion or indiscretion of each individual was very much limited by what Mr. Lowell termed "grand-motherly legislation." Before this Act, Dicey wrote, "his conduct no more concerned the State than the question whether he should wear a black coat or a brown coat." [57] But even in 1887 Professor Maitland, warning his students against taking too narrow a view of modern English law, spoke of the active duties which modern statutes have cast upon Englishmen in general.[58] Yet the first critic believed that "the statesmen who have introduced unemployment insurance by the State have, whether they knew it or not acknowledged in principle the *droit du travail* for the sake of which socialists died behind the barricades of June 1848." [59] Mr. Keir Hardie, moving the Labour party Right to Work Bill in 1911, declared, that "this Bill seeks to set up quite a new and distinct principle in modern politics"; but he based his argument on a statute of Elizabeth (43 Elizabeth, c. 2).[60]

The linking of this Act, "An Act to Provide for Insurance against Loss of Health, and for the Prevention and Cure of Sickness and for Insurance against Unemployment and for purposes incidental thereto," with the Coal Mines (Minimum Wage) Act, 1912, made it certain that such was not the belief of the Prime Minister. Mr. Asquith specifically denied such an intent in the Act.[61] But the leader of the Labour party, Mr. MacDonald, found the principle one which all parties could accept, and typical of a very decided advance in public opinion. "If this Bill had been introduced ten years ago,"

[57] *Op. cit.*, p. xxxvii.
[58] Cf. F. W. Maitland, *The Constitutional History of England*, p. 505.
[59] Dicey, *op. cit.*, pp. xxxviii–xxxix.
[60] *Parl. Deb.*, H.C., 1911, vol. 25, pp. 1218–1220.
[61] *Parl. Deb.*, H.C., 5 S., 1912, vol. 35, p. 42; also *Parl. Deb.*, H.C., 5 S., 1911, vol. 21, pp. 627–638, the Government statement on the Right to Work Amendment of the Labour Party.

he said, "it would not have found, I think, a single supporter from either of the Front Benches. The point of view which the Chancellor and the Government have taken is one which is quite new, and which marks a fundamental change of public opinion, and the most extraordinary thing for those who are sitting on these benches is to find that point of view is not challenged by any section of this House. The old assumption upon which we used to approach questions of legislation, by which State aid and State organizations were regarded as something which ought to be suspected by every wise man, has been thrown over, thrown over not only by those who sit in this quarter of the House, but thrown over by everybody. That is a very substantial advance, one of those advances which one finds in public opinion happening periodically about once every century, and I think it is an indication that to-day in the times that have come upon us the old political parties are largely losing their significance; and the combination which has taken place during the last week or two, on both sides of the House, to praise this Bill and facilitate its passing is one that is welcome, at any rate, very heartily and most sincerely by those who sit with me here. For the first time in a clear, unmistakable, systematic way a Government has come before the country and has said that these breaches in the way of life are a responsibility imposed upon the Government, and an Opposition has also offered to say to the Government: 'We support you in your efforts and agree with your general position.' " [62]

The Bill passed second reading without division, following a final summing up by the Chancellor of the Exchequer on the debate [63] in which he again invited all parties to join with him in making the Bill what it was intended to be. The House as a Committee of the Whole began consideration of the Bill on July 5,[64] the main effort of the Labour party in the Committee being to secure an increased contri-

[62] *Parl. Deb.*, H.C., 5 S., 1911, vol. 26, pp. 718–719; pp. 718–736, entire (MacDonald).

[63] *Parl. Deb., ibid.*, pp. 756–782 (Lloyd George); note Opposition speeches of second reading: Forster (pp. 287–299), Bonar Law (pp. 511–525), and A. Chamberlain (pp. 736–756).

[64] Committee Stage: *Parl. Deb.*, H.C., 5 S., 1911, vol. 27, pp. 1148–1294; 1361–1390; 1483–1560; and Financial Resolution, pp. 1390–1462. Vol. 28: pp. 31–168; 207–340; 382–456; 697–840; 881–955; 993–1244. Vol. 29: pp. 37–152; 201–342; 381–542; 720–766. Vol. 30: pp. 57–105; completing 14 days in Committee, and on Oct. 25, the Government put through its motion on the Business of the House (pp. 111–267), and until November 21, 16 days were allotted: *ibid.*, 307–414; 426–498; 542–660; 721–836; 878–963; 1017–1120;

bution from the State.[65] Between the second and third readings of
the Bill, Mr. Lloyd George made two important speeches in defence
of the measure and conducted a campaign before the people explaining the Bill, with special reference to the Friendly Societies, Trade
Unions and all existing institutions and agencies which would be affected by the operation of the Bill.[66]

It must be taken into account that the Chancellor of the Exchequer
had no easy task to convince the nation of the wisdom of the Insurance Bill. It was similar to M. Loncheur in France in 1929 and
1930, in defending the French national system of insurance. It is
likely that his agitation and speeches on this subject did as much to
arouse personal antagonism to him and to "inflame the masses," as
his opponents said, as the Budget campaign. The temper of the country in 1911 was different from 1909, and the full effect of the social
policy of the Government in arousing popular interest was more in
evidence in 1912. The indictment made against social evils in the
first decade of this century was not more popularly put than by Mr.
Lloyd George. One has only to read the Parliamentary debates with
their great wealth of personal reference to understand why Mr.
Clynes thought he had done more than any man of his time to reveal
the ugliness of the social system, and why Lord Hugh Cecil believed
he was responsible for arousing the bitterest class hatred. His speech
at Birmingham may illustrate this divergence of view. "What is
the evil of this country?" he asked. "Side by side with great and most
extravagant wealth you have got multitudes of people who cannot
consider even a bare subsistence as assured to them. What do I mean
by a bare subsistence? I don't mean luxuries; I exclude even com-
forts. By a bare subsistence I mean that a minimum of food, raiment,
shelter, and medical care which is essential to keep human life in its

1485–1590; 1667–1777; 1826–1941; 1963–2032. Vol. 31: pp. 41–155; 208–332;
389–479; 532–650; 832–984; 1030–1155; the Financial Resolution, November
15, pp. 383–389; and important report on Part II (Unemployment Insurance),
Standing Committee B. November 2–16, pp. 1637–2120. Vol. 32: Report Stage,
November 28 to December 4, pp. 215–329; 420–543; 599–835; 853–954; 1033–
1159; allocation of time discussion, pp. 836–852.

[65] *Parl. Deb.*, H.C., 5 S., 1911, vol. 27, pp. 1391–1400 (Snowden); pp. 1441–
1499 (MacDonald).

[66] Cf. *The People's Insurance*, by the Rt. Hon. D. Lloyd George (2nd. ed.
1911), Part IV, pp. 175–188; Part II, replies to letters addressed to Chancellor
of Exchequer before the Bill was finally amended; and pp. 33–63 contains
the scheme of the Bill compiled from explanatory *Memoranda* issued by the
Treasury and the Board of Trade at the time the Bill was introduced.

tenement of clay at all." [67] He made plain that that was not his idea of the Government's aid: "We aspire to something more. Our object, our goal ought to be enough to maintain efficiency for every man, woman, and child. The individual demands it, the State needs it, humanity cries for it, religion insists upon it." [68]

The value of this National Insurance of 1911 Act as a lesson in practical politics for great numbers of people was brought out fully in the debates, and with this the Government was in sympathy. Mr. George said, "There is nothing more marked in this country, in most countries, than the contrast between the relentlessness and the rigour with which the laws of property are enforced and the slackness and sluggishness with which the laws affecting the health of the people are administered. These health committees, these societies will be administered by the men themselves. It will be a great lesson in self-government. It will be the first time the workers of this country have been really federated for the purpose of administering affairs which are essential to their very happiness and comfort." [69] This point of view was given by Sir John Simon on the 1911 Act, when he said "few modern Acts of Parliament have occupied more time in discussion and certainly no modern Act of Parliament has been more widely discussed." [70]

The Chancellor of the Exchequer delivered a speech at Whitefield's Tabernacle which was unusually full of the strange popular appeal touched by humour and imagination, which made many of Mr. Lloyd George's campaign utterances seem far removed from the authoritative words of a member of the Government. These speeches were responsible ones, for which their author had to make allowance that back in the House of Commons they would have to be validated. At the late date, October, the Chancellor spoke of the effects of the Bill on the country at large. "Next year it will be in operation" he said, "in the following year the benefits will be flowing, and the stream of benefits will get wider, greater in value—swollen year by year, and by the time the general election comes, what

---

[67] *Op. cit.*, p. 192; for the Birmingham speech, June 10, 1911, pp. 191–204. Mr. Lloyd George's speeches on land reform, 1925–1928, were reminiscent of the earlier period of his activity, as were his Liberal address of 1927–1929 on unemployment.

[68] *Op. cit.*, p. 193.

[69] *Op cit.*, p. 203.

[70] His Preface to *The Law of National Insurance* (1912) by Orme Clarke.

will be the use of misrepresentations of this Bill? Why, there will be living refutations of every falsehood springing up in every street, town, city and hamlet of the land. There won't be a village where you cannot point to lives having been saved by the Insurance Bill. There won't be a town or hamlet where you cannot point to households saved from privation and hunger by the Insurance Bill. There will be the man who has come back from the sanatorium fit for work, strong, vigorous, who but for that Bill, would have been a poor wretched consumptive, staggering to the grave. There will be children who will be saved. There will be the slums which have defiled our great cities for generations cleansed and swept out of the way by the health provisions of this Bill. They say, 'Why not wait?' Wait for whom? Wait! For what are we to wait? Wait until the stream, that dark stream of human misery has all flowed past? Or are we to wait until it surges up and swells and breaks over the banks of law and convention which hem it in and devastates the land with its horrors. . . . This Bill was promised three years ago. It has been on the table six months, discussed and advertised in every paper. No; we will have it through. We want to get on with other work. This is not the end of social reform. It is a good beginning. Some of these provisions are only palliatives until we can get deeper. But it does more than that. It amasses information, and gathers it from all sources as to social evils—analyses and collects it; and all this will be of enormous benefit when we come to deal with the great problems. I never said it would do everything. It will help, and then we will go on. I am taunted that I promised 'a new heaven and a new earth.' They seem to think that phrase was uttered by me. But I am a humble believer in it. I should like to be able in a humble way to help its advent—a new earth, where the health of the multitude would be more precious in the eyes of the law than the wealth of the few; a new earth, where the super-abundance with which Providence blesses labour can be directed and controlled so that the home of the labourer shall be saved from wretchedness, penury, and privation; a new earth, and the best of all to be concentrated and organized to avert the worst from each." [71]

This same temper is reflected in Labour's closing speech on the third reading of the Insurance Bill, Mr. J. Ramsay MacDonald said. "The great value of this Bill is not what it is going to do as a

[71] *The People's Insurance*, pp. 222–223; pp. 205–223, entire speech.

remedial measure immediately, but that it is going to compel us to face problems that we would not have faced if it had not been introduced." [72] If one is tempted to discount the natural fervour in Mr. Lloyd George's speaking to popular audiences, it need only be recalled that the same speaker could drive a sleepy House in the early morning hours through the almost endless drudgery of the Bill's amendments, and later in the same day begin skilfully once more to bring the Bill to completion.

The quotations given were the statement of the responsible Minister, and it can be taken fairly for the social purpose of the Government in their programme of legislation, implied by Sir Henry Campbell-Bannerman when, in his opening speech in 1906, he declared that England must be "less of a pleasure ground for the rich and more of a treasure house for the nation." [73] The Prime Minister, Mr. Asquith, on the third reading [74] of the Insurance Bill, December 6, added his authority to the principle by which politics is an instrument of service in bringing about social justice. "Political machinery," he said, "is only worth having if it is adapted to and used for worthy social ends, and this Bill confers upon millions of our fellow countrymen by the joint operation of self-help and state help the greatest alleviation of the risks and sufferings of life that Parliament has ever conferred upon any people." [75] Though in effect only a short time before the War the National Insurance Act even by 1914 had contributed much valuable information with regard to the condition of the people; and the administration of the Act involved directly or indirectly every type of social question as well as a necessary examination of the whole machinery of enforcement.[76]

[72] *Parl. Deb.*, H.C., 5 S., 1911, vol. 32, pp. 1433–1441.

[73] *Parl. Deb.*, 4 S.H.C., 1906, vol. 152, pp. 164–179, entire.

[74] *Parl. Deb.*, 5 S.H.C., 1911, vol. 32, pp. 1419–1530, third reading entire; note speeches of Forster (pp. 1419–1433), Bonar Law (pp. 1504–1518), and Lloyd George (pp. 1451–1470) ; see pp. 2785–2796 for Lords amendments' consideration. Progress of National Insurance Bill in House of Lords : *Parl. Deb.*, 5 S.H.L., 1911, vol. 10, pp. 736–765, introduced by Lord Haldane, Secretary of State for War ; second reading debate entire, pp. 736–800 ; Committee, December 12–14, pp. 806–808, 990–1091.

[75] *Parl. Deb.*, 5 S.H.C., 1911, vol. 32, p. 1522; pp. 1518–1522, entire.

[76] See *Report for 1912–1913 on the Administration of the National Insurance Act, Part I, Health Insurance,* (Cmd. 6907, 1913) ; and *First Report of the Proceedings of the Board of Trade* under *Part II* of the *National Unemployment Insurance Act, 1911,* (Cmd. 6965, 1913). Note Budget statement of

ADMINISTRATION OF ACT OF 1911.

The Act of 1911 insured compulsorily, with certain exceptions, all "employed" persons, British or alien, from 16 to 70 years of age, and persons not "employed" could insure under certain conditions during the same age period, against the risk of ill-health, and in the employments specified in the Act, against unemployment. Compulsory health and unemployment insurance, with state aid and under state control, were established.[77] Part I of the Act, Health Insurance,[78] was placed under the control of Insurance Commissioners appointed by the Treasury, to whom power was given to effectively carry out the Act by making regulations which, if not annulled became part of the Act itself. This power to make regulations was probably the widest power of subordinate legislation ever conferred by Parliament upon any body of officials.[79] Over 100 matters were specifically left to be dealt with by regulations.[80] It was provided that "The Insurance Commissioners may make regulations for any of the purposes for which regulations may be made under this Part (I) of this Act or the schedules therein referred to, and for prescribing anything which under this Part of this Act or any such schedules is to be prescribed, and generally for carrying this Part of this Act into effect, and any regulation so made shall be laid before both Houses of Parliament as soon as may be after they are made, and shall have effect as if enacted in this Act."

The Administration of Part II of the Act, Unemployment Insurance,[81] was placed in the hands of the Board of Trade, with similar

---

1911 on the finances of the National Insurance Bill; *Parl. Deb.*, 5 S.H.C., 1911, vol. 25, pp. 1868–1870; pp. 1849–1870 entire (Lloyd George). Also the extended debate the next year on the Insurance Commissioners and the politics of the time as affected by the Insurance Act, in Civil Service (Supplementary Estimates) Committee: *Parl. Deb.*, H.C., 5 S., 1912, vol. 34, pp. 1558–1624; and on Estimates for 1912–13, National Insurance Act (Administration): *Parl. Deb.*, 5 S., 1912, vol. 37, pp. 523–600, 1108–1164, 1948–1996; vol. 38: pp. 1943–2002; vol. 39: pp. 257–261; vol. 40; pp. 2173–2220; vol. 41: pp. 1739–1774.

[77] Act of 1911, Sect. I.

[78] *Ibid*. Sects. 1–83.

[79] Dicey, *op. cit.*, p. xl.

[80] Compare Sections 1 and 3 of the Ministry of Health Act, 1919, "An Act to establish a Ministry of Health to exercise in England and Wales powers with respect to Health and Local Government."

[81] Act of 1911, Sects. 84–107.

comprehensive powers of making regulations for the administration of the Act with regard to unemployment,[82] and the power of adding to the number of insured trades.[83] As early as 1913 Part I, Health Insurance, of the 1911 Act was amended and in 1914 Part II, Unemployment Insurance, was amended by the law of that year; both amending Acts being directed mainly to removal of certain administrative difficulties.[84] The scope of this Act was necessarily widened during the War. These Acts were: The National Insurance (Navy and Army) Act, 1914; The National Insurance (Navy and Army) (Session 2) Act, 1914; The National Insurance (Part I, Amendment) Act, 1915, providing for total disablement; The National Insurance (Part II, Amendment), 1915, and 1916, extension to workers abroad and munition workers; The National Insurance (Temporary Employment in Agriculture) Act, 1916; The National Insurance (Part I, Amendment) Act, 1917, disablement from War. Legislation since the War designed to meet unusual post-war conditions has steadily confirmed the principle established in the Act of 1911, and, in many ways, has established a new system of national insurance.

III

Post-war Legislation

The immediate post-war years, 1918–1920, affected disastrously the working of the national unemployment insurance scheme. A good deal of the criticism of the unemployment insurance system of Great Britain neglects to give the important place that should be given to the fact that a nation was mobilised for four years on a strict military basis, and, following the war, used the national insurance systems as a demobilising agency. In fact it was a welfare agency in the transition period. Between the War Acts and the principle Act of 1920 were passed the National Insurance (Unemployment) Acts, 8 April 1919, which increased the rate of unemployment benefit.

The Unemployment Insurance Act, 1920, carried out the Govern-

---

[82] *Ibid.* Sect. 91.

[83] *Ibid.* Sect. 103, and Sixth Schedule.

[84] See *National Health Insurance, Report of Second Year's Working* (Cmd. 7496, 1914) wherein the 1913 Act is fully considered along with the whole problem of administration.

ment policy of bringing the great majority of the wage earners of the country under a comprehensive compulsory scheme of contributory unemployment insurance, domestic servants and agricultural labourers being about the only classes excluded. An additional 8,000,000 workers were included by this Act, among them non-manual workers receiving less than £250 a year. This Act enlarged powers granted for making Special Orders.[85]

The Minister was given the power to make regulations for any of the purposes for which regulations may be made under the Unemployment Insurance Act or the Schedule thereto, and for prescribing anything which under this Act or any such Schedules is to be prescribed; and, "Generally for carrying this Act into effect." (g). It is required that all regulations made under this Act shall be laid before each House of Parliament as soon as may be after they are made, and if not declared annulled within the next subsequent twenty days on which the House has sat next after such regulation is laid before it, all regulations under this Act shall have effect as if enacted in the Act. The Act of 1920 further provided, by adoption in the Sixth Schedule, that the power to make regulations under sections eighty and eighty-one of the Factory and Workshop Act, 1901, should apply to Special Orders under this Act. It was enacted that "before a Special Order comes into force, it shall be laid before each House of Parliament for a period of not less than twenty days during which the House is sitting, and, if either of those houses before the expiration of those twenty days presents an address to His Majesty against the Order or any part thereof, no further proceedings shall be taken thereon without prejudice to the making of any new Order. Any Order or Special Order made under any of the provisions of the Act may be revoked, varied, or amended by an Order or Special Order in like manner." [86] The procedure for regulations and Special Orders in the Act of 1924 is the same as that for the principal Act of 1920,[87] which is also true of the Act of 1927. The Act of 1920 is "the Principal Act" in citing the Unemployment Insurance Acts.

The Act of 1920 also provided for the placing of unemployment insurance on an "industry basis" which Labour has opposed except

[85] Act of 1920, Sect. 36.
[86] See Sections 35–37 of the Act of 1920.
[87] See Sections 12 and 13 of the Act of 1924.

it be under state control.[88] The Act of 1927, however, withdrew the power of the Minister of Labour to make or approve a special scheme for an industry. But amending and extending Acts followed fast on the passing of this principal Act in 1920, almost as if Parliament were playing hide-and-seek with the problem of unemployment. In 1922 the Minister of Labour issued a Memorandum addressed to the National Confederation of Employers' Organizations and the Trade Union Congress General Council, asking the co-operation of these bodies in considering steps which might be taken to improve the system of national unemployment insurance. It was generally agreed that the state should administer the system, the employers and the workers both agreeing to this.[89] The Unemployed Insurance (Temporary Provisions Amendment) Act, 1920; the two Unemployment Insurance Acts of 1921, providing for an increase of the contribution rates and the period of benefit; the Unemployed Workers' Dependents (Temporary Provisions) Act, 1921, (repealed in 1922), and the Unemployment Insurance Act, 1922, supplementing the allowance of an unemployed person; the Unemployment Insurance Act, 1923, continuing for further periods the payment of unemployed benefit; and the Unemployment Insurance Act, 1924, were all superseded by the Unemployment Insurance (No. 2) Act, 1924. This last Act provided that an unemployed person might claim one week's benefit for every six contributions paid in respect of him and for periods not exceeding in the aggregate 26 weeks in a benefit year. This meant that for half the year an unemployed person might be legally entitled to an allowance benefit, which was fixed at 18s. a week for men, 15s. for women, 7s.6d for boys and 6s. for girls.

THE UNEMPLOYMENT INSURANCE ACT, 1927

An amending Act of 1925 changed the law with respect to the period on the expiration of which benefit under the Acts relating to unemployment insurance becomes payable and with respect to the

[88] Act of 1920, Sections 18–20. Cf. *Report on the Administration of Section 18 of the Unemployment Insurance Act, 1920,* and on the Action Taken with a View to Investigating the Possibility of Developing Unemployment *Insurance by Industries* (Cmd. 1613, 1923). Also *The Labour Year Book,* 1924, pp. 41–43; and see Section 11 of 1927 Act.

[89] See *Ministry of Labour Gazette,* December 1922, and February 1924; and a Report for the Trade Union Congress and the Labour Party, *Social In-*

rates of contribution under the Unemployment Acts. Slight changes in the provisions of the 1924 and 1925 Acts were made in the Unemployment Insurance Act of 1926, and then followed the Unemployment Insurance Act, 1927, which came into force, with certain exceptions, in April, 1928. Sir William Beveridge has described the period between 1921 and 1927 as "a welter of vacillating legislation."

The 1927 Act was based upon the Blanesburgh Report on Unemployment Insurance appointed by the Conservative Government in November 1925, to "consider, in the light of experience gained in the working of the unemployment insurance scheme, what changes in the scheme, if any, ought to be made." The final report submitted was unanimous, after hearings and investigations, although the membership of the committee included both employers and trade union leaders. The historical review in the report traced the development of unemployment insurance from voluntary trade union effort to the Act of 1911, which applied to about two and a quarter million workers. The large fund accumulated by 1920, £21,000,000 was swept away by post-war depression, and the practical extension of the Act in 1920 to all manual workers, except those in agriculture and domestic service. Heavy unemployment before the general strike had created a deficit, and the general trade depression combined with the general strike and the coal stoppage caused the deficit to increase beyond twenty million pounds.

It is important to note that the Blanesburgh Committee regarded an unemployment insurance scheme as a permanent part of the English code of social insurance. This very fact has had its disquieting effect in the minds of many people, for it seems to indicate a complacent attitude toward the whole problem of industrial organization in Great Britain. Very early after the War the im-

---

surance and Trade Union Membership (1923) which discusses fully the advantage to the worker of having social insurance administered by the Government. From the workers' point of view are also two Reports, one the *Memorandum on Unemployment Insurance by Industry (1922)* issued by the National Joint Council, formed to represent the Trade Union Congress, the Labour Party Executive and the Parliamentary Labour Party, and the other *Unemployment: A Labour Policy (1921)*, being the report of the joint committee on unemployment appointed by the Parliamentary committee of the Trade Union Congress and the Labour Party Executive, together with the resolution unanimously adopted by the special Trade Union and Labour Conference in London, January 27, 1921. This report includes a copy of the Labour Party's Prevention of Unemployment Bill.

plications of such an accepted fact were seen by Professor Henry Clay, who gave his views in the Manchester *Guardian Commercial* in the "Reconstruction in Europe Supplement", October 26, 1922. He concluded his study by saying, that "finally, the community should face its obligations of maintaining its unemployed members adequately and continuously, instead of inadequately and intermittently. If it does it will realize the expense involved, and will apply itself to the problem of understanding and controlling the trade fluctuations which are the chief cause of unemployment." Professor Clay's later studies have been directed to the argument that a determined system of rationalization must be followed out before there can be any appreciable attack on England's unemployed problem.

The terms of reference for the Blanesburgh Committee included only a contributory scheme, and because the Act of 1927 embodied the major proposals of the Committee and because this report is a commentary on the whole of state policy with regard to unemployment, the principles of a satisfactory plan as determined by the Blanesburgh Committee are given. The Minister of Labour, Miss Bondfield, in the second MacDonald Cabinet, was a member of the Blanesburgh Committee. First, the Committee recommended, the worker's contribution must be moderate in amount. It should never exceed 5d. a week, and, supplemented by the contribution of his employer and the state, should secure him an insurance sufficient in the great majority of cases to save him, during inevitable unemployment, from recourse to public assistance. Second, the scheme must not, by the extent of the benefit promised, tempt the insured contributor to improvidence when in receipt of good pay. Third, it should provide benefits definitely less in amount than the general labourer's rate of wage, so that there may be no temptation to prefer benefit to work. Fourth, it must not interfere unduly with the mobility of labour in the country. Fifth, it must not deter from emigration those who would be benefited by a life overseas. And finally, subject to these conditions, the scheme should be made as attractive in its benefits to the insured contributor as, on an actuarial basis, it is possible to make it. In accordance with these principles, the committee recommended, first, that there should be an unemployment fund to which employers, employed, and the state should contribute in equal amounts. Second, the scheme should apply to substantially the same persons as those included in previous Acts.

Third, the rates of benefit and of contribution should be revised, the former slightly and the latter substantially in a downward direction.

The Minister of Labour, Sir Arthur Steel Maitland, in moving the second reading of the Unemployment Insurance Bill, 1927 declared that "the proposals in the present Bill meant a remodelling of the whole system of unemployment insurance." Subject to transitional provisions the aim of the Act of 1927 was to place the insurance scheme on a permanent basis. It provided unemployment benefit was to be payable as a right, where the requisite statutory conditions were satisfied, and the discretionary power of the Minister of Labour to place restrictions on the grant of benefit came to end. The Act provided a new scale of benefits. The weekly rate of benefit for men with no adult dependents was reduced from 18s. to 17s.; while the rate in respect of an adult dependent was increased from 5s. to 7s.; and, two shillings, the old benefit, in respect of each dependent child. The Act also provided that, after a transitional period, it would be a condition for the receipt of benefit that at least 30 contributions had been paid in the two years preceding the date of claim.[90] The Minister of Labour stated in the debate on the benefits that it had never been considered that any benefit should be a maintenance allowance. It was merely intended as a help to people to tide over a period of unemployment; and to fulfil this purpose the employer, the worker and the state made contributions, but not in equal amounts. The principle of a maintenance allowance was not accepted by the Conservative Government.

THE NEW ATTITUDE TO UNEMPLOYMENT IN ENGLAND

The debates on the Unemployment Act of 1927 were indicative of the new attitude in England towards the problem of unemployment. There was general recognition that the Act would not solve the unemployment situation, and that Acts of Parliament cannot provide a remedy. A new national energy was demanded in the whole of industry. The devastation wrought upon the moral and economic resources of the nation by the long years of unemployment is known by all the responsible leaders of Parliament. In the year of the passing of the Unemployment Insurance Act of 1927 the London

[90] Note Sections 1, 4 and 5 of the 1927 Act.

Times, November 24, 1927, expressed in an editorial the view of many, when it declared that the adoption of a sound administrative system of unemployment insurance could only serve as a definition, not a solution, of the problem of pauperism and unemployment. On the second reading of the Government Bill of 1927, the opposition of the Labour party was expressed in the following amendment: "This House declines to assent to the second reading of a Bill which fails to effect a fairer distribution of the burden of maintaining the unemployment fund and will further increase the excessive charges upon the rates, reduces already inadequate scales of unemployment benefit and imposes certain conditions for the receipt of such benefit which in many cases will be impossible to fulfil." But a Labour Government in power again in 1929 has had to confess that the failure of the unemployment scheme was not in administration, and that any attack upon unemployment to have a permanent effect had to be joined with a national industrial policy fully agreed upon by all responsible for production.[91] It is likely that a political truce by all parties could be agreed upon on unemployment if the vote-getting appeal of electoral promises could be discarded.

The policy of the Conservative Government with regard to unemployment was briefly summed up in the Unemployment Resolution of December 19, 1927 offered by Sir W. Greaves-Lord in lieu of a Resolution submitted by Mr. Thomas Johnston for the Labour party. The Labour Resolution called for the adoption of "a comprehensive national policy which will, in the first place, stimulate production, relieve industry in the necessitous areas from its exceptional burdens and provide work or, alternatively, training and adequate maintenance of the unemployed, and aim at the absorption of that section of the population for which the present economic system offers no prospect of steady employment with a decent standard of life." This Resolution was defeated by a vote of 258 votes to 104, and the Government Resolution was carried. It was: "That this House notes with satisfaction that, in spite of the grave set-back caused by the general strike and the prolonged coal dispute in 1926, the number in employment during 1927 has been greater than at any previous

[91] See debate on salary of the "Minister of Unemployment," Mr. J. H. Thomas, Lord Privy Seal in the Labour Government, *Parl. Deb.,* 5 S.H.C., November 4, 1929, pp. 657–770. Cf. *Report of the Industrial Transference Board* (Cmd. 3156, 1928). See also *Labour Year Book, 1930,* pp. 74–94.

period since 1920; and is of opinion that the absorption of those who remain unemployed cannot be effected by Socialistic measures, and can best be assisted by a policy directed to encouraging the recovery of industry, promoting industrial peace, and, while preventing hardships to those unavoidably out of work, taking all steps that are practicable to forward the readjustment of labour forces to the changing needs of modern industry." Unemployment was thus resolved upon by party announcements.

The unemployment debates in the House of Commons since 1920 have increasingly shown the serious condition not only of the finances of the Unemployment Fund, but the debates have convinced no one that any party has a remedy for unemployment. But there have been new Acts each year. The Unemployment Insurance Act, 1928, provided that, for the purpose of the power of the Treasury to make advances to the Unemployment Fund during the period ending December 31, 1930, the total amount of the advances which might be outstanding during the emergency period should be increased to £40,000,000. The Unemployment Insurance Act, 1929,[92] provided for an increase in the Exchequer contribution to the Unemployment Fund to one half of the aggregate contributions of the unemployed persons and their employers. The Memorandum issued in explanation of the 1929 Act, when it was introduced, estimated the increase of the annual Exchequer contribution to the revenue of the Unemployment Fund would be about £3,500,000. The startling fact was in this official report that revenue of the Unemployment Fund on the existing basis was sufficient to cover the expenditure arising from an average live register of the employment exchanges of 1,000,000 workers. This meant that of the working population of Great Britain it was estimated that one million unemployed would be a normal social expenditure. Before the Act of 1929 the Exchequer contribution was rather less than 40 per cent of the aggregate contributions of the other parties—workers and employers, and this by

[92] For unemployment debates in 1929 see *Parl. Deb.,* 5 S.H.C., vol. 229, Debate on Labour Government Address, July 3–10, pp. 91–214, 255–378, 383–466, 530–654, 723–846, 919–1034, for the most part unemployment policy; *ibid.,* pp. 1123–1218 (Unemployment Insurance Money); *Parl. Deb.,* vol. 30, July 15, 1929, pp. 130–159, second reading Unemployment Insurance Bill, pp. 130–132 (Bondfield); *Parl. Deb.* vol. 232, November 21, 1929, second reading Unemployment Insurance (No. 2) Bill, pp. 737–851; pp. 737–752 (Bondfield); Nov. 25, *ibid.,* pp. 1027–1099; Dec. 2, 3, 5, Committee: pp. 1963–2095, 2217–2327, 2599–2722.

the 1929 Act became equal. The estimated cost of Unemployment Insurance for the financial year 1928–1929 was £10,442,000, of which the state paid £5,309,000, and the Unemployment Fund contribution was £5,133,000.[93] The number of insured persons aged sixteen to sixty-four in employment reached an estimated average of 10,191,000, as compared with 10,007,000 in 1928 and 10,003,000 in 1927. The total number of weekly payments of benefits during the twelve month period ending May, 1929 was about 50,000,000. The total number of separate individuals who claimed benefit at some time within the period was approximately 4,900,000, or one-third of the insured workers under the Unemployment Insurance Acts. The average rate of unemployment among insured persons was 10.5 per cent in 1929, as compared with 10.8 per cent in 1928; but in both 1928 and 1929 the wholly unemployed of the insured persons of Great Britain was 8.2 per cent. During the whole of 1928 and 1929 the number of persons, insured and uninsured, registered at Employment Exchanges, never was less than 1,000,000 a month; the lowest figure was in March, 1928, 1,033,845 and the highest in December, 1928, 1,520,730. In 1929 each month the number was over 1,100,000, being most in January and February 1929, respectively 1,434,000 and 1,430,000. The average rate of unemployment among *insured* persons in Great Britain in the years 1921 to 1929 has been:

Year	Per Cent
1921	17.0
1922	14.3
1923	11.7
1924	10.3
1925	11.3
1926	12.5
1927	9.7
1928	10.8
1929	10.5

The second Labour Government of Mr. MacDonald had no more baffling problem than that of unemployment. It was the cause of

[93] The statistics are taken from the *Report of the Ministry of Labour for 1928*, pp. 13–73, and from the *Ministry of Labour Gazette*, November and December, 1929, and January, 1930, pp. 2–6, and p. 16.

bitter controversy within the party and of unremitting attack from without the party. The facts were month by month telling the story of England's industrial plight. The percentage of *insured* unemployed mounted in August, 1930 to 17.5 per cent and on the register at September 8, 1930 there were 2,139,571 men and women, boys and girls.

The Labour Government did what every other Government did, they passed Acts of Parliament to deal with unemployment. The Unemployment Insurance (No. 2) Act, 1929 provided for an increase as from April 1, 1929, in the Exchequer contribution to the Unemployment Fund to one half of the aggregate contributions paid by employers and employees, or in the case of an exempted person, paid by the employer. The Unemployment Insurance Act, 1930, which came into force March 13, 1930, and continues in force until June 30, 1933 (the time-limit was part of the obstructionist tactics of the House of Lords) lowered the minimum age (before it was 16) to the school-leaving age if and when the school-leaving age is raised to not less than 15, and the Government pledged itself to raise the school-leaving age to 15 as from April 1, 1931. This pledge was re-affirmed in the King's Speech in October, 1930. This provision, it may be pointed out, is to come into operation by regulations to be made by the Minister of Labour. The Minister of Labour may also make regulations providing that boys and girls under 16 continuing their education may be credited with unemployment insurance contributions at the rate of one contribution for every two weeks attendance at the school, instruction centre, etc., subject to a maximum credit of 20 contributions. Such credited contributions will not be taken into account for benefit purposes after the age of 18 has been attained. It is now laid down that the Minister of Labour shall make arrangements with local education authorities for the provision, so far as is practicable, of approved courses of instruction for persons under 18 claiming benefit. Attendance at such courses is already a condition of receiving benefit, but the Act also makes failure to attend a disqualification for benefit, subject to conditions, to be prescribed by the Minister. The adult dependents' benefits and children's allowances of the 1930 Act increase the costs of the unemployment scheme. It is officially estimated that in 1930–1931 the increase in the total Exchequer contribution as a result of the 1930 Act will be about £10,500,000. It is worth pointing out that the statutory limit of borrowing for the unemployment fund is £40,000,000; the debt in 1921 was only £75,000, but in November 1929 it was at £36,850,000.

It would be a mistake to assume that the passing of one Unemployment Insurance Act after another since 1918 has indicated a passive reliance upon the state aid on the part of the people of Great Britain. The truth is that perhaps in the whole field of social legislation there has never been so much time and thought given to lasting solutions than in the unemployment crisis of Great Britain, by individuals and by organized workers' and employers' associations. In an immediate way the Unemployment Acts have been a means of preventing human suffering, but they have not diminished the intent of any political party in England to rid the nation of the economic evil of unemployment. The Trade Union Congress and the Labour party do not base a constructive economic programme upon subsidized unemployment, and the 1929 general election indicated that each party, while promising much, knew the limits of a national unemployment insurance system. There are increasing signs that new means of cooperation are opening up. The Federation of British Industries, the employers, and the Trade Union Congress, the workers, have finally seen a large duty devolving upon all engaged in industry to add their contribution to the common cause. These encouraging factors are best discussed in the chapter dealing with Labour and Trade Union post-war policy. But at a time when Great Britain has faced a prolonged crisis, and borne for years millions of unemployed in some standard of decent living, it would be a mistake to fail to give great credit to an insurance system that had been the means of protecting a national security standard. A great industrial nation will not accept always such a make-shift industrial policy for her workers. The limitations of the insurance schemes have already served to bring attention to basic problems of industry and economic organization in Great Britain. The challenge has been put most insistently since 1927, a year of re-awakening, upon the self-directing and voluntary agencies of organized industry and labour. This is a new direction of social policy which can be of tremendous importance in working out the complex problems of an old industrial country.

IV

HEALTH INSURANCE

With regard to Part I (Health Insurance) of the Act of 1911, it may be noted that changes have been mainly administrative. The National Health Insurance Act, 1918, sought to bring the working of the Act up to date; and the National Health Insurance Act, 1919, besides altering the rates of benefit and contribution raised the rate of remuneration for exemption from compulsory Health Insurance from £160 per year, as set by the 1911 Act, to £250, for all manual workers and those whose income fell below that amount.[94] The period of disorganization, mixed with dismay, is reflected in the National Health Insurance Acts, 1920, 1921, and 1922, which were largely concerned with the financial provisions of the Acts and their amendment. The National Health Insurance Act, 1921 and the National Health Insurance (Prolongation of Insurance) Act, 1921 extended temporarily the period during which persons who were employed might remain insured, under general provisions of the National Health Insurance Acts, 1911–1921.

The Ministry of Health Act, 1919, transferred the powers exercised by the Insurance Commissioners for England and Wales, under the 1911 Act, to the Minister of Health, and in the Ministry was set up the Insurance Department for the National Health Insurance Act.[95] The powers and duties of the new Ministry were to include the supervision and administration of the entire insurance

---

[94] Act of 1918, Part I. Sections 1–6 for Financial Provisions; Act of 1919, sect. 1.

[95] Act of 1919, Sect. 3. *The Report of the Inter-Departmental Committee on Public Assistance Administration*, (1924, Cmd. 2011) is a useful summary of the historical development of forms of assistance, and gives recommendations for linking these services more closely together, so as to prevent failure or overlapping of assistance in case of need. The Committee was appointed to work out a system of coördination for administrative and executive arrangements for the grant of assistance from public funds on account of sickness, destitution and unemployment. Cf. *The Inter-Departmental Committee on Health and Unemployment Insurance, First and Second Interim Reports* (Cmd. 1644, 1922), and the *Third Interim Report* (Cmd. 1821, 1923). It is significant that the Minister of Labour gave an adverse report to a change in the present principle of the benefit and insurance system in his *Memorandum on the proposal to use unemployment benefit in aid of (a) wages on relief work, or (b) wages in industry* (1923).

system.[96] The Scottish Board of Health Act, 1919, gave that body control in Scotland. Co-operating with the Minister of Health is the National Health Insurance Joint Committee, consisting of representatives of England, Wales and Scotland, with the Minister of Health as Chairman. The Minister, acting through the Insurance Department takes the place of the former body called the Insurance Commissioners. The Minister may appoint such employees as are needed, has general charge of the system, and is authorized to issue regulations controlling all subordinate officers and organizations. The Acts governing National Health Insurance were consolidated in the National Health Insurance Act, 1924.

The National Health Insurance (Amending) Acts of 1926 and 1928, the latter going into effect January 1, 1929, dealt with the administration of the principal Act and provided changes sought by the Ministry of Health which had to do with the working of schemes under the Approved Societies, and, additional benefits. The additional benefits and exemptions applied particularly to persons continuously insured for some time, and the 1928 Act provided that persons who became unemployed shall remain insured for all benefits for a period averaging over twenty months. Provision was also made whereby insured persons are relieved from any penalties, in the form of reduction or suspension of benefits, by reason of arrears of contributions during periods of proved genuine unemployment. This again is a commentary on the chronic unemployment of British workers. Also under the National Health Insurance Act, 1928, new classes of persons became liable to compulsory health insurance, from January 1, 1929, with a corresponding liability to insurance under the Contributory Pensions Act, 1925. These classes comprise persons whose economic position is similar to that of the general body of workers already insured, but who had hitherto been outside the scope of the Acts for the technical reason that their employment was not under contract of service.

[96] See *Ministry of Health, First Annual Report, 1919–1920*. Part I—(i) Public Health; (ii) Local Administration; (iii) Local Taxation and Valuation. (Cmd. 923). Part II—Housing and Town Planning (Cmd. 917). Part III—Administration of the Poor Law, the Unemployed Workmen Act, and the Old Age Pensions Act (Cmd. 932). Part IV—Administration of National Health Insurance (Cmd. 913). These Reports of 1920 indicate the scope of the Ministry of Health, and Reports since then provide the best account of the workings of the Acts.

The principles of the National Health Insurance Acts are the protection of the health of individual and community, and the provision of a weekly sum to safeguard the home during sickness. The Acts are compulsory and universal in their application to the working classes. They are contributory by employers, work-people, and the state and are worked principally through Approved Societies, closely supervised by the Minister of Health whose power of control by regulations is very strict. The Acts are administered by the Ministry of Health as the central authority and the local administration is in the hands of the Insurance Committee, consisting of a minimum of 20, and a maximum of 40 members. The magnitude of the Acts may be seen in the fact that the number of persons entitled to benefits at December 31, 1929, in Great Britain were approximately 16,000,000.[97] In England alone the number entitled to health benefits was 13,798,000. Between 1912–1918, benefits under the Act—sickness, disablement, maternity, medical, sanitorium and other benefits—totaled £63,438,000. The total benefits expenditure in Great Britain in 1928 was over thirty million pounds, and for England alone the sum was £27,223,000. When these figures are translated into health benefits they recall the high hopes of the social insurance debates of 1910 and 1911.

The Minister of Health may make regulations under this Act for any of the following purposes:[98] (a) for any purposes for which regulations are expressly authorized to be made by any provisions of the Act; (b) for prescribing anything which under this Act is to be prescribed; and (c) generally for carrying this Act into effect. All regulations made under this Act shall be laid before Parliament as soon as may be after they are made, and shall have effect as if enacted in the Act if not annulled by Parliament within twenty-one days. The Minister is empowered to make Special Orders under this Act,[99] and these he shall publish in such manner as he may think best adapted for informing persons affected. Before a Special Order comes into force, it must be laid before each House of Parliament for a period of not less than thirty days, and after thirty days if not annulled it becomes part of the Act.

---

[97] All figures are taken from *Tenth Annual Report of the Ministry of Health, 1928–1929*, pp. 155–178, and appendices, pp. 227–235.
[98] Section 93 of the Act of 1924, Part V. Central Administration.
[99] Section 94 of the Act of 1924, Part V. Central Administration.

The National Health Insurance Act, 1928, extended the power of the Minister of Health under "the principal Act" (Act of 1924) to make Special Orders.[100] The Act of 1928 provided that as soon as the Minister has published notice of the proposal to make a Special Order he may, if he certifies that it is expedient that the Special Order come into operation forthwith, make the Special Order to come into operation forthwith as a Provisional Special Order, but such Provisional Special Order shall only continue in force until the Special Order made in accordance with the usual Special Order procedure has come into force. The same rule of approval by Parliament is required of Provisional Special Orders as for Special Orders, and the procedure is identical.

The Administration of the system of Health Insurance was fully gone into by the Royal Commission on National Health Insurance which was appointed in 1924. The Reports and Evidence of this Commission describe fully the present system, and are a mine of information on the whole problem of social insurance in England. The aim of the Commission was to make a full and impartial investigation into the working of the system set up under the Act of 1911, with a view to securing the fullest possible advantages for the fifteen million workers who are compulsorily insured under the scheme. The terms of reference for this Commission were: To inquire into the scheme of National Health Insurance established by the National Health Insurance Act, 1911–1912, and to report what, if any, alterations, extensions, or developments should be made in regard to the scope of that scheme and the administrative, financial, and medical arrangements set up under it.

One of the most significant of the results of public discussion and official investigation of the system of health insurance was that the Government had the benefit of expert advice with regard to all schemes of social insurance. The Widows', Orphans', and Old Age Pensions Act, 1925, was one indication of this, and the movement for a unified system of social insurance is another. In Parliamentary debates since 1918 there have been many references to a system of unified insurance, and the Government is committed to the idea, but as yet no satisfactory scheme has been brought forward. The Local Government Act, 1929 represented administrative reorganization

---

[100] Section 17 of the Act of 1928, becoming sub-sections 7 and 8 of the Act of 1924.

with regard to Poor Law Reform. Such reform has a close connection with the programme of the state with regard to unemployment and health insurance, in fact, all the public social services. Labour held that probably the chief way in which the new Unemployment Act of 1924 operated in this connection was that it enabled the Poor Law authorities to discontinue or reduce payments in supplementation of unemployment benefit. In 1929 a Cabinet Committee of the Labour Government began a study of all existing state schemes of social insurance with a view of reorganization of such services in England.

V.

Poor Law Reform

It is outside the scope of this study to consider the case of "the legal poor", but because of the close connection between Poor Law Reform and social legislation brief mention may be made of the Local Government Act, 1929, which went into force on April 1, 1930. The importance of poor relief and the expenditure on pauperism in England is gained from knowing that the expenditure in 1926–27, was £49,774,916, the highest total in Poor Law history. The estimate of the Minister of Health for the year 1928–29 put the cost of pauper relief at £40,890,000. The average number relieved weekly in 1928–29 was 1,110,205, or 281 in each 10,000 of the population. In August 1930 the poor relief per 10,000 estimated population was in England and Wales 290, and in Scotland 434. After April, 1930 the work of Poor Law administration devolved upon County and County Borough Councils with their dependent Assistance Committees and the secondarily dependent Guardians Committees.

The Minister of Health, Mr. Neville Chamberlain, in December, 1925, addressed a letter to the Boards of Guardians in England and Wales, together with a *Memorandum* containing provisional proposals for a measure of Poor Law Reform. It will be remembered that the whole question was exhaustively considered by the Royal Commission which was appointed in 1905 and reported in 1909. In July, 1917, a Committee known as the Maclean Committee was appointed by the Minister of Reconstruction to consider and report upon the steps to be taken to secure the better co-ordination of public assistance in England and Wales and upon such other matters affecting the system of local government as might from time to time be referred to it.

The Committee in a number of instances reconciled the majority and the minority reports of the Royal Commission of 1909. It recommended the abolition of the Boards of Guardians and the transfer of their functions to local authorities—normally County and County Borough Councils—on certain stated lines. The provisional proposals that were later put forward by the Ministry of Health were drawn on the lines proposed by the Maclean Committee. The Local Government Act, 1929 embodied these proposals. In making the proposals the Minister of Health wrote that he was in no small degree influenced by the fact that the existing organization of local government was such as seriously to detract from the value to the community of the devoted personal service rendered by so many members of Boards of Guardians. In case after case, he pointed out, Parliament had recently decided to assign not to the Guardians but to other authorities new social services where the work to be done was either wholly or mainly of the nature of public assistance, and the Minister believed that a single local authority should be wholly or mainly responsible for the local administration of its area. If the proposals were carried out, the Minister wrote, Boards of Guardians would disappear, "and with them much of the unpalatable flavour associated with the Poor Law and its administration today." By the proposals applicable to the country generally, the objects sought, briefly (and apart from the reduction in the number of local elections and local administrative bodies) ;

1. The co-ordination and improvement of the provision made for the prevention and treatment of ill-health both institutionally and otherwise, and the inclusion in this provision of all public assistance required as the result of sickness, accident, and infirmity. In county boroughs a complete unification of the health service can be secured, and as regards administrative counties there is contemplated a concentration in the county council of a general responsibility for the administration of health services in the hands of borough and district councils acting within the county.

2. The co-ordination of all forms of public assistance, and especially an improved correlation between Poor Law relief and unemployment benefit.

3. The decentralization of the responsibility at present falling on the Minister of Health.

4. The simplification of the financial relations between the Ministry and the local authorities and the freeing of the local authorities from the financial restrictions in matters of comparative detail which are necessary concomitant of the present system.

5. The correction of certain anomalies of historic origin, such as the association of the registration service (births, deaths, and marriages) with the provision for the relief of the poor.

These proposals for the reform of the Poor Law in 1926 brought forward by the Minister of Health and embodied in the Local Government Act, 1929 need only be enumerated to indicate the remarkable changes that have taken place in the principles of relief since the beginning of the nineteenth century. If this change means anything at all it means that human life has become of more value, that the individual is more important. It means also that the state is determined to aid in bringing in the good society in every way that it can. The moral earnestness of social effort is today a tremendous factor in laying the foundations of a new order in which the purposive will of the state can interpret its intent that conditions of life shall be good. A century and a quarter of progress has really given to the modern state a new citizen. This citizen believes in the state because in a great many ways the state is competent to carry out reforms and to maintain high standards of collective action. The Local Government Act, 1929, represents not only reform in social policy but a better technique of administration. Thus, as Professor Gilbert Murray, has suggested, one of the great objections to state interference in the last century—that the state did not possess enough knowledge or enough organization to do the proposed work effectively or intelligently—does not obtain.[101] Now it often does. And the conclusion is reached that the state has become a far more self-conscious unity, and where it has knowledge, it can act.

[101] *Contemporary Review,* vol. 128, No. 720 (December, 1925), from an address to Liberal candidates on October 26, 1925, "What Liberalism Stands For," pp. 681–697.

CHAPTER X

THE POLITICAL AND INDUSTRIAL ALLIANCE OF THE BRITISH LABOUR MOVEMENT: SOCIAL LEGISLATION AND THE TRADE UNIONS.

The history of the British Labour movement is best understood when it is seen to be rooted deep in the British soil. The development of legislation and administration with regard to social services is distinctly British and existing agencies of government and voluntary organization have always been utilized. There has been from the beginning an appeal to the facts of the condition of life and industry as they are known to the British people, and the validity of Labour's appeal at its best has been in the claim to understand what could be done for the nation's welfare as a whole. This direct contact with the facts of English life and industry has made the Labour movement a British institution. The inclusion of a body of writers, civil servants, and intellectuals, as represented by the Fabians, early strengthened the political movement. The long years of political struggle in Parliament prepared the way for a constitutional Labour party, and the earlier Liberal-Labour candidates broke down a great deal of middle class opposition. This was later a source of solid strength for social legislation.

But the originality of the British Labour movement is best proved by the growth and organization of the Labour party. The alliance of the political and the industrial Labour movements has given reality to the whole Labour programme. The background of this alliance can be seen in the political agitation for the extension of the franchise, the rights of trade unions in the Acts of 1871–76, and in the practical opportunist policy of the Trade Union Congress from year to year. Finally the alliance between the two wings of the Labour movement was perfected in the organization of the independent political Labour movement on the basis of trade union support.

The demands for reform, and for the extension of old Acts and the passing of new ones affecting the life and labour of the people, have been a unifying force in the British Labour movement. The industrial organization is based, and has been based, on the Trade Union movement, and upon the strength of trade unionism the political movement has been able to build a national party. It is well to connect this alliance to the legislative programme in a direct way. Yet it would be a serious error in making a general survey of social legislation in England to imagine the progress of public social services to be the achievement, or, in the keeping, of any single political party. This important fact is recognized, yet the special and direct connection of the political Labour movement to social legislation is a matter of practical politics and needs to be taken into account. The alliance of the political and industrial Labour movements in England has not only given a broad basis for the working out of the problems of social legislation, but has been of importance in the development of modern democratic government.

The chief features of social legislation in England have now been considered. This legislation showed to what extent the state made an effort to control industry by protecting the conditions of work and by advancing the standards of living for the individual. The state prescribed positive duties with regard to the health and safety of the worker, beyond this the state inaugurated a general system of social insurance based upon the principle of a minimum standard of life and security. The intervention of the state made it necessary to consider the organization of the workers within the community and the rights that could be given special recognition. It is thus of interest to see how the Trade Union Congress, the "Parliament of Labour", reflected the changing opinion of Labour. The bitter controversy over the laws defining the status of trade unions is especially important. The public, greatly concerned in that long conflict, had seen the case fully presented in the Parliamentary debates on industrial unrest. The programme of the Trade Union Congress, the status of trade unions and industrial unrest may now provide an opportunity to judge the tendency of public opinion with regard to state action in the social politics of this century. They provide the background for a larger understanding of the work of Parliament with regard to social legislation.

I

The Trade Union Congress

The Plymouth and Huddersfield Trade Union Congress of 1899 and 1900 can be compared with the first and second general Congress at Paris in the same years of the French Socialist organizations. The Labour movement of each country was making an effort more clearly to outline economic and political functions. The Congresses reflected the progress of the Labour movements of France and England, indicating that though the development of the movements had been different, common problems were faced by both countries. From two major points of view the French and English leaders at that time were not far apart. It was accepted as essential that political power through Parliamentary representation must be increased, and that the Labour movement had to be recognized and reconstituted to meet the demands of the new century. The tendency to uniformity in the Labour movements of France and England was, of course, only an expression of the general tendency toward an internationalization of the Labour movement.[1] Industrial expansion and commercial development forced modern nations to find a way out of their problems; workers' legislation was a necessity in each nation; the development of the laws relating to labour being a measure of the extent to which a country was industrialized. The expected result was that by 1900 the inner political programmes of the Labour parties, and the parliamentary questions of all parties on industrial problems should be moving toward uniformity in expression and purpose.

The chairman of the Huddersfield Congress in his opening address declared there never was a time when the hearty co-operation of all the workers was more required, not only if they wished to secure a reasonable proportion of the reforms which the Trade Union Congress advocated, but to preserve those rights and privileges which for years they had believed they were in full enjoyment of but which

[1] Cf. Sombart, *op. cit.*, pp. 178–211; for a discussion of the tendency of the French and English inner political programmes toward uniformity, see pp. 211–253; also Paul Louis', *Histoire de socialisme français*, pp. 273–4 and *Histoire du mouvement syndical en France, 1789–1910*, p. 13; Floignet and Dupont, *op. cit.*, p. 45.

were in danger of being whittled away by recent decisions in the court. The president, William Pickles, in his address assumed what had been said by an earlier speaker, that the Congress were repre- sentatives of the great democracy, and he had faith in that great democracy, but it had its destiny in its own hands. With this in mind he discussed the Trade Union method and aim from the point of view of natural science and evolution, marking a departure from the usual presidential efforts of the Congress. He purposely neglected the political and industrial phases of the Labour movement to deal with what he called the "philosophical" aspect of the Trade Union world. The president affirmed that all were convinced a great change had taken place in the Trade Union movement, both in the minds of those who might be called the leaders of the movement and also in the character of the problem which these men had to solve. Ten years ago the problem was, "How best to determine the rights and duties of the working class in the existing social orders?" But from the resolutions agreed to by the last two or three Trade Union Con- gresses, it could be judged that Trade Unionists had gravely de- cided that the existing social order was not worthy of such adjust- ment, for they had pledged themselves to a programme which if carried into effect, would entirely sweep away the capitalistic basis of society and substitute for it a collectivist basis. The capitalist had socialized production, and the people would socialize ownership and distribution. This address concluded with the famous dictum of Engels on the approaching hour when man would become master of his own social organization. The London *Times* commented at length editorially on this presidential address, and it was taken by some to indicate a new spirit in the Trade Union outlook.[2]

This further outlook was further defined by the Report of the Parliamentary Committee which urged and put forward two changes in the Standing Orders, affecting the choice of officials, and the con- trol of business, "in order to make the Congress a good practical legislative assembly." The first change was that the president of the Congress should be, instead of chosen by delegates, *ex officio* the chairman of the Parliamentary Committee for the past twelve months, and that similarly the vice-chairman and treasurer of the

[2] The London *Times*, Sept. 5, 1900, p. 7; and see *Economic Journal*, p. 573, vol. X, December, 1900. J. Ramsay MacDonald, "The Huddersfield Trade Union Congress."

Parliamentary Committee should be the vice-president and secretary-treasurer of the Congress. The second change gave the Parliamentary Committee authority to place on the programme of the Congress only such propositions as came within the objects of and aims of trade unionism. The vote on the first was 657,000 for, 549,000 against; for the second 572,000 for, 394,000 against. There were at the Congress 386 delegates, representing 1,225,133 Trade Unionists.

The changes at the Huddersfield Congress made clear the purpose of the Trade Union leaders, that the annual gatherings of representatives of the various workmen's organizations must be for the purpose of deciding the chief points of some practical programme in legislation, and of supporting with the whole force of its affiliated membership trade union struggles of more than local importance. The other idea which a section of the Congress had of its utility, wrote Mr. Ramsay MacDonald, was that it was to guide and inspire the trade union aim, and that in consequence, it was its duty to take the widest possible view of what is known as "the working class movement."

The report of the Parliamentary Committee presented at Huddersfield, having in mind this idea of the function of the Congress, was mainly taken up with a record of Parliamentary Bills, lobbyings and divisions, deputations to Government officials; and reports on Workmen's Trains, Education, Banking, Picketing, Labour Representation, Eight Hours Bill, Federation, and Co-operation. The resolutions passed at the Congress indicate the acceptance on the part of the rank and file of the purposes of the Parliamentary Committee. The following resolutions were among those passed at the Huddersfield Congress:

1. An eight hour day in all trades and occupations in the United Kingdom, and that this should be a test question at all parliamentary and municipal elections.
2. In favour of the principle of Old Age Pensions, and, "that the only legislation that will solve the problem presented by age and poverty in modern industrial life is that which recognizes the pension as a civic right, which may be claimed by any citizen."
3. Abolition of employment of children under fifteen years of age.
4. Cheaper and better trains for workmen.
5. Increased legislation on the Housing difficulty.

6. Taxation of ground rents and values.
7. For Bills relating to inspection of mines and compulsory Shop half-holidays.
8. Fair Wages contracts in Government departments and by Government contractors.
9. The amendment of the Workmen's Compensation Act so as to include all workers in its provisions.
10. The extension of the right to organize to the postal employees.
11. That education be extended and that the Government assume this work as one of its chief obligations to the people.

The purpose of the Labour leaders was to devise some machinery by which the will of the Congress would become effective. That was a major duty, for there was a growing feeling that the Trade Union Congress had no definite work to do. The paralysis of the Parliament of Westminster, it was said, had been closely followed by the paralysis of Labour's Parliament. Socialist resolutions had been passed, and there the matter seemed to end—at least no particular effort was made to put them into force. Critics within and without the Labour movement were convinced that the limitations of trade unionism were more apparent. It was recognized that the Trade Unions had done great work in educating and safeguarding the work-people, in providing "countless opportunities for men to learn the meaning of democratic government and administration," and in making plain that amongst the work-people of Great Britain could be "found men competent to take the responsibilities of the highest offices of state." It was said "the methods that are available when Labour is organized and the capitalist is alone are useless when the capitalists are also organized in strong combinations. The strike has become an antiquated and clumsy method of fighting—a method, moreover, that in most cases now leaves the workmen the worse at its conclusion. As friendly societies and as co-operative fraternities the limitations of trade unionism are even more apparent. What then is to be done? The political power of the trade unionist must be brought into operation. Some common ideal—social, political, industrial—must possess the members of trade unions in this country, and for the realization of this ideal every effort must be made. It is neither likely nor desirable that all workmen will think alike on matters affecting the commonwealth. The important thing is that there should be in the Labour world some common democratic ideal of citizenship. Without this ideal there can be no future for trade unionism and no room for the palaver of a Trade Union Congress." [3] Such writing as this is vigorous even after the lapse of a quarter of a century.

The Parliamentary Committee were determined on the problem of making the decisions of the Congress effective, for in their report it was pointed out that although the Boiler Inspection and Registration Bill and the Miners' Eight Hours Bill secured a second reading debate, neither was passed into law. This they regarded as an indication of the strength of the industrialist vote in the House of Commons. "Every effort," they urged, "should be made during the election to secure the election of members more in sympathy with the legislation required by, and the aspiration of, the working class."

The next year the presidential address at the Swansea Congress declared that matters affecting the social and industrial welfare of the masses had been disregarded during the last Parliamentary session. The fact that the Factory and Workshop Amendment Bill was placed upon the Statute Book was taken to mean a victory for the power of organization. The report of the Parliamentary Committee was even more definite. The slaughtering of the Miners' Eight Hours Bill was used as an illustration of their belief that, "it must be obvious to every one who has watched the proceedings of Parliament during the past few years that it is useless to expect any drastic measures of industrial reform from the House of Commons, composed as it is at the present time." Further disapproval of the Government was expressed by the Parliamentary Committee because they declared that the Government instead of helping higher grade education, had endeavoured to destroy it on every possible occasion. They had resisted to the uttermost the creation of any democratic governing body; every friend of popular education was to be vigilant, otherwise the Government would change the whole educational policy of the country, to the injury, if not the destruction, of the higher interests of the people.

So far as Labour and the Trade Unions were concerned the opposition to the Government was given the greatest possible inspiration by the famous Taff Vale Case, a dispute between the Taff Vale Railway Company in South Wales and its workers. The Amalgamated Society of Railway Servants, after the railwaymen had

---

[3] *The New Age,* Sept. 13, 1900; editorial article, "The Annual Trade Union Congress: Its Past, Present and Future."

struck in 1900, came to their assistance. In the subsequent litigation the Taff Vale Railway Company successfully sought an injunction to restrain the Society and its officers from committing acts which had the effect of supporting the strike, and also damages were assessed against the Society. The House of Lords, after a succession of appeals, upheld the decision.[4] This decision made the cause of industrial and political Labour identical. The Labour party was given its greatest popular support by this unexpected decision, which seemed to the workers to destroy the rights given by the Trade Union Acts of 1871–76. From these earlier Acts of 1900, although Trade Unions had been fought and their methods attacked, yet there had been no action against a trade union. A judicial decision accomplished at once what years of active propaganda had not achieved, and direct results of the political and industrial alliance were soon seen. The Labour party now had a popular argument for the trade unionist to support. At the same time there was a growing demand that the industrial organization of the Labour movement more effectively represent the enlarging claims of the worker. The trade union was to become a more important agency of representation.

THE DEVELOPMENT OF ORGANIZED POLITICAL POWER

The consequences of the decision of the House of Lords in the Taff Vale Case had just begun to be fully understood by the Trade Unionists, and at the Swansea, 1901, Congress the necessity of strict organization and reconstruction, "because of the employers' fight," was urged by the official legal counsel of the Congress. The recommendations of the Parliamentary Committee with reference to the Taff Vale Case were unanimously passed. The Committee were empowered to take a test case to the House of Lords to ascertain how far picketing might be carried on without infringing the law, and rendering the funds of the societies liable for damages. A fund was created for this purpose.

The day following the handing down of the Taff Vale decision the London *Times* editorially remarked that it would "commend itself to the natural sense of justice of the British people."[5] But John

---

[4] *Taff Vale Railway Company* v. *Amalgamated Society of Railway Servants* (1901), A.C. 426.

[5] The London *Times*, editorial article, p. 9, July 23, 1901.

Burns at the London Congress of 1902, which can well be compared with the Tours Congress in France of that year for practical results, stated the views of the Trade Unionists. While signs were not lacking, he pointed out, that their organization was regarded as a menace both politically, socially and commercially, the Trade Union Congress of 1902 must mark an epoch, "because it registered by the unions the taking up of the challenge thrown down that Labour should be smashed and combination overthrown, so that the large aggregation in former times of wealth in the hands of unscrupulous men shall lead to the re-introduction into this country of ours of Slavery under the mask of Freedom, industrial oppression under the mask of Liberty. You must tear this mask off, the re-barbarization of industry must be opposed." [6]

The leaders of the English Labour movement and the Congress knew that another period of crisis in trade union history had been reached corresponding to the periods of 1824–5, 1867–76, and which came again in 1911.[7] Another such crisis came in 1927, with results that are noted below. But it is not exact to say that the leaders of the Labour movement had not decided upon the policy which was made more necessary by the Taff Vale crisis, and which, of course, was given great impetus by it. By the means of a strong Parliamentary Representation Committee and effective Trade Union workers the Taff Vale case was used to unify the English Labour movement. The political Labour movement, it is certain, would not have reached anywhere near the strength represented by the 1906 Parliament if it had not been for the Taff Vale decision. From 1875, when Trade Unions were finally legalized, political redress for their grievances was one of the major concerns of the Labour movement. It has been said that "the Socialists made rapid progress under the shadow of the Taff Vale case," [8] in the ranks of organized Labour; but one has to look much further back in the Trade Union history for the growth of the collectivist idea. In 1894 the Norwich Trade Union Congress adopted a resolution in favour of the socialization of all the instruments of production. Although in 1901, it is interesting to note that the Congress changed, in the resolution calling a con-

---

[6] *Trade Union Congress Report, London, 1902*, pp. 29–30.

[7] Cf. Sidney Webb's *Preface to the Theory and Practice of Trade Unions*, by J. H. Greenwood (1911), pp. 5–6.

[8] Walter v. Osborne and Mark H. Judge, *Trade Unions and the Law*, (1911), pp. 6–7.

ference to consider a comprehensive scheme for old age pensions, the phrase "Socialist societies," to "and other societies." [9] The leaders were determined that the Trade Union movement was not to be a stumbling block in the path of the Labour movement in England, but the basis of its progress. The wisdom of the policy of the industrial and political movements has been vindicated, which has not been true in France nor in Germany.[10]

The resolutions passed at the 1901 Congress further carried out the purpose of the leaders with regard to the will of the Congress becoming effective. The reconstruction of the Labour movement and the aims of its leaders in directing the affairs of the workers, while looked on by some as destructive and revolutionary, seem from this distance to have definitely marked a period where Labour took upon itself a larger share in the common task of organizing the industrial system of England. A wider view of the responsibilities of Parliamentary activity was becoming more manifest. The report of the Parliamentary Committee on the Miners' Eight Hours Bill, the keystone to regulation of hours of labour by law, and the Factory and Workshops Acts Amendment and Consolidation Bill, set forth the fact that Labour representatives were giving themselves with vigour to all the work of the House of Commons in which their knowledge and personal equipment could be best used. The Committee in their report advocated the passing of consolidation Act, similar to that which codified all the Acts dealing with factories and workshops, of all other Acts affecting Labour, such as the Mines Regulation Acts and the Education Acts. The amendment and extension of the Workmen's Compensation Act, the Mines Regulation Act, and the enlargement of the powers of Factory Inspectors were included in the report.

While often the narrower and meaningless jargon of early days was used (and this is true of all the contemporary movements), the Labour forces were approaching the problems of democracy with a less class-conscious point of view. Better organization was being often followed by better judgment, and, it was thought—especially among the higher trade union officials—by a quiet determination to take an all-round, instead of a purely partizan view, of industrial

---

[9] The London *Times*, Sept. 6, 1901, p. 6.

[10] Sombart, *op. cit.*, p. 215; supported years later by the views of Egon Wertheimer in his *Portrait of the British Labour Party* (1929).

relationship. This is, as was then seen, a matter upon which it is rash to generalize, but the comments of trade unionists on the question of education, the wider recognition of the threatening reality of foreign competition, the prominence given to the discussion and elucidation of technical processes in some of the journals of the Trade Unions, and the growing tendency for the unions to become something wider than protective organizations of small sections of workers, were taken to be among the most hopeful signs of the movement; while probably at no time in the past were the unions so widely recognized as providing on the side of "labour" the machinery of pacific adjustment of difficulties that may arise.[11]

The Parliamentary Committee in 1901 pledged themselves to support Sir Charles W. Dilke in his Shops Bill, and the 48-Hour-Week Bill. The 1901 Congress expressly instructed that the Eight Hours Day should be fought for "through various local administrative bodies" where the question of strong Parliamentary opposition would not be met. This same idea was expressed by John Burns at the 1902 Congress when he suggested copying the tolerant, practical, useful work that the Labour group of the London County Council had been able to do in combination with the sympathetic men of all religions and all views on politics on those municipal problems which did not divide them as the political problem did. He declared that a critical time was upon the Labour movement; trade was on the decline, wages were beginning to fall, the Press was more bitter, Parliament was often unsympathetic, and the law, with heavy strokes, was descending upon them, and not with strict impartiality. Public opinion was heavily against them. But their business was to head off the stream of reaction. The Congress was told that, "they must so focus their aim, so express their object and so formulate their demands that the depth of grievance and misery should be the justification for all their actions in that place, where Labour, inarticulate no longer, was determined that its grievances should be removed." [12] The words of John Burns were a prophecy.

The introduction of the Report of the 1902 London Trade Union Congress surveyed the progress of the Labour movement of England towards the ideals of Labour which were comprised in the

---

[11] See *The Economic Journal*, vol. XI, March 1901, pp. 136–7, "Labour Notes."

[12] *The London Trade Union Congress Report, 1902*, pp. 29–30.

terms "a living wage," "full legislative protection," and "an adequate and equal representation in Imperial Parliament and on local governing bodies." It was pointed out that in 1867 Labour's voice was almost inarticulate in Parliament, on local governing bodies, and also on the magisterial bench. In 1902 Labour's representatives were to be found by the hundred on local governing bodies, by scores on the magisterial bench, and by thirteen or fourteen direct Labour members in the House of Commons. Thirty-five years ago, the Report continued, there was practically no Mines Regulation Act, an imperfect Factory Act, no laws regulating railways so far as safety was concerned, no Truck Act worthy of the name, and no Workmen's Compensation Act. By 1902 there were improved mining legislation, a fairly good Factory Act, moderate regulations in regard to safety on railways, a great improvement in laws in regard to "truck," a valuable installment in reference to workmen's compensation for injuries, in addition to many other valuable reforms affecting the interests of Labour.

The keynote which was sounded at the London Congress of 1902 is clear and unmistakable, namely, that the primary and most important weapon that the industrial classes could use at the time was to secure "a large body of Labour representatives in the House of Commons to voice and give effect to the rising hopes of the present generation of workers, with a view of ameliorating the lot of the industrial classes. If this is done we shall soon see a radical change in regard to the laws on the Statute Book of England." [13] The report of the Parliamentary Committee at the 1902 Congress covered the questions of Old Age Pensions, Education, Corn Tax, Steam Engines (Persons in Charge) Bill, Workmen's Compensation and Fair Wages Questions, Miners' Eight Hours Bill, Postal Questions, and the Woolwich Arsenal and Dockyard Labourers' Wages.[14]

The address of the president pointed out that while much work had been done by the Parliamentary Committee of the Trade Union Congress however, that not a single measure of benefit to the working classes had been put upon the Statute Book during the Parliamentary session; on the contrary, the Education Bill of the Gov-

[13] Introduction to *Report of the London Trade Union Congress, 1902*, pp. 27-28.
[14] *Ibid.*, 29-56, for Parliamentary Committee Report.

ernment was a decidedly reactionary measure, no provisions being made in the way of elementary education. The duty of the state was clear, children should not be stunted in their physical or intellectual growth. The Bill was attacked by the Congress president because it abolished the School Boards, placing the schools under the municipal or borough councils, with power to nominate a given number to form a Schools Committee, they in turn having the power to co-opt other members,—this in itself, he believed, being a blow to democratic representation, an interference with the right of citizenship, and public control stunted and arrested. The president believed the moral and intellectual advance of the people depended on the spirit and success with which they faced the situation, and that no measure could be regarded as satisfactory that did not provide one authority directly elected by the people for all educational purposes and free from sectarian bias.[15]

The Congress of 1901 had instructed the Parliamentary Committee to convene a national conference on old age pensions of the trade unions, co-operative, friendly and other societies. This conference was held January 14–15, 1902 at Memorial Hall, London, attended by representatives of three million working men and women. The following resolution was passed: "That this Conference urges upon the Government the urgent necessity of establishing a national system of old age pensions which shall be universal in its application to all citizens, male and female, on attaining the age of sixty years, the pension to be at the rate of at least five shillings a week, and that the entire cost of such scheme be met entirely by means of Imperial taxation."

Two other Conferences were held which indicated the interest of the Trade Union world in the affairs of the nation. The first was the Corn Tax Conference, May 27, 1902, in London, following the introduction of the Budget by the Chancellor of the Exchequer. Over a million organized workmen were represented by 170 delegates, and after the adjournment of the Conference the Chancellor of the Exchequer received a deputation from the delegates. The Education Conference was held in London, May 28, 1902, with the same representation as the Corn Tax Conference.[16] The discussion

[15] *Report Trade Union Congress of London, 1902,* pp. 27–28.
[16] See Speeches of Mr. Asquith and Viscount Bryce in the House of Commons, July 23, 1901, on Education Bill; also Campbell-Bannerman on the

of Education in the sessions of 1900–2 ranked closely behind the questions of the Housing of the Working Classes, the Miners' Eight Hours Bill, and the Old Age Pensions Bill. Early in the first session of 1900 a resolution had been put before the House providing an opportunity for the discussion of the proposed modifications in the system of elementary education.[17]

The Resolution passed at the Education Conference was, "That, as the Government Bill will destroy popularly constituted bodies of education this Conference expresses its dissent to the Government policy on Education; and further it is of the opinion that the abolition of School Boards will be detrimental to the interests of the education of the people, and will take away the advantages which the workers have in direct representation in the management of School Boards." [18] The important fact was that Labour concerned itself with national education. The phrase "direct representation" indicates the spirit of the Congress, finding expression in the report of the Parliamentary Committee "that steps should be taken at the next Parliamentary election to secure the defeat of every member of the present House of Commons and all Parliamentary candidates who may not promise to vote for a solution of the education problem in accordance with the declared policy of the Parliamentary Committees' Report and in consonance with the expressed desire of the Trade Unionists." [19]

At the opening of the Parliament in January, 1901, Campbell-Bannerman declared, in the Liberal Opposition speech on the Address, that the social reforms of the day must be about Education, Housing and Temperance, and that a new spirit was in Education, which brought about "the dreadful dilemma" of the Unionists. "They have to please the powers of reaction and privilege," he

---

political situation and the Education Bill, a speech reported in the London *Times,* July 3, 1901, p. 10; and the London *Times,* Sept. 5, 1901, p. 10, "Education Reform—Possible or Practicable."

[17] The Jebb Resolution: "That, in the opinion of this House, the proposals contained in the Code of Regulations for Day Schools and in the Minutes of the Board of Education laid before Parliament during the present sessions are conducive to the interests of Education." Ayes 188, noes 105. *Parl. Deb.,* 4 S.H.C., vol. LXXXII, p. 596. Viscount Bryce referring to this Resolution declared that the discussion on it lacked the conventional topics of educational controversy. *Ibid.,* p. 693.

[18] The *Report of the London Trade Union Congress, 1902,* pp. 41–2.

[19] *Ibid.,* p. 42.

stated, "and yet they must satisfy popular sentiment and popular demands. They have trusted to the respite given to them by Royal Commissions, and they hoped that those Royal Commissions would find for them some way of reconciling the irreconcilable forces." [20]

The London Congress could not fail to take note of the controversy which had been begun in the London *Times* in a series of articles from October 7, 1901, to December 27, 1901, headed "The Crisis in the British Industries." "Is Trade Unionism destructive of British Industry?" was taken up by the Congress, at the same time that its Parliamentary Committee was seriously studying the legal position of the Trade Unions. Through action of the Labour members and the aid of Sir Charles W. Dilke, a debate on this subject took place in the House of Commons on a motion moved by Mr. Beaumont. The Government majority on the motion was only twenty-nine. The president of the Congress defined the attitude of organized Labour when he said that "modern industrial society is based upon freedom, and it is a serious matter for our organizations that this should be now challenged by the Law Court, as it has been in certain recent judgments. Let us face facts as we find them in a bold and honest manner and go out for an alteration in the law. In order to do this we shall have to reconstitute the House of Commons. We must build up a great Labour party in Parliament from the ranks of the Trade Unionists, and not only make ourselves a great industrial but also a political force in the country." [21] For this reason, the president pointed out, the Trade Unions had a moral as well as an economic effect, for by them "we are schooled and educated in thrift, self-restraint, and the practical wisdom of social politics." The duty of all was to build an empire consisting of men working together for the common good and the uplifting of its inhabitants.

The Management Committee of the General Federation of Trade Unions made a statement on the "crisis," affirming that so far from the aggregate product being less per head and decreasing, they were convinced, on the evidence of employers themselves, that greater sobriety, greater regularity, increased intelligence, and improved methods of remuneration made the manual labour of the country

---

[20] *Parl. Deb.,* 4 S.H.C., vol. LXXXIX, 1901, pp. 82–99; pp. 99–109, Prime Minister's reply (Balfour).

[21] *Report of the London Trade Union Congress,* 1902, pp. 32–36.

(irrespective of the results of machinery) far more productive than it ever was before. They further declared that at the time the influence of trade unionism as a whole, was more effective in increasing than in reducing the productivity of its members.[22] But to other critics "the whole system, as now being worked, is in fact, the direct outcome of trade unionism coupled with advanced Socialism." [23] Such criticism was preceded by the conviction that whatever political leaders may or may not be able to do, there was much that employers and employed can and should accomplish, on their own initiative, in the way of putting their mutual relations on a better footing.[24] There were disinterested critics who held that the falling behind of English competition was not due to the supposed average inefficiency of British Labour or on account of trade restrictions imposed by labour organizations. The discussion on the decadence of British industry, which had been continued for some time, partook "at best of the unphilosophical character . . . while at times it degenerates into an avowed polemic against Trade Unions." [25]

II

The Reality of the Political and Industrial Alliance

The most informed of the observers of the English Labour movement at that time did perceive the fact that there would be a great expansion of the political activity of the Trade Unions. This is evident from the reports of the Congresses which have gone before. The development of a Labour party in England having a great effect on the two older parties and under the direction of leaders like Millerand in France and Bernstein in Germany, was a not uncom-

[22] The London *Times,* December 20, 1901; also the defence of the English Trade Unions and their methods by Mr. and Mrs. Sidney Webb, the London *Times,* December 6, 1901. Compare with this early controversy the Reports of the Winter Conference of the Institute of Public Administration in March, 1928, on "Trade Unions and Efficiency," in *Journal of Public Administration,* vol. VI, 1928, pp. 116–161.

[23] E. A. Pratt, *Trade Unionism and British Industry* (1904), p. 27. (Reprinted from the *Times* series.)

[24] Pratt, *op. cit.,* pp. 17–18.

[25] G. B. Dibblee, "The Printing Trades and the Crisis in British Industry," the *Economic Journal,* March, 1902, pp. 1–2; see also Paul Mantoux and Maurice Alfassa, *La Crise du Trade-Unionisme* (1903), chapters II and III.

mon view, being emphasized at that time by certain French students of the English movement.[26] It appears to the writer to be a mistake to ascribe the growth of the Labour party in a large measure to the "tactical craft of the astute intellectuals of the Labour party." [27] This overlooks the solid advance toward working class representation and influence which was a phenomenon of politics in France, England, and Germany in the early years of the twentieth century. However this attitude has even lately been clearly stated by a student of English politics and institutions. In the view of this critic "A clever advertizing coterie, has, for the time, dragged in its train, with unwilling, if it be polite, acquiescence, the less vocal, if not less statesmanlike, Trade Unionist officials of the older, soberer, more responsible type, while younger inexperienced agitators have vented defiantly their enthusiasm in glad clamorous response to the red flag held out to them of internecine enmity to Capitalists and Capitalism. Yet we must allow that we do not see how in these circumstances it was possible to consider or describe, the political Labour movement, even in this country, as not becoming more and more tightly tied outwardly to the fetishes and dogmas, the positive large overthrow and the vague negative reconstruction, for which open and avowed Socialists feel, and exhibit a complacent but servile regard." [28] This statement could certainly be revised in the light of events which have transpired since the general strike in 1926.

The drift in the direction of a fighting political machine for Labour set in when the Trade Union leaders began to turn away from Gladstonian Liberalism. When it became apparent that Labour could determine the failure or success of certain measures and that direct control over legislation was possible the creation of a Parliamentary party became the first duty of the hour.[29] An Act of Parliament

[26] Cf. Paul Mantoux and Maurice Alfassa, *op. cit.*

[27] Cf. L. L. Price, "Industrial Policy," two reviews, the *Economic Journal,* September, 1923, p. 357.

[28] Price, *ibid.*, pp. 357–8.

[29] See the *Nation* (London) for 1907, for an indication of the force of Labour politics, and note especially the series of articles by Mr. J. A. Hobson, October 26–December 7. The books of 1907–9 provide a commentary also, see especially: A. Griffith-Boscawen's *Fourteen Years in Parliament* (1907); J. Ellis Barker, *British Socialism: An Examination of its Doctrines, Policy, Aims, Practical Proposals* (1908), *Practical Socialism: A Remonstrance,* Edited by Mark H. Judge (1908), being Papers of the British Constitution Association; H. O. Arnold-Foster, *English Socialism of To-Day* (1908); B.

has, the Webbs' have pointed out, at all times formed one of the means by which British Trade Unionists have sought to attain their ends. The fervour with which they have believed in this particular method, and the extent to which they have been able to employ it have varied according to the political circumstances of the time.[30] France and England from 1890 were fighting ground for the Labour leaders who were trying to build up a Parliamentary strength; the legislature of 1893–8 in France and the great victory of 1906 in England of the Labour party were well prepared for by years of planning and leadership.

This tendency toward Parliamentary representation has through every period of Labour history in France and England been linked with a recognition that there were duties that the Trade Unions could not perform acceptably in the modern State. Tom Mann and John Burns of the Amalgamated Society of Engineers were among the first to insist that the Trade Unions were becoming ineffective in handling the problems that the state should look after. John Burns asserted that the "reckless assumption of the duties and responsibilities that only the state or whole community can discharge, in the nature of sick and superannuation benefits, at the instance of the middle class, is crushing out the larger unions by taxing their members to an unbearable extent. The result of this is that all of them have ceased to be unions for maintaining the rights of labour, and have degenerated into mere middle and upper class rate-reducing institutions." [31]

This attitude became more common as the organization of Labour and its increasing influence in governmental investigations and industrial disputes forced it to assume an increasingly important rôle in arbitration. The growth of Labour in this regard is an outstanding contribution of the Trade Union movement to the slow work of

---

Villiers, *The Socialist Movement in England* (1908) ; Jane T. Stoddart, *The New Socialism* (1909), *The New Order: A Forward Policy for Unionists,* Edited by Lord Malmesbury (1908) ; *Towards a Social Policy: Suggestions for Constructive Domestic Reform,* by various writers, representing the conclusions of a committee consisting of Messrs. C. R. Buxton, J. L. Hammond, F. W. Hirst, L. T. Hobhouse, J. A. Hobson, C. F. G. Masterman, and others (1907) ; and J. Kier Hardie, *My Confession of Faith in the Labour Alliance* (1909).

[30] Cf. Sidney and Beatrice Webb, *Industrial Democracy,* vol. I, p. 247.

[31] Quoted by J. F. Rees, *A Social and Industrial History of England 1815–1918* (1920), p. 135.

building up an industrial peace in England. This important work was recognized by the Royal Commission on Labour in their final report in 1894, while Lecky believed "there can be little doubt that the largest, wealthiest, and best organized Trade Unions have done much to diminish labour conflicts." [32] The real value of this development of arbitration proceedings is in the patient work of conciliation; and its growth is among the hopeful signs that industry will command a leadership that will save modern society from the anarchy of economic disruption and warfare. The view of Trade Unions as agencies of industrial co-operation has not become less in England, in fact, one of the chief arguments for strong, well-organized unions is the responsible part they can take in the control of industry. The reports of the Minister of Labour each year emphasize this fact.

In this connection it is worth while noting the attitude of the early Trade Union Congresses in this century toward the annual resolution brought forward on the establishment of a Court for compulsory arbitration. Compulsory arbitration in labour disputes was defeated at the 1900 Congress by 939,000 votes to 246,000; at the 1901 Congress it was rejected by 676,000 votes to 366,000; and the London 1902 Congress voted against it by a majority of 658,000 votes. [33] The majority at the 1903 Congress at Leicester was 618,000 against the resolution; and at the 1904 Congress at Leeds the majority against was 486,000,[34] while the 1905 Congress at Henley the majority against compulsory arbitration was even larger. The vote at the 1900 Congress was explained as due to the suspicion which trade unionists still had of the "outsider" and it was plain from the debate that if a satisfactory method of choosing the arbitrator could be devised, the unions would accept compulsory arbitration.[35]

Just before the 1900 Trade Union Congress, Lord Avebury, president of the British Chambers of Commerce, declared in favour of joint conciliation boards to settle industrial disputes.[36] The attitude of the Government had been given by the President of the Board of Trade on December 15, 1898, when receiving a deputation of trade unionists. He pointed out the evils of industrial warfare, but be-

[32] Lecky, *Democracy and Liberty,* vol. II, p. 355, quoted by S. and B. Webb, *Industrial Democracy,* p. 239; cf. 241 ff.
[33] *Report Trade Union Congress,* 1902, pp. 66–68.
[34] *Ibid.,* 1904, pp. 103–5.
[35] *Economic Journal,* vol. X, Dec. 1900, p. 574 (J. Ramsay MacDonald).
[36] The London *Times,* p. 4, Sept. 6, 1900.

lieved that those evils could not be remedied by any legal enactment
making arbitration in labour disputes compulsory.[37] The decision
of Mr. Justice Farwell in the Taff Vale Case was reflected in the attitude of the Trade Union Congress of 1900,[38] and for several sessions the Penrhyn quarries dispute tempered the arguments of the
trade unionists.[39] It has been held that at the time that the 1902
resolution was submitted to the Congress "one would have indeed expected that the Taff Vale decision would have influenced the Trade
Unionists strongly in favour of compulsory methods." [40] But it was
not until the Sheffield Congress of 1910 that Mr. Tillett succeeded
in getting the Congress to instruct the Parliamentary Committee "to
prepare a report on the various existing forms of conciliation and
arbitration in industrial disputes both British and foreign." The
Committee carried out the instructions of the Congress, and their report was published in the Report of the Trade Union Congress, 1911.
The Committee made no recommendations. However, the Congress
of 1903 instructed the Parliamentary Committee to draft a Bill for
the establishment of a Court which should be authorized to demand
evidence compulsorily in any trade dispute in which the parties had
not agreed to settlement after a month had expired since the declaration of a strike or lock-out. The power to call for an investigation
was given to either of the parties or a public authority, and in the
event of disagreement between the parties concerned a public report
should be made. An equal number of employers' and trade union representatives should constitute the Court and should appoint a chairman, or in case of disagreement the Board of Trade should appoint a
chairman. The Court should be movable and have the power to call
for Special Commissions of investigation and report. This Bill, offered as an Amendment to the Conciliation Act, 1896, was presented
by Mr. R. Bell in 1904.[41] This Act was the only instrument dealing
with the settlement of trade disputes which was in force at the beginning of this century. No results came from this effort to follow

---

[37] *Economic Journal,* vol. IX, March, 1899, p. 85.

[38] See especially the speech of the Secretary of the Railway Servants, Mr.
Bell.

[39] Mr. Lloyd George, as counsel for the strikers, appeared before the 1902
Congress on their behalf. He referred to the owner as one who had "feudal
ideas." For his speech see *Report of the Trade Union Congress, 1902,* p. 64.

[40] De Montgomery, *op. cit.,* p. 338.

[41] See *Report of the Trade Union Congress,* 1904, p. 71.

out the recommendations of the trade unionists. The Report of the Parliamentary Committee to the Leeds Congress of which Mr. Bell was chairman, declared that in 1904, a year in which no greater political or industrial questions could have been before the workers, "we have been under the rule of one of the strongest reactionary Governments of modern times." [42]

III

THE STATUS OF THE TRADE UNIONS

The view of the Trade Union Parliamentary Committee was a general one. In the year 1904, Sir Charles W. Dilke believed that an "extraordinary paralysis had overtaken Government legislation." [43] He brought forward on February 28 the Trade Union and Trade Disputes Bill (No. 2), "to legalize conduct of Trade Disputes and to alter the law affecting the liability of Trade Union funds." [44] Mr. Paulton on February 5 had introduced a similar Bill,[45] which was supported by Sir Robert Reid and Mr. Robert Bell, but to which the Prime Minister found very serious fault, and, while not making it a party issue, declared his opposition. The proposal to put the Bill before a Standing Committee failed.[46] The debates on this Bill indicated the struggle that was yet to come on the question of the legal status of the trade unions. The same ground had been gone over in 1903, at which time a similar Bill was before Parliament. Sir Frederick Banbury and Mr. Cripps saw in the law a revolutionary doctrine of the rights of combination on the part of the workmen, while others believed that the whole progress of the organized Labour of England was at stake. The main point for this study is that Parlia-

[42] Report of the Parliamentary Committee, *Trade Union Congress Report, 1904*, p. 54.

[43] *Parl. Deb.*, 4 S.H.C., 1904, vol. 132, p. 795, in debate on the Shops Bill.

[44] House Bill No. 91, 1904; *Parl. Deb.*, 4 S.H.C., 1904, vol. 130, p. 574.

[45] House Bill No. 8, 1904; *Parl. Deb.*, 4 S.H.C., 1904, vol. 133, pp. 858–962 for speech of Mr. Paulton on second reading of Bill, April 22.

[46] The debate on second reading: Prime Minister (pp. 974–979), Sir Robert Reid (pp. 979–984), Mr. Cripps (pp. 983–990), and Mr. Bell (pp. 990–996), *Parl. Deb.*, 4 S.H.C., vol. 133, pp. 958–1008. The vote for adjournment which prevented any further proceeding of the Bill was only carried by a majority of 39 votes, 238–199. This is indicative of what was to be.

ment had before it several years the problem of the legal status of the trade unions, about which was centred the fullest discussion of the rights of Labour, of the community and the state.

In the debate on the King's Speech in 1905 the leader of the Opposition condemned the lack of any reference to the question which above all others was on the minds of the working classes of the nation the status of the Trade Unions. This was one of the main problems before all parties, and its history in the 1905 session "did not exhibit either the Government or the House of Commons in a very happy light." [47] On February 17, Mr. Whittaker introduced into the House of Commons the Trade Unions and Trade Disputes Bill, 1905.[48] The Bill provided that it should be lawful for the agents of a trade union to picket premises for the purpose of peacefully persuading any person to abstain from working; but a combination to do any act in furtherance of a trade dispute should not be ground for an action, if such act might be done by one person with impunity; and that an action should not be brought against a trade union for the recovery of damage sustained by reason of the action of any of its members.

The Bill was read a second time in the House of Commons on March 10, passing by a majority of 122 (252–130), and was referred to the Standing Committee on Law.[49] The mover, Mr. Whittaker, on second reading,[50] urged that recent judicial decisions revealed a danger to the progress of the Trade Unions and the industrial peace of the nation. Better conditions between the employers and workmen had prevailed during the past thirty years, mainly due to the position in which the Trade Unions had been put. This belief was strongly supported by Mr. Asquith, who thought there had been introduced "by a recognition of the practice of combination a sense of responsibility and of statesmanship in the conduct of industrial relations which was of equal value to employer and employee." It was, he said, "not a matter of party controversy, the general principles of which the vast majority of the House fa-

---

[47] *Annual Register 1905,* p. 82.

[48] Two Bills were presented, House Bills No. 2 and No. 205, both being withdrawn.

[49] The Minutes and Report of the Standing Committee are published as Report No. 154, 1905.

[50] *Parl. Deb.,* 4 S.H.C., vol. 142, 1905, pp. 1054–1069 (Whittaker) for seconder (Wilson), pp. 1069–1075.

voured.[51] He maintained that in view of the recent judicial decisions legislation was not only expedient but absolutely necessary. The Attorney-General, Sir R. B. Finlay, was of the opposite opinion, believing that it would be nothing more than passing class legislation in favour of the workmen, and would not define the law but would put the Trade Unions above the law. The Attorney-General announced that he would vote for the rejection of the Bill, but that no pressure would be taken to put the followers of the Government in line of opposition, recognizing, on the authority of the Prime Minister, that a practice had grown up of regarding the second reading of private Bills as more in the nature of an abstract Resolution which had the support of the members than as a stage in legislation.[52] In 1904 a similar Bill passed second reading by a majority of only 39, and those who voted against it were 199. In a year the majority was increased to 122, and those voting against were 130.

The first clause of the Bill, to legalize peaceful picketing, was in Committee amended by a proviso to the effect that no picketer should after being requested by any person annoyed by his conduct, or by any constable instructed by such person, to move away, to so act as wilfully to obstruct, insult or annoy such person. This was, of course, unsatisfactory to the friends of the Bill, and Mr. Whittaker, who was in charge of the Bill, moved to withdraw the Bill. This was refused, by a vote of 26 to 22. It was the unanimous opinion of the Labour members and of those who represented the organized Labour of the country, that the proviso was "fatal to the Bill" and made it "an absurdity." The promoters of the Bill complained that they had received no help from the Government in the Grand Committee, and that on the contrary Ministers, particularly the Solicitor-General, Sir Edward Carson, had voted for every "destructive amendment." Sir Henry Campbell-Bannerman at the Council of the National Liberal Federation, Newcastle-on-Tyne, May 18–19, 1905, referred to the "deplorable spectacle of the last few weeks" when the Trade Unions and Trade Disputes Bill, intended to revive the original intention of Parliament, had been so mauled and maimed in the Committee under the inspiration of the Government led by their own Solicitor-General, that the Labour and Liberal Members had

[51] *Parl. Deb.*, p. 1093, p. 1097, pp. 1092–1098 entire.
[52] *Parl. Deb.*, *ibid.*, pp. 1106–1107; pp. 1098–1108 entire. Speeches against the Bill: Sir Thomas Wrightson (pp. 1075–1080), Mr. Duke (pp. 1080–1085) and Sir W. Tomlinson (pp. 1091–2); for, Mr. Atherley-Jones (pp. 1086–1090); debate entire second reading, pp. 1054–1127.

been obliged to leave the room. A resolution was unanimously passed at this Council declaring that immediate steps ought to be taken "to restore to workmen the right of effective combination of which they have been deprived by recent decisions of the courts."

In its amended form the Whittaker Bill was reported to the House by the Grand Committee, where the Bill was withdrawn by its friends. The Report of the Parliamentary Committee of the Trade Union Congress at Henley in September, 1905, said that "above all the past year will be remembered as the one in which the Trade Unions and Trade Disputes Bill, after passing its second reading by a large majority was finally so mutilated in the Standing Committee on Law as to render it not merely practically useless but positively harmful to trade unions." In its conclusion the Committee recognized the great assistance of the trade unions in promoting legislation for the benefit of the workers. The time was ripe for great effort on every side. Capital was arrayed against the workers, organized as it had never been before supported by the immense influence of an unjust state of law. It was the opinion of the Parliamentary Committee that the first and foremost need was for more Labour men to be sent to Parliament. Mr. Sexton, in the presidential address, advocated unity among all sections of the Labour party, urging the importance of securing increased independent Labour representation in Parliament. The 1905 session had taught a valuable lesson because of its fruitlessness, he believed.[53] Such determined and consistent criticism of the Government told on the nerves of the leaders of the Conservative party, combined with the open dissensions in their own ranks. On May 5, at Birmingham, Mr. Chamberlain declared it would have been better to have the elections sooner, and to let the people, if they wished it, change their rulers, and see how they liked their substitutes, who were "calling their political followers from every point of the compass, not to decide a policy, but as vultures come to a feast."

It is difficult to over-emphasize the effect that the judicial decisions in the early years of this country had on the Labour movement of England.[54] The Report of the Royal Commission on Trade Disputes

[53] *Annual Register, 1905,* p. 150.
[54] See Introduction to the 1902 edition of *Industrial Democracy,* Sidney and Beatrice Webb, for series of legal decisions. Also the article by Professor W. M. Geldart, *Economic Journal,* June, 1906, pp. 189–211, on the principles which have been developed by judicial decisions almost entirely since 1894. This article also reviews the Report of the Royal Commission.

and Trade Combinations,[55] appointed in 1903, reported early in
1906. The Commission had been opposed from the first by the Parliamentary Committee of the Trade Union Congress and the Labour
members of Parliament, who in joint meeting on January 17, 1903,
protested "against the appointment of the Trade Disputes Commission, as being calculated to hinder the early settlement of the
point at issue; and in addition to this fundamental objection, we
protest against the composition of the Committee, which include a
majority of members already publicly committed to a course of
action in relation to the subject they have to examine and report
upon, and in addition contains representatives of the organized employers, but no representatives of the organized workmen, and is
therefore, neither impartial nor judicial." The Parliamentary Committee at the Leicester Congress, September, 1903, recommended
that no trade union or trade union official recognize or give evidence before the Trade Disputes Commission. The Congress
gave this mandate, and again in 1904 determined that "in consequence of its inequitable and non-representative character, no
evidence or information should be supplied to it by the Trade
Unions." [56]

The controversy centring about the legal status of the trade unions
gave an opportunity for general political discussions on the place
of politics in the Labour movement, and the necessary attitude of
the organized workmen to the direct representation of Labour in
Parliament.[57] The Taff Vale judgment had thrown wide open the
flood gates of recrimination, on both sides, and from 1901 to the
general election in January, 1906, it was the centre around which
the political forces of the time played. When the new Government
came in, one of their first duties was to settle definitely the status
of the trade unions.

[55] Cmd. 2825, 1906.
[56] *Report of the Trade Union Congress,* Leeds, 1904, pp. 55–56.
[57] Cf. A. W. Humphrey, *op. cit.,* chap. X, pp. 142–163; also Geoffrey Drage,
Trade Unionism (1906), for an opposing point of view. French comments can
be seen in M. Morin, *La Situation Juridique des Trade Unions en Angleterre*
(Caen, 1907), and M. Barrault, *Le droit d'association en Angleterre* (1908).
S. and B. Webb's Trade Unionism, chap. X, pp. 594–676, for the views of
these writers on the period from 1890–1920, including of course, the Taff
Vale judgment.

Trade Union and Trade Disputes Act, 1906, and the Trade Union Act, 1913

The Prime Minister, Sir Henry Campbell-Bannerman, in his Albert Hall address, December 21, 1905, stated the attitude of the new Government on the law of combinations. "It has been gravely effected by a series of judicial decisions," he said, "and it will be our desire with the least possible delay so to amend it as to give freedom and security to the Trade Unions in the pursuit of their legitimate ends."[58] This promise was fulfilled when on March 28, 1906, the Attorney-General, Sir John Walton, introduced the Government Bill.[59] Under legal decisions, he held, a construction had been put upon the law of conspiracy, so loose and so wide that it was now impossible to tell beforehand what was the legal quality of action which a Trade Union might take; the right of peaceful persuasion had been seriously impaired, and provident funds had been made liable for claims founded on the acts of unauthorized officials. All this had created a feeling of insecurity and injustice and the Government had received a mandate to redress the grievance.

The Attorney-General claimed that the Government Bill was an honest attempt to do justice to Trade Unions without inflicting injustice upon the community at large and that it accorded with the mandate that the Government had received at the election. The Government Bill met with the opposition of Conservatives,[60] because it set up a "class privilege" for trade unions, while Labour members declared that the Government Bill could not be accepted.[61] On second reading [62] of the Government Bill the leader of the Opposition, Mr. Balfour, attacked the Government for its surrender to Labour on the Trade Disputes Bill.[63] The Government was accused of following the dictates of Labour.[64] The second reading of the

[58] The London *Times*, December 22, 1905, p. 7.
[59] *Parl. Deb.*, 4 S.H.C., 1906, vol. 154, pp. 1295–1311, speech of the Attorney-General; pp. 1295–1352, entire debate on the first reading.
[60] *Parl. Deb.*, 4 S.H.C., 1906, vol. 154, pp. 1320–1328 (Sir Edward Carson); pp. 1331–1335 (Lord Robert Cecil).
[61] *Parl. Deb., ibid.*, pp. 1328–1331, Brace; Bell, pp. 1335–1342.
[62] *Parl. Deb.*, 4 S.H.C., 1906, vol. 155, pp. 1482–1496 (Sir W. Robson, Solicitor-General).
[63] *Parl. Deb., ibid.*, pp. 1524–1536.
[64] *Parl. Deb., ibid.*, pp. 1496–1502 (Bowles).

Government Bill was agreed to, and along with the Labour Party Bill [65] went before the Committee. When the Labour Party Trades Disputes Bill was being debated on the second reading, the Labour leader, Mr. Hardie, had hoped "that as the Government was pledged to the country to deal with this question they would deal with it in such a way as to remove it forever from the field of politics." [66] This point of view was expressed in the debate on the Government Bill, when a Labour member, Mr. Shackleton, declared that the problem was one that was outside of party politics and should be so treated.[67] It was from the Conservative members that chief opposition to the Hudson Bill came, both in the Committee stage and the first and second readings.[68]

The Government, in the Bill brought forward by the Attorney-General, proposed to limit the liability of trade union funds for damages to cases where the act complained of was that of the executive committee of a trade union or of its authorized agent acting in accordance with its express or implied orders, or, at least, not contravening them. The Hudson Bill would prevent trade unions being sued or their funds becoming liable for damages resulting to employers from any act of any member of the trade union. It was because the Government Bill was unsatisfactory on this point that the Labour party pressed forward their own Bill, which was read a second time on March 30, the Government themselves voting for it. The Prime Minister, after declaring that trade unions were beneficial institutions, said he had voted two or three times previously for Bills on the lines of the Hudson Bill, and he proposed to vote for the second reading of the Bill.[69] The Prime Minister held that the difference between the Labour Members' Bill and the Government Bill was one of method rather than of principle. For that reason he asked the House to pass the second reading of the Bill, and details could be arranged in Committee. The second reading passed by a vote of 416 to 66.

The strength of the Labour party for their Bill can be seen

---

[65] House Bill No. 5, 1906. Reached Committee stage and withdrawn.

[66] *Parl. Deb.*, 4 S.H.C., 1906, vol. 155, p. 51; pp. 47–51, entire.

[67] *Parl. Deb.*, 4 S.H.C., 1906, vol. 154, pp. 1311–1316.

[68] *Parl. Deb.*, 4 S.H.C., 1906, vol. 155, pp. 21–83, debate on Hudson Bill; especially F. E. Smith, pp. 28–33.

[69] *Parl. Deb.*, 4 S.H.C., 1906, vol. 155, pp. 51–54.

from the vote on the clause upon which the trade unionists put the whole emphasis. It is this clause which protected from liability for any tort or wrong by or on behalf of the Trade Union. It is section four of the Trade Disputes Act, 1906. "An action against a Trade Union, whether of workmen or masters, or against any members thereof on behalf of themselves and all other members of the trade union for the recovery of damages in respect of any tortious act alleged to have been committed by or on behalf of the trade union, shall not be entertained by any Court; provided, that nothing in this section shall affect the liability of the trustees of such unions to be sued in the events provided for by the Trade Union Act, 1871, section 9." [70] This was carried by a vote of 259 to 29 in Committee stage.[71] One observer wrote that the Act conferred a privilege quite foreign to the fundamental principles of the Common Law, contrary to the report of the Royal Commission appointed to inquire into the subject, which was unanimous on this point, and contrary to the original intention of the Government. Yet in deference to the strong electoral pressure of the trade unions it was accepted by the Liberal cabinet, and passed by the Conservative House of Lords without a division, except on subsidiary amendments relating to picketing and to interests in land.[72] It was the reversal of the Taff Vale judgment that the Labour party wanted, and opinion upon this statute continued to be widely different, according to the place given in industry to Trade Unions and the powers they were expected to exercise, with or without special privileges.[73]

The Trade Union Act, 1913, was Parliamentary intervention to meet the situation created by the Osborne judgment, in December, 1909, which decided that the Amalgamated Society of Railway

---

[70] Trade Disputes Act, 1906, sec. 4, sub-sec. 1.

[71] *Parl. Deb.*, 4 S.H.C., 1906, vol. 162, pp. 120–204, pp. 1607–1785; for Committee consideration July 26th and August 3rd; *Parl. Deb.*, vol. 163, pp. 1349–1440, pp. 1452–1520, for consideration as amended (House Bill No. 342) on Nov. 1st and 2nd; *Parl. Deb.*, vol. 164, pp. 145–236, pp. 856–916, for further consideration Nov. 5th, and third reading and passing, without division, on Nov. 9th. Note especially concluding speech of Sir John Walton, Attorney-General, pp. 912–915, and Mr. Balfour, pp. 906–911. For progress in House of Lords, all stages, *Parl. Deb.*, vol. 167, pp. 272–320, 810–820, 1465–67.

[72] Lowell, *op. cit.*, vol. II, pp. 534–5.

[73] See S. and B. Webbs' *Trade Unionism*, pp. 604–8; Dicey, *op. cit.*, pp. xliv–xlviii.

Servants, a registered Trade Union, could not lawfully collect levies from its members for the formation of a Parliamentary fund, and apply such fund for political purposes, even if a rule of the union authorizing this had been duly made in accordance with the constitution of the society.[74] This decision in the House of Lords seriously threatened the Labour party and its political programme, for its financial resources were mainly in Trade Union funds. When the Osborne judgment was given there were 1,153 trade unions registered at the Board of Trade, with a membership of 2,350,000. Shortly after the decision a resolution was moved in the House of Commons: [75] "That, in the opinion of this House, the right to send representatives to Parliament and to municipal administrative bodies, and to make financial provision for their election and maintenance, enjoyed by trade unions for over forty years, and taken from them by the decision in the case of Osborne *v.* Amalgamated Society of Railway Servants, should be restored." A Bill was introduced in that session, being withdrawn, but the Government introduced in 1911 their Bill,[76] which after two years became the Act of 1913.

The two general elections of 1910 were fought under the handicap of this decision, and Labour constantly agitated for the complete reversal of the decision. The Government was in the long, bitter conflict with the House of Lords, and there was delay. The temper of the times may be indicated by the question on March 6, 1912, when Mr. Claude Lowther asked the Prime Minister, "whether he would consider the introduction of legislation designed to substitute in Trade Unions the secret for the open ballot on questions vitally affecting the interests of the whole nation?" and he further asked "if he were aware that the opinions of members of Trade Unions are very often gotten by bullying and intimidation? Is it not the

---

[74] See the full and clear article of Professor W. M. Geldart, "The Present Law of Trade Disputes and Trade Unions," *"Political Quarterly,* No. 2, May, 1914, pp. 17–61, for a friendly, yet critical estimate of the changes in the law and the principles of judicial decisions. The Acts of 1906 and 1913 are analyzed at length.

[75] *Parl. Deb.,* 5 S.H.C., 1910, vol. 16, p. 1321; moved by J. W. Taylor, pp. 1321–1325. See speeches of Attorney-General, pp. 1349–1359 (Robson); Vivian, pp. 1337–1346; Pringle, pp. 1328–1334; and Shackleton, pp. 1356–1362.

[76] *Ibid.,* moved by J. W. Taylor, pp. 1321–1325. See speeches of Attorney-General, pp. 1349–1359 (Robson); Vivian, pp. 1337–1346; Pringle, pp. 1328–1334; and Shackleton, pp. 1356–1362.

desire of the Government to obtain the opinion of the men themselves, and not that of syndicalist Socialists?" [77] Mr. Asquith replied: "I am sorry the honourable gentleman should have used such language. I think the methods adopted for the purpose of ascertaining the opinions of Trade Unions are a matter of internal regulation, and I have every confidence in the good sense and good faith of my fellow countrymen to whatever class they belong." [78]

After much delay the Government finally passed the compromise Trade Union Act of 1913, accepted by Labour and the Trade Unions, which remained in force until the passage of the Trade Unions and Trade Disputes Act of 1927. This Act provided that a trade union might have power to apply its funds, without restriction, for any lawful objects or purposes—other than political—authorized under its constitution.[79] There were definite restrictions imposed on political activities, and before engaging in such activities a ballot was required which had to secure a majority of those voting. The Chief Registrar of Friendly Societies had to be furnished with the special political rules drawn up, and all payments for political purpose, as defined in the Act, were to be made out of a distinct political fund.[80] It was further provided that any Trade Union member who objected to paying the political fund could, by signing an approved form, be exempted from payments towards it without forfeiting any of his rights as a member of the Trade Union.

The Act of 1913 was not satisfactory to Labour, for it appeared to exact duties from the Trade Unions which were not required of other voluntary bodies. From the Osborne judgment to 1914 the dealings of the Liberal and Labour leaders were less and less friendly, and the constitutional crisis, no less than the extended debates on the national insurance legislation widened the breach between the two parties.[81] The tremendous energy of Liberalism had spent itself, a new force seemed to be stirring within Labour, and the life of England seemed to be at the parting of the ways.

---

[77] *Parl. Deb.*, H.C., 5 S., vol. 35, 1912, pp. 374–375.

[78] *Op. cit.*, p. 375. See answer to similar question a week later, *op. cit.*, p. 1096.

[79] Act of 1913, section 2.

[80] Section 3 of the Act of 1913 gave the procedure on the formation of a fund for certain political purposes.

[81] Cf. G. D. H. Cole, *A Short History of the British Working Class Movement*, (1927), vol. III, chapter III.

PARLIAMENT, THE LABOUR PARTY, AND TRADE UNION
ACTION TO 1914

The Acts of 1906 and 1913 represent the development of the purposes of Trade Union action, and in this study interpret well the expansion of the political Labour movement.[82] How unsatisfactory
was payment by Trade Unions to members of Parliament was plainly
put by the leader of the Labour party, Mr. MacDonald, during the
Budget debate of 1911. He declared it was "an exceedingly bad
thing for Trade Unions to provide income for the maintenance of
members of Parliament. We are not Trade Union servants here in
this House. Members of the Labour party ought to be national
servants." [83]

The contrary was intimated by Mr. F. E. Smith (Lord Birkenhead), who quoted Mr. J. Keir Hardie, when he said, "Labour representation means more than sending a member to the House of Commons. It is a means to an end, and that end is not trade unionism, but
socialism." [84] This same point of view was in the resolution of the
Miners' Federation at the Lambeth Congress of 1913, which asked
that the Labour Party Conference direct its attention more to urgent
political questions, with a view to having adequate discussion thereon,
and allow the Trade Union Congress to deal with industrial questions
and all other matters affecting the Trade Unions not of a political
nature.[85]

Such an attitude has been taken to represent a British compromise
between social democracy and syndicalism, and Mr. Beer believes
that "the Trade Unions Congress since 1915 onwards have taken up
the question of control in the sense of a forward move of Labour
toward a higher conception of social justice." [86] The president of

---

[82] See *Report of the 10th Annual Conference of the Labour Party, Newport,
1910*, Appendix I, pp. 101–110, for Report of the Special Conference on the
House of Lords Decision on Labour Representation. See also the Parliamentary
Committee Report of the Trade Union Congress on the Trade Unions (No. 2)
Bill, pp. 149–150, *Report of the 46th Trade Union Congress, Manchester, 1913*.

[83] *Parl. Deb.*, 5 S.H.C., vol. 25, 1911, p. 1887, pp. 1883–1888, entire (Mac-
Donald).

[84] *Parl. Deb.*, 5 S.H.C., vol. 26, 1911, p. 938, pp. 931–942, entire.

[85] See *Report of the 14th Annual Conference of the Labour Party. Glasgow,
1914*, (January), p. 18.

[86] Beer, *op. cit.*, vol. II, p. 376.

the 1913 Trade Union Congress, W. J. Davis, who is also the historian of the Trade Union Congress, having written its history in two volumes, could say that although the Congress was the mother of the great Labour movement, the Labour party was, and should be mainly political. The political force of Labour was its greatest force.[87] The progress of Labour, Mr. J. R. Clynes said at the same Congress, was to be judged by the greatly improved outlook and higher standard of understanding which possessed the working classes, showing by the wisdom of their decisions and the calmness of their judgment, that Labour can be trusted with the destinies of the nation.[88]

The subjects of Bills and motions as agreed upon at the opening of the Parliamentary Session in 1914 by the Labour party indicate the wide scope of Party action on industrial politics. Up until 1914 at the opening of each session it was the practice of the Parliamentary Labour Party to review the various resolutions of the Labour Party Conferences, which were accepted as general guidance upon Parliamentary matters. The National Executive of the Party sat with the Parliamentary Party in joint meeting at the opening of each Session for the purpose of compiling a list of party Bills and subjects for motions. Members agreed if successful in the ballot for Bills to put forward the party Bills in the order of priority decided upon by the Joint Committee, but members were free to select the subject of any motion on the party list they preferred. The list of Bills in the 1914 Parliamentary Session follows:

Prevention of Unemployment.
Education (Administrative Provisions).
Representation of the People.
Education (Provision of Meals) Amendment.
Nationalization of Mines.
Agricultural Labourers (Wages and Hours).
Agricultural Labourers (Scotland) Half-Holiday.
Prevention and Cure of Sickness and Destitution.
Provision for Minimum Wages and Maximum Hours of Labour.
Minister of Labour.
Prevention of Sickness and Destitution amongst Children.
Old Age Pensions (Amendment).

[87] *Report of the 46th Trade Union Congress, 1913, Manchester,* p. 56, pp. 55–61 entire.
[88] *Ibid.,* pp. 52–53.

Compulsory Weighing.
Railway (Eight Hours).
Local Authorities (Enabling).
Abolition of Fines.
Saturday to Monday Stop.
State Aid for the Blind.
Abolition of Artificial Humidity.
48-Hour Week in Cotton Trade.
Enginemen's Certificate.
Factory and Workshop (Underground).
Hairdressers' Sunday Closing (Wales).

It is not remarkable that the Labour Party won many men and women who believed that at last in Parliament the needs of the people could be discussed. The Labour party came at a time when the industrial workers' movement could give it power, and the programme of the party reflects in a direct way the influence of the highly organized trade union world of Great Britain. To the list of Bills consider the list of Subjects for Motions, and together compare these with the programme at the beginning of the century. One can thus gain a fair idea of the growth of the industrial and political Labour movement in England, and the direct relation to social legislation. The list follows:

General 30s. Minimum Wage.
Eviction of Workmen During Trade Disputes.
Atmosphere and Dust in Textile Factories.
System of Fines in Textile and other Trades.
Inclusion of Clerks in Factory Acts.
Eight-Hour Day.
Truck.
Hours in Bakehouses.
Maladministration of Fair Wages Clause.
Factory Inspection.
Poor Law Reform.
Railway and Mining Accidents.
Labour Exchanges Administration.
Extension of Particulars Clause to Docks, etc.
Workmen's Compensation Act Amendment.
Railway and Canal Nationalization.
Nationalization of Hospitals.
National Factory for Municipal Clothing.
Land Nationalization.
Socialism.

House of Commons Procedure.
Day Training Classes.
School Clinics.
Commission of Inquiry into Older Universities.
Inquiry into Industrial Assurance.
Payment of Jurors.
Militarism.
Abolition of the Right of Capture of Private Property at Sea.

The British Labour Party, like the French Socialists, have always recognized the value of debates in the House of Commons as good publicity for the party. With increasing Parliamentary influence their contribution to the cause of good government has been substantial. Of the 29 members returned by the Labour party in 1906, under the auspices of the Labour Representation Committee only four had had any previous Parliamentary experience. This was a handicap in a body skilled in legislative discipline, but party procedure was immediately put upon a regular business basis.[89] Prior to the outbreak of war in 1914 the party had special Committees on the following subjects: Foreign Affairs, Electoral Reform, Unemployment, Party Policy, Municipal Affairs, Workmen's Compensation, Railway and Transit, Government Workers' Conditions, Finance, Education, and Truck.

When war came in 1914 Labour was called upon to take a responsible part in carrying on the Government and in prosecuting the work of winning against a common foe. For a time the immediate problems of work and wages and industrial organizations were forgotten, but very soon in England men began to think of what the world would be like when peace came. They set forth aims, elaborated principles of reconstruction, and it is well to briefly note the political and industrial labour movement since 1918, which is done in a succeeding chapter. 1914 provides a logical division in this study of the social politics of England. The strength of a Labour party dependent upon the alliance of political and industrial movements became fully evident in the election of 1918. From that time on this unique experiment in effective democratic representation has had increasing significance both for British social history and for all students of popular government.

[89] See *The Labour Year Book, 1916*, pp. 318–319. Post-war developments are given in later chapters.

IV

TRADE UNION REACTION TO LABOUR LEGISLATION

The period in England from 1910–1914 has definitely come to be considered years of industrial unrest. The political activity of the Trade Unions from 1899 to 1910 had kept constantly before the country the major problems of industrial conflict, and the way out of the social struggle as conceived by Labour. The political Labour movement could not limit the rapid expansion of the industrial movement which not only had a strong economic argument for revolutionary action in the position of the wage earner, due to the phenomena of falling prices and almost stationary wages, but there was the added strength of an intellectual revival going on in the Labour movement. There were the combined forces of the effort to reorganize the economic structure of trade unionism and to interpret the expanding consciousness of the working class by a new economic theory.

The Seamen's and Dockers' Strike of 1911 began the definite expression of the new movement, followed by the National Railway Strike of the same year. In 1912 was the National Miners' Strike; in 1913 the Dublin strike; and in 1914 the London Building Dispute. Direct effect on the structure of trade unionism was seen in the formation of the National Union of Railwaymen in 1912–1913, "on an industrial basis, which made it to some extent the twentieth century 'new model' of Trade Union structure." [90] Then followed the Triple Industrial Alliance proposed at a conference of the Miners' Federation of Great Britain, the National Union of Railwaymen, and the National Transport Workers' Federation, held on April 23, 1914. The idea of such a conference was first brought into prominence at the Miners' Annual Conference in 1913, when a resolution was passed, "That the Executive Committee of the Miners' Federation be requested to approach the Executive Committee of other big Trade Unions with a view to co-operative action and the support of each other's demands." [91] Action was to be confined, the president of the Miners' Federation wrote, to

[90] Cf. G. D. H. Cole, *The British Labour Movement* (3rd ed. 1924) p. 17.
[91] Robert Smillie, *"The Triple Industrial Alliance," The Labour Year Book, 1916,* p. 103-104.

joint national action. Sympathetic action was no longer to be left to the uncontrolled emotions of a strike period, but it was to be the calculated result of mature consideration and careful planning. The predominant idea of the alliance was that each of these great fighting organizations, before embarking upon any big movement, either defensive or aggressive, should formulate its programme, submit it to the others, and that upon joint proposal joint action should be taken. Mr. Smillie considered the Triple Industrial Alliance "one definite concrete result of the industrial unrest," made necessary by the progress of industrial development which forced capital to attack Trade Unionism and defend itself against Trade Union advance. That this attack would further the amalgamation of Trade Unions and Federations, leading to the further extension of the principle of common defence was seen by the leaders of the Triple Alliance. The membership of the three bodies was considerable, the miners numbering 800,000, the railwaymen 270,000, and the transport workers 250,000. The miners considered that the two industries most comparable with their own were the railwaymen and the transport. While the scheme at the moment was not intended to include more than the three trades referred to, there was the belief that "it may well be found advisable later on to extend the scope of the alliance in the general interests of Labour as a whole. Even now, indeed, it has already been discussed whether the Triple Alliance might not be in a position to assist our fellow workers in the textile industry if, at an adverse moment, they were threatened with a lockout. Under such circumstances there is every probability that a stoppage of production would cause an immediate settlement. In every case the results of joint action on a large scale should be rapid and decisive, and all the suffering and loss inseparable from trade troubles of the past could be prevented in the future."

The growth of the amalgamation movement in the Trade Union world was part of the unusual extension of the influence of organized Labour by an enormous increase in membership in the first years of the century. In 1899 there were 1,310 separate Trade Unions in the United Kingdom, with a total membership of 1,860,913; in 1910 there were 1,195 Trade Unions with a membership of 2,446,342. By 1914 the number of separate Trade Unions had decreased to 1,123, but having a membership of 3,959,863, which was an increase in 105.3 per cent compared with 1905. The growth of Trade Union membership was due in great measure to the industrial revival from 1910 onwards, which was characterized by the disputes which involved all of the United Kingdom, English, Welsh and Scottish miners, English railwaymen and Irish transport workers. It was due also "to the growing feeling among the workers that only by industrial organization can organized capital be combated." [92] This is confirmed by the statistics on Trade Unions for 1910–1914:

Year	No. at end of year	Membership	Per cent Increase (+) decrease (−)
1910	1,195	2,446,342	+ 3.3
1911	1,204	3,018,903	+23.4
1912	1,149	3,287,884	+ 8.9
1913	1,135	3,987,115	+21.5
1914	1,123	3,959,863	− 0.7 [93]

In a group of special trades the Insurance Act was a factor in the increase, combined with the fact that the Trade Union Congress was giving more attention to the organization of the unskilled worker. It was the unusual growth of Trade Unionism and the extension of the benefits of organization to include many millions more of workers and their dependents in the United Kingdom that gave to Labour politics the necessity of bringing before Parliament the question of Industrial Unrest.

The Government in 1910 was compelled to give most of its attention to the controversy between the Commons and the Lords, while the death of King Edward VII was the occasion of a general truce. But the Government had foreshadowed a comprehensive programme of reform in their legislative measures, and the Ministerial declarations embodied an acknowledgment of the principles of reform which had been fought for in measures which had been introduced or supported by the Government. At that time the Labour

[92] *The Labour Year Book, 1916*, p. 105.
[93] *The Labour Year Book, 1916*, p. 105. See also for a comparison of French and English and German Trade Union membership the *Third and Fourth Abstract of Foreign Labour Statistics by the Board of Trade* (1906 and 1911), pp. xx and xxxv respectively.

Party wanted nothing better than to debate all questions on the floor of the House of Commons. The Government was constantly aware that every important debate on social questions or industrial peace would be a review of their record from 1906.[94] It was also face to face with the problem of Trade Unionism in all of English industry and the measures of control that were made inevitable by the social reform legislation of the Government. There was a considerable change of attitude about several Government measures between 1909 and July 23, 1912; when Mr. Lloyd George spoke on the Port of London Authority Dispute. The Government was in somewhat of the same position as the Trade Union Congress and the Labour Party: the swiftly moving forces of industrial progress, the economic development of the nation, swept aside nicely laid plans and Ministerial programmes. The economic movement was larger than the conception of the Trade Union Congress and the political consequences could not be adequately handled by the Government, nor was the Labour party any closer to an effective understanding of the unrest and revolt.

There was no conflict between the Trade Union Congress and the social programme of the Government. At the Ipswich Trade Union Congress in 1909 there was special consideration of the Labour Exchanges Act and the National Scheme of Unemployed Benefit, and a careful reading of the Report of the Congress is convincing proof that there was no Trade Union opposition on the basic principle of the proposed social reforms which the Government had put forward.[95] There was some fear that the power and place of the Trade Unions would be injured by the remedial measures of the Government, but this feeling was not shared by the members of the Parliamentary Committee or by those Trade Union leaders who saw that the Trade Unions would more than likely have the influence of a larger share in the administration of social and industrial schemes. The period was as full of incessant turmoil and perturbation for the Labour party and Trade Unions as for the Government, all were nonplussed by the series of economic crises that made this

[94] See *Report of the Parliamentary Committee to the Trade Union Congress, 1913*, pp. 77–170, of the Congress Report; also *Report of the Executive to the 14th Annual Conference of the Labour Party, 1914*, pp. 3–32.
[95] The *Report of the Trade Union Congress, 1909*, pp. 55–59. The Parliamentary Report at this Congress, pp. 53–106, is most interesting, covering in detail the chief questions before the Congress and Parliament of 1909.

period a definite background in the struggle "between State Social-ism and Revolutionary Trade Unionism." [96] There had to be a re-vision of the method of the Trade Union leaders as well as for the party in power which seemed to have reached the period in which its evolution had most fully expressed itself in a "Neo-Liberalism" or "Socialism of the State." [97]

INDUSTRIAL UNREST AND BRITISH LABOUR

Parliamentary debates in 1911 on labour disputes clearly revealed that all parties within the State were equally at a loss to offer a satis-factory means of adjustment, though the labour leader, Mr. Mac-Donald, could denounce the Home Secretary, Mr. Churchill, be-cause he had not given in a debate "one single idea regarding the reasons why there is industrial unrest." [98] For their part, he said, they had succeeded in converting the nation at least to the great truth of individual and national prosperity, that unless a man can possess enough at the end of the week to give his individuality free play, then you can talk about your constitutional liberties as much as you like, that man cannot possibly fulfil his duties as a citizen and his responsibilities as an individual.[99] The employment of the mili-tary in Labour disputes, had stirred the deepest hatred, though the Home Secretary, Mr. Churchill, stated that he did not know "whether in the history of the world a similar catastrophe (referring to the railway strike of 1911) can be shown to have menaced an equally great community." [100] Mr. MacDonald declared that "the Depart-

---

[96] Cf. M. Beer, vol. II, p. 363.

[97] Cf. Edouard Guyot, *Le Socialisme et l'Evolution de l'Angleterre Con-temporaine, 1880–1911,* (1913), pp. 241–315; chap. V, *"Le Socialisme d'Etat et l'Evolution du Parti Liberal"*; also Jacques Bardoux, *L'Angleterre Radicale (1905–1913), Essai de Psychologie Sociale* (1913); and André Siegfried, *L'Angleterre d'Aujourd'hui, son Evolution Économique et Politique* (5th ed. 1924).

[98] *Parl. Deb.,* 5 S.H.C., 1911, vol. 29, pp. 1948–1949, pp. 1948–1959 entire; pp. 1943–1991, debate entire on August 16, during debate on Appropriation Bill; for August 17, 18, pp. 2193–2204, 2247–2250.

[99] *Parl. Deb.,* 5 S.H.C., 1911, vol. 29, p. 2293; debate entire, August 22, on employment of military, pp. 2282–2378. See speeches of Prime Minister (pp. 2291–2293); A. Chamberlain (pp. 2299–2301); J. H. Thomas (pp. 2301–2304); Barnes (pp. 2315–2321); Chiozza Money (pp. 2304–2309); Hardie (2333–2341); Lloyd George (pp. 2345–2354).

[100] *Parl. Deb., op. cit.,* p. 2327, pp. 2323–2333 entire.

ment which has played the most diabolical part in all this unrest is
the Home Department. This is not a medieval state, and it is not
Russia. It is not even Germany. We have discovered a secret which
few countries have heretofore discovered. The secret this nation
has discovered is that the way to maintain law and order is to trust
the ordinary operations of a law-abiding and orderly-inclined public." [101] The tactics of Mr. Churchill were compared with those of M.
Briand, who made, said Captain Wedgwood, "an exactly similar
speech justifying the use of the military in order to maintain the
supplies of food at the time of the great strike in France a year
ago." [102]

The Labour party in November, 1911, offered a resolution declaring that the refusal of the railway companies to carry out the Railway Conciliation Agreement of 1907 had no justification, and asked
the Government for the "public interest" to bring both sides into
a conference.[103] The unrest which flourished in July and August,
Mr. MacDonald said in November, had a characteristic which was
far more than that of a mere passing agitation. It had the characteristic of a fundamental upstirring, of fundamental discontent with
everything in general, which could only let itself go in ways which
were familiar with the public. All classes, rich and poor together,
the capitalist class and the labouring class in those extraordinary
months were seized with a sort of revolutionary spirit.[104]

This phase of the industrial unrest was suggested forcibly by
Dr. Gore, Bishop of Birmingham, in a farewell diocesan letter on
his transfer to the bishopric of Oxford. It was written during the
railway and dockers' strike, 1911. "There is," he said, "a profound
sense of unrest and dissatisfaction among workers recently. I cannot but believe that this profound discontent is justified, though
some particular exhibitions of it are not. As Christians we are not
justified in tolerating the conditions of life and labour under which
the great mass of our population is living. We have no right to say
that these conditions are not remediable. Preventible lack of equipment for life among the young, and later the insecurity of employ-

---

[101] *Parl. Deb., op. cit.,* pp. 2296–2298.
[102] *Parl. Deb.,* 5 S.H.C., 1909, vol. 29, pp. 2341–2345.
[103] *Parl. Deb.,* 5 S.H.C., 1911, vol. 31, pp. 1209–1329, debate entire, November
22, on railway companies and their employees. See speeches of Prime Minister
(pp. 1229–1233) ; Bonar Law (pp. 1233–1237) ; J. H. Thomas (pp. 1238–1245).
[104] *Parl. Deb.,* 5 S.H.C., 1911, vol. 31, p. 1211, pp. 1209–1223 entire.

ment and inadequacy of remuneration and consequent destitution and semi-destitution among so many people, ought to inspire in all Christians a determination to reform our industrial system." [105]

The Labour party amendment on Industrial Unrest in the 1912 Parliament provided a full opportunity for a debate on the "state of England question" and the reform of the industrial system.[106] The Amendment regretted, "That, having regard to the existing industrial unrest arising from a deplorable insufficiency of wages, which has persisted notwithstanding a great expansion of national wealth, and a considerable increase in the cost of living, your Majesty's Government's speech contains no specific mention of legislation securing a minimum living wage and for preventing a continuance of such unequal division of the fruits of industry by the nationalization of railways, mines and monopolies." The leader of the Labour party declared that there were 2,000,000 families in the nation with an income of only £45 a year. Between 1901–1911, according to the Board of Trade returns, there was a drop of £57,500 in wages. In 1910, in the transport trade, as classified by the Board of Trade, wages were increased by the sum of £341 per week in the gross, and 3,900 were affected. In 1911, owing to strikes, that £341 per week increase became £12,270 per week, and the number of people affected rose from 3,900 to 77,000. "You cannot shut your eyes," he said, "to the moral to be drawn from that state of things. As a matter of fact, it is because those men are demanding to see something better and are beginning to appreciate that width of life we all like—that enormous and unfulfilled possibility of the human mind acting in a state of freedom—that you are hearing now not the calm counsels of men who can sit and hold on, but the hasty, angry, enraged counsels of men who have got nothing to hold on to."

[105] Quoted by S. P. Orth, *Socialism and Democracy in Europe,* (1913), pp. 221–222. Cf. J. W. Scott, *Syndicalism and Philosophical Realism* (1919); G. D. H. Cole, *The World of Labour* (1913), and the allied books of this writer and the Guild Socialists; Bertrand Russell: *Principles of Social Reconstruction* (1916), and *Roads to Freedom: Socialism, Anarchism and Syndicalism* (1st ed. 1918, 3rd ed. 1920), especially chap. VIII. Mr. Scott wrote of British workmen's unrest 1910–1919, that they were "seeking something vaguer and vaster, something, they knew not what, something, as far as could be judged from their spokesmen, suggestive of fundamental alteration of the whole condition of labour, if not the abolition of the industrial system altogether." (p. 12, *op. cit.)*

[106] *Parl. Deb.,* 5 S.H.C., 1912, vol. 34, pp. 44–98, debate entire on Labour Amendment (p. 45).

There was a strange lack of confidence about in everything that was reasonable. If workmen were asked to submit their case to conciliation and arbitration, they said, "We have been cheated so often we will not do it again." Mr. MacDonald said, that in 1906, and before, his colleagues and himself went all over the country saying "a strike is an antiquated weapon which involves suffering and pain and trouble, and in the end the side that is right does not win. Trust the House of Commons. Build up a political party." They did; they adopted conciliation. As a matter of fact, between the years when they were telling them to build up a party and the delivery of the Osborne judgment conciliation was tried as it never was before. They did more by that propaganda, it was claimed, than anything that was ever done before to persuade the workman to put his care in writing, lay it on a table, to argue it out in reason, and that he was going to get more by that method than any other he might adopt. But no sooner was the worker persuaded that peaceful methods were right than conciliation was smashed by the railway directors, and Parliamentary methods were smashed by lawyers that might or might not have been good law, but was exceedingly bad common sense, and exceedingly bad and false history. As a matter of fact it was the red tape of the lawyers that stood side by side with the red-flag of the syndicalist—the two things were absolutely the same. The type of mind that gave that decision, and that regarded that type of labour combination from the merely static and legal point of view was what had whistled up the very worst elements inside the Labour movement; and so long as that judgment remained so long would the unrest and lack of confidence in civil and peaceful methods remain in the minds of the very best men in the Trade Union movement.

Despite any condemnation of the Labour leaders social progress was inevitably joined with legislation. The national minimum wage was, along with trade union status, a patent illustration. Industry could only be carried on if the living minimum wage was made the first charge on an industry. The view was emphasized most clearly. "Legislation has to come," declared Mr. MacDonald, "it has to embody the moral requirements which nobody can resist, and the time has come when we ought to translate these abstract moral propositions into effective Acts of Parliament. Labour unrest must be dealt with by this House. This House cannot afford to shut its eyes to it; and, if it tried, it would not be allowed to do so. Both outside and inside, this House will hear voices explaining and explaining what labour unrest means, asking for legislation, asking for administrative interference, the intention of which will be to do justice to men who are not economically strong enough to see justice is done to themselves. And that must be the intention of this House more and more. We cannot possibly allow capital and labour to fight out their own battles, we, standing on one side, looking on. There are three sides to every dispute; there is the side of capital, and there is the side of labour, there is the side of the general community; and the general community has no business to allow capital and labour, fighting their battles themselves, to elbow them out of consideration. This House and its officers, this Government and its administration must represent the third party, the general public." [107]

The Chancellor of the Exchequer's Birmingham speech was quoted by Mr. J. R. Clynes, a Labour member.[108] Mr. Lloyd George had said that the protection of property in England was the most perfect machine ever devised by the human brain. The guardians of property patrolled every street, and if the transgressor eluded them their vigilance pursued him to the end of the earth. But compare that with the way in which the Public Health Acts and the Housing Acts were administered, asked Mr. Lloyd George. Public Health Acts the country had had for years and years, now Housing Acts on the Statute Book, and yet there was no city or town, nay not a village, but you had the reek of insanitary property.[109] Labour seemed to be content in this debate to quote from contemporary sources, and Mr. Lansbury read into the record the Lambeth Resolution of the whole College of Bishops, "That the labourer, the workman and his wife and children, should and ought to be, from every point of Christianity and national morals, the first charge upon industry.[110] He asked the House to remember when it talked of Syndicalism, that if it refused to deal with the wrongs of the people, if ever it was powerless to deal with them, there was nothing for the people to do but to attend to the matter outside that House. For his part, while the House refused to deal with the social problem, he was going to join with all men outside who would join with him in doing what was

---

[107] *Parl. Deb., op. cit.*, pp. 51–52 (MacDonald).
[108] *Parl. Deb., op. cit.*, pp. 54–56 (Clynes).
[109] *Parl. Deb., op. cit.*, p. 60.
[110] *Parl. Deb., op. cit.*, pp. 80–89.

possible to stir up and foment revolt against revolting conditions. He was going to do all he could to make the poor hate poverty, to make them hate their poverty—never mind about hating their social conditions. He did not want them to hate the rich, but to hate the idea that they and their children should live under untoward conditions. Soon after Mr. Lansbury's appeal his indictment found a response in the statement of Lord Hugh Cecil that he thought "it is true that the great sufferings and sorrows of which we are hearing so much are the fruit of the industrial system. I think it is also true that the competitive system depends upon a side of human nature which is fundamentally unchristian, and appeals to and is animated by those motives of self-interest, which are essentially inconsistent with the profession of Christianity." [111]

But profit-sharing, upon which Lord Hugh Cecil placed emphasis, was no part of the concern of Syndicalism. This was evident in the debate on March 27, 1912, when a resolution was offered, "That in the opinion of this House, the growth and advocacy by certain Labour agitators of an anti-social policy of Syndicalism based upon class warfare and incitement to mutiny constitute a grave danger to the State and the welfare of the community." [112]

The mover, Mr. Ormsby-Gore, referring to France as the natural home of Syndicalism, believed that one of the reasons for the growth of Syndicalism was the failure of the Parliamentary Labour parties of France and England to carry out their lavish promises. The Government, through the Chancellor of the Duchy of Lancaster, Mr. Hobhouse, declared that Syndicalism did not create unrest in England.[113] It was due to two reasons. First, looking back over a series of years there had been a much greater rise in the cost of living than in wages, and on the other hand, on the intellectual side, there was an increased *mental sense* of the poverty among the working classes in the country, as compared with those more fortunate than they are, which had not been accompanied by any corresponding advancement in their material welfare. Those were the two reasons if Syndicalism, or anything approaching it, had obtained a foothold in England. The Labour spokesman,[114] considering the conditions of

---

[111] *Parl. Deb., op. cit.,* pp. 107–108, pp. 107–113 entire.
[112] *Parl. Deb.,* 5 S.H.C., 1912, vol. 36, p. 537; pp. 535–559 debate entire.
[113] *Parl. Deb., op. cit.,* pp. 552–555.
[114] *Parl. Deb., op. cit.,* pp. 555–559 (Roberts).

the time an inevitable form of capitalistic development, yet declared he was not a believer in the class war, nor had he sympathy with Syndicalism. If the nation were to be rid of the enemy, as Syndicalism had been called, the causes would have to be removed. The causes were poverty, low wages, and those incidental miseries which affect the working classes. The Labour party, he said, were prepared to associate themselves with any party or any section of any party who were genuinely desirous of removing the causes that brought those things about, and that curse which fell upon the working classes because of no inherent evil on their part, but because of conditions over which they had no control—the curse of undeserved poverty.

Faith that the Government could be used as a means toward understanding the causes of industrial unrest was indicated once again in the resolution on May 8, 1912, in the House of Commons, which declared, "That this House is of the opinion that the recent industrial disturbances show the necessity of a thorough and authoritative investigation into the causes of the present industrial unrest, and into possible remedies therefor, and, in view of the prospective recurrence of such disturbances calls upon the Government to prosecute such investigation by all appropriate means and in the speediest manner compatible with adequate inquiry into the issues involved." [115] The mover, a Liberal, Mr. Crawshay-Williams, thought that the situation was serious, but that the unrest was not in itself a bad thing. It was part of a struggle for better conditions on the part of the workers of the country.[116] It was part of a long development which began with the first Factory Act. From being a blind and groping movement it became a conscious and connected effort. Not only had labour learned its power, but Labour had obtained an ethical conviction of its causes. Unrest was part of a deliberate revolt against the untrammelled nature of wealth getting, and this in itself was not bad. It was only the symptoms which were considered bad, and it was remembered that strikes were not the unrest; they were the symptoms of unrest. "It is an idealism; it may be crude idealism; it may be blind idealism; but it is an idealism, and the cruder and blinder it is, the more it needs our guidance and assistance . . . We are in a period of change, and unless we recognize that we are in a period of fundamental change, unless we take

[115] *Parl. Deb.*, 5 S.H.C., 1912, vol. 38, p. 487; pp. 487–534 debate entire.
[116] *Parl. Deb.*, *op. cit.*, pp. 487–503.

the matter in hand today, not only we but those who come after us will rue it. The spirit behind this movement is a right spirit, it will prevail. Labour will get, and rightly get, a larger share of this world's goods. Our duty, as the ruling body in this great nation, is to see to it that Labour gets its due without the miseries and calamities of industrial strife." [117]

There was no lack of faith either in the attitude of the veteran Hardie,[118] who declared that Booth and Rowntree had showed facts enough, as Campbell-Bannerman in 1906 stated, and he warned the House and the Government that if any make-believe Committees were set up no single working-class organization would appear before them. The working class would give no evidence. They had formulated their demands, and if the House did not satisfy the demands, so much the worse for the House. Syndicalism was the direct outcome of the apathy and indifference of Parliament toward working-class questions, and he rejoiced at the growth of Syndicalism. The more Syndicalism outside, the quicker would be the pace that Parliament moved. Parliament never moved except in response to pressure, and the more pressure the more likelihood there would be of real drastic reforms, and the conditions of the workmen improved. Conditions in respect to railway wages were aptly put by Mr. J. H. Thomas, when he said that in ten years there had been an increase of a halfpenny a man.[119]

But at the close of the debate the Government was brought to the issue for their share of the responsibility in the cause of industrial unrest, because of the doctrines which underlay the legislative programme of the Government since 1906. Mr. Peto specifically mentioned as causes of industrial unrest the Coal Mines (Eight Hours) Act, 1908, the Coal Mines (Minimum Wage) Act, 1912, the Budget of 1909, and the Parliament Act of 1911.[120] The Government, through the Chancellor of the Exchequer, Mr. Lloyd George, found one answer in the fact that in their indictment of the present order the Labour leader Hardie and the distinguished Conservative apologist Lord Hugh Cecil were in accord.[121] Great needs had brought men together. The "state of England question" could never more be downed.

[117] *Parl. Deb., op. cit.,* p. 503.
[118] *Parl. Deb., op. cit.,* pp. 513–520.
[119] *Parl. Deb., op. cit.,* pp. 520–521 (Thomas).
[120] *Parl. Deb., op. cit.,* pp. 521–532 (Peto), pp. 532–534 (Lloyd George).
[121] *Parl. Deb., op. cit.,* pp. 508–513 (Cecil).

CHAPTER XI

THE BRITISH LABOUR MOVEMENT AND SOCIAL POLICY: THE POST-WAR YEARS TO THE GENERAL ELECTION OF 1929

The post-war years in England and France have been years of upheaval, quick reaction and unceasing change. Consequently there have been sharp differences in political opinion and there have been strong antagonisms in national policies. These years, therefore, provide illustrative material in the development and expansion of the Labour movement for an understanding of the problems which this study has presented. This and the succeeding chapter on the British Labour Movement and social policy, is an account of the post-war years to the general election of 1929, and of the extension of the political and industrial alliance to the second Labour Government in Great Britain.

The British Labour movement in common with all political agencies of the modern democratic state has had to bear the indictment so often given since 1918 of the inadequacy of Parliamentary government. The failure of the political democratic institutions to adjust the economic machinery of the modern state to the changed conditions has become a less effective argument as the complexity of present day industrial civilization is seen by more people. The easy challenge of the incompetency of democratic government has not been given with as much assurance by capital and labour since the state has asked often from 1918 for these two organized agencies of production to help solve the difficulties in the working of the industrial system of the twentieth century. It has been seen that democratic government and its institutions have not been the cause of industrial discord, but that the methods of persuasion and debate and consultation which are essentially democratic in their nature may contribute to the working out of saner industrial relationships.

It is a matter of record that in every country the workers did their duty from 1914 to 1918 in the struggle which almost destroyed Europe. The material and economic dislocation of the war cannot be adequately estimated even twelve years after the armistice. In both France and England the major problems since 1918 have been those which have arisen out of the war and its aftermath. If there is today lacking the high mood which is reflected in the British Labour party manifesto of 1918, *Labour and the New Social Order,* and the Trade Union Congress aims of 1918 to 1920, there is not denied for these times the serious determination to make the conditions of industry better and to build more soundly the economic structure of peace. There seemed to be the expectation of a new world in 1918. The calmer mood was given expression in a letter dated September 11, 1914, written by Mr. J. Ramsay MacDonald, later to be Prime Minister, who well said that incalculable political and social consequences would follow upon victory; that the quarrel was not of the people, but the end of it would be the lives and liberties of the people. Against many difficult odds the peoples of France and England have had to find a stable way to peace, and their Governments have reflected the changed conditions of the post-war Europe. The internal problems of adjustment have been always insistent, while foreign policy, as never before, both in its economic and political aspects, has been joined to the issues of prosperity within the country.

The survey of social legislation in Great Britain has given the quick and rapid changes which necessarily took place with regard to the administration of the social services by the state. During the war there was nothing to be done but carry forward the services as they were organized before 1914, and to adjust as fairly as could be done the working of the general schemes to the individual. In fact since 1918 the time of Parliament, has been given more to the elaboration of the old systems than to any original schemes of social legislation. The account of political and industrial activities in the Labour movement which follow below will give the story of a nation hard pressed by untoward economic conditions. But there has been no lesser aim than that out of the distress and dislocation a better understanding of the needs of England would result. There have been hard and prolonged years of unemployment, industries had to be reorganized, and a war had to be paid for after it was over. There can be no doubt that these years have revealed the conditions of industrial and social life in England. What has been attempted to meet these needs may be partially seen in the account of the political and industrial Labour movement and the programme of social legislation.

I

THE GROWTH OF THE LABOUR PARTY

The British Labour movement has faced since the war the lively issues growing out of the difficult problem of adjusting a political party to a new economic conditions. The Labour party has, in spite of almost overwhelming obstacles, achieved a party discipline under sustained Parliamentary leadership. Since 1918 no party in England has had a more united front than Labour, although often the leadership of the party has been set some difficult internal problems to settle. The opposition press has delighted in the antics of the Labour members, has emphasized the real divergence in point of view of Mr. MacDonald and some prominent men in the party, especially of the Left Wing, but the Labour forces have held their own in the state. They have increased their poll since 1900 by over eight million votes; and from a vote in 1918 of 2,244,945, they reached the total of 5,487,620 in 1924, although they lost 40 seats in the October, 1924, election. The Labour party contested 570 seats in 1929, and elected 287 candidates, polling a vote of 8,362,594. The electoral progress of the Labour party can be readily seen in the summarized history here given:

General Election	Seats Contested	Members Returned	Labour Vote
1900	15	2	62,698
1906	50	29	323,195
1910 (January)	78	40	505,690
1910 (December)	56	42	370,802
1918	361	57	2,244,945
1922	414	142	4,236,733
1923	427	191	4,236,733
1924	514	151	5,487,620
1929	570	287	8,362,594

In the General Election, 1924, the total number of votes cast was 16,120,735. Of this number the Conservatives polled 7,385,139,

Labour, 5,487,620, Liberals, 2,982,563, and scattering, 265,413. The state of the parties in December, 1924, was: Conservatives, 402 members, Labour, 151, Liberal, 41, others 9. The total vote in the 1929 election was 22,639,117. The Conservatives polled 8,644,-243, the Liberals 5,300,947, and Labour, 8,362,594; and other parties 311,333. Of the 615 seats in the House of Commons, Labour secured 287, the Conservatives, 260, the Liberals 59, and Independents 9.

After the General Election of 1918, the Labour party entered a new period of activity and influence. The election of that year was the first test of the popular hold of the party on the people since 1910, and the returning of 57 members to the House of Commons, representing a total electoral strength of 2,244,945 votes, gave enthusiasm to the cause of Labour. The Labour party was the largest opposition group in attendance on Parliament, for the representatives of the Sinn Fein party, while more numerous, did not attend at Westminster. The party was not recognized as the official Opposition, as it wanted to be, but the procedure adopted by the Speaker was to grant precedence on all occasions of first class importance to the Labour Party and to the Independent Liberals alternately.

The Parliamentary Labour Party, 1919–1924: Policy and Influence

The Session of 1919 of the new Parliament opened on February 11, and on the Address in answer to the King's Speech, the Labour party moved an amendment regretting the absence of any mention of definite proposals for dealing with the causes of industrial unrest and for securing, as regards wages and working hours, conditions of labour that would establish a higher standard of life and social well-being for the people. The Labour party brought forward a number of Bills for Second Reading in 1919, being fortunate in the ballot for Bills. Among these Bills were the Prevention of Unemployment Bill, which was thrown out; the Women's Emancipation Bill passed through all stages, but did not become law because the Government introduced instead their own Sex Disqualification Bill, which became a law; the Checkweighing in Various Industries Bill passed all stages and became law; the Local Authorities (Enabling) Bill, which sought to extend the powers of local authorities in matters of finance and municipal trading, was rejected on Second Reading. The Labour party also gained from the Government, in their debate on the motion on Pensions for Mothers, an expression of agreement with the principle.

On the Address, in answer to the King's Speech in the Parliamentary Session of 1920, the Labour party moved an amendment expressing regret at the absence of any proposal to nationalize the coal mines of the country. This amendment, along with an amendment practically demanding a revision of the Peace Treaties, was defeated. The Labour party Bills in this session were its Women's Emancipation Bill, introduced as the Representation of the People Bill, which received a Second Reading and went to Committee, and this stage was not concluded; the Local Authorities (Enabling) Bill came up for Second Reading and was again rejected; and the Blind (Education, Employment and Maintenance) Bill, secured a Second Reading, but the Government brought forward their own provision, the extension of Old Age Pensions and the Labour Bill was dropped.

The official party Amendment to the Address in the Parliamentary Session of 1921, was an amendment expressing regret that in view of the serious distress consequent upon unemployment and the lack of preparedness on the part of the Government to deal with the situation, there was no legislation recognizing the right of the genuine unemployed to work or to adequate maintenance. During the year the Labour party by motions and questions kept the important problems of housing and unemployment in the first place of legislative interest. Again in 1922 the Labour party amendment to the Address dealt with unemployment and expressed regret, in view of the disaster to British trade, and the amount of unemployment, that there was no indication that the Government were prepared to recognize and deal effectively with the course of unemployment, or to provide the opportunity for useful productive work; and further, in view of the exhaustion of national funds provided for the assistance of local authorities, and the approaching cessation of unemployment insurance benefit, regretted that there was no apparent intention on the part of the Government to grant substantial financial aid to the local authorities who could not be expected to bear a national burden. The amendment was defeated by 270 to 78.

From 1918 to 1922 was "a cycle of profound economic disturbance and political unsettlement, marked by trade depression, falling prices, heavy wage reductions, and abnormal unemployment." [1] It was a critical phase of Labour history in which forced readjustments took place and heavy losses were sustained by the working-class movement. But the British Labour movement from 1918 has had an unfailing interest for all who study the politics of democracy. Mr. Arthur Henderson, quite qualified to judge, wrote in 1922 that this was, perhaps, due in measure to two outstanding facts: (a) that the organized movement in Britain was regarded almost universally as the most powerful, highly organized, and progressive organization in the world, and (b) that the political labour movement was expected soon to be called upon to assume the responsibilities of national government. [2]

Professor W. G. S. Adams, Gladstone Professor Political Theory and Institutions, Oxford, declared that a new complex of problems —constitutional, political and economic—was the result of the rapid rise of Labour since 1918. This was especially significant in a great political society with strong traditions and understandings marking out lines of natural social progress. Professor Adams' interpretation is suggestive. [3] "Temporary appearances may seem to contradict what experience and study may suggest. Yet there is a logic underlying the development of human society, and the study of what has been and of what is reveals in some measure what is to be. Even great convulsions in society, marking a new ferment of thought which leavens the whole body politic and, it may be, over-throwing a long established order, settle down into a development in which we can trace a continuity through change. England has been notably free from violent convulsions, and a characteristic steadiness has marked its long political evolution. But with this stability there has been a power of readjustment to new conditions and of further development. The English constitution has been peculiarly flexible, and with age it does not become less but rather more so. There is in it, somehow, a wonderful power of shock absorption."

On October 26, 1922, following the resignation of the Prime Minister, Mr. Lloyd George, Parliament was dissolved. The newly

---

[1] J. Ramsay MacDonald, *The Labour Year Book, 1924,* "Foreword."

[2] In his "Introduction" to Paul Blanshard's *An Outline of the British Labour Movement* (1923), p. v.

[3] See his "England after the Election," *Foreign Affairs,* vol. II, No. 3 (March, 1924), pp. 351–365.

elected Parliament, which met on November 23, 1922, with Mr. Bonar Law as Prime Minister, contained 142 Labour members, representing a Labour vote of 4,236,733. The party made an early claim to be regarded as the Opposition, which carries with it the exclusive occupation of the Front Opposition Bench. The Speaker, however, ruled that he must take into account the existence of other parties in opposition, and it was ultimately decided that the major portion of the Front Bench should be allocated to the Labour party, which should be regarded as the chief Opposition. At the first meeting of the party, Mr. J. Ramsay MacDonald, regaining his hold securely on the Labour party, was elected Chairman and Leader; Mr. J. R. Clynes and Mr. Arthur Henderson were elected Deputy-Leader and Chief Whip respectively.

II

Labour and the "Capitalist System" Debate, 1923

The influence of the Labour party in the House of Commons from the election of 1922 has met no serious setback, so far as losing its hold on the loyalty of its supporters. The official amendments of the Party in these years, when in Opposition, have dealt mainly with old age pensions, unemployment, housing, and questions arising out of the peace treaties of the War of 1914–1918. These problems remain unsettled, but honest effort is continually given by the best minds of Great Britain to understanding "the state of England" question. Perhaps the early post-war attitude of the Labour party can be well set forth in the agreed motion on the Capitalist System, offered March 20, 1923. The debate was initiated by Mr. Philip Snowden, the Labour Chancellor of the Exchequer in the first and second MacDonald Governments. The resolution read as follows: "That, in view of the failure of the capitalist system to adequately utilize and organize natural resources and productive power, or to provide the necessary standard of life for vast numbers of the population, and believing that the cause of this failure lies in the private ownership and control of the means of production and distribution, this House declares that legislative effort should be directed to the gradual supersession of the capitalist system by an industrial and social order based on the public ownership and democratic control of the instruments of production and distribution."

This was answered by an amendment by Sir Alfred Mond as follows: "To leave out from the word 'That' to the end of the Question and to put instead thereof the words: "This House, believing that the abolition of private interest in the means of production and distribution would improverish the people and aggravate existing evils, is unalterably opposed to any scheme of legislation which would deprive the State of the benefits of individual initiative, and believing that far-reaching measures of social redress may be accomplished without overturning the present basis of society, is resolved to prosecute proposals which, by removing the evil effects of monopoly and waste, will conduce to the well-being of the people." The vote taken at the end of the second day's sitting, July 16, 1923, resulted in a vote for Socialism of 121, for Capitalism 368. The minority consisted entirely of members of the Labour party; the majority was composed from every other party in the House.

The debate in 1923 brought very little new material together, but it did serve the function of indicating the useless waste in human life that the economic system based on exploitation demands. This indictment was just as sincere from the ranks of the Liberals and the Conservatives as from the Labour benches, and therein is the hope of the struggle for a sounder social order. Mr. Lloyd George, who is excelled by no one in indicting social waste, pointedly said that "those who are most anxious to preserve the present system ought to be the most anxious to remedy the evils which arise from it. Unless they do so, I am certain that the bulk of the workers of this country will come to the conclusion that they are evils which are inherent in the system . . . I should like . . . to point out to the House of Commons circumstances which fill me with a great deal of apprehension from the after-effects of the War. Those facts are greater than we apprehended, and I think they are more potent. If anyone doubts that the war had made a permanent impression upon the people of this country he has only got to look at one fact, that Hon. Members who challenge the existing order of things, at the last election, for the first time, polled 4,250,000 votes. The House will make a very great mistake if it goes away with the idea that everything is all right, because it has demolished an impossible proposition made by the Hon. Member for Colne Valley (Mr. Snowden), because the facts will remain. It is not his arguments, powerful as they are, but the facts that we have to consider."

Sir John Simon believed that the most important thing of all was to humanize industry: "You cannot humanize industry by the vain and dreary repetition of an arid formula. The way to humanize industry is not to put it into the straight jacket of universal Socialism; it is to use the force of public opinion, the power of Parliament, to correct the rigours of unrestricted selfishness by putting public needs and human rights before private interests, and by doing it, as I believe it can be done, without sapping the energies or undermining the liberties of the British people." Mr. Arthur Henderson reviewed, somewhat in the fashion of Mr. Snowden, the history of the industrial and labour movement in the thirty preceding years in his indictment of the existing system. The war, he added, brought into operation new ideas of social possibility, of economic reconstruction, of unity, of responsibility, and of human rights. Labour indicted the capitalist system because, in its opinion, the system condemns large numbers of honest, decent, self-respecting and law-abiding citizens of long periods of undeserved and unrelieved misery, and to conditions of life which any person with a spark of human feeling would not defend as tolerable, let alone just.

There is no one in the Labour movement who can more ably put what the opponents of its doctrines call the "metaphysics of Socialism," than Mr. J. Ramsay MacDonald. He concluded the debate in 1923, as follows: "I object to the human spirit being limited and confined in its freedom by embattled economic power such as capitalism affords today. Talk about liberty today! Why, we have not got a whiff of liberty yet. The great mass of our people are not free to choose a destiny for their own children, and to live lives that would be good lives. The great mass of our people are not free to say what they like and to think what they like. I object most strongly to this domination of materialism, which is capitalism, over life, absolutely. Moreover, what is the great problem we have all got to face? I say it is the problem of production to begin with. What is the appeal of capitalism for more production? Absolutely nothing at all. It cannot be the appeal of property. Until you can enlist the soul of your worker you are neither going to have duty coming from his heart nor amplitude coming from his efforts. Capitalists cannot lift the man up to that; they may give him big positions and managing posts, but this is gross materialism which moth and dust doth corrupt and which thieves break through and steal, and until society has discovered that fine, impalpable, spiritual effort it will never solve this great problem of production."

THE FIRST LABOUR GOVERNMENT

In a very short time this spokesman of Labour was to be called upon to form a Government, for on November 13, 1923, when the Session of 1923 was resumed, Mr. Stanley Baldwin, the Conservative Prime Minister, announced the decision of the Government to advise a Dissolution of Parliament in order that they might ask for a mandate from the country to carry out Protectionist proposals for the cure of unemployment. The action of Mr. Baldwin was bitterly censured by some of his followers, and the country was greatly surprised at the Government's policy. The events which followed somewhat balanced the feeling of popular disapproval which at one time threatened the leadership of Mr. Baldwin.

The Labour party put the following Motion on the Paper, and it was debated on November 15: "That this House censures the neglect of His Majesty's Government to deal with the pressing needs of the unemployed, regrets its failure to devise and pursue a national policy calculated to restore the influence of the country abroad and re-establish international peace and trade; condemns the decision of the Government to leave millions of British people in want in order to fight an election of an undisclosed scheme of tariffs and imperial preference, conceived by sections of capitalists in their own interests, and the effect of which must be to increase the cost of living and encourage the formation of anti-social trusts and combines." This motion was defeated by 285 votes to 190. The Country then awaited the General Election which took place in December. The Government returned 258 members, the Liberals 158, Independents 8, and Labour increasing its number by 149 returned 191 members in the House of Commons. The Labour total vote polled was 4,348,379.

The Conservative Prime Minister decided to meet Parliament on January 8, 1924, and on the 15th of that month Parliament was formally opened with the King's Speech prepared by the Conservative Government. The Conservative Government framed the Speech

knowing that there would be little chance of carrying out the proposals contained in it, which proposed to give effect to the recommendations of the Imperial Conference on Imperial Preference,
and extension of the existing methods of dealing with Unemployment and Agricultural, and additional bonus to pre-war Pensioners,
and legislation to deal with the discouragement of thrift operating
under the Old Age Pensions Acts. Even this was not a bold programme, though there was no chance of it having to be vindicated.

After two days of debate on the Speech, during which period
many questions regarding foreign affairs, education, housing, unemployment, and feeding of school children was raised, the Labour
party moved the following Amendment to the Address in answer:
"But it is our duty respectfully to submit to your Majesty that your
Majesty's present advisers have not the confidence of this House."

This Amendment was debated for three days, and was then carried
by 328 to 256, a majority of 72, the Liberals voting with the Labour
party. The following day, January 22, the Prime Minister announced
the resignation of the Government, and the House was adjourned
until February 12. The King called upon Mr. J. Ramsay MacDonald
to form a Government, exactly twenty-four years after he had been
organizing secretary of the Labour Representation Committee which
met in London. Prior to the opening of Parliament, when it was
almost a certainty that the Conservative Government would be defeated on the Address, the National Executive of the Party and the
Parliamentary Executive met and decided in favour of the party
taking office should the opportunity offer. When Parliament re-
assembled on February 12, the first Labour Prime Minister made a
statement of Government policy dealing with such questions as Dis-
armament, the League of Nations, Housing, Unemployment, Agriculture, Recognition of Russia, and the Peace of Europe. Mr. Mac-
Donald recognized the situation that his Government was in, a position representing a new constitutional problem, for the election of
1923 left no one of the three parties in the position of having a
majority, and brought into the sphere of practical politics the programme of a third party. He announced that the Government would
only go out on the defeat of a question of policy when the will of the
House was definitely expressed.

It is unnecessary here to make any attempt to estimate the nine
months in office of the first Government formed by the Labour

party. There is no better statement of the matter than Mr. Mac-
Donald gave in Albert Hall, London, May 13, 1924: "No minority
ought to be asked to do the work of a majority. It is not sound democracy." Four months before in the same place, January 8, Mr. Mac-
Donald set forth what he thought a Labour Government might do
and what its attitude to problems of the state would be. This Albert
Hall address made a great impression on the country, and was en-
thusiastically welcomed by his followers. One thought at the time
of what MacDonald in 1921 had written of Hardie: "His life was
but the manifestation of the spirit, and to him "the spirit" was something like what it was to the men whose bones lay on the Ayrshire
moors under martyrs' monuments. It was the grand crowned authority of life, but an authority that spoke from behind a veil, that
revealed itself in mysterious things both to man's heart and eyes." [4]
MacDonald wrote of the leader: "When the great labour leader
comes he must possess the power which is to purify society and expose
the falseness and vulgarity of materialist possession and class distinction. The mind of the labour leader must be too rich to do homage
to 'tinsel show', too proud of its own lineage to make obeisance to
false honour, and too cultured to be misled by vulgar display. A
working class living in moral and social parasitism on its 'betters' will
only increase the barrenness and futility of life."

The Albert Hall speech thus was well begun with a reference to
the pioneers who had made the whole adventure of modern labour
possible. "You and I, my friends," he said, "their successors, the
heirs of their labour, must cherish with religious zeal the inspiring
memories they have left behind, and guard with all the care that
tender human hearts can show the lamps they lit before the altars
of democracy and Socialism. We are upon a pilgrimage. We are on
a journey. . . . We shall take office if we have the chance in order
to try and settle the manifold and pressing difficulties that beset our
nation, Europe, and the whole world at the present moment. My
task, and my colleagues' task, is going to be to mobilise all men and
women of good-will and sane judgment."

The audience that heard the man who in a few days was to become
the Prime Minister knew that he did not underestimate the difficulty
of the problems at home that were equalled by the tremendous
tasks of foreign policy. Europe, Russia, the League of Nations were

[4] His "Introduction" to William Stewart's *Keir Hardie*.

talked of, along with the problems of housing and unemployment. In a few days he was to be leader of the Government, and it is interesting to note Mr. MacDonald's closing passage: "I want a Labour Government so that the life of the nation can be carried on; 1924 is not the last year in God's programme of creation. We shall be dead and gone and forgotten, and generation after generation will come, and still the journey will be going on, still the search for the Holy Grail will be made by knights like Hardie. The shield of love and the spear of justice will still be in the hands of good and upright men and women. And the ideal of a great future will be in front of our people. I see no end, thank God, to these things. I see my own horizon, I see my own sky-line, but I am convinced that when my children and my children's children get there, there will be another sky-line, another horizon, another dawning, another glorious beckoning from Heaven itself. That is my faith, and in that faith I go on and my colleagues go on, doing in their lifetime what they can to make their generation contribute something substantial to the well-being and happiness and holiness of human life."

III

The Labour Party in Office and the 1924 General Election

With the Labour party in office, a new situation, from the point of view of Parliamentary internal organization, arose. All the officers of the party and many of those who served on the Executive in the previous Session of Parliament had become Ministers, and it was decided, therefore, that instead of an Executive composed mainly of the officers of the party, there should be an Executive composed of twelve Members not in the Government, plus three Ministers, to act as a liaison committee between the party and the Government. It was convenient to the Government to be able to consult a representative committee of the party at short notice, and it was convenient to the party as a whole to have a committee to make representations to the Government when considered necessary.

The Labour rule of nine months, declared Mr. Arthur Henderson, "Upheld all that was best in the British Constitution," doing more in nine months to restore the peace of the world than its predeces-

sors accomplished in as many years, and "demonstrated by its legislative and administrative record that the ability to govern can no
longer be regarded as a monopoly of any one particularly privileged
class." [5]

The party Bills and motions in the first short Labour Government followed exactly the line that had been pursued by Labour
from 1918. There was one serious criticism of Labour, that they did
not attempt to put into effect the reforms that very easily might have
won Parliamentary support. The attitude of Labour with regard to
industrial legislation is noted in the part of this study dealing with
actual statutes, and it is only worth recording here that other Bills
of the Labour party brought forward were, the Rent Restrictions
Bill, which was abandoned in Committee; the Representation of the
People Bill, providing for equality in the franchise by conferring
the vote upon women at the age of twenty-one, assimilating the Parliamentary and Local Government franchises, abolishing the University fee for registration, and removing the disqualification resting
upon members of certain local authorities who may have received
poor relief, passed Second Reading but got no farther; the Nationalization of Mines and Materials Bill, promoted by the Miners' Federation and approved by the Party, was rejected on Second Reading;
and the Motions on a National Minimum Wage and Mothers' Pensions were accepted without division.

The importance of administration is emphasized in all of the
propaganda literature of the Labour Party. After the fall of the
first Labour Government and upon the formation of the second
Labour Government, its supporters cited often the sympathetic and
the constructive administrative policy of the Labour Government
which, so it is claimed, is a double benefit to the people with regard to
the provisions of old age pensions, unemployment, and housing requirements. Friends of Labour believed that the record of the first
Labour Government compared favourably with any other Governments. It was officially declared that if the full programme for the
Session had been completed in the Autumn, it would have comprised
a great Housing scheme, a good working-class Budget, a welcome
improvement in the Old Age Pensions Scheme, a substantial amendment of the Unemployment Insurance Scheme, an agreement with
Russia which, if ratified by the Parliament, would have helped con-

[5] Foreword, *Labour Year Book, 1925,* p. iii.

siderably towards increasing the volume of employment, an Inter-Allied agreement with Germany which it was hoped might pave the way to durable peace and economic restoration of Europe, a Factories Bill which would have conferred great benefit upon many workers, an Eight-hour Day, Equality in the Franchise, and a national scheme of Electricity Supply. Such a record for the year would have been phenomenal! All of which, of course, is part of the unpredictable in politics, and has no more value than any other unfulfilled promise. It also proves that the Labour party does not neglect the publicity value of promises.

The Labour Government fell after nine months of office on the issues arising out of the famous Communist prosecution, initiated against the acting editor of the *Workers' Weekly,* Mr. Campbell. The weekly was the organ of the Communist Party in Great Britain, and the Government decided to withdraw the prosecution on the ground that it would not be in the public interest to attach an entirely unwarranted importance to the seditious articles in question or to those responsible for it. The action of the Attorney-General in withdrawing the prosecution was raised, and the Conservative Opposition asked for a day to discuss the matter. On October 8, 1924, the Conservatives moved a Motion of censure, to which the Liberal party offered an amendment, which was finally accepted by both Conservatives and Liberals in order to insure the defeat of the Government. The Liberal amendment was: "That a Select Committee be appointed to investigate and report upon the circumstances leading up to the withdrawal of the proceedings recently instituted by the Director of Public Prosecutions against Mr. Campbell."

The Prime Minister said the motion demanding an inquiry by a Select Committee, practically gave the lie to the solemn assurances of the Ministers, and if carried the Government would go to the country. By a vote of 364 to 198 the Liberal amendment was carried, and the next day, October 9, 1924, the Prime Minister announced that the King had acceded to his request to dissolve Parliament.

In the General Election of 1924, which quickly followed dissolution, Labour contested 514 seats, polled 5,487,620 votes, and returned 151 members to the House of Commons. Polling over a million more votes than ever before the party nevertheless lost 40 seats. But the coming into office of Labour gave it a prestige that greatly strengthened the Party and its hold on the country. At the same time Labour came to grips with the disillusioning facts of politics. The Labour Party for a long time had gained much from the ardent and eager spirits of reform and revolution in England, and the season of training as a Government dealing with knotty problems of finance, trade and administration, did a good deal to clarify their thinking. The party received a discipline which has meant since 1924 a larger and fuller share in the government of Great Britain. The first experiment of Labour as a minority Government in 1924 made it easier for Labour to form a minority Government in 1929.

The Labour party programme was well outlined in the Election Manifesto in the General Election of 1924 issued with the united support of the Parliamentary Labour Party, the General Council of the Trade Union Congress, and the Executive Committee of the Labour Party. This Manifesto emphasized the work for international peace of the Labour Government; the Budget, the housing, education, agriculture and unemployment programme of the Labour Government were indications of a new spirit at Westminster, it was affirmed. The Labour Government's Bills before Parliament were cited as evidence of the capacity of the party to understand the needs of the people and to use Parliament as an instrument of reform. Under the caption "The Spirit That Giveth Life," the Election Manifesto of 1924 concluded with the following: "It is along such lines as those marked out in this Appeal, and in the spirit of public service herein indicated, that the Labour Party, in conformity with its consistent public declarations, would work in Parliament towards the transformation, gradual as it must be, of the existing economic and industrial system into a genuine Commonwealth of Labour. We know the facts. We realise the difficulties. The path to our goal is long and narrow and sometimes so hard to travel that men and women faint by the way. But we have faith in humanity. We refuse to believe that there is nothing to be done but conserve the present order, which is disorder; or that the misery, the demoralization and the ruin it causes to innocent men and women and children can be remedied by the perpetual repetition of the abstract principles of Individualism. We appeal to the People to support us in our steadfast march—taking each step only after careful examination, making sure of each advance as we go, and using each success as the beginning of further achievements towards a really Socialist Commonwealth, in which there shall at least be opportunity for Goodwill to conquer Hate and

Strife, and for Brotherhood, if not to supersede Greed, at least to set due bounds to that competition which leads only to loss and death."

LABOUR AND THE PARLIAMENTARY SYSTEM

Such an appeal illustrates what one English critic believes to be by far the greatest asset of the Labour Party—its vision of a new political, social and economic order.[6] Of course, in the great economic organization of Labour there lies ready to hand an instrument of political propaganda and social organization possessed by neither of the old parties. But Labour "has brought freshness into the rather stale atmosphere of political controversy and there is much more widely extended sympathy with its programme than would have seemed possible before the war." This has been increased by a growing recognition of the essentially constitutional character of the Labour movement. In recent times the leaders of the party have taken marked pains to insist on this point. The English constitution is their possession and heritage as much as that of any other party; their allegiance to it is as true as that of any other party. They have observed the Parliamentary system and have regarded it as the right means for the expression of the will of the people.

What this has meant to the politics of Great Britain all serious students of affairs recognize. Parliament has again become a place where debate and discussion of great policies takes place, and here the Labour Party has made a contribution to the cause of good government. "It is, however, in domestic affairs," Professor Adams believes, "that Labour marks a great departure from either of the old parties. A new school of thought is coming into power and responsibility, a school which may be called that of the socialization of national life. It is not a school of Communism, but one which seeks much more than any other party to organize community action and to control the sources of power within the nation. Responsibility for action is bound to exercise a great influence on the formulation and practical expression of this school of thought. The application of its underlying ideas in different fields of public life is taking shape in various definite proposals, the difficulties and advantages of which can now be considered, deliberately if not altogether dispassionately. Parliament will again become the great debating centre in which discussion will focus. The country will also be schooled in the same

---

[6] W. G. S. Adams, *op. cit.*, p. 355 ff.

problems, and the quickening of thought in the country will react on the work of Parliament." [7]

Somewhat the same conclusion was reached concerning the whole of postwar Europe and socialism by M. Emile Vandervelde, chief of the Socialist party in Belgium. His thesis is that the workers must wrest political power from the State. "In short, the ultimate progress of socialization depends largely on the political progress of the working class, and such progress is itself a function of industrial development, of the growth of the proletariat, and of the consciousness and organization of the working class. From this standpoint there can be no doubt that the war has given a definite impulse to previously existing tendencies and has laid the way wide open to the socialist conquest of power." [8]

The practical effect of the Labour party seeking to organize community action and definitely to build upon the democratic doctrine of consent is seen in the constructive programme which it has given to the nation. Its failures have been significant, because there has been a capacity for criticism in the party. Also the Labour movement has widened its appeal by welcoming professional men, educators, even peers,—anyone who accepts its creed. The programme of the Labour party in and without Parliament, whether one agrees with it or not, is at least comprehensive, constructive, and arguably practicable. There have been controversies and always Labour representatives in the Parliament of England have fought for specific reforms, but with increasing meaning the advocates of Labour have declared that the best interests of the wage earner are not in conflict with the national interests.[9] They have stated their ideal in human terms and the power which has come to the Labour party is based upon this fact rather than upon a doctrine of class warfare.

IV

BRITISH LABOUR AND SOCIAL POLICY

A clear statement of the philosophy of the British Labour party was given by Mr. J. Ramsey MacDonald at the 28th annual Confer-

[7] *Op. cit.*, p. 357.

[8] *Foreign Affairs*, vol. 3, no. 4 (July, 1925), "Ten Years of Socialism in Europe," pp. 556–566.

[9] This view is emphasized by an American writer, Professor W. B. Munroe, in his *The Governments of Europe* (1925), pp. 257–258.

ence of the Labour party, at Birmingham, October 4, 1928. This Conference considered the programme of Labour as given in their official party manifesto in 1928 and issued under the title of *Labour and the Nation*. The Conference devoted several sessions to the programme, which was submitted for approval by Mr. MacDonald. The document, he said, had been drafted in such a way as to make the Labour party's outlook and conception of a society clear. It was not merely something for the present, but something for the years to come, "pregnant with programme after programme which would carry out Socialist ideas and make society respond to the Socialist conception of itself." The pledge of the Labour party as a national party was upon this programme. Because of this fact, *Labour and the Nation* summarises the progress of the British Labour Movement in the twentieth century the chief legislative and administrative measures demanded in this programme are given here:

Industrial Legislation.

The repeal of the Trade Unions Act and the restoration of trade union rights.

The establishment of a 48-hour week.

The improvement and extension of Factory Acts, Mines Regulation Acts, Minimum Wage Acts, and other industrial legislation.

Unemployment.

The establishment of adequate provision for unemployed workers, under the control of a National Authority.

The withdrawal from the labour market of children under 15, with the necessary provision of maintenance allowance.

The improvement of the provision made for widows and orphans and for the veterans of industry.

The repeal of the Eight Hours Act in the coal industry.

The transference and migration of unemployed miners.

The establishment of a superannuation scheme for aged miners.

The Development of Industry and Trade.

The establishment of a National Economic Committee to advise the Government as to economic policy, and of a National Development and Employment Board to prepare schemes for the development of national resources.

The transference to public ownership of the coal, transport, power, and life insurance industries.

The relief of industry by the readjustment of the relations between national and local finance and by the taxation of land values.

The more stringent control of Banking and Credit, and their closer adaptation to the needs of industry.

The protection of the consumer against exploitation and the extension of the powers of the Food Council.

The establishment of the fullest possible publicity with regard to costs and profits.

The promotion of scientific research, with a view to the improvement of industrial technique.

The extension of the powers of the Economic Section of the League of Nations.

Agriculture and Rural Life.

The transference of land to public ownership.

The establishment of security of tenure for efficient farmers.

The provision of credit on easy terms.

The stabilisation of prices by the collective purchase of imported grain and meat.

The elimination of waste by the development of collective marketing.

The establishment of efficient services of electrical power and transport in rural areas.

The protection of the agricultural worker by the effective enforcement of an adequate minimum wage and of reasonable hours of labour.

The improvement of the services of health, housing and education in rural districts.

The provision of facilities for the acquisition of land, and of an adequate supply of untied cottages.

The Development of the Social Services.

The passage of legislation to enable the larger local authorities to undertake such services as their citizens may desire, subject to due safeguards in respect of efficiency and capital expenditure.

The provision of an adequate supply of houses at rents within the means of the workers, the establishment of cottage homes for the aged, and the prevention of profiteering in land and building materials.

Slum clearance and the extension of town and regional planning.

The provision of medical care before and after childbirth, and the extension and improvement of the school medical service.

The amendment of the Health Insurance Acts, and the extension of insurance, including additional medical benefits, to the dependents of insured workers and to sections of the population at present outside its scope.

The improvement of pensions for the aged and of the allowances provided for widows and orphans.

The break-up of the Poor Law.

Education and the Care of Childhood.

The creation of a democratic system of education, adequately financed, free from the taint of class distinctions, and organized as a continuous whole from the nursery school to the university.

The fullest possible provision for the physical well-being of children, by the establishment of the necessary number of nursery schools, open-air schools and special schools for defective children, by the extension of school meals and by the further development of the school medical service.

The adequate staffing of primary schools and the drastic reduction of the size of classes.

The improvement of school buildings and the provision of books, equipment and amenities on a generous scale.

The regrading of children in such a way as to secure primary education for all children up to 11, and secondary education of varying types for all children above that age.

The extension of the school-leaving age to 15, with the necessary provision of maintenance allowances.

The establishment of easy access to universities and other places of higher education, and the provision of adequate financial assistance for them.

International Co-operation.

The promotion of international economic co-operation, as recommended by the International Economic Conference of 1927, and cordial co-operation with the International Labour Office.

The British Commonwealth of Nations.

The establishment of safeguards against exploitation of indigenous peoples by European capital, the prevention of forced labour and of injurious or inequitable conditions of employment, the protection of such peoples in the occupation of their land and in the exercise of civic rights, and the development among them of the services of health and education.

The strengthening and extension of the authority of the Mandates Commission of the League of Nations.

The statement of J. Ramsay MacDonald on the meaning of *Labour and the Nation* indicates the growth of political independence [10] in

[10] See signed article in *Daily Herald,* July 9, 1928, pp. 1–2.

the British Labour movement. He declared that the Labour Manifesto of 1928 "not only maintains in so many words the independence of Labour, but establishes it upon the foundations of idea and principle." "We are independent of Communism," he wrote, "on the one hand, and of Reformism on the other—not because they have fought us in our organization and at elections, but because we hold different views, and because, by being mixed up with them, we should present to the country a rabble and confusion. We have borrowed neither from a Moscow Thesis nor from a Liberal Yellow Book." This political purity was perhaps over-emphasized. The leader in Parliament, however, plainly put the cause of political and industrial alliance, declaring that in the Manifesto some seventy of the evils of society today were mentioned. "Some can be rectified by the stroke of a Ministerial pen, others only by long and severe Parliamentary fighting. Some present no difficulties; others bristle with difficulties, financial and administrative." It was his belief that the clearness of the intelligence with which the party held to its ideas, the volume of instructed public opinion which could be placed behind them, and the capacity of Labour administration upon whom will devolve the task of pioneering leadership, would determine how fast or how slow would be the progress of the Labour Party. The party demanded allies—the industrial organization of Labour and the business organization of Co-operation and these by placing a majority in Parliament would help to bear the brunt of the Parliamentary fight which would lay the foundations of a new social order and relieve immediate distress. In his earlier Foreword to the Manifesto the ex-labour premier had stated that, "Acting with our Trade Union colleagues we can command the industrial and political power which together will enable society to control its economic resources and re-fashion its organization so as to secure justice."

The fact that a Labour Government has been formed since this was written does not lessen the conviction that Labour as an organized political influence can only be adequately challenged as a great national party when it is a majority and not—as the 1924 and 1929–1930 experiments—a minority Government. Then finally it will be brought directly and unescapably to answer for its years of propaganda. It will be then judged, and rightly, by what answer it can give to "the State of England question."

CHAPTER XII

THE BRITISH LABOUR MOVEMENT AND SOCIAL POLICY: THE EXTENSION OF THE INDUSTRIAL AND POLITICAL ALLIANCE OF LABOUR

The survey of social legislation in England has shown the close working alliance of the Trade Union movement and the Labour party. The industrial and political movements are separate, yet with regard to social legislation there has been in Parliament unified action. This unity today is, of course, given a formal expression in the National Joint Council of the British Labour movement, representing the General Council of the Trade Union Congress, the Executive Committee of the Labour Party, and the Executive Committee of the Parliamentary Labour Party, this last representing the members of the Labour Party in the House of Commons.

The duties of the National Joint Council are to consider all questions affecting the Labour movement as a whole, and make provisions for taking immediate and unified action on all questions of national emergency; to endeavour to secure a common policy and joint action, whether by legislation or otherwise, on all questions affecting the workers as producers, consumers and citizens. The National Joint Council is to consult, when necessary, a Joint Conference, consisting of the General Council of the Trade Union Congress and the Labour Party Executive, together with a number of Parliamentary members, which, with the Labour Party Executive, will be equal in numbers to the numbers of the General Council of the Trade Union Congress.[1] At the Sixtieth Trade Union Congress, at Swansea, September, 1928, Mr. Arthur Henderson, fraternal delegate of the Labour Party, said that Labour stood on the threshold of power and responsibility, and used this as an argument in favour of the better co-ordination of its sections. He advocated the formation of a Grand Joint Council representing the General Council, the Co-operative movement, and the Labour Party. Mr. MacDonald in first giving the General Election Manifesto of 1928 to the nation

[1] See the *Labour Year Book, 1927*, p. 2.

urged this joint alliance as the practical political basis for Labour's victory. The chairman of the 1928 Labour Party Congress, Mr. George Lansbury, welcomed the proposal put forward at the Trade Union Congress of "a Labour Trinity," for a National Joint Council, representative of the Trade Unions, Co-operative Societies, and the Labour Party.

The Trade Union Congress since the first programme of 1868 to the agitation, after the passing of the Trade Union Act 1927, for a new law with regard to Trade Union, and relief for the miners, has sought to bring direct influence to bear upon Parliament. It is significant that even down to 1921 the executive body of the Trade Union Congress was the old Parliamentary Committee. The work of the Parliamentary Committee dealt with the advocacy of Bills before Parliament and Bills to be drafted, interviews with Ministers, and direction of the general interests of organized labour between sessions of the Congress. The Parliamentary Committee was replaced in 1921 by the General Council, at present made up of representatives from 18 groups in the Trade Union Congress; including such groups as mining and quarrying with a total membership in 1927 of 840,641, and the agriculture group, representing only 30,000. The purpose of the General Council is to provide a powerful directing executive body for the whole British Trade Union movement.

Besides the National Joint Council, an executive Joint Committee with the Labour party, there are two other Joint Committees with the Labour party, one on the Living Wage, and one on Workmen's Compensation Insurance. There are also five other Joint Committees with other Bodies : the Joint Consultative Committee on Professional Workers, the Trades Councils Joint Consultative Committee, the Trade Boards Advisory Council, the Standing Joint Committee of Industrial Women's Organization, and the Social Insurance Advisory Committee. And there are seven departments of the Trade Union Congress, Finance, Organization, International, Trade Boards, Research, Social Insurance, and Publicity. The Social Insurance Department was instituted in 1928, and represents a new phase of the study of social insurance systems and their relationship to the workers. This interest was defined in the resolution, passed at the Belfast 1929 Trade Union Congress, requesting the Government to appoint a Commission of Inquiry with a view to consolidating and merging the various contributory schemes of social insurance, to be administered by a Department charged with the special duty of social insurance administration. Further, that the Commission should also inquire into the various non-contributory social services for the purpose of reporting upon the possibility of the same being reorganized.[2] Of course the comprehensive schemes of unemployment, sickness, invalidity, and compensation insurance in Great Britain, with their dependence upon Acts of Parliament, are another strong reason for alliance between the political and industrial Labour movements.

The influence of the Trade Union movement is of course strong in the twelve Advisory Committees of the Labour party, which are: (1) Agricultural and Rural Problems, (2) Army, Navy and Pensions Problems, (3) Education, (4) Finance and Commerce, (5) Home Office, (6) Industrial Affairs, (7) Land, (8) Legal System and Administration of Justice, (9) Local Government, (10) Machinery of Government, (11) Public Health, and (12) Science.

The unity of the Labour movement has been, of course, a conscious aim of the Trade Union executives and the Labour Party leaders, but it is a remarkable fact that events outside of their control have done as much as anything else to keep the Trade Union movement in close dependence upon the Parliamentary Labour party. The necessity for a fighting alliance was given by the Taff Vale decision; the Osborne judgment came just at the time when the Labour party was gaining independence in the House of Commons, and there was urgent need of spurring the Government to action for a more liberal trade union law; and finally, the Trade Disputes and Trade Union Act, 1927, united the two divisions when there were indications that insurgency in the industrial movement would weaken the leadership of the Labour party.

I

The Strength of British Trade Unionism

An indication of the Trade Union movement's power is to be gathered from the statistical summary below of the membership of the affiliated unions, 1900 to 1929, represented at the annual Trade Union Congress.[3]

[2] *Report Trade Union Congress, Belfast,, 1929*, p. 376.
[3] See *Belfast Trade Union Congress Report, 1929*, pp. 4–5, *Nineteenth Abstract of Labour Statistics of the United Kingdom* (1928), pp. 165–181.

Year	Number of Unions	Members Represented at Trade Union Congress (in Thousands)
1900	184	1,250
1901	191	1,200
1902	198	1,400
1903	204	1,500
1904	212	1,423
1905	205	1,541
1906	226	1,555
1907	236	1,700
1908	214	1,777
1909	219	1,705
1910	212	1,648
1911	202	1,662
1912	201	2,002
1913	207	2,232
1914	—	—
1915	215	2,682
1916	227	2,851
1917	235	3,082
1918	262	4,532
1919	266	5,284
1920	215	6,505
1921	213	6,418
1922	206	5,129
1923	194	4,269
1924	203	4,328
1925	205	4,343
1926	207	4,365
1927	204	4,163
1928	196	3,874
1929	202	3,673
1930	—	3,750

The membership of the Trade Union Congress since its foundation is shown in the following table, for decennial periods:

Year	Number of Unions	Members
1868	—	118,367
1878	114	623,957
1888	138	816,944
1898	188	1,184,241
1908	214	1,777,000
1918	262	4,532,085
1928	196	3,874,842
1930	—	3,750,000

Unity in the Trade Union Movement: Expulsion of Communists

The growth of the British Labour party is largely due to the fact that organized labour in England has been won over to its side. The political programme of the Parliamentary party and the electoral promises of its candidates have been supported by the highly organized industrial movement in Great Britain. There has been no long drawn out struggle between the Parliamentary and the industrial labour movements, though there has been from time to time a sharp conflict with regard to specific economic questions and the proper tactics of a united Labour party. The Syndicalist agitation before the war in England centred largely around the movement for the minimum wage, and was not the anti-parliamentary struggle that the militant Syndicalists in France carried on in the pre-war France. The National Minority Movement in England, especially to be noted during 1924–1926, was a revival of the old Syndicalist campaign led by Mr. Tom Mann, but did not have the response that the similar effort in the industrial unrest of 1911 and 1912 had. The writings of Mr. Harry Pollitt and Mr. Tom Mann in the *Labour Monthly,* provided a running account of this movement, and the insurgent spirit in trade unionism was noted in the efforts to give larger powers to the General Council as a central authority of the industrial workers. This, of course, would have weakened the federal principle upon which Labour movement is based.

The practical politics of the Labour party and the Trade Union Congress are well illustrated in their relations with the Communist party, whose openly avowed policy is to scrap the present methods and objects of the Labour party and to transform it into a Communist organization. At the London Conference of 1924 the chief debate at the Conference centred around the party's attitude to members of the Communist party, and this question again came to the place of first importance at the Liverpool Conference in October, 1925. Both of these Conferences, as well as the Blackpool and Birmingham and Brighton Conferences of 1927, 1928 and 1929, showed that the hold of "MacDonaldism," as the National Minority leaders called it, was unshaken. There was in 1925–1926 a revival of the familiar discussion of the antagonism between political democracy and the militant worker, but there has not been the tedious, vague

polemics that characterized the pre-war social movement in France.
The Trade Union Congress has been able to direct its new energy
and the Labour party has formed two Governments. It is certain that
whatever direction the industrial movement of the next few years
takes in England, the political Labour movement will continue to be
a powerful factor in establishing ideals of public service. Since the
general strike of 1926 and the failure of the miners to gain their
objectives, there has been a reaction favourable to the Parliamentary
activities of the Labour party. The recurring crises in the negotiations of coal-owners and coal-miners has served to consolidate the
British interests of the political and industrial Labour Alliance.

The Labour party realizes that England possesses a wholly enfranchised adult population and a Parliament and a system of
government that will respond to the direction of the working people
as soon as they express intelligent desire for change through the
ballot box. Mr. Sidney Webb (as he then was) a member of the first
and second MacDonald Cabinets, and a Labour leader of unfailing
energy, declared at the Labour party Conference in 1923 that
"Violence persuades no one, convinces no one, satisfies no one . . .
violence may destroy but it can never construct. Moreover, in our
practical British way we can see that by the very nature of the case
violence can be much more easily and effectively applied on the
conservative side, to keep things as they are because this requires
only acquiescence, than on the side of change." The British Labour
party and the Trade Union Congress have fully supported this view.
The 25th annual Labour party Conference, Liverpool, 1925, by a
vote of 2,954,000 to 321,000 defeated the motion which meant the
reopening of the Communist party's demand for affiliation; on the
motion to ban the Communists from individual membership in local
Labour parties the vote was, for 2,870,000, against 321,000. Thus
the Communists were repudiated by an overwhelming vote. The
Margate Labour Party Conference of 1927 affirmed the Liverpool
Conference action by a vote of 2,706,000 to 349,000. The Trade
Union Congress action has been equally firm. The Edinburgh Congress of 1927 supported the General Council's refusal to recognize
Trade Councils affiliated to the minority Movement by a vote of
3,746,000 to 148,000; the Swansea Congress of 1928 instructed the
General Congress to "institute an inquiry into the proceedings and
methods of disruptive elements within the Trade Union movement,

whether among the unions or within the General Council, and to submit a report with the recommendations to the affiliated unions."

The Executive Committee of the Labour party in making their recommendations to the 1924 Conference to refuse affiliation to the Communist party squarely put the issue: [4] The Birmingham Labour Conference, 1928, endorsed by a vast majority a recommendation of the Executive Committee that persons belonging to political parties ineligible for affiliation to the Labour party (that is, members of the Communist party) should not be eligible for appointment as delegates to national or local Labour party conferences. The Belfast 1929 Trade Union Congress showed the determined effort of organized Labour to prevent the "disruptive tactics of the New Minority Movement or the Communist party."

"The Communist party believes that Parliament and other Administrative Authorities are simply machines that should only be exploited to their own destruction; that there is no hope in the masses of the people rising to the height of their political responsibilities; and that, therefore, as soon as a Minority in the community feel that they are sufficiently powerful to revolutionize the present political and industrial system, they are justified in using power, armed and otherwise, to achieve that purpose. Pending the speedy conversion of the masses, should they disagree with this procedure, the correct position is that they should be held down by force, deprived of liberty of speech, organization and Press, and such expressions in the direction of opinion will be dealt with as counter-revolutionary symptoms." But the Labour party differences are fundamental and unchanging, as is evident from their stated opinion that, "The Labour party holds a fundamental objection to tyranny, quite apart from the social, political, or industrial standing of the tyrant. In its opinion intelligence wisely directed is more enduring in its results than coercion, no matter how well intentioned. It objects to the limitations at present suffered by the masses of the people, but aids and welcomes their increasing desire for a freer and a fuller social life. The advances made during its short existence form the justification for steady and continuous effort in the direction of securing the suffrage and support of the greater masses of the nation. So-

[4] *Labour Year Book, 1925*, pp. 1–12, and *Report of the Labour Party Conference, London, 1924*. See also the extended report of the Executive Committee to the Labour Party Conference in 1922 when the same question was considered.

cialism that will secure the freedom under which men and women can develop their finest faculties and lead to a still higher social organization must essentially be based on freedom. The jargon of the Communist party is as foreign to the British worker as to the British Capitalist. The failure of the British Communist party, as represented in their "secret" Conference of 1929 is proof of this. Their membership is only a few thousand in a highly industrialized England.

The history of British democracy is convincing evidence that Labour politics can be used to strengthen the constitutional guarantees of freedom, and promote conditions of good-will which will bring to the state a larger liberty of action. Good will can inspire a new allegiance which is sorely needed by the state if its aims are to be social. The experience of the war and the years since the war have had much to do with the interest that many labour leaders take in the work that a Labour party must do in present-day governments. Labour politics as Mr. MacDonald has often said, has come into the open, and never again can Labour refuse to bear its share in the carrying on of the nation's business. The 1925 Labour party conference defeated by a very large majority a resolution demanding that no Labour Government be formed unless there was a working majority in the House of Commons. The party did not want to bind the future to a barren policy dictated by no higher principle than socialist orthodoxy. By a vote of 2,587,000 to 512,000 the Conference defeated the resolution on minority government moved on behalf of the Transport and General Workers' Union by Mr. Ernest Bevin: "That this Conference is of opinion in view of the experience of the recent Labour Government it is inadvisable that the Labour party should again accept office whilst having a minority in the House of Commons." Mr. MacDonald said, "In an absolutely blank political landscape you are asked to say that if you are returned at the next election with 308 members you will take office, but if you have only 306 members you will not. That sort of tactics won't do."

II

THE OBJECTIVES OF TRADE UNIONISM

The English Labour movement has been strengthened in Parliamentary prestige by the failure of industrial struggles on an unprecedented scale after the war which has resulted in men's minds being directed more to the political field. An early indication of this was the Hull Trades Union Congress in 1924, which was the 56th Annual Congress of the Trade Unions, and was attended by delegates representing 4,328,235 members. The Hull Congress adopted unanimously a resolution offered by the General Council, which constitutes a seven-point programme known as the Industrial Workers' Charter. This Industrial Workers' Charter is now incorporated in the Trade Union Congress Orders as Objects of Congress. It can be taken with the sections of *Labour and the Nation* on industry to constitute the present-day Trade Union objectives. The resolution of this Hull Congress re-affirmed the decisions of past Congresses with regard to necessary and fundamental changes in the social, economic, and political systems, and decided to formulate the said decisions in an Industrial Workers' Charter, pledging itself to secure by every legitimate means the fulfilment of the objects constituting the Charter, which, subject to such additions as the Trade Union Congress might from time to time approve, was accepted as follows:

(1)   Public ownership and control of natural resources and of services—
    (a)   Nationalization of land, mines, and minerals.
    (b)   Nationalization of railways.
    (c)   The extension of State and municipal enterprise for the provision of social necessities and services.
    (d)   Proper provision for the adequate participation of the workers in control and management of public services and industries.

(2)   Wages and Hours of Labour—
    (a)   A legal maximum working week of 44 hours.
    (b)   A legal minimum wage for each industry or occupation.

(3)   Unemployment—
    (a)   Suitable provision in relation to unemployment, with adequate maintenance of the unemployed.
    (b)   Establishment of training centres for unemployed juveniles.
    (c)   Extension of training facilities for adults during periods of industrial depression.

(4)   Housing—
    Provision of proper and adequate housing accommodation.

(5) Education—
>Full educational facilities to be provided by the State from the elementary schools to the universities.

(6) Industrial accidents and diseases—
>Adequate maintenance and compensation in respect of all forms of industrial accidents and diseases.

(7) Pensions—
>(a) Adequate State pensions for all at the age of 60.
>(b) Adequate State pension for widowed mothers and dependent children and mothers whose family breadwinner is incapaciated.

The Hull Congress decided that it should be the duty of the General Council to institute a vigorous campaign in all parts of the country with a view to mobilizing public opinion in support of the objects of the Charter and their fulfilment. The 1924 Congress further decided that it should be the duty of the General Council to report to each Annual Trade Union Congress on the extent of the propaganda work carried out and the progress made in relation to the Charter, and no motion having for its purpose the re-affirmation or the deletion of any object contained in the Charter should be allowed to appear on the Congress Agenda for a period of three years from the date such object was adopted by Congress, unless the motion was, in the opinion of the General Council, of immediate importance.

This Charter can be compared with the Trade Union programme of 1868 and 1900 given in this study, and it is an important commentary on the progress of the Labour movement since 1868. This Charter demands an acceptance of a standard of life for the workman, and it goes much farther than that challenging fact—the movement demands proper provision for the adequate participation of the workers in control and management. Thus, the whole problem of the organization of industry is today under discussion. And in this connection the following resolution, adopted at the Hull Congress on the motion of the Miners' Federation of Great Britain, seconded on behalf of the Associated Society of Locomotive Engineers and Firemen, is also of note. This Congress declared that the time had arrived when the number of Trade Unions should be reduced to an absolute minimum. That the aim should be as far as possible, organization by industry with every worker a member of the appropriate organization. That it was essential that a united front be formed for improving the standards of life of the workers. And, accordingly, the General Council was instructed to draw up (1) A scheme of organization by industry; and (2) A scheme which secures unity of action, without the definite merging of existing Unions, by a scientific linking up of same to present a united front.

This united front that was demanded in a "scientific linking up" was referred as a special study to the General Council of the Trade Union Congress. Some writers in 1924 seemed to see in the trend of events the break-up of the Labour party and the Trade Union alliance, which since 1900 had given the political movement increasing power. In fact, as Mr. Cole has pointed out, since 1909 when the Miners' Federation joined the Labour party, the party had become "almost as representative of the Trade Union movement as the Congress itself." [5] But the fact that the General Council, representing every phase of the industrial movement, was moving toward the establishment of itself as a centralized authority, able to exert the full power of the Trade Union movement in applying a national Trade Union policy, appeared to some observers to minimize the Parliamentary Labour movement. The proposal for the General Council as central authority of the industrial movement sponsored by the Left wing, and at the Scarborough Congress in 1925 some tactical gains were made by the Left wing of the General Council. The proposal was that the General Council should have its own machinery, its own set of departments, and should have that importance of first position which the industrial movement, as some believed, naturally demanded. Yet the General Council's report to the 1925 Trade Union Congress asked for no extension of powers, contenting itself by saying that "valuable experience has been gained and the mining dispute has shown that when the Trade Union movement is united and determined in defence of the standards of the workers the forces of reaction can be successfully withstood." Events since 1925 have not justified predictions of the predominance of the industrial movement, at least so far as this meant the Parliamentary Labour party becoming less effective as a political party in the life of the nation.

[5] *Organized Labour*, p. 109.

Increasing Interdependence of Political and Industrial Movements

The Liverpool Conference of the Labour party in 1925 marked a swing to the Right, and at that time the militant Miners' secretary, Mr. A. J. Cook, declared that "the tendencies prevalent at Liverpool show that the Labour party is drifting to political disaster." He believed it was becoming a new Liberal party and not a "Workers' party." His later support of the second MacDonald Government in their Coal Mines Bill and their international economic policy was unaffected by earlier opposition. The immediate cause of the active leadership of the political leaders in 1925 in defining the work of the party was the militancy of the Scarborough Trade Union Congress of 1925, and the offensive tactics of the radical Left wing. The militancy of that Congress was defined merely in a resolution, but this declared "That the Trade Union movement must organize to prepare the Trade Unions in conjunction with the party of workers to struggle for the overthrow of capitalism." Even to this resolution there were 1,218,000 votes of opposition to the majority vote of 2,456,000. At the Labour party Conference in Liverpool a few weeks later, Mr. MacDonald and the party chiefs stopped the Left Wing advance. The Liverpool Conference, he said, showed "right up to the hilt" that Labour's success depended on "the most complete co-operation" between the political and industrial wings. He did not believe that all the differences were corrected, but his faith was unshaken in an united Labour movement. A quarter of a century of progress had not made him less inclined to trust the processes of democracy or put less faith in Parliament. He further declared that the political Labour movement was responsive to the large hopes of the Trade Union world for workers' control, and the political leaders could be depended upon to make progress toward the "Commonwealth of Labour" as quickly as the industrialists prepare for social control. The Labour party, it was made plain, would not abdicate in favour of the new Minority Movement. The Trade Union Congress of 1926 at Bournemouth indicated the change from 1925 and the proceedings also reflected the reaction of the Trade Union movement to the General Strike. The mining controversy was unsettled, and this, together with the disastrous effects of the General Strike, overshadowed the Congress. The Trade Union Congress interpretation of the General Strike was given by the President, Mr. Arthur Pugh, who believed the strike reflected the growing discontent of the workers with the whole structure and policy of the industrial system. The Government were warned lest they attempted the destruction of the Trade Union movement by legislation. His hopes for the mining industry were those of Labour: National ownership, the scientific evolution of the industry, and the invoking of a spirit of new endeavour and co-operation between workers by hand and brain. This Congress and the Margate Labour Conference of 1926 marked definitely the turning of the united Labour movement from the depression of the General Strike, for the determination of the Government to introduce their Trade Disputes and Trade Union Bill was known. The Government united their Opposition, and once again Labour had found a rallying ground for the party and the Trade Unions. The new battle was to be one of ballots. The presidential address gave the keynote: "While the Communist party and the Minority Movement still believe in the General Strike, the Labour party would look forward with confidence to the General Election." The best answer of what Labour had learned from the general strike was to be in the Election Manifesto. In three years Labour again formed a Government.

III

The General Strike, 1926

It is well now briefly to consider the General Strike of May, 1926, because it marks an epoch in the history of social reform and because the whole Labour movement was affected by its results. The postwar years of industrial discord in England were symbolized in the long expected General Strike. The immediate causes have been given in the sections dealing with the nation and the coal-mines, and reference is here made to the General Strike because it was the means by which the industrial and political Labour movements were united as they had not been since the armistice. It is well known that a national sympathetic strike had been for a long time discussed in the Trade Union world and in the political Labour movement. The sympathetic strike, or the general strike, was often referred to in the years of industrial unrest in 1911 and 1912. Before the War and in the troubled days of 1919 and 1926 in England, the general strike was never in the minds of the British worker as a revolutionary idea. The British worker was not contemplating attacking his national government. His Annual Congresses were not taken up with theorising about state action. His attitude toward his government was common sense and conventional. He was patriotic, and saw no necessary conflict between Labour ideals and his patriotism. There was no "myth" of the general strike in England, so far as there was any belief that its use could bring about the control of the government by the workers. The British Labour movement is a constitutional movement, and the leaders in England have never believed that the sympathetic strike was illegal or unconstitutional. They did not so consider the general strike of 1926, whatever may have been their opinion of its usefulness or its wisdom. The general strike of 1926 was not a revolutionary political strike; the strikers were following orders and workers were attempting to aid the miners. It was even considered a defensive measure in the industrial struggle going on between the forces of organized capital and labour. The general strike of 1926 was an indication of the post-war industrial discord, arising directly out of the chaotic conditions of the coal industry. It was a further indication of the failure of the trade union leaders, the mine owners, and the Government to provide the leadership which would have established a working basis for the reorganization of the industry. The general strike revealed the bankrupcy of post-war industrial leadership, and cleared the way for a fresher attempt to better industrial relationships in Great Britain.

It is worth noting that one of the results of the general strike was to inspire attempts to carry out conferences between industrial and labour groups which may be of some aid in creating the conditions of peace. The British worker could not believe his problems would be all solved by a general strike, and the peace-in-industry programme since 1926 is a proof of it. Mr. Tawney, though writing before the general strike of 1926, had stated the fact clearly and has given an interesting comment on this subject. Later events substantiated his point of view. He told a Williamstown audience in 1925 that, the thousands of members of the Labour party who had acquired administrative experience in connection with local governing bodies, as well as with Trade Unions and co-operative societies, "are well aware that if any serious change is to be made, it requires prolonged discussion and preparation, and that it can be permanent only if based on general consent. They are not disposed, therefore, to provoke a reaction by attempting a *coup d'état,* which if successful would leave all the larger questions of social reorganization unsolved." [6] His conclusion was that the implications associated with the general strike are not congenial to the traditions or temper of the British Labour movement. The general strike, however, did come in May, 1926, and now, as a matter of history, it can be looked upon as one of the phases of the industrial labour movements which will not recur. The proof is abundant that it is not a British method.

The acceptance by the Trade Union Congress of the duties of the alliance with the Labour party has been most vigorously given since the general strike. The president of the Edinburgh Trade Union Congress, 1927, Mr. George Hicks, made this plain by declaring before the Congress that the immediate task for the Trade Union movement was to use every atom of strength it possessed in preparing for the return of a Labour Government at the next general election. This would be the best method, he said, of ridding the Trade Unions of the shackles which the Trade Disputes and Trade Unions had riveted upon them. The Swansea Congress of 1928 carried forward the spirit of close co-operation with the Labour party, and, as will be noted, advanced the cause of industrial peace by "the method of discussion," that is, by the acceptance of the Mond negotiations and the agreements reached on trade union recognition, victimization and rationalization.

The Constructive Period of Trade Unionism

The 1927 Congress clearly marked the progress of opinion in the Trade Union movement toward what the Chairman of the Congress called "the beginning of the constructive period of Trade Unionism." Industrial peace became a practical objective of the movement when it was urged that the machinery of joint conference between the representative organizations entitled to speak for industry as a whole be extended. Everyone knew, said Mr. Hicks, employers as well as trade unionists, that the vexatious, toilsome, and difficult period though which they were passing was a transitional period.

[6] R. H. Tawney, *The British Labour Movement* (1925).

Much fuller use could be made under these conditions of the machinery for joint consultation and negotiation between employers and employed. They had not reached the limits of possible development in this direction. It was more than doubtful whether they had seen the fullest possible development of machinery for joint consultation in particular industries. And practically nothing had yet been done to establish effective machinery of joint conference between the representative organizations entitled to speak for industry as a whole. There were many problems upon which joint discussion would prove of value. It was pointed out that a direct exchange of practical views between representatives of the great organized bodies who had responsibility for the conduct of industry and know its problems at first hand would be of far greater significance than the suggestion which had been made by the Government for a national conference to discuss "a vague aspiration towards 'industrial peace.' " Here Labour was decrying Government direction! The argument given was formerly the argument of the industrialists only; but now the Trade Union Congress chairman was convinced that discussion by those responsible along practical lines would bring both sides face to face with the hard realities of the present economic situation, and might yield useful results in showing how far and upon what terms co-operation was possible in a common endeavour to improve the efficiency of industry and to raise the workers' standard of life. It was important, the Congress was told, that their movement should frame a clear-cut and coherent policy on practical lines. They should not be deterred by allegations that in entering into such discussions they were surrendering some essential principle of trade unionism. On the contrary, they would lead to a much clearer understanding on the part of their own organized movement of the immediate practical objectives at which they ought to aim.

This same Congress did not even put to a vote the motion "to condemn the propaganda of industrial peace carried out by leading Trade Union officials." But the formal reply to the Prime Minister's advances for industrial peace was given in the motion below which was carried unanimously: "This Congress, having noted the repeated appeals of the Prime Minister to the leaders of Labour on the subject of collaboration for industrial peace, is compelled to inform Mr. Baldwin that the greatest hindrance to a response to these appeals is the legislative and industrial policy pursued by him and his Government, especially their action in lengthening the miners' hours and the deliberate class bias displayed in the Trade Unions Act. The immediate repeal of such repressive legislation would be the best evidence of the sincerity and honesty of Mr. Baldwin and his Government."

This statement on industrial peace is given at length because the attitude of the Trade Union Congress was a direct expression of their faith in social legislation, and their confidence of Government action was to be gained from legislation approved by the Government with regard to the law of Trade Unions and the Miners' Eight Hours Act. This view was confirmed by the action of the 1928 Swansea Congress which asked the Labour party to put in the forefront of their programme the repeal of the Miners' Eight Hours Act and the ratification of the Washington Convention. Industrial peace was again brought to the front in the report of the General Council on the Mond negotiations, and the Congress by a vote of 3,075,000 to 566,000 adopted the Report. This decision carried the approval of the setting up of a national Industrial Council for the appointment of Joint Conciliation Boards. The statement of Mr. Cook that the Trade Unions exist to fight capitalism was taken up by Mr. Bevin, representing transport workers, who maintained that they could "fight by discussion as well as by starvation." The General, Council by joining in negotiations and the Mond conversations was demanding for trade unionism a new status and influence. This view of the constructive duty of the Trade Unions certainly met the approval of the Trade Union Congresses of 1927, 1928, 1929 and 1930. Likewise, it is necessary to point out, that there was no less determined opposition to the Government's "attack on the Labour Movement by forcing the Trades Disputes and Trade Union Bill through the House of Commons without any attempt at impartial preliminary inquiry or mandate from the people," as the Congress of 1927 defined by resolution their attitude. The concluding paragraphs of the resolution follow:[7] "This Congress hereby affirms its determination to maintain in their entirety the rights and liberties which the past efforts of the organized workers have secured, including the full right of combination by all workers, and the application of the strike, to be used as and when, and in what manner may be found necessary

[7] *Labour Year Book, 1928,* p. 8.

either to secure improvements in their working conditions, to establish a rightful status of labour in the economic life of the country, or to resist any attempts to depress the workers' economic conditions. "This Congress pledges itself to work steadfastly for the repeal of this iniquitous measure, and calls upon the working class of Great Britain to exercise its fullest political power to remove from office the present Government, which dominated by organized capital and heredity class privilege and prejudice, has so unscrupulously used its position to injure the industrial and political organization of the workers." The 1928, 1929 and 1930 Trade Union Congress passed similar resolutions.

The most direct evidence of the combined political and industrial organization of the Labour movement was given by the National Conference of Trade Union Executives, called at London, April 29, 1927, to protest against the Government's Bill. It was there declared that "the Trade Unions do not recognize the artificial and mischievous division of their work into rigid, water-tight compartments, industrial and political. When is the question of Workmen's Compensation or the Prevention of Accidents industrial and not political? When is the question of Unemployment, a shorter working week, a Factory Law industrial and not political? Surely the welfare and protection of the workers, by legislative and administrative action, are an essential part of the work of every Trade Union." [8] Mr. Arthur Henderson reminded the delegates that the Labour party owed its origin to the conviction of the Trade Unions that the only effective way of carrying out the purpose for which the unions were formed was for the unions to combine industrial and political action. "It is a travesty of historical truth," he continued, "to say that the Trade Unions have been snared into unwilling alliance with the Labour party. The party is the child of the unions. It was created by the unions as a deliberate act of policy after years of discussion in the Trades Union Congress. In the mind of the Unions there never was any idea of separating their political

[8] *Report of the National Conference of Trade Union Executive Representatives*, London, April 29, 1927, p. 22, speech of Mr. Arthur Henderson, M.P. Cf. The Trade Union Defence Committee's Pamphlets, Nos. 1 and 2, *The Government's Attack on Trade Union Law*, by Arthur Henderson, Jr., with Introduction by W. M. Citrine, and *Union-Smashing by Law*, both published in 1927.

work from their industrial work. The two things were one and indivisible. The party was a natural, a legitimate, and a necessary extension of the activities of the Trade Unions."

This extended account of the political and industrial alliance of Labour since the war is given because it provides a background for the programme of the Labour party with regard to social legislation, and it is a necessary part of the story of the work of the party in Parliament. With this combined support in mind the Labour General Election Manifesto of 1928 with regard to social legislation and the Hull (1924) Industrial Workers' Charter are better understood. They are both a commentary on the past of British social policy and a promise of the future. It is clear that one of the results of the general strike was to direct the Labour movement again to the old familiar method of political and industrial combination. The industrial leaders were fortunate in England in being able to salvage the disaster of the national stoppage with the aid of a strong political party.

The advantages which the alliance of the industrial and political labour movements brought to the British Labour party have often been given, and it has seemed that the direct results of this alliance on the Trade Union movement have been sometimes neglected. But in the long years of collaboration and joint leadership of the Labour movement the British Labour party has contributed to the Trade Union movement a constructive and democratic aim which is national in its appeal. The controversies of the legislative programme in Parliament about the minimum wage, unemployment, old age pensions, and the status of the Trade Unions have gone on with unabated zeal. Yet these issues have not been the end of the workers' idealism, and, in fact, they have been only the beginning of what is hoped for with regard to the place of the worker in the life of the nation. The British Labour party has consistently kept before the industrial movement an ideal of a responsible organized labour machinery which would take its part in the direction of the national interests of Great Britain. It is not the genius of the British to detail the plans of their Utopias, and the programme of the Trade Union Congress has kept very little ahead of the actual state of opinion in the rank and file on labour reforms. This phase of the question was given an interesting turn in the debate on Syndicalism in 1912 in the House of Commons, when a member confessed, "I would far rather be

governed by Tom Mann than by Mr. and Mrs. Sidney Webb." [9]
But the reply of the whole Labour movement was put in the blunt
language of Hardie, who said "to dogmatize about the form which
the Socialist State shall take is to play the fool." [10] The political education of the working class would progress and their policy would
extend in an increasing degree in the direction of transfiguring the
state from "a property-preserving to a life-preserving institution."

IV

THE GENERAL ELECTION OF 1929

The fifth general election since the armistice, the general election
of 1929, found the British Labour party endorsing 569 candidates,
and electing 287 members of Parliament. The 1900 general election,
with which this survey was begun, sent 2 Labour members to the
House of Commons. The total number on the Voters' Register in
1928 was 28,502,265, including 5,000,000 new voters (extension of
franchise to women at 21 years of age on equal terms with men), and
a total of 22,639,117 votes were cast. The progress of thirty years
from the Labour Representation Committee to the responsible Government of the day is a remarkable political achievement, which is
likely to be under-estimated by those long familiar with British
politics. It is significant in a country which has strongly developed
political traditions and prejudices. The meaning of this brief electoral history for this study, is the strong evidence given that social
questions are dominant in British party politics today.

The Annual report of the National Executive of the Labour party
presented to the party Conference at Brighton in September 1929,
statistical tables of the growth of the party and its position at the
polls. Attention was drawn to a comparison of the votes cast for
the candidates of the three parties.

	Candidates	Average vote per candidate	Increase or decrease over 1924 vote
Conservatives	590	14,685	23
Liberal	513	10,333	+1,770
Labour	569	14,694	+4,018

[9] *Parl. Deb.,* 5 S.H.C., March 27, 1912, vol. 36, p. 537; pp. 535-544, speech
entire of Mr. Ormsby-Gore.
[10] K. Keir Hardie, *From Serfdom to Socialism* (1907), p. 96.

The Executive Committee gave the comparison between the results of the election of 1924 and 1929 with reference to majorities to show what was termed the "increasing hold" of Labour on the constituencies.

Majorities	1924	1929
Over 10,000	4	67
Between 5,000 and 10,000	25	91
Between 4,000 and 5,000	27	19
Between 3,000 and 4,000	18	28
Between 2,000 and 3,000	21	38
Between 1,000 and 2,000	31	17
Under 1,000	28	26

The changing character of the Labour party, so far as its national appeal is concerned, is reflected in the relative decline in the Trade Union strength in the party. This is illustrated by the fact that of the candidates who went to the poll 365 were put forward by constituency Labour parties against 139 by Trade Unions, 53 by the Independent Labour party, and 12 by the Co-operative party. This is also reflected in the elected members of the Labour party in the House of Commons. The 289 Labour members of Parliament represent the following divisions of the Labour movement:

Divisional Labour parties	132
Trade Unions	115
Independent Labour party	33
Co-operative party	9

There has been much discussion of minority and majority representation in the House of Commons since the definite fact of a three-party system has had to be recognized. The following table indicates the position of the Conservative, Liberal and Labour parties in respect of majority and minority representation in 471 single-membered constituencies where more than two candidates went to the poll in 1929.

	Majority	Minority
Labour	98 or 45.5%	118
Conservative	60 or 28.6%	150
Liberal	4 or 9.1%	40
Independent		1

"The figures prove beyond any doubt," the National Executive report declared, "that the Labour party has a larger number of majority seats, absolutely and relatively, than any other party. It can claim that its members of Parliament are, on the average, more representative of the constituencies which have elected them to Parliament than the members of other political parties. The Liberal party only secured one majority seat out of every eleven won by them, where more than two candidates went to the poll." This then is the background of the 1929 general election, and upon this strength the second Labour Government was formed by Mr. MacDonald.

THE SECOND LABOUR GOVERNMENT

The first King's Speech ever to be offered by a Labour Government was read on July 2, 1929, and outlined the Labour programme for Parliament. Industrial and social questions had a large place in the promised Parliamentary business of the new Government. The Government, it was said, had under consideration the question of the re-organization of the coal industry including hours and other factors and of the ownership of the minerals. Those proposals were put forward in December, 1929 in the Coal Mines Bill. Inquiries were to be undertaken immediately into the condition of the iron and steel and the cotton industries in order to discover means for co-operation with them to improve their position in the markets of the world. Bills were promised for amending and consolidating factory legislation, and for giving effect to the obligations of the Washington International Labour Conference in 1919. It was also proposed to introduce legislation to promote an extensive slum clearance and to make further provision for housing in urban and rural areas. A general survey was promised by the Government of the various National Insurance and Pensions schemes, and meanwhile a Bill was being prepared to amend the Widows', Orphans', and Old Age Contributory Pensions Act, 1925 so as to modify the conditions applicable to certain pensions, and to make some increase in the classes of persons entitled to them. This was the 1929 Act. Finally, a measure was to be introduced "to remedy the situation created by the Trade Disputes and Trade Unions Act, 1927." This was the Parliamentary programme framed by the second Labour Government. The president of the 1929 Trade Union Congress, Mr. Ben

Tillett, said at Belfast, "We are confident that the Government intends to ratify its pledges in respect of the Trade Dispute and Trade Unions Act, 1927, the Miners' Eight-Hour Act, the Washington Convention, Factory legislation, and other matters of vital interest and importance to the Trade Unions." [11]

The several days of debate on the King's Speech made it plain that the Labour Government was a minority Government, a suggestion emphasized by Mr. Baldwin, the leader of the Conservative Opposition, when he said that the Government was a minority Government, and, therefore, the House of Commons as a whole had its rights. Mr. MacDonald in reply said that he knew perfectly well that his Government was, as they were in 1924, if a combination were made against them, in a minority. He then made his oft-quoted statement of a Council of State. "I want to say something else," he added. "It is not altogether because I happen to be at the head of a minority that I say this, because this thought must be occurring to the mind of every one of us who are aware of the very serious problems that this country has to face—problems at home and problems abroad. I wonder how far it is possible, without in any way abandoning any of our party positions, without in any way surrendering any item of our party principles, to consider ourselves more as a Council of State and less as arrayed regiments facing each other in battle. It is perfectly true that the condition of the House at the present moment invites us to make these reflections, and so far as we are concerned co-operation will be welcome—this applies to a majority Government as much as it applies to a minority Government—by putting our ideas into a common pool and bringing out from that common pool legislation and administration that will be of substantial benefit to the nation as a whole."

The idea of Parliament as a Council of State, while not a new idea, nevertheless never had such insistent reasons, behind its appeal than in the Parliament which began its work in July, 1929. The necessity of Parliament acting in its corporate capacity, as it always does when the conditions of the nation are grave, represented a new way of looking at the economic recovery of England. It may mean a new constructive period of party politics in England.

This same temper was in evidence at the annual Labour party Con-

[11] *Report of Trade Union Congress, Belfast, 1929,* pp. 79–83, President's address, pp. 61–70, Report of General Council.

ference at Brighton in September 1929, when for three days the delegates listened to responsible Cabinet Ministers tell of their work and of their difficulties. Never before had the British Labour movement been brought so close to the actual problem of seeing how their programmes on paper could be worked out in governmental administration. This is a sobering experience which has already redirected the energies of many in the party to thinking out afresh the relationship of the modern democratic Labour movement to the organization of community interests as a whole. However, the stereotyped programmes of social reform have never attracted the British Labour party in the way that the French and German Socialists have adhered to "Theses". There have been from year to year a critical sense in the British Labour party, combined with a sense of humor and a practical understanding of what could be done in social politics. This had an interesting development in 1929 when the Parliamentary Labour party, the members in the House of Commons, decided to hold a regular monthly meeting of the party, rather than the weekly meeting of the party as was the custom when they were in Opposition. They did not wish to hinder the Labour Government's work. Just as the first Government of 1924 made changes in the Labour party organization, so the 1929 Government did. An innovation was the election of a Consultative Committee of 12 members to act as a channel of communication between the Parliamentary Labour party and the various Ministers.

The most significant indications of the actual power of the organized labour movement is in the responsible place that the Trade Union Congress has taken in the post-war discussions, and especially since 1926, of the organization of industry. For example, when the Trade Union Congress met at Belfast in 1893 there were no more than 900,000 organized workers represented and at the 1929 Congress in that city there were approximately 4,000,000 represented. A Parliamentary political fund was discussed at that Congress; but in 1929 a Labour Government's programme was debated. The Trade Union movement in 1893, as the president in 1929 said, was struggling for mere recognition and toleration. The Trade Unions today, however, were an integral part of the organization of industry. They hold an unchallenged position as representatives of the workers in all negotiations affecting conditions of unemployment. The whole range of collective bargaining is wider now, taking account of economic questions which, in former years, the employers jealously insisted upon excluding from the purview of the unions. There is nothing in the organization and direction of industry that can be now regarded as the exclusive concern of the employer. "Our unions negotiate now," it was pointed out, "as equals with the power of the organized masses behind them. Their negotiations deal not only with wages, hours, and conditions of employment, but with policy and economic organization in the widest sense." Nor are the activities of the Trade Union Movement confined to the problems of specific industries and trades. Collective agreements are now framed for multiple trades on a national scale, and common conditions are prescribed for a whole range of industries, while the General Council, in the exercise of a mandate conferred upon it by the unions affiliated to the Trade Union Congress, prosecute steadily the policy of improving the status of the workers and securing a continuously rising standard of life for all by industrial re-organization and a betterment of industrial relations.

The leadership of the Trade Union Congress in the field of industrial relationships is strong evidence of the new constructive period of Trade Union activity. The General Council of the Trade Union Congress by accepting the invitation of the organized employers of the country took a forward step of great significance in the development of trade union policy. "It brings us, as I believe," said Mr. Tillett at Belfast, "within sight of the goal which our Congress has been aiming, when the responsible bodies representing the wage-earners on the one hand and the organizers of industry on the other can sit down together to consider their mutual relations and the problems of industrial re-organization without sacrifice of principle. The organization we have built up is disciplined, powerful, realistic in temper, with resources, knowledge and experience which are unrivalled." It was these resources which were "at the disposal of the nation in a genuine endeavour to promote the regeneration of economic life, to recover lost markets, open new channels of trade, and to modernize our methods of production and distribution." A democratic nation that can produce such a spirit in organized labour certainly can feel that the liberty which has been granted has been well used. At the 1929 Congress four million workers were represented by leaders who gave this evidence of the responsible progress of a great industrial movement.

Co-operation in Industry

The responsible leadership of the Trade Union Movement gave full support to industrial co-operation when on December 19, 1929, at a meeting of representatives of the General Council of the Trades Union Congress, the National Confederation of Employers' Organizations, and the Federation of British Industries, a permanent method of consultation and co-operation was approved. The scheme established formal and friendly relations between the national body of trade unionists and the two national bodies of employers. This was a notable step in industrial co-operation and it was a new thing in British industrial history. The resolution to accept the procedure agreed upon was moved by Mr. A. J. Cook, representing the Trade Union Congress, and was unanimously adopted by the three organizations concerned.

This beginning of conferences between the Trade Union Congress and the Employers' Organizations was so important, and so closely joined with the social politics of the British Labour movement that the proposals and the practical machinery accepted are here given. The proposals were as follows :—

(1) The Trades Union Congress (T.U.C.), Confederation, or Federation of British Industries (F.B.I.), can propose as subjects for discussion any matter within their respective provinces which is of common interest to British industry, it being understood that these discussions will not invade the provinces or trespass upon the functions of the individual constituents of the T.U.C., Confederation, or F.B.I.

(2) Having regard to the separate spheres and functions of the Confederation and the F.B.I., and the necessity for the T.U.C. knowing which of these two organizations will be responsible for the employers' side of any question proposed for discussion, the Confederation and the F.B.I. will set up an Allocation Committee, whose sole function will be to say whether any given subject proposed by the T.U.C., or which the Confederation or F.B.I. proposes to raise with the T.U.C., is one which concerns the responsibility of the Confederation or the F.B.I., or both.

(3) The question of allocation having been settled, the future procedure will be carried through direct between the T.U.C., on the one hand, and the Confederation or F.B.I., or both, on the other hand, without further reference to the Allocation Committee.

(4)   When the T.U.C., on the one hand, or the Confederation or F.B.I. (or both), on the other hand, accept a subject for discussion, the organization so accepting shall take up with the organizations which proposed that subject the question of the size of the Committee for the purpose and the other arrangements of procedure for its discussion.

(5)   If the T.U.C., on the one hand, or the Confederation or F.B.I., on the other hand, considers itself unable to discuss a subject, it is understood that the organization declining will explain its reasons therefor to the organization proposing.

(6)   All discussions at meetings, and correspondence arising out of the procedure proposed, shall, unless otherwise mutually agreed, be confidential to the T.U.C., Confederation, and F.B.I., and when a subject proposed for discussion has been accepted and discussed, no action shall be taken on any conclusions reached until these conclusions have been specifically approved by the organizations concerned.

These proposals given above provided the practical machinery for the selection of subjects and their discussion, but the Joint Committee considered that, for the purpose of examining these proposals, they should be accompanied by way of illustration by some indication of the types of subjects in regard to which the machinery could operate. The following list was drawn up by the Joint Committee for that purpose, and they include the outstanding problems which every modern democratic government has to constantly consider in its national and international policy. Royal Commissions in England have studied the most of them since the War. They are the same type of questions which the National Economic Council in France as will be noted, has been given by the French Government for study. The list of the Joint Committee follows:

1.   *Unemployment.*
2.   *Industry and Finance.*—Macmillan Committee.
3.   *Taxation of Industry:*—
     (a)   General effect of taxation on industry.
     (b)   Inadequate allowances for obsolescence and depreciation, taxation of wasting assets, taxation of moneys put to reserve, and similar points.
4.   *Social Services.*—Co-ordination.
5.   *Education and Industry.*—"Shaftesbury" and "Elgin" Councils.
6.   *Delegated Powers of Government Departments.*—Donoughmore Committee.

7. *Inter-Empire Trade.*—Imperial Conference and Imperial Economic Conference.
8. *International Trade:*—
   (a)   Tariff Truce Proposals;
   (b)   Proposals for multilateral customs agreements;
   (c)   Most favoured nations treatment;
   (d)   Import and Export Restrictions Convention, and similar problems.
9. *Trade facilities.*
10. *Insurance of export credits.*
11. *General international labour questions.*
12 *Industrial and commercial statistics.*

The proposals of the National Joint Committee composed of representatives of the three national bodies were approved by the Trade Union Congress General Council, December 18, 1929, by the Grand Council of the Federation of British Industries, January 8, and by the Council of the Confederation of Employers' Organizations, January 15, 1930.

The development of co-operation between the government and employers' and workers' organizations in the re-organization of industry is further illustrated by the decision of the Labour Government to establish an Economic Advisory Council. This decision was taken on January 16, 1930, and the non-Ministerial personnel of the Economic Advisory Council was announced February 12, 1930. The list included leaders in industry and trade, Trade Union executives, economists, and bankers, chosen by the Prime Minister "in virtue of their special knowledge and experience in industry and economics." The Ministerial members are the Prime Minister, the chairman, the Chancellor of the Exchequer, the Lord Privy Seal (Mr. J. H. Thomas in the Labour Government as "Minister of Unemployment"), the President of the Board of Trade, and the Minister of Agriculture and Fisheries, with such other Ministers as the Prime Minister may from time to time summon. The Council will meet when summoned by the Chairman, and as regularly as found possible, the official announcement declared; and also the Chairman may appoint standing committees and also such committees for special purposes as may be required. The Economic Advisory Council has a secretary, and assistant secretaries, and may have such a staff as may be necessary.

The functions of the Economic Advisory Council, as set forth in

the Treasury Minute of January 27, 1930, are not as broad as the
authority which it was suggested such an Economic Council should
have, when the Trade Union Congress discussed this subject. Providing that it acts after receiving the approval of the Prime Minister,
the Council may initiate inquiries into, and advise upon, any subject
falling within its scope, including proposals for legislation. The
Council shall consult Departments and outside authorities in regard
to any work in hand or projected and shall collate such statistical
or other information as may be required for the performance of its
work. The Council shall also cause to be prepared a list of industrial, commercial, financial and working-class experience, and persons who have made a special study of social, economic and other
scientific problems who might assist the Council by serving on Committees or as advisers in matters of which they have expert knowledge, or in other ways. The Prime Minister on February 12, 1930
told the House of Commons that such a list had been prepared. The
reports and work of the Advisory Economic Council will be confidential unless the Council advises the Prime Minister otherwise,
and any action arising out of these reports will be taken on the sole
responsibility of the Government.

The Trades Union Congress and the Labour Party Conference of 1930

The 1930 Trades Union Congress at Nottingham during the
first week in September, and the thirteenth annual conference of
the Labour party at Llandudno in October 1930 reflected the mood
of the political and industrial movements. The annual meetings
accurately revealed the conflicts and disappointments within the
Labour movement, and there was again the indication that criticism
within the party was becoming better defined. Mr. John Beard,
in the presidential address at the Trade Union Congress, declared
he had little use for "Socialism in our time," and he described this
propaganda slogan of the Independent Labour Party as "at best
an epistemological profundity of neither use nor ornament." "Ex-
pediency," he said, "in the broadest sense of that term must be
our guide, and not some abstract principle which may have no relation to the actual facts and problems with which we are faced."
Here is British opportunism with a vengeance! It is an echo of

the earlier post-war Trade Union Congress address of the then Mr. Sidney Webb who expounded the doctrine of "the inevitability of gradualness" in his presidential message. At the 1930 Trade Union Congress two members of the Labour Government took part in the deliberations, Mr. Clynes and Mr. Thomas, and again the Trade Union Congress and the Labour Party Conference were opportunities for the Labour Cabinet members to defend official Government policies. They also were not spared criticism.

The 1930 Trades Union Congress passed a resolution on rationalisation calling upon the Congress "to urge affiliated unions when facing this problem to press for reduction of hours in order to limit displacements, to institute generally in connection with the reorganisation of industry adequate compensation for persons displaced, and to press for an adequate state pension for persons 65 years of age and over in order to provide avenues of employment for younger workers." The Congress passed resolutions dealing with a demand for a statutory 44-hour week, inclusive of meal times, for the employment by the Government at Trade Union rate of all unemployed workers, and for the immediate reversal of the Trade Disputes Act of 1927. "Socialism in our time" had not conquered the British Trades Union Congress as these resolutions attest, nor had the results of the second Labour Government in its long months in office served to destroy faith in political action. The typical trade unionist was true to his doctrine of the inevitability of gradualness!

The Labour Party Conference at Llandudno under the presidency of Miss Susan Lawrence, Parliamentary Secretary to the Minister of Health, proved that despite the failure of the MacDonald Government with regard to unemployment and the revolt of the militant Left Wing of Labour in Parliament, the members of the party were unwilling to refuse confidence to their official leaders. Miss Lawrence reviewed the record of the Government, and she emphasised the handicaps imposed by the minority position of the Government. The overwhelming effects of the trade crisis in England and the repercussions of a worldwide depression were pointed out as obstacles of the Government. This same view was skillfully presented by Mr. MacDonald in his address to his party conference, and the prime minister made much of the old human appeal in his labour philosophy. He spoke mainly about unemployment, but gave ample indication of his opposition to tariffs and to a return to protectionism. At any rate the resolution of confidence in the Government, which urged them to carry out the programme of reform advocated by the party in *Labour and the Nation,* passed by the large vote of 1,803,000 votes to 334,000 votes.

The 1930 Trade Union Congress and the annual Labour Party Conference, convening after nearly two years of the second Labour Government, provided ample proof that there is determination in the organised industrial and political Labour movement to use the party as an instrument of political and economic change. The achievements of the Government were far below the hopes of the most ardent members of the party, but in spite of the failure to fulfil election promises there was remarkably little active opposition to the Government. The important problems of agriculture and unemployment were left unsolved, and the promises of the Government with regard to the Trades Disputes Act had to be repeated again in the second Labour Address in October 1930. Always the fact that the second Labour Government was a minority Government softened the criticism of the party's failure, and combined with this were the problems of India and unemployment which no party was prepared to risk an election over. But sooner or later the Labour Government which comes to power will have directly to deal with the industrial measures which Labour has long declared its Parliamentary objective, and it is a great misfortune that the first and second Labour Government were minority Governments. The fact that they were made it possible to avoid criticism within the party and to escape responsibility before the people of the nation. This is however part of the general problem of the Parliament of England.

INDEX

(The index to the material in the second volume should also be used by the reader in connection with the topics covered in this volume)

A

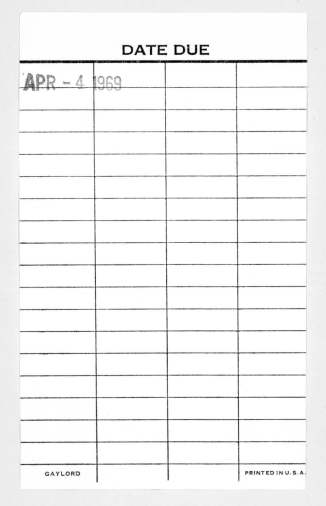

DATE DUE

APR - 4 1969			
GAYLORD			PRINTED IN U.S.A.